From Volga to Ganga

AF518108

From Volga to Ganga

Rahul Sankrityayan

Translated by
V.G. Kiernan and Kanwal Dhaliwal

Edited by
Kanwal Dhaliwal and Maya Joshi

LeftWord

First published in February 2021 by
LeftWord Books
2254/2A Shadi Khampur
New Ranjit Nagar
New Delhi 110008
India

Digital print edition, March 2021.

LeftWord Books and Vaam Prakashan are imprints of
Naya Rasta Publishers Pvt. Ltd.

First published in Hindi by
Rahul Sankrityayan, 1942

Translated by
Dr. V.G. Kiernan, 1946

Volga se Ganga © The Estate of Rahul Sankrityayan

Translation of the first 19 chapters of
From Volga to Ganga © The Estate of Victor Kiernan

Translation of the 20th chapter of
From Volga to Ganga © Kanwal Dhaliwal

Introduction © Maya Joshi

This volume © LeftWord Books

leftword.com

ISBN
978-81-940778-1-7 (paperback)
978-81-947287-6-4 (e-book)

Contents

Dedicated to
The human capacity to reason

Volga se Ganga
Text and Context

Maya Joshi

Volga se Ganga is Rahul Sankrityayan's most popular work. It is as iconoclastic as it is iconic. The riverine route that Rahul Sankrityayan (1893–1963) traces here attempts at sketching nothing less than 8,000 years of human history. Astoundingly audacious in ambition, it is a genre-defying work of historical fiction that seeks to track the migration of peoples from the bank of the Volga in 2000 BCE to the banks of river Ganga in Patna, Bihar, in 1942. The vagueness of the first date and locale and the precision of the last are only to be expected. The book takes into its grand sweep a vision of *human* development, struggle, and evolution, while keeping the focus on the landmass we now call India and Pakistan.

It concerns itself with material history – tools and trades, food, clothing, and language, familial and social structures – and increasingly, towards the end, the region's political destiny. It does so via stories knit together by a slender thread of a single family's migration, stories that leap across centuries, peopled with characters historically known and vividly imagined, who fall in love, fight each other, write poetry, expound philosophy, debate ideas, sacrifice their lives for causes, eat, drink, entertain, dress, love, and hate in terms that would be recognizable to a historian as being appropriate to their times. At least that is the intention. Rich in finely imagined detail, yet cognizant of grand sweeps, it locates its human drama within a materialist-historical framework. This grand narrative of a forest, however, houses quite diverse and individually, even idiosyncratically, imagined trees. Its high seriousness of purpose is fleshed out in vibrant, youthful, colloquial, humorous detail, rendering it delightful and accessible, and accounting in no small part for its enormous popularity. It is history in the *longue durée* brought alive. His most translated work, with versions in Bangla, Marathi, Malayalam, Panjabi, Odia, Urdu and Telugu and Tamil being prominent among Indian languages, and Chinese, Czech and Russian among the foreign ones, Sankrityayan has arguably been synonymous, for most Indian readers, with *Volga se Ganga*. Victor Kiernan's English version, which this edition builds upon, ought to have made it more visible to a global readership than it has.

In order to understand the significance of the text and its multiple locations, it is useful to begin by considering the circumstances of the text's production. Part of the large body of literature produced by Indians – and some non-Indians who were co-travellers in the anti-imperial struggle – during incarceration in British jails, *Volga se Ganga* is necessarily the product of its historical moment. Its political concerns are those of the author's, and of large swathes of the population. While it reflects the shifting zeitgeist, it does so from a perspective largely shaped by Sankrityayan's Marxist sensibilities and convictions, honed by political activism. But it also carries traces of all that he was – prior to, in addition to, and alongside his communist orientation.

By this time in his life-journey, defined as much by flowing continuities akin to a river's progression as by sharp drops and departures, Sankrityayan was an avowed Marxist. How he arrived there, and how that journey informs the unique character of this book, requires a biographical note. Compressing into a few paragraphs a life that in effect packed several in its 70-year span calls for a radical editing out of details. What follows is a bare-bones sketch that tracks the major landmarks, both biographical and writerly, getting more detailed as we inch closer to the date of the text's composition (1940–42) and publication (1942).

A Traveller's Tale

I know of three men from my father's generation who were inspired in three different directions by 'Rahul-ji', as he was called. One became a Buddhist scholar, one ran away from home and eventually became a writer, especially of travelogues in Hindi, and the third became a communist. How did one man come to mean so many things to so many people?

He was born Kedarnath Pandey into a Brahmin family of modest means in Kanaila village, Azamgarh district of present-day Uttar Pradesh. The year was 1893. The name by which he is known, Rahul Sankrityayan, came into being in 1928 in Kelaniya district in distant Sri Lanka. That journey, from Kedar to Rahul, bears telling.

Acts of naming are significant – they shape and mark identity, arguably more so in traditional India. This renaming was part of the process of taking ordination as a Buddhist monk at the Vidyalankara Pirivena, a monastic college in Kelaniya that exists to this day. He had gone there in 1927, keen on studying the Pali canon – Tipitaka, or Tripitaka in Sanskrit. The young Kedarnath Vidyarthi's disgruntlement with the Arya Samaj – to which he was drawn in 1915 – and attraction towards Buddhist philosophy were an ironic result of the zeal that served him well as a proselytizer for the Samaj, in which role he was required to study rival schools of philosophy for purposes of logical refutation. Contrary to expectations, he found himself increasingly convinced by the logic and epistemology he found in Buddhist schools. Specifically, he found himself being unable to accept the belief in the Veds as authority, in a God as creator, and a Soul as a permanent entity.

He had arrived at the Arya Samaj via a similar process of disillusionment with other schools of what we might loosely call Hindu philosophy. Before turning to the Arya Samaj, he had been part of *maths* such as the Parsa math in Bihar and Tirumishi in Tamil Nadu, both *Vaishnav* in orientation. This, in turn, was preceded by a brief youthful brush with *Shaiv* practices.

Why a young man from a farming family, with a maternal grandfather in the army, became a *sadhu* can be attributed as much to an unfortunate biographical circumstance as to a strong desire for learning. Married off at the age of eleven in keeping with tradition, he rebelled and saw in running away the only means of continuing his education and escaping a life of stifling domesticity. Over three decades later, he would write *Ghumakkar Shastr*, a treatise for roamers, half-humorously celebrating this impulse for *ghumakkari* as the highest impulse, impelling the seeker to great heights and wider horizons. *Koop-mandookt*, the frog-in-the-well mentality, one he knew too well from his early life experiences, was the enemy to enlightenment and must be fought and defeated, by individuals and by societies and nations alike. Running away from the parochial is thus a noble act, one the book not only recommends but acts as a guide for. It is the highest religion of man-(and woman-)kind, he argues, in obvious iconoclastic delight. It is, indeed, a youthful duty. Ismail Meeruthi's *she'r* brightens his path, running like a leitmotif in his autobiography:

> *Sair kar duniya ki ghafil zindagaani phir kahan*
> *Zindagi agar phir rahi toh, naujawani phir kahan*

> (Wander the wide world, Heedless One, where will life last
> Life might yet linger, in bits, but where will youth last)

The other source of light that serves as his beacon are the words of the Buddh, in the Pali text *Majjhim Nikaya*, said to have been Shakyamuni's final teaching to his disciples. Sankrityayan adapts that for his own motto, and makes it the epigraph of his autobiography:

> *I took ideas/thoughts as a raft to carry me across, not as a load to be carried on the head.*

Young Kedar made his journey of discovery through many temples of learning, moving on when he found them either bound in orthodoxy or mired in petty power politics. Shaiva *sadhus* attacking Vaishnavs with *trishuls*, Vaishnav *maths* tempting him with offers of heir apparent-ship to the *gaddi* (the seat of power), internecine rivalries that went against the spirit of what was professed, and growing discontent with orthodox beliefs he could no longer rationally accept, drove him onwards. He settled on Arya Samaj as a reformed, progressive, socially ameliorative school of thought, only to find Buddhism drawing him away with more credible philosophical foundations, and the promise of recovering a deep, neglected past, whose archaeological and textual riches were only then beginning to be fully discovered and appreciated. A growing sense that there was a concerted suppression of this heterodox past drew him to this restorative project, already initiated in Sri Lanka by Anagarika Dharmapala. Not given to Buddhist proselytization, however, Sankrityayan participated in the intellectual project. He did this through his own quest for learning, his epic journeys in the 1930s to Tibet to retrieve lost Buddhist texts preserved in the original or in Tibetan translations, and his subsequent work as translator/editor of these works and teacher of Buddhist philosophy, even as a card-carrying communist. His respect for and engagement with the Buddh thus outlived his next move, of rejecting the concept of rebirth, and accepting dialectical materialism as 'the most relevant philosophy for the times'. The name he had fashioned from a slice of Buddhist history and a sense of a past (Rahul being Siddharth Gautam's son, and 'sankritya' being the *gotr*) stayed with him through his Marxist years.

The exact time for this transition from Buddhism to Marxism is hard to fix. While still an Arya Samaji, Sankrityayan writes glowingly of the 1917 October Revolution as a powerfully transformative historical event, one that inspired his utopian fiction *Baisvin Sadi* ('The Twenty-Second Century'), which, though finally completed in 1924, was first conceived in skeletal form in his imagination over the year that followed the Russian Revolution. In 1935 he would recall this book when commenting on what he saw during his first visit to the Soviet Union:

> The picture of villages, cities, men and women that I had portrayed in *Baisvin Sadi* had been a thing of the imagination. But here it was being given solid shape in the real world. Is it any surprise then that I consider Soviet soil to be worthy of reverence?[1]

Baisvin Sadi had been written while he was still an Arya Samaji, his transformative visit to Sri Lanka was further yet in the future, and he was yet to take on Buddhist robes. But the seeds for his turn to Marxism had been sown and they germinated and grew roots through the 1920s, watered by a temperament he describes as *buddhivadi* (rationalist), which subjected received ideas to a relentlessly sceptical intelligence. Dialectics certainly provided a bridge between the two traditions.[2]

Parallel to this intellectual/philosophical journey was a life of enthusiastic immersion in the politics of the day. The Arya Samaj had opened him to a world of nationalist politics, a cause to which he was galvanized by the Jallianwala Bagh massacre of 1919. He offered *satyagraha* in Bihar as a member of the Congress party in 1921–22, serving prison terms in Buxar Jail in 1922 and Hazaribagh Jail in 1924–25. He would eventually move away from the Congress, disillusioned with its inability to address the problems of the peasantry in rural Bihar. He got involved with the peasant movement with Swami Sahajananda but eventually parted ways with him to help establish the Bihar unit of the Communist Party in 1939. Having already co-translated *The Communist Manifesto* into Hindi with Acharya Narendra Dev in 1930 (a manuscript now lost), in which year he was also founder member of the Socialist Party, he had now declared his allegiance to communism.

In between, he travelled. Always a *ghumakkar*, he had travelled extensively through India before making his way to Sri Lanka in the 1920s. From Sri Lanka, he went to Europe (1932–33) and then made pioneering journeys into the remote Himalayan regions of Kinnaur and Ladakh, and the four epic journeys to Tibet (1933, 1934, 1936, 1938). In 1935, he finally made it to the Soviet Union. Making his way via Malaya, Japan, Korea and Manchuria, he took the trans-Siberian Railway. In the Soviet Union, he was at the Institute of Oriental Studies, Leningrad, at the invitation of the legendary Indologist Fyodor Scherbatsky, who, having heard of his discovery in Tibet of Dharmkirti's *Pramanvarttik*, a classic text in Buddhist logic long presumed lost, had reached out to him for what would turn into a longer academic association. He travelled to Baku, besides Moscow, and returned via Iran. When he returned and re-entered the political scene as a communist, he was arrested during the Amavari Satyagraha, and subsequently, in 1940, elected president of the All India Kisan Sabha. It was as a peasant leader on the left that he found himself incarcerated in the Deoli Internment Camp in Rajasthan.

Volga se Ganga (published in 1943) thus carries traces of all these spaces – of travels, physical and mental, through books, and on foot, by rail, sea, and air. It brings together the creative and purposive impulses and commitments that drove Sankrityayan's wider worldview. Written during a two-year hiatus in his itinerant life, in that hub of creative energy that the British colonial prison turned out to be for an entire generation, first at Hazaribagh and then at the Deoli Internment Camp in Rajasthan where leftists were incarcerated, this book was birthed alongside two other books that point us to the nature of Sankrityayan's concerns at this point in his life. One was an equally monumental but entirely discursive tome called *Darshan Digdarshan*, a majestic survey of world philosophy, filtered via a palpably Marxist lens, and the other, a slimmer volume titled *Vaigyanik Bhautikvad* ('Scientific Materialism'). While these two books anticipate it in scale and political intent, they do not prepare us for the creative effusion that characterizes *Volga se Ganga*.

The book must also be seen in terms of what immediately followed the writer's release and the publication of the three books above. After release, Sankrityayan returned to the Soviet Union in 1943–44, teaching Buddhist Logic and Sanskrit, while also researching for a book that he eventually published in 1956–57 – a two-volume history of Central Asia, the Sahitya Akademi Award-winning, pathbreaking *Madhya Asia ka Itihas*, drawing extensively upon researches by Soviet archaeologists. His interest in Central Asia was fuelled by a strong sense of civilizational exchange and the intention of demonstrating that Central Asia had been transformed for the better under Soviet rule. His aim had been to bring the history up to the 1920s, but he was denied permission to enter Soviet Central Asia. In any case, this phase of his creative output is extraordinary in grandeur of scale, painting on a large canvas, narratives across genres as varied as a polemical tract, a survey/compendium of philosophical ideas on a global scale, a book of history on a neglected but crucial region, and a work of eminently readable historical fiction. In doing this, he was not only producing fresh frameworks for thinking about India's place in world history, he was also producing an *oeuvre*, in Hindi, that would provide road maps for imagining alternative futures.

Volga se Ganga: Themes

How to read *Volga se Ganga*? How *does* one comprehend a work of 'fiction' that encompasses 8,000 years of human history, attempting all the while a fidelity to a historical vision in adherence to facts then believed to be true and accessible to a non-specialist? The problem is but obviously exacerbated by the fact that history as a discipline is constantly evolving fresh models and narratives in the light of fresh facts.

A kind of frame that might help us navigate this text is expressed in the following alliterative trio: migrations (of peoples, ideas, and cultural forms, which it traces), maps (which it redraws by virtue of opening up an alternative 'route' to accessing modern India), and miscegenation (which it celebrates in both its genetic and cultural-linguistic variants). Needless to say, the three 'M's overlap and are merely offered here as suggestive modes for a possible reading of this rambling, rich romp through a massive swathe of history.

For this lively book wears its learning and its mission lightly, exhibiting a fertile, sensuous, and playful imagination at work. It was meant to be a simplified version of his book *Manav Samaj* ('Human Society') which he intended to be 'a scientific survey of social evolution'. Here, Sankrityayan says, he intended to 'give a simpler picture, and make the outline easier to grasp' (Author's Preface to the first Hindi edition). Given the burden that history has to bear in narratives of national mythmaking, the book was expectedly received as iconoclastic in certain quarters. There was even a call for it to be banned, but his extraordinary erudition had earned him the title of 'Mahapandit' in Sanskrit from Kashi *pandits*, and his proficiency in other classical languages such as Pali, Tibetan, Chinese, and Persian, rendered him a formidable opponent. So, the call was unsuccessful.

Volga se Ganga rests on an unusually wide range of travel, reading, and active politics, assimilated and presented in a readable format by a public-spirited intellectual passionately committed to shaping a new, progressive, India. As history and narrative, it seeks to educate, entertain, and inspire; its target audience a Hindi-speaking, reasonably literate Indian who might get a sense of the past, present, and likely futures of a people in the throes of an anti-imperialist struggle at home, but also part of a global anti-fascist struggle.

Sankrityayan's own ideological preferences – a secular, modern India which nevertheless maintains an affective connect with a rich, heterodox, cultural past – are apparent in the narrative's choice of episodes and characters. While its status as fictionalized history absolves it of the responsibility of absolute historical verisimilitude, the shifting terrain of historiography itself (especially in the hotly contested understanding of the 'Aryans', a debate that has recently gathered heat due to the coincidence of new findings via scientific genetic research and a revival of older anxieties about national origins) renders any dismissal of its 'lapses' moot. The book's strengths are what one would expect of a *longue durée* epic, warts and all. What's most valuable here is a unique coming together of political, historical and philosophical vision and creative imagination. Sankrityayan, with characteristic humility born of *ghumakkari* as a kind of epistemic mode, writes this book as he does others – in the spirit of an ongoing, collective, search for understanding. As he puts it in his Preface, he is glad to be corrected, satisfied with his role as pioneer.

The book is ambitious in its range, historical and affective. It begins in 6000 BCE with an unsentimental depiction of a mother drowning her own daughter in the Volga in a bitter power struggle. It is the beginning of the matrilineal clan but niceties such as the incest taboo have not yet entered the human domain. After this initial shock to the senses, the remaining early chapters, which owe much to Engels's *The Origin of the Family, Private Property and the State*, tend to be celebratory of matrilineal clans and 'primitive communism'. As human beings evolve finer emotions, romance enters relationships and the book teems in them, often in the form of star-crossed lovers enacting historical and social conflicts across time. Eros, in fact, emerges in the narrative as a revolutionary force. Story after story gives to young lovers lines that challenge the status quo, be it in questioning the logic of war, or the prevalence of communal or religions divides. In each era, the presence of slavery, poverty, and the suppression of women are especially prominent as markers of societal backwardness and are clearly marked as such in a fairly straightforward pedagogic manner. As the narrative moves into periods of recorded history, a galaxy of known names figure in the drama, intermixed with invented ones. Dress, food, and modes of hospitality from the many cultures and regions that have fed the civilization we call India today receive special attention, bringing the past come alive in vivid detail. However, debates about political systems and transformative possibilities run like a thread, clearly indicating the larger narrative intent. In the course of the narration, later inventions of India's 'authentic' or 'pure' cultural pasts get demolished and are exposed as anachronistic interpolations. India is seen, as Nehru famously also has it, as a palimpsest. We meet characters from Persepolis and Athens, while Swat, Tajikistan, Gandhar, Panchal are action zones. Taxila's Naagdatt debates 'dharm' and the forms of government with Chanakya. In Ayodhya, a young Ashvghosh romances a Greek girl Prabha as he writes the first Indian play *Urvashi Viyog*, borrowing freely from Greek dramaturgical practices. (The revered Buddhist Ashvghosh, author of *Buddhcharit* is given a pre-history that is somewhat more 'secular', decidedly more romantic.) Buddhist philosophers Dingnag and Vasubandhu make an appearance, and Dharmkirti and Naagarjun are subjected to a comparative analysis in terms of the political implications of their views. Later, we meet Jalal-ud-din Muhammad Akbar, Birbal, Abul Fazal and Todar Mall hanging out together (disguised as commoners 'Jalua', 'Fazla', 'Biru', and 'Todu'!), joking and discussing the finer points of statecraft and religion, even as Todar Mall's son and Abul Fazal's daughter enact yet another star-crossed romance. A few centuries later, we meet a grandson of the king of Banaras in England, discussing with his English girlfriend Annie Russell, among other matters, his friend Karl Marx's views on India and the relative freedom of women in the two countries. Gandhi, Ambedkar and Marx inform the conversation in the last chapter, as its protagonist, Sumer, a Dalit, debates his, the nation's, and the world's future with his friends on a summer evening in a park in Patna. Sumer, as it turns out, will die flying a fighter plane downing fascist Japanese planes, contemplating high in the air the dubious journey of man's progress from the Stone Age to the rise of fascism. The year is 1942.

The question that plagues Sumer, and most of the young

protagonists in the book, is still with us in 2019. And Sankrityayan's miscegenated history of the region arguably speaks to us with greater urgency than it did in his own time.

Volga se Ganga: Frames

In preparing this edition, I thought it fit to include, by way of frame narratives, two crucial readings, each by one of his illustrious contemporaries whose paths almost never crossed. They reflect the diversity of the worlds Sankrityayan inhabited as well as the complex texture of the text's varied reception. One is his long-term younger associate and friend from his Buddhist world, Bhadant Anand Kausalyayan, with whom he made common cause for the revival of Buddhist Studies in India, and who was his close confidante and colleague. His insights are invaluable. The other his formidable comrade S.A. Dange. One wrote in Hindi, the other in Marathi. Each has been translated in full and reproduced as an Appendix at the end of this edition. But, a brief note on each.

S.A. Dange was Sankrityayan's informal interlocutor at the Deoli Internment Camp that they shared for the duration of the writing not only of this book but also of the tome *Darshan Digdarshan*. He offers one window to the book. In his introduction to the original Marathi edition of *Volga se Ganga* (reproduced as Appendix 2 to this volume), Dange explains the book's purpose and offers a kind of review:

> As Mankind changes, each age succumbs to progress and gets pushed to a level higher. Rahulji has tried to present these levels in totality, for a combined view, through his stories in this anthology. Objections could be raised regarding some of the inclusions, that they have more than a touch of the logical or philosophical, and lack literary merit. But one finds impressive prose in most of the stories. The description of the very ancient epochs is excellent.

Dange's Introduction expectedly dwells at length on Marxist theories of human development and class conflict and raises questions inspired by the book:

> How are these eras recognized? Does the arrival and decline of each take Mankind towards 'progress' at all? Who or what is responsible for the commencing and culmination of the eras? Are they man-made or otherwise destined? These questions could give rise to many others.

Dange proceeds to offer some interesting readings of his own on the meaning of such 'Aryan' practices as *yajna* and the concept of *Brahman*:

> Their method of making things was the *yajna* method or *yajna-karm*. A civilization like that considers it a part of the larger world of inanimate things and living creatures, and it considered the universe to be '*brahman*'. One can confidently state that '*brahman*' means the way the ancients lived, or commune-living.

Moving between his own exposition and a book review, he acknowledges the affective range of the book. 'This book is not a narration of history; it divulges much more. It brings alive, era by era, Man's passions, thoughts, feelings and behaviour.' Finally, he considers and dismisses some objections that the book elicited: 'some of the portrayals of the prehistoric living conditions are so engaging, that complaints have come from some quarters that they are quite unbelievable, difficult to comprehend and that they don't fit into the social documentation of "Hindi culture". Those objections are baseless.'

Bearing testimony to the breadth of Rahul Sankrityayan's reach is the addendum to *Volga se Ganga* written by his long-term friend, monk and fellow-traveller in the project of Buddhist revival on the subcontinent – Bhadant Anand Kausalyayan. This fascinating and informative note (see Appendix 1) is invaluable in contextualizing the reception of the book in its own time for a different readership. Kausalyayan refers to the controversy the book generated in its time, with an anonymous 'Swamiji' (most likely Swami Karpatri) writing in *Vishwabandhu* (a contemporary Arya Samaji periodical), asking that the book be banned on grounds of what we would call 'hurt sentiments' today. Rahul Sankrityayan offends 'Swamiji' by preaching the virtues of nudity and as an open critic of the Veds ('*Nagnvadi Ved-nindak*'). This is a reference to some of the early chapters' matter-of-fact and unabashed descriptions and celebration of youthful bodies, beginning but not confining themselves to the cave-dwellers. Anand Kausalyayan, while taking gentle swipes at the ignorance and callowness of the unnamed 'Swamiji', launches on a defence of the book that rests on a systematic enumeration of its breathtaking range of scholarly reference that ranges from well-known classical texts, scriptures, travelogues, historical studies, and theoretical treatises in an array of languages.

Since quite a few of the sources are from Sanskrit and 'Vedic' traditions, the Swamiji and his ilk are exposed as ignorant of their own traditions, unable to appreciate and live by the vaunted ideals of 'Arya' culture – namely an ability to engage with ideas and transform minds through debate.

Kausalyayan thus brilliantly subverts the Swamiji's critique from within the presumed locations of its origin. Further, in naming well-known travelogues by Chinese pilgrims, a range of Buddhist texts in Pali and Sanskrit, and later books such as Engels's *The Origin of the Family, Private Property and the State*, he not only reveals Rahul Sankrityayan's erudition and research, he opens up for the general reader of this Hindi book a world of reference that can only be called cosmopolitan. It is an act of audacity and defiance to bring this world of ideas – clearly unorthodox – to the notice of the moribund world of the Swamiji. Anand Kausalyayan desists from offering his own readings, content to lay out in painstaking scholarly detail the specific sources that Rahul Sankrityayan relied upon in shaping *Volga se Ganga*.

Together, the two frame the book in its own time and ours, and provide lively glimpses into the rich, layered, universe that Rahul Sankrityayan, and an entire generation, inhabited.

A short note on the text and by way of acknowledgements:

The history of this edition coming together is befittingly meandering and involves varieties of *ghumakkari*. There are many firsts in this project. For my unusual interest in Rahul Sankrityayan I must thank an unusual family, especially my late father, whose own trajectory was inspired at least partly by that of 'Rahulji', as he was called at home, and my own recalcitrant obsession with his life and work, leading me to what seemed at that time a foolhardy adventure with doctoral research (on a man who wrote nothing in English) from within the English Department. It was a pleasure to hear from Vijay Prashad that he wanted to reprint the Kiernan translation with a fresh introduction. As a member of the somewhat solitary world of Sankrityayan readers in the anglophone world, I was delighted to hear that not only had he heard of Sankrityayan, he actually had read and enjoyed the book while at school. The project grew with the serendipitous discovery that an intrepid fellow-traveller and Sankrityayan enthusiast, Kanwal Dhaliwal, had translated the last chapter left untranslated by Kiernan, thus making it a complete volume. He had also 'restored' to the text some of its original flavour by retaining some of the Sanskrit words, an intervention that was accepted by all of us as an enhancement. A desire to make it a good resource book for serious students led me to track other translations as well as the book's reception history, in the course of which I heard of an Introduction by S.A. Dange who had been a part of the original production of the book. Tracking the Marathi Introduction and getting it translated was a minor feat of sleuthing in which colleague Dhananjay Kapse was of help. A translator in Pune, Sheela Jaywant, helped us make it accessible to English readers. As always, Jeta Sankrityayan and Jaya Parhawk, Sankrityayan's children and literary executors, provided much needed information, clarifications, and clearances. Finally, Vijay Prashad and Sudhanva Deshpande's enthusiasm, cooperation, and patience with this unexpectedly long, stretched-out project has been truly commendable. I thank them above all.

Some curated suggestions for further reading of Sankrityayan's works. All works are in Hindi, unless specified.

Sankrityayan, Rahul. *Akbar.* Allahabad: Kitab Mahal, 1957.

———. '*Bhadant Bodhananda Mahasthavir*'. In *Rahul Vangmaya - 2.2: Jeevani aur Sansmaran.* Delhi: Radhakrishna Prakashan, 2008.

———. *Baisvin Sadi* [The Twenty-Second Century]. Allahabad: Kitab Mahal, 1998. First published in 1931.

———. *Baisvin Sadi* (translated excerpts). In *The Gollancz Book of South Asian Science Fiction.* Edited by Tarun K. Saint. Translated, with an Introduction, by Maya Joshi. Gurugram: Hachette, 2019.

———. 'Buddhist Dialectics' (English translation). In *Buddhism: The Marxist Approach.* New Delhi: People's Publishing House, 1970. Reprinted in 1990.

———. *Darshan Digdarshan* [Survey of Philosophy]. Allahabad: Kitab Mahal, 2007. First published in 1944.

———. *Ghumakkar Shastr* [Treatise for Roamers]. Allahabad: Kitab Mahal, 1992. First published in 1948.

———. *History of Central Asia: Bronze Age - Chengiz Khan.* Kolkata: New Age Publishers Ltd., 1964, 2007. Partial translation of *Madhya Asia ka Itihas.*

———. *Manav Samaj* [Human Society]. Patna: Granthmala Karyalaya, 1943.

———. *Mere Asahyog ke Saathi* [My Comrades in Non-Cooperation]. Allahabad: Kitab Mahal, 1956.

———. *Meri Jeevan-Yatra* [My Life's Journey]. 4 vols. New Delhi: Radhakrishna Prakashan, 2005. Originally published in 1944 (Vol. I), 1950 (Vol. II), and 1967 (Vols. III & IV).

———. *Dimagi Ghulami* [The Enslavement of the Mind]. Allahabad: Kitab Mahal, 1937.

———. *Samyavad hi Kyon?* [Why Communism?]. Allahabad: Kitab Mahal, 1934.

———. *Selected Essays* (English translation). New Delhi: People's Publishing House, 1984, 2009.

———. *Tumhari Kshaya* [Your Ruin]. Allahabad: Kitab Mahal, 1977. First published in 1939.

———. *Vaigyanik Bhautikvad* [Scientific Materialism]. Kolkata: Adhunik Pustak Bhavan, 1944.

———. *Volga se Ganga* [From Volga to Ganga]. Allahabad: Kitab Mahal, 2007. First published in 1942.

Translator's Note

Kanwal Dhaliwal

In 2013, I published a Panjabi translation of *Volga se Ganga* from its original Hindi version. I was curious, at that time, about whether there was an English edition of the book. I found one on the internet, published from Varanasi. It was a curious edition, one which had several problems. First, it did not mention the name of the author – Rahul Sankrityayan – and only mentioned the translator's name, 'Victor Keirman'. Second, the edition spelled the translator's name incorrectly, for his real name – as I discovered – was Victor Kiernan (1913–2009), a Marxist scholar from the United Kingdom who lived in India from 1938 to 1946 during which time he translated the work of Muhammad Iqbal and Faiz Ahmad Faiz. Thirdly, the edition from Varanasi only had nineteen chapters – rather than twenty chapters from the original Hindi version. Why was the final chapter missing? Kiernan's edition of Rahul Sankrityayan's *Volga se Ganga* appeared in 1946 from People's Publishing House.

I began my project by translating the twentieth chapter of the book. This led me to go through the entire translation by Kiernan, which is a marvellous achievement. There were some interesting discrepancies, which I think were due to the fact that Kiernan may not have had the time to delve into the mythology and ancient history of India, in spite of his great interest in the history of the subcontinent. Fully unlocking the linguistic potential of the Indologist Sankrityayan, I am sure, would also have been the greatest challenge for a non-Indian translator. I shall list some examples to show where and how I felt it important to modify Kiernan's original translation.

Certain names of Indian places and locations have been introduced to the world by the British. For centuries, these have been wrongly pronounced and incorrectly spelled, simply for the fact that the English-speaking rulers did not pronounce them correctly. Many such names, as often surface in the media, are now being respelled in India, for example Bombay as 'Mumbai', Calcutta as 'Kolkata', Benares as 'Varanasi', etc. I have decided to keep the corrected version only where it is descriptive. If the names are mentioned by a character, then depending on who is speaking, an appropriate version has been chosen. Additionally, I opted for the correct version of names, which are still being used in their distorted forms, like Punjab (Panjab), Jhelum (Jehlam), Sutlej (Satluj), etc.

Keeping some of the names and words that have a Proto-Indo-European root un-translated is an important addition to this edited version. I noticed that Kiernan had translated these words as accurately as possible, but I felt it necessary not to translate them but to explain the meaning of the words in endnotes. This is to convey the hidden message of the author, who in his original Hindi text had kept them un-translated. I understand that the author tried to point towards the possibility of those words being used as part of the commonly used language in those regions and in that particular time in history. For example, words such as *medved* (bear), *chashak* (cup), or *shvak* (dog), Mahapitar (Great-Father), and Jambudvip (India), etc.

Apart from these historically remote words, I also felt it important to keep all the words, as originally given by the author, which have been used as titles of people of certain authority such as Chakrvarti (paramount-Imperial-ruler), Parambhattarak (His Highness), or honorific titles for Buddhist clergy – such as Dharmrakshit or Mahasthavir. These titles have a peculiar character which cannot be simply substituted with equivalent words in English or Christian terminology.

I felt it important to leave alone – in their original form – the names of animals and plants. I admire the depth of the author's knowledge of the flora and fauna of the Indian subcontinent. On almost every occasion he mentions the names of such animals or trees which are only found in that part of the world, hence have no parallel words apart from some botanical terminology. *Jamun*, *neem*, *peepal*, *bakul*, *palas* (among trees), as well as *nilgai* (a type of antelope) and *mangur* (a type of fish) are some examples.

Then there are the Indian units of weights, measures and distances, which Kiernan must have researched painstakingly to calculate their equivalents in English pounds, pints and miles. I decided to retain the original words so as to make the readers aware of ancient Indian terms for such units. Interestingly enough Sankrityayan has mentioned such words which have their root in antiquity and are not in use in contemporary Hindi either, for example *yojan* (8 miles), although units like *ser*, *kos* and *ratti* have been in use until recently.

Multi-meaning words and words that invite great debates and controversies like Arya and Indr did need to be left as they are, untranslated and without entry into the contemporary debates around these terms. Kiernan's translation contains confusion at times – where the word Arya is rendered as 'sir' and Indr as 'prince', which are not accurate in certain instances.

The trend of spelling Indian names/words (ones that end in a consonant) of historical importance with an extra 'a' at the end, for example 'Shiva' for Shiv, 'Buddha' for Buddh, 'yoga' for *yog*, etc., also came under scrutiny. It was decided to spell all such names as close as possible to their original pronunciation, moving away from the tradition. I must add that such a trend has been so damaging to the understanding of the original pronunciation, the manipulated spellings are being considered 'correct' even by the younger generation in India, let alone in the rest of the world.

Semantics and phonetics was the rather easy part while editing the text. The major challenge I faced which, I believe, must have been the case for Kiernan as well, were the metaphors and similes. There were so many occasions where I found that the true expression of the original had not been conveyed or wrongly conveyed. Obviously, there were linguistic issues as well as cultural ones at play. I have tried to resolve the issue either by giving my version or through the endnotes. For example, Kiernan's translation of one sentence reads: *She made her way down towards the margin of a stream laughing its way among the stones*. It should have been translated as: *She made her way down towards the margin of a stream roaring its way among the stones*. The mistake is rather funny. The word normally used in Hindi to express loud/harsh noise is used for a kind of loud-laughter; however, the word does not literally mean laughter. Besides, the present participle verb 'roaring' here is attributed to the object (stream) and not to the subject, 'she', which appears to be the cause of the imprecision. Then there are cases where mythology has become a hurdle in conveying the true sense of an expression. '*My* chandr, *you have come back from the shadows*', is Kiernan's translation for '*My* chandr, *you have returned safe from the mouth of Rahu!*' I can understand that for an English reader it would have made no sense if the myth of Rahu or the meaning of '*chandr*' were not explained. For obvious reasons, therefore, the translator here appears to have chosen a simplified version, which I preferred to replace with the original expression explaining the myth in the endnotes.

It would be unfair to claim that I accomplished this project on my own. There are many, near and dear, who participated with their expertise to enable me to declare 'mission accomplished'. I would like to first thank Uwe Groth, a scholar of Sanskrit and Russian with a good knowledge of English and of course his mother tongue – German. Uwe, a good friend from Hamburg, had provided me great help even during the project of my Panjabi translation of the same book, in making me understand all the references that the author had quoted in Sanskrit. He not only retyped all the Sanskrit verses that were mentioned in the book, in a modern font system, but he also translated them into English for me to understand exactly what they meant.

Dr. Kamakshi Balasubramanian, an excellent author herself, a scholar of Russian language and literature and my teacher at university in the city of Hyderabad, India, a dear friend of course, was so kind to read through my draft of the twentieth chapter that I had dared to translate 'on my own'. Shaun Jeffery, a dear comrade from Suffolk was also kind to look at my first attempt on the last chapter and to offer advice for improvement. The scrutinizing eye of Nazeef Mollah, editor at LeftWord Books, further enhanced the text. The story of 'Sumer' would never have been a flawless translation without their help.

I must thank Dr. Madhu Bala from the city of Patiala, India, a scholar of Sanskrit, Hindi and Panjabi and author of numerous books in these languages. Mrs. Bala is not only a close friend but an ex-colleague during my teaching days in India. She has been a great help in eliminating some discrepancies that were either typing errors in the

Hindi text or were not written correctly in the first place. She helped me to understand many words that I was not sure of the pronunciation of in the original, since I still have gaps in my understanding of the Devanagari script. While mentioning all those who helped with my Hindi, I cannot forget another name – Ms. Satnam Kaur, a close friend, who, being a native Hindi speaker, and to my luck, a resident of London, often removed my doubts about certain difficult-to-pronounce words. Satnam is a poetess and an art graduate.

I thank my dear friend Preetinder Singh Bajwa, an expert graphic designer and a fellow artist, for the map and illustration that appear on pages 38 and 144 respectively.

My wife Kamaljit deserves all the credit for letting me carry on with my work uninterrupted, while I should, in fact, have been helping her in the day-to-day responsibilities at home. She had not only to fulfil the demanding responsibilities of her teaching job, but also to care for two teenage kids. I am so grateful to her and to my son Livtar and daughter Livleen.

Translator's Note

I undertook this translation at the suggestion of Mr. P.C. Joshi, General Secretary of the Communist Party of India, who is proud of having read Tulsi Das seventeen times, and even now, amid his enormous daily work, keeps in touch with arts and letters even in mellower moments, talking of a holiday some day in the Welsh hills. I found the book as interesting as he had led me to expect, but very much more difficult. The author, whom I had had the pleasure of meeting, left India soon after I began work, to undertake research in Indology in the USSR, and thus escaped the numerous questions with which I should otherwise have plied him. His diction, in the first part of the book, is very heavily Sanskritized, as is natural in view of the demands of his subject and his profound knowledge of the Sanskrit language. In the latter part, dialect phrases are introduced, and a certain number of errors in the Hindi text assisted to complicate my problem.

The task would have been quite beyond my inadequate knowledge, had I not been liberally helped by my Hindi-speaking colleagues of Aitchison College, Lahore. I take this opportunity of thanking Dr. Hardev Bahri, Ph.D. D.Litt., and Mr. P.C. Jain – the latter of whom, on one occasion, ransacked no fewer than fourteen lexicons in a vain search for a word which had baffled all of us. Mr. Maharaj Krishan Anand was my most constant guide, rescuing me with unwearied energy from the quicksand which beset my path. Mr. Ramesh Sinha, of the Hindi staff of *People's Age*, undertook the laborious task of revising my entire manuscript. I cannot sufficiently express my gratitude to these friends for their generous help. If, as may be inevitable in the translation of so long and difficult a work, some errors have managed to survive, I can only blame myself.

V.G. Kiernan Bombay, 24 July 1946

Author's Preface

(Second Hindi Edition)

It is gratifying to an author to see the first edition of his work exhausted within seven or eight months; and still more gratifying is the resentment it has aroused among conservatives, which sometimes expresses itself in the form of unrestricted nonsense and abuse. But I believe that the stream of abuse has now diminished. Certain respectable persons, making decidedly unsuccessful efforts to keep their tempers, have indulged in pedantic criticisms, and have wished me to write a defence of myself. In general I have no desire to avoid writing; but there must be something solid to write against. I have had a good deal of material as the basis of each story: various languages and their comparative philology; records deducible from or written on clay, stone, copper, bronze, iron; unwritten songs, tales, customs, magic rites. It was my hope while writing, and still is, to publish an indication of these materials in the shape of an appendix; but this would be a heavy task, and lack of time has hindered me from undertaking it. In any case, it could not be included in this volume, as it would more than double its length. I do, however, intend to see about it.

In this second edition, I have made very few changes, except to add a small touch here and there. I had hoped to include illustrations with each story, but wartime difficulties have not permitted this.

Rahul Sankrityayan Allahabad, 4 November 1943

Author’s Preface

(First Hindi Edition)

Man at the Outset was far from standing where he stands today; many conflicts have been a necessary part of his development. I have tried to give a scientific survey of social evolution in my book *Manav Samaj* [‘Human Society’]. The wish to give a simpler picture, and make the outline easier to grasp, has led me to write the present book. It deals with the Indo-European race, with which Indian readers will feel more at home. This race had forerunners, centuries earlier, in the Egyptians, Assyrians, and Indus Valley people, but an attempt to deal with all these would multiply difficulties – for author and reader alike. I have tried to give an authentic account of society as it was at each stage, but errors will inevitably creep into a pioneer attempt like this. If my work helps other writers to build up a clearer picture, I shall consider myself to have been successful.

About the period to which the story ‘Bandhul the Malla’ in this volume belongs, I have written a separate novel – *Singh Senapati* [‘The Lion-Hearted Commander’].

Rahul Sankrityayan

Central Jail, Hazaribagh
23 February 1942

From Volga to Ganga

Map

LOCATIONS WHERE EACH STORY IS SET

Nisha

REGION : BANKS OF THE UPPER VOLGA
PEOPLE : INDO-EUROPEAN
TIME : 6000 BCE

This story takes us back some 360 generations of human life. The white races of India, Iran and Europe formed one clan then. It was the early dawn of mankind.

—1—

It is afternoon. Today, after how many days, the blessing of sunshine has returned. Although, with only five hours' daylight, there is no vigour in the sun's warmth, still, there is no cloud, snowfall, fog, or strong wind. The sun pours its rays everywhere delighting the eyes and, with their warm touch, releasing joyful feelings in the mind. What is visible all round? Under the blue sky's roof the earth is covered with snow, white as camphor. There has been no fresh snowfall in the last twenty-four hours, and the snow on the ground has crystallized and hardened. But it does not conceal the earth under one unvaried covering. Running from north to south is something like a silvery, crooked line, several miles long. From far away on the hills, on each side, it can be made out as the edge of a dark range of forest. Let us look at this forest from a nearer point. Two kinds of trees are the commonest in it. One is the birch, with its skin of white bark, but at present bare of leaves. The other is the flawlessly straight pine, shooting out its branches at right angles from high up on the trunk, with needle-like leaves of bright or darker green. Where snow has rested on the trees, the ice that has formed here and there on the branches and trunks makes an arresting pattern of black and white.

And what else? Stretching in every direction lies one unbroken realm of terrible silence. Nowhere heard the chirp of the cricket, the caressing music of birds, or the sound of any animal.

Let us climb the pine that stands at the summit of the hill and look all round. Perhaps something else will come in view besides snow, earth, pines. Is nothing growing here except giant trees? Is there no room in this land for little plants, for grass? We cannot guess. We have left two parts of the winter behind, and are now in the third and last. We have no means of measuring how deep is the snow these trees appear to have dug into. It may be twelve feet deep, or even more. This year the snowfall has been very heavy, everybody complains about it.

What is this that can be seen from the top of the pine? The same snow, the same forest-range, the same region of hills – high and low. Yes, but at one point on the other side of the hill, smoke is rising. In this lifeless and soundless wilderness, it is strange to see a wreath of smoke. Let us make for it, and satisfy our curiosity.

The smoke was really at a great distance, though in the transparent cloudless atmosphere it seemed quite close. Now we have got very near to it. A smell of fat and meat cooking on a fire enters our nostrils. And now voices can be heard, those of small children. We must move softly, not letting our footsteps, even our breath, be heard, or else these creatures will become aware of us, and there is no knowing what sort of welcome they or their dogs might give us.

Yes, it really is a half-dozen of children, all in one house, the biggest not more than eight years old, the youngest only one year. The 'house' is in fact a natural hill-cave. How far inward its sides and rear extend, we cannot see, for they are in darkness, and we had better not try to see! As for grown-ups, there is an old woman, whose hair, the colour of flax or of smoke, hangs in tangled and matted locks so as almost to cover her face. But just now she has pushed it back with one hand. Her eyebrows also are pale, and her whole face is lined with wrinkles that seem as if they were growing from inside it. The smoke and warmth of the fire fill the cave, especially just where the children and our old grandmother are. On the latter's body is no clothing, no covering. Her two shrunken hands rest on the ground near her feet. Her eyes are deep-sunk, and their pale blue pupils dull as though empty: still, in their depths a spark still flickers, to show that their light is not quite extinguished. As to her ears, they seem to be doing their duty. She evidently hears the children's voices very well. Now one child has set up an outcry, and she turns her eyes that way. There are a couple of children – a boy and girl, two years old or a little more, who are very much of the same size. Both have pallid hair with a tinge of yellow, like the old woman's, but with a stronger sheen, with more life. Their bodies are plump and well nourished, tawny or yellowish in hue; they have big, deep blue eyes. The boy is crying noisily, the girl standing up and sucking a small bone she has pushed into her mouth. In the quavering voice of old age the grandmother says – 'Agin! Come! Come here. Agin! Granny here!'

Agin stays where he is without getting up. At this juncture an eight-year-old boy comes, lifts him up in his arms, and carries him to the grandmother. This boy's hair has more gold in it than the small child's, but is longer and more matted. His body, naked from head to foot, is of the same white colour; it is less plump, and streaked here and there with dark dirt stains. The bigger boy sets the little one down on his feet near the grandmother, saying – 'Granny! Rochna has snatched the bone. Agin crying.'

Then he goes away, and the grandmother lifts Agin up in her withered hands. He keeps on crying, and the flowing stream of his tears washes a thick line of skin across his dirty cheeks. Kissing and fondling his face, the old woman says – 'Agin! Don't cry! I beat Rochna!' – and she smacks one hand against the cave floor, bare soil soaked thick with the grease-droppings of many years. Even now Agin's whimpering does not stop, and his tears go on rolling. The grandmother wipes them with her dirty palm, reducing the streaks of tawny skin showing on his face to a uniform grimness. Then, to soothe the child's weeping, she puts him to her skinny breasts that hang down like dried half-grown pumpkins in the framework of ribs starting out from under her shrivelled skin. Agin closes his mouth on one breast and stops crying. At this moment a sound of conversation comes from outside. Agin peeps in that direction, the dry breast dragging at his mouth. A soft, pleasant voice is heard – 'Agi... i... i... n!'

Agin begins to cry afresh. Two women enter, and bang down in one corner the bundles of wood piled on their heads. Then one of them runs up to Rochna, the other to Agin. The latter, crying all the harder, howls 'Ma-ma!' His mother frees her right hand, and undoing above her right breast a hairy white bull-hide dress pinned with porcupine-quills, lets it slip down. There is too little flesh on her young body, because of the scarcity of food in winter, but it is remarkably graceful. She has bright, clean cheeks of the same tawny complexion as the children, and flaxen hair, not matted but flowing loose and falling over her forehead. Round, red-tipped breasts stand out from her broad spare chest; her waist is curved inwards, her hips medium-sized healthy, her thighs rounded and muscly; plough-shaped[1] calves, that are clearly accustomed to hard exercise. This eighteen-year-old girl lifts Agin up with both hands, and kisses his mouth, eyes and cheeks. His little white teeth show between his red lips, glistening, his eyes half-closed; and small dimples appear in his cheeks. The young woman, sitting on the bull-skin she had dropped, puts Agin's mouth to her soft breast. He clutches it with all his fingers, and begins to suck. Just now the other young woman, equally naked, carries Rochna over and sits down near her. Watching their faces, one sees that the two women are sisters.

—2—

Leaving them talking, hidden inside the cave, we take a look round outside. Across the snow, in one direction, runs a trail of imprints of many skin-shod feet. Let us follow them up quickly. The trail slants, and reaches the hill-forest on the other side. We make haste and go on climbing, but there is no end to the fresh footprints. At one moment we are crossing a white snowfield; at another we penetrate the thicket straddling the ridge of a hill and mount a new snowfield and new tree-clad slopes. At last, staring up from below, we catch sight of the skyline of a ridge bare of trees. There the white mass of the snow rises to meet the blue sky; silhouetted against this blue, several figures of human beings are in the point of being lost to view behind the hill. If the bright sky were not at their backs, we should certainly not be able to make them out. The bull-hides thrown over their bodies are white like the snow. The weapons in their hands seem to borrow the same white colour. It would be very hard to recognize their shapes on the vast, white snowfield.

Going closer, we see at their head a woman of between forty and fifty, with a body powerfully developed. Her bare right arm is enough to reveal her strength. In her hair, her face, and all her limbs she resembles the two young women in the cave, but is much bigger. In her left hand is a stout, sharp pointed stick of birchwood, four or five feet long. Her right hand holds a stone axe sharpened by friction, its head lashed with leather thongs into the wooden handle. Behind her walk four men and a pair of women. One man may be a little older than the leading woman; the others range from a youth of twenty-six to a boy of fourteen. The big man has long, straw-coloured hair like the rest, while a thick moustache and beard of the same hue overspread his face. His physique is muscular like the woman's, and two weapons of the same sort as hers are gripped in his two hands. Two of the other three males have exactly his bushy moustache and beard, and only differ from him in age. Of the females, one is twenty-two, the other sixteen or nearly sixteen. Having seen the faces of the grandmother and the rest of the cave-brood, we can compare them with these, and are left in no doubt that the old woman is the mould that has shaped all these men and women.

From the implements of wood, bone and stone in their hands, and from the intentness of their motions, it is obvious on what mission they are bound ...

Descending from the crest, the leading woman – the Mother, as we may call her – turned off to the left, the rest following in silence. As they moved over the snow, not the faintest sound came from their skin-wrapped feet. Suspended in front of them was a high rock face, with boulders strewn about it. The hunters were advancing now very slowly and with extreme caution, in open order, drawing out each stride to its greatest extent as they lifted foot after foot, and finding holds on the rock with their hands. It was the Mother who was first to reach the entrance of a cave. She stared intently at the white snow outside it, but there were no tracks of any kind. Then she stole into the cave, alone. When she had gone a few feet it bent to one side, and the light became dim. She paused awhile to let her eyes grow accustomed to it, and then, going further, found three big bears – a male, female and cub fast asleep, if not dead, with heads sunk on the ground; no sign of life could be detected in them.

Stealthily the Mother re-joined her troop. At the first sight of her animated face they guessed that she had made a 'find'. Pressing the little finger down with the thumb she held up the other three fingers spread out. Two men gripped their weapons and followed her inside; the rest stood still, waiting with bated breath. Once inside, the Mother approached the he-bear and stood beside it; the big man took up his position next to the she-bear; the other took the cub. Then, simultaneously, their pointed sticks were plunged downward with such force as to pierce the flank and penetrate to the heart. The animals never stirred. The end of their six-month winter sleep had been still more than a month distant. But the Mother and her brood could not know this; they had to be on their guard. Three or four times more they drove the points of their sticks into the bellies, before rolling the he-bear over. Then they fearlessly seized the bears by their forepaws and snouts, and dragged them to the cave entrance – all laughing exultantly and talking at the top of their voices.

Laying the big bear out flat, the Mother drew a flint knife from inside her dress of skins and, starting from where the wound gaped, skinned off the fur from the belly. To remove a fur so accurately with a stone knife is work for strong and experienced hands. Cutting off a morsel from the soft heart she put it in her mouth and then another in the mouth of the youngest, the boy of fourteen. All the rest squatted round the bear and she went on cutting bits from the heart and distributing them. When the first bear's heart was finished, and the Mother was laying her hands on the second, the sixteen-year-old girl went outside and stuffed a piece of snow in her mouth. The big man also emerged, put some snow in his mouth and caught hold of the girl's hand. She resisted slightly then quietened. The man put his arm round her and led to one side.

When the two of them returned to the bears, each holding a big handful of snow, there was a brighter colour in their cheeks and eyes. The man said – 'I'll cut, Mother! You are tired.'

The Mother handed the knife to him, and, turning, caressed

the face of a youth of twenty-four, took him by the hand, and went outside. They ate up the hearts of all three bears, on which, since they had been hibernating for four months without food, little fat could be expected to remain. The cub's flesh, however, was rather more tender and appetizing, and of this they devoured a good deal. Then all lay down side by side to take a little rest.

Now they must turn back for home. The he-bear and she-bear were hoisted up by two men each, all four feet bound together with thongs of hide to a staff resting on the men's shoulders. One girl carried the cub, and the Mother, grasping her stone axe, moved ahead.

These savages had no notion of clock-time, but they knew that the night would be a moonlit one. They had covered some distance, when the sun appeared to sink below the horizon. Actually, it had not gone right down, and twilight lingered for several hours; by the time it vanished moonlight was reigning on earth, in heaven, everywhere.

Their cave-home was still distant when at a certain point, in a tract of open country, the Mother halted, listened with concentrated attention, and caught a sound. All stood in silence. The sixteen-year-old girl moved close to the man of about twenty-six, saying – 'G'rr, g'rr ... *vrik*! *vrik*!'[2] Nodding her head, the Mother repeated, 'G'rr, g'rr – *vrik*! *vrik*!' and added in a tone of breathless excitement – 'Ready!'

The game was laid on the ground, and they all took a firm grip of their weapons and stood back to back, peering in every direction. All of a sudden, a pack of seven or eight wolves rushed towards them with lolling tongues; they came close, snarling and began to circle round them. Seeing the wooden spears and stone axes in the hunters' hands, they hesitated before attacking. Meanwhile the boy, who was standing in the middle, detached from his staff a length of wood tied to it, unwound from his waist a thin strip of stout leather, and with the two made ready a bow. Pulling out some sharp stone-headed arrows that had been concealed somewhere about him, he thrust them and the bow into the hands of the youth of twenty-four, pulled him into the middle, and stationed himself in his place. The young man tightened the string and drew the bow, and an arrow released with a sharp twang struck one wolf in the flank. The wolf rolled over, but recovered, and was about to make a desperate attack when the man shot another arrow. This time the wound was mortal. Seeing the wolf motionless, the rest of the pack came close, licked the hot blood pouring from its body, and then tore it to pieces and began to devour it.

Observing them preoccupied with their feast, the hunters lifted up their game, and running with stealthy steps began hastening on their way again. This time the Mother was in the rear, turning to stare back from time to time. Today no snow had fallen, so they could easily find their way through the moonlit night by retracing their own footmarks. The cave might have been less than a mile distant when the wolf pack caught up with them once more. For the second time they laid their game down and grasped their weapons. The archer shot several arrows, but could inflict no injury on the wolves, which were never still for a moment together. The wolves manoeuvred about them for a while, and then four of them in one rush sprang upon the girl of sixteen. The Mother, who was at her side, thrust her spear into one wolf's belly and stretched it on the ground, but the other three fastened their claws in the girl's thighs, pulled her down, and instantly ripping open her stomach began to tear out her entrails. Just when everyone's attention was fixed on trying to rescue the girl, the remaining three wolves pounced on the unprotected back of the youth of twenty-four, not leaving him the slightest possibility of defending himself, and dragging him to the ground began tearing open his body also. And while his friends were engaged on that side, the girl had been dragged thirty or forty feet away. The Mother looked around: the young man was gasping out his last breath, close to the bleeding wolf. One of them thrust his spear into the dying wolf's open jaws, a second seized hold of its front jaws, and the rest, pressing their mouths to the wound, gulped the flowing, hot brackish blood. The Mother made it easier for them by cutting the jugular vein. All this had taken place in a few minutes; they knew that as soon as the wolves had finished eating the girl, there would be a new attack. Abandoning the dying man where he lay, and raising the three bears and the dead wolf, they set off running, and reached their cave in safety.

The fire was burning and crackling, and in its red glow all the children and the two girls were lying asleep. The old woman caught the sound of their approach, and in a trembling, deep voice said –

'Nisha! You have come!'

'Yes,' answered the Mother, as she first stacked her weapons on one side and then, unfastening her skin dress, emerged naked. The others put down the game, removed their wrappings of skin, and allowed the warm comfortable glow of the fire to steal over their entire bodies.

By this time all the sleepers had woken up. These people were accustomed from childhood to awake at the most ordinary sound. It was only by the most careful husbanding of resources that the Mother had kept her family alive until now. The hunting of deer, hares, wild cattle, sheep, goats and horses had come to an end before the onset of winter, because these creatures had migrated to the sunny, faraway lands of the south. The Mother's group should also have moved somewhat further south, but the girl of sixteen had just then fallen ill. According to the code by which Man lived in that age, it was no part of the duty of the Mother, the family head, to jeopardize the lives of all for the sake of one; but the Mother's heart had weakened and today they had lost two members instead of one. Two months still remained before the return of the game; in this interval it was still to be seen how many more lives would be lost. Three bears and one wolf were not enough to get them through the winter.

The children were overjoyed; poor things had gone to bed with empty stomachs. The Mother began by cutting up the wolf's heart and giving it to them, and while they were smacking their lips and feasting she removed the skin without doing it any injury, for fur is a very useful thing. When meat had been cut and was being distributed, the hungriest ate some raw; then they roasted it on the embers of the fire and all fell to feeding. Each one pressed the Mother to take a bite from their morsels of the roast, but she only said – 'Well, today eat your bellyful; from tomorrow there will not be so much!'

Later, she got up and brought from one corner of the cave a swollen bladder, saying – 'Here, here is honey-wine, tonight drink, dance, enjoy yourselves.'

The little ones were allowed a mouthful each from the wineskin, their elders got more, and tipsy merriment sprang up. Their eyes reddened, bursts of laughter broke out. Someone sang a song. The big man started banging one stick against another while the others began dancing. It was a night of overflowing happiness. They had a ruler – The Mother, but hers was no rule of injustice. All but grandmother and the big man were the Mother's offspring, while she and the big man were both children of the old woman, so that there could be no question of 'mine' or 'thine' among them. In fact, a very long time was still to elapse before the coming of age of 'ownership'. The Mother, it is true, had paramount authority over all males equally. It would be untrue to say that she did not regret the death of the youth – her son and husband at once; but the conditions of life in that epoch forced people to think more about the present than the past. The Mother now had two 'husbands' left with her, and a third, the boy of fourteen, would soon be ready. Of the children living under her rule, one could not know how many would grow up to take their place as husbands. The Mother being fond of the young man of twenty-six, only the fifty-year-old man was left for the three young women.

One day, when winter was drawing to a close, the old grandmother fell asleep forever. Wolves carried off three of the children, and when the snows were melting the big man fell into the boiling current of a stream.

With all this, only nine survivors remained of the family of sixteen.

—3—

It was springtime. Long-dead nature was undergoing her transformation into a new existence. Shoots of leaves were coming out on birch trees that had been sterile for six months. Snow was melting, greenery overspreading the earth. A damp intoxicating scent of vegetation and fresh soil was wafted by the breezes. A lifeless universe was again filling with life. Here in the trees, birds warbled their varied notes; there the cricket kept up its perpetual chirping. Perched on the banks of channels filled with melted snow, thousands of water-fowls were easily pecking for grubs; the swan engaged in its amorous sports. Amid the green hill-forests, herds of deer could be seen skipping or grazing; there were sheep, goats, stags, cows, and here and there crouched the panther and the wolf, eager to devour them.

Just as the streams frozen by winter resumed their flow, each group of human beings which had been immobilized in one place, also put itself in motion. Loaded with weapons, skins and children, and bearing with them their household fire, men were making for the more open areas. With the passing of the days, they, like the animals and plants, regained their vigour, and layers of flesh and fat accumulated under their shrunken skins. Sometimes their shaggy dogs pulled down a sheep or a goat; sometimes they themselves captured some game with snare, arrow or wooden spear. There were fish, besides, in the river and at this season these dwellers along the upper reaches of the Volga never drew up their nets empty.

It was still cold at night, but the days were warm, and the family whose mother was Nisha had now fallen in with other such groups on the bank of the Volga. In those days it was a mother who held sway not a father. It was, indeed, impossible to say who the father of any individual was. Nisha had had eight girls and six boys born to her, of whom she still had now, when she had reached her fifty-fifth year, four daughters and three sons. There was no doubt about their being her children, since there was the evidence of their birth to prove it, but to say who the father of each was, not possible. While Nisha's mother, the old grandmother, had occupied the chief position before her, the old woman, then in her maturity, had had numerous husbands, some of them her brothers, some her sons: and often enough these, singing and dancing with Nisha, had succeeded in making themselves the objects of her love. Later, when she herself became the leader, none of her brothers or grown-up sons ventured to deny her constantly varying choice of a love-partner. Hence the lack of any means of settling the paternity of her surviving seven children. In Nisha's family she herself was the biggest and oldest, as well as the most powerful; though her superiority was not likely to last much longer. In a year or two she herself would be turning into an old grandmother, and Lekha, the strongest of her daughters would take her place. When that happened, there would be sharp quarrelling between Lekha and her sisters. On each mother-chief devolved the duty of preserving her family from extinction – for every year some were bound to fall victim to the jaws of wolves or panthers, the claws of bears, the horns of bulls, or the Volga's flood. Of Lekha's sisters, one or two, as always happened, would succeed in founding separate families. This proliferation of families would come to an end when one man came to be the centre of a group of women, as now one woman was the centre of a group of men.

Nisha saw her daughter Lekha win success after success in the hunt; she was as quick as a deer at climbing the hills. One day they came in sight of a beehive, so high up on the rocks that even the *medved*[3] would not be able to get at it. But Lekha fastened several poles end to end, and in the night swarmed up them like a lizard, scorched the big stinging bees away from the hive with a torch, and made a hole in it. Not less than thirty *ser*[4] of honey dripped into the skin bag she held underneath. This daring act of Lekha's won the commendation of neighbouring families as well as her own. But Nisha did not rejoice at it. She saw that the more eager the young men of the family were to dance at Lekha's signal, the less they welcomed her own advances, though at present they had not the courage to flout her openly.

For a long time now Nisha had been trying to think of a remedy. Sometimes the thought came to her of seizing Lekha by the throat and killing her in her sleep; but she realized that Lekha was the stronger, and that single-handed she could not hope for success against her daughter. She might seek the help of another, but why should anyone agree to become her accomplice? All the men of the family desired to win Lekha's affection and love. Nisha's daughters would be equally reluctant to assist her. They were afraid of Lekha – they knew that if such an attempt failed they would suffer a miserable death at Lekha's hands.

Nisha was seated by herself, turning something over in her mind. Suddenly her face lit up – an expedient for getting the better of Lekha had occurred to her.

The day was three hours old. The families, each behind its own skin tent, were lying or sitting naked to enjoy the sunshine, but Nisha was in front of her tent. Near her was playing Lekha's three-year-old boy. In Nisha's hand was a leaf-cup containing some bright red strawberries. The Volga was flowing close by, and before Nisha, the ground sloped down to the steep bank of the river. Nisha let fall one strawberry, the boy ran and picked it up and ate it. Then she sent another rolling and to pick this up he had to go a little further. Nisha went on quickly throwing the berries, and as fast as she threw them, the child scampered to catch them, till the moment came when its foot slipped on the brink, and it fell with a splash into the swift current of the Volga.

As Nisha's glance fell on the river, she screamed. Lekha was sitting a little distance away, watching. As her son vanished, she hastened towards the bank. The boy was floating half-submerged in the stream. She plunged in, and succeeded in catching hold of him. The child had swallowed a great deal of water, and lost its strength: the icy water of the Volga pierced its body like a spear. It was only with great effort that Lekha could force her way through the current towards the bank. With one hand she was clutching her son; with the other, and her feet, she was trying to swim. And now she felt the grip of a pair of strong hands fastening itself round her throat. Lekha had no need to wonder what was happening. She had long noticed the change in Nisha's attitude to her. Today, Nisha meant to remove her like a thorn from her path. She was still able to make Nisha feel her strength, but the child encumbered one hand. Seeing her calling up all her energy, Nisha strove to force her down, her breast pressed against Lekha's head. Lekha for the first time sank under the surface, and while she struggled the child slipped out of her hold. By now Nisha had reduced her to helplessness. But suddenly her fingers closed on Nisha's throat. Lekha was senseless, and Nisha powerless to swim with this weight dragging her down. She fought on, but in vain. Both, locked together, were swept away by the Volga.

Rochna, now its strongest surviving woman, became the matriarch of the Nisha family.

Diva

REGION : BANK OF THE MIDDLE VOLGA
PEOPLE : INDO-SLAV
TIME : 3500 BCE

This story is about an Aryan clan, some 225 generations ago. At that time, the white races of India, Iran and Russia made one common race, which is called the Indo-Slavs or the 'Hundred Families'.

—1—

'Diva![1] The sun is so strong, look, your body is covered with sweat. Come, sit down here on this stone.'

'All right, Surshrava!' and Diva came and sat down beside him on the flat rock in the shade of a big pine tree.

No wonder Diva's forehead shone with drops of perspiration like tawny pearls, for it was summertime, and noon, and they had been running after deer. But the scene was one which might quickly charm away weariness. From base to summit, the mountain was covered with greenery; great pines, with their spreading branches and sharp leaves, broke the force of the sun's rays. Underneath, between their trunks, flowers, creepers and plants of many kinds were growing. After resting awhile the young pair forgot their weariness, and began to take pleasure in the variegated colours and sweet scent of the vegetation growing all round them. The youth put down his bow and arrows and stone axe on the rock, and began to pick white, purple, red flowers from among the plants growing at the edges of a stream of crystal-clear water that flowed peacefully nearby. The girl, too, laid aside her weapons and passed her hand through her long golden hair; her scalp was still damp. For a moment she looked towards the bank of the Volga, rolling calmly on below. Then the pleasant murmur of birds for a moment charmed her attention; she turned, and her eyes fell on the young man picking flowers. He had the same golden hair, but she could not think of comparing her own with it: his hair seemed to her far more handsome. The youth had a thick yellow beard, above which could be seen the tawny skin of his nose, cheeks and forehead. The girl's glance fell on his strong, hairy arms, and the recollection came to her of a day when he had broken the back of a big long-tusked boar with a single blow of a stone axe, wielded by those same arms. How mighty they had looked that day and now, as he picked flowers, how gentle they seemed! But even now the firm flesh of his forearms, and the veins standing out on his wrists as he tensed them, allowed his strength to be seen.

The idea came into the girl's mind once of going to him and caressing those arms: they seemed to her so fascinating just now. She stared at his thighs, and noticed how the muscles stood out at each step. To Diva they appeared truly wonderful, these thighs not fat but sinewy, and these strong calves and narrow ankles. Sur[2] had, at times, betrayed a desire to win Diva's love; not by words, but by his expression. Sometimes in the dances he had tried to please her by displaying his skills; but while she had often linked arms with other young men of the clan and danced with them, had sometimes given them her lips to kiss, or laid down with her head in their lap, the unlucky Sur had been left disappointed of a single kiss or embrace, and even of ever holding her hand in the dance.

Now he was coming towards her, with his cupped hands full of flowers. As she sat, conscious of the full bloom of his naked body, the fine shape of his broad chest and slender, muscular waist, Diva had a feeling of regret. Why had she never thought about Sur? But really, it was not she that was so much to blame; it was the bashfulness that had chained Sur's tongue. '*A door opens only to him who knocks*'.

As Sur approached, Diva smiled and said –

'How pretty these flowers are, and how nicely they smell!'

'If I twine them into your golden hair,' said Sur, putting his flowers down on the stone, 'they will look even prettier.'

'Sur! Was it for me you were bringing these flowers?'

'Yes. I looked at them, and looked at you, and I thought of the water-fairies.'

'Water-fairies?'

'Yes, the beautiful water-fairies who make all your wishes come true when they are pleased, and when they are angry won't even leave you alive.'

'And which kind of fairy do you think I am, Sur?'

'Not an angry one.'

'But I have never shown pleasure in you.' Diva sighed and became silent.

'No, Diva,' repeated Sur. 'You have never been angry with me. Do you remember our childhood?'

'Even then you were bashful.'

'But you did not get angry with me.'

'I kissed you myself in those days.'

'Yes; how sweet those kisses were!'

'But when these round breasts of mine began to swell, then all the young men of the clan began to look out for me,' said Diva regretfully, 'and then I forgot all about you.'

'But it was not your fault, Diva!'

'Then whose?'

'Mine; because when the young men of the clan begged you for a kiss, you gave them a kiss; if any of them wanted an embrace, you gave them an embrace. You have never disappointed the hopes of any young man of the clan who was a successful hunter and good at dancing, and had a strong fine body.'

'But you were like that, Sur, you were even more active and nimble and well made, and I disappointed your hope.'

'But I never showed my desire, Diva.'

'Not in words; even in childhood when we used to play together, you never put your wishes into words, but Diva used to understand. Then Diva forgot her Sur. Does this other Diva (Day) ever forget that shining Sur (Sun)? No! Diva will never forget you now.'

'So we shall be the same Sur and Diva as we used to be!'

'Yes, and I'll kiss your lips.'

Like a pair of children, the two naked graceful creatures pressed together their full lips, and then Diva, gazing into Sur's blue eyes with her own, blue as the linseed flower, said –

'And you are the son of my own mother, and I forgot you!'

Her eyes were wet. Sur, brushing her tears away with his cheek, said –

'No, you didn't forget me. When you grew up, your voice and eyes, all your body, began to seem different, and I ran away from you.'

'Not in your thoughts, Sur!'

'Well ...'

'No! Tell me you will never be afraid of me again!'

'I won't be afraid ... Come, let me fasten these flowers.'

Sur pulled the fibres out of a long stalk, and with it began twining together his red, white and purple blossoms, arranging them artistically. Then he gathered Diva's hair together and let it fall over her back. In these warm days, the young men and women of the Volga banks often indulged in bathing and swimming, so Diva's hair was fresh and free from tangles. Sur hung his garland round it like a three-fold girdle, and finally slipped into it over her forehead a spray of purple flowers at each side with one of white flowers between. Diva was still sitting on the stone. Sur stood back a little and gazed at her face. How beautiful she looked! He moved away a little further; she seemed even more beautiful, but from there he could not smell the scent of the flowers. He came back and sat near her, leaning his cheek against her. Diva kissed her companion's eyes, and laid her right hand on his shoulder. Sur, clasping Diva's waist in his left arm, said –

'The flowers are prettier than before.'

'The flowers are, or I am?'

Sur could think of no reply, but after a pause he said –

'I looked at you from a little way off, and you were even more beautiful, and when I looked from further off I found you were beautiful still.'

'And what if you were to look from away on the bank of the Volga?'

'No, not so far!' A flicker of alarm showed in Sur's eyes.

'When I go too far away your scent fades, and your face is blurred.'

'Well, which do you want, then – to look at me from a distance, or to be near me?'

'To be near you, Diva! Just as the bright Sun keeps close to Day!'

'Will you dance with me today?'

'Of course!'

'Will you stay with me today?'

'Yes.'

'And all night?'

'Of course!'

'Then today I won't stay with any other young man of the clan,' said Diva, embracing him.

Meanwhile a band of hunters, youths and girls, approached. In spite of hearing their voices, the pair went on clasping each other as closely as before. The newcomers came up, and someone cried –

'Today you have chosen Sur as your companion, Diva!'

'Yes. Look,' she answered, turning towards them – 'Sur has arranged these flowers.'

'Sur!' exclaimed a girl, 'you arrange flowers very well! Do my hair as well.'

'Not today!' said Diva. 'Today Sur is mine; tomorrow.'

'Tomorrow Sur will be mine.'

'Tomorrow? No, he will be mine then too.'

'Is Sur to be yours every day, Diva? That isn't right.'

'Not every day,' said Diva, realizing that she was in the wrong. 'Today and tomorrow, *svasr*.'[3]

As time went on, many other seasoned hunters appeared. A big black dog came close and began to lick Sur's feet, and he remembered about the sheep he had killed. He whispered something into Diva's ear, and ran off.

—2—

The clan dwelling was a huge hut, with wooden walls and straw thatching. Stone axes may be sharp, but to cut such heavy timber alone is impossible. Though their axes had done a great deal of work, the builders had also made use of fire to help them in cutting their logs. And this big hut? Yes, it should be called a big-hut. The hut had to be big, for in it lived the whole Nisha-Jan[4]: the descendants of some woman of bygone days named Nisha. All the clan members lived under the same roof, hunted together, gathered fruit or honey together. All obeyed one chieftainess, and a committee managed the affairs of the whole body. Managed? – Yes. No aspect in the lives of the individuals of the clan escaped from its common life; hunting, dancing, love-making, house-building, making cloths out of skins. In all kinds of business, guidance was sought from the committee, among whom the matriarchs held the highest position.

In this big-hut the hundred and fifty members of the Nisha clan were living. They could all in a sense be called one family, or they might be described as several families; while a mother was alive, she and her children formed a kind of sub-family, all the more so as all the individuals composing it were known by the mother's name. For instance, if Diva were to have children, and her own mother were not alive, these children would be known simply as Diva-Sunu[5] or Duhita.[6] The food – meat or fruit, brought in by them – however, would not be their own. All the men and women of the clan alike pooled whatever resources they came by, and consumed them jointly. If none were forthcoming, the clan would starve to death collectively. Individuals, as distinct from the clan, had no rights of their own. To be faithful to the commands and customs of the clan seemed to these people as natural as to follow their own impulses.

And the big-hut? It was only a temporary dwelling. As soon as the game moved away from its vicinity, and fruits and roots became scarce, the whole clan would shift to a new district. From the experience of ages they knew when and where the game would be found. When they departed, this thatched roof would fall, but timber or stone walls would remain standing for some years. In their new hunting ground they would build a new home, roofing the walls with new thatch. One part of it would be for storing their possessions, and another for cooking; for they made earthenware, shaping it by hand, besides using animal skulls as vessels. They ate meat sometimes raw, sometimes roasted while fresh, for cooking dried meat was not considered allowable. Honey was plentiful along this stretch of the Volga, and consequently the *medveds* also were often met with. The Nisha clan was very fond of honey, both for eating and for drinking in the form of wine.

What about this music? Men and women are singing, with fresh and clear voices. Are they beating the hides that are used as clothes? The Jan not only did all the work collectively but also combined it with distraction; singing was an integral part of their communal toil, and as they joined their voices in chorus their fatigue was forgotten. But this music does not seem to be a song of labour. At one moment there came a pure, soft flow of sound from women's voices, at another the deeper and harsher notes of men. Let's go and see.

Inside the big-hut, on one side, which was partitioned off, were assembled the men and women, children, old folk, and adolescents of the clan. In the middle blazed a fire of pinewood, with a hole above it in the roof. Men and women were singing something in a rolling chorus, in which were distinguishable the sounds –

'O... o... o... g... n... a ... A... y... a... a ...'[7]

It seemed as if they were praying to this fire in their midst. Presently the chieftainess and those who belonged to the clan council began throwing on the fire meat, fat, fruits and honey. This season, plenty of game had fallen to the clan; there had been abundance of fruit and honey, and the clan folk had not been worsted by animal or human foes. Now, therefore, on the night of the full moon, the clan was offering its gratitude and prayers to *Agni*, the Fire-god. The chieftainess poured on the fire a *chashak*[8] of honey-wine, while the clan stood all round, all as naked as when they were born. It was not winter, and in warm weather to have their skins covered with another skin they would consider a discomfort. But what well-shaped bodies! Not a single protuberant belly; no layers of fat to swell out the skin. One calls this beauty, this is health. All these faces were very much alike – naturally, since they were all the descendants of Nisha, children of the same fathers, brothers and sons. Health and strength were likewise common to all. The rickety and the weak would not survive this life, in face of the hostility of Nature and of the animal world.

The chieftainess rose and led the way into the biggest section of the hut. The clansfolk sat on the mud-plastered floor. Skin after skin of honey-wine made its appearance, and cups were filled – one man had a skull goblet, another a vessel hollowed out of bone or horn, a third a cup of pine leaves. Youths and girls, grown-up men and women, grandfathers and grandmothers, fell to eating and drinking. Each group sat by itself; but this was not a matter of rule. Old women remembered how they in their time had relished the joys of life, and knew that now it was the turn of the youths and girls; and there were girls willing to pour a mouthful of nectar for some of the old men in the evening of their lives. There among them was Diva, with a throng of young men and women sitting round her. Her hand was on Ribhu's shoulder; Sur was sitting with Diva.

Food, drink, singing, dancing, and then, in the same big room, lovers pillowed on each other's laps. ... In the morning when they awoke, some of them, men and women, would do the work of the house, some would go off to hunt, others to collect fruits; as to the rosy-faced children, they would be in their mothers' lap, or on furs spread out in the shade of the trees, or riding on the backs of elder children or sitting in their laps; and many would go jumping and skipping on the sandy margin of the Volga.

The old men and women of this epoch were more peaceful and contented than in the days of Nisha's reign. The clan was no longer under the rule of a single mother; the families of many living mothers now made up a single family or clan, and there was no unrestricted authority of a matriarch. It was the clan council that ruled. Here there was no need for a Nisha to drown her daughter in the Volga.

—3—

Diva had become the mother of four sons and five daughters, and at the age of forty-five had been chosen as chieftainess of the Nisha clan. The clan had trebled its numbers in the last twenty-five years, and for this whenever Sur kissed Diva's lips to congratulate her, she would say – 'It is all by the mercy of Agni, it is all the glory of the Sun-god. Whoever has the protection of Agni and of the Sun, will find honey flowing like the streams of the Volga wherever he goes, and herds of deer will come to feed among his *darus*.'[9]

But things had grown difficult for the Nisha clan. Wherever the clan went in its migrations, it would not be satisfied with the same area of forest as it had occupied before. It was not only necessary to build a communal house three times as big; they needed a hunting ground three times as wide. And now, beyond the hunting grounds where they had pitched their settlement, lay those of the Usha clan. Between the two was a stretch of unoccupied jungle. At times the Nisha clan went hunting not merely in this unclaimed area, but even in the Usha territory. The clan council saw the likelihood of a quarrel arising with the Usha folk, but they could think of no means to avert it. One day in the council Diva said –

'God has given us so many months; these forests are meant to fill them with food. Except from these forests there can be no food for all our mouths. The Nisha clan cannot afford to give up the bears, cattle, horses, that live among these trees, any more than it can do without the fish of the Volga.'

The Usha clan saw them committing manifest injustice. Once or twice the Usha council met the Nisha council in discussion, recalling that since ancient times there had been no war between the two clans and arguing that they had always been coming to this area in the winters. But the Nisha clan, faced with starvation, could not be expected to think of justice. When all other laws grow feeble, recourse must be had to the law of the jungle. Each clan gradually began making preparations. No news of the one would reach the other, for each clan married, lived and died within its own circle.

A band of the Nisha people went out looking for game in the neighbouring hunting ground and was ambushed by the Usha clan. Attacked, Nisha men stood their ground and fought, but they had come out unprepared and there were not enough of them. They were forced to retreat, leaving some of their dead and carrying the wounded with them. The chieftainess heard their story, the council met to deliberate, and finally the assembly of all the men and women of the clan gathered. Every detail was recounted, the names of those who had been killed were recited, wounded were produced, their mothers and sisters and daughters clamoured for a sanguinary revenge. Not to shed blood for blood would be completely against the clan ethics and no infringement of clan ethics conceivable. It was resolved that the blood of the dead clansmen must be avenged. The music of the dance was transformed into battle music. Leaving a few men and women to protect the children and the old folk, the rest marched out; armed with bows, stone axes, wooden spears and clubs, and wearing their toughest hides to protect their bodies. In front went the musicians, and after them the armed men and women. Diva, as the chieftainess, was in the lead. The blare of the instruments echoed far and wide till the whole forest resounded with the tumult, and birds and beasts fled this way and that in alarm.

They crossed from their own territory into the intervening strip. Even without any boundary marks, every tribesman knew his own frontier, and could not tell a lie about it; the art of lying was still an unfamiliar skill among human beings, and could only be practised laboriously. Men of the other tribe who were out hunting carried word to their people, and the Usha warriors took the field. They were fighting for their rights. It is true they only wanted to protect their own hunting grounds, but their enemies were not disposed to think of right or wrong. Battle was joined between the two clans in the Usha territory. A rain of sharp flint-headed arrows hissed through the air, stone axes brushed against each other, spear-thrusts and club blows were exchanged. When their weapons were broken or lost, the warriors, male and female, fought on with their bare hands and teeth, or with stone snatched up from the ground.

The Nisha clan outnumbered its rival by two to one, so that victory was beyond the latter's reach. But there was no choice but to fight – as long as a single boy remained. The battle had begun when the day was already a full three hours old. Two thirds of the Usha clan were killed in the forest, but the wounded were not killed, for in tribal warfare it would be a grave breach of the code to touch a wounded enemy. The surviving third fell back to the bank of the Volga, and resisted to the last gasp. Some mothers, along with the old folk and children, fled from the settlement and attempted to escape, but it was too late. Their savage foes pursued and overtook them, dashed the suckling infants against rocks, and drowned the old men and women in the Volga with stones hung round their necks. All the flesh, fruit, honey, meat and other valuables stored in the settlement were brought out, and then all the women and children left alive were shut up inside the hut, and it was set on fire. The Nisha clansmen exulted in the shrieks that arose from the living wretches in the midst of the leaping flames; they gave thanks to Agni, and regaled their gods and themselves with the food and drink stored up by their enemies.

Diva was rejoicing. She had torn three women's babies from their breasts and dashed them against a rock, and the sound of their cracking skulls had thrown her into fits of ghoulish laughter. After the feast dancing began; by the light of the same fire Diva was dancing with her young son Vasu. At moments, in the rhythm of the movements, these two naked creatures kissed or embraced each other, or separating and circling round each other went through the gestures of the dance. Everyone knew that for tonight Vasu was the leader's chosen partner, and Vasu had no mind to slight his mother's passion while she was wild with the intoxication of triumph.

The clan's hunting grounds were now more than four times as extensive as before, and all anxiety about where to live through the winter had disappeared. Only one thing troubled them, that the Usha folk they had killed were now dead and transformed into ghosts, trying to accomplish what they had failed in while still alive. The place where the hut had been burned had become an abode of ghosts, which none of the Nisha clan dared to pass by singly or even in couples. Many a time the hunters saw hundreds of naked shapes dancing before a great fire. When the time had come to shift the settlement, the clan was obliged to pass that spot, but then it was moving in full strength and in bright daylight. There were still times when Diva, in the darkness of night, would see suckling infants jumping up from the ground to cling to her hands, and would wake up screaming.

—4—

Diva had lived to be past seventy. She was no longer chieftainess but she was still treated with respect in her old age, for in the twenty years of her leadership she had done much for the prosperity of the growing clan. During those years they had had to fight several times against outsiders and had suffered heavy losses, though they had always won in the end. At present they had hunting grounds sufficient for some months. To Diva all this was a sign of the Bhaga's[10] favour;

though those children destroyed by her hands were still at times a trouble to her dreams.

Winter had come. The Volga had frozen, and looked from a distance, with its covering of the snowfall of months, like a trail of silver powder or of carded cotton wool. Away from the river, lifeless, immobilizing frost lay heavy on the woods. The Nisha clan had by now increased still further in numbers, so that it required a still larger food supply; at the same time there were more hands that could be set to work, and on the days devoted to labour they were able to add a bigger stock of food to their board. Even in winter men and women went out to hunt with the dogs they had tamed, and found some sort of game or other. They had also devised a new method of hunting. Owing to lack of food, the animals they chiefly hunted – deer, cattle, wild horses and so on – used to roam from forest to forest. The clansmen had noticed seeds germinating when they fell on the ground; so they began bedding grass seeds in moist earth. When the grass sprouted up, the animals would remain a few days longer to eat it.

One day Rikshshrava's dog had set off in chase of a hare, and he had gone running after it. Sweat was pouring from him, and he halted to remove his heavy fur jacket and throw it over his shoulder before hastening forward again. The dog was out of sight by this time, but its footprints were clearly visible across the snow. Out of breath, Riksh sat down on the trunk of a fallen tree to rest himself. Before he had recovered his breath, his ear caught the far-off barking of the dog. He got up at once and ran on. The sound came closer and closer and then as he got near, he saw, leaning against a pine tree a handsome young woman. She was wrapped in a coat of white fur; from under her white cap, wisps of golden tresses could be seen. A dead hare lay at her feet. The dog, at Riksh's approach, came up to him, barking furiously. Riksh stared at the girl's face. She smiled, saying –

'This is your dog, friend?'

'Yes, mine. But I have never seen you.'

'I belong to the Kuru[11] clan. This is their district.'

'The Kuru clan!'

Riksh stood lost in thought. The Kurus were the neighbours of his own clan, and there had been discord between the two for several years; at times it had come to fighting. The Kurus, however, were more sensible than the Usha clan had been, and realized that they had no chance of winning a war; they usually put their trust in flight, and though the strength of their arms could not give them victory, the speed of their legs enabled them to survive. The Nisha warriors had, indeed, vowed the destruction of the Kurus, but so far they had not succeeded in carrying their resolve into effect.

'It was your dog that killed this hare,' said the girl, seeing Riksh silent, 'so you take it.'

'But it was killed in the Kuru hunting ground.'

'Yes, it was killed there, but I was waiting for the dog's master.'

'Waiting?'

'Yes, to give him the hare.'

At the name of Kuru a sensation of hatred had stirred in Riksh's mind, but it vanished at the girl's conciliatory words. Moved by an impulse of friendliness he said –

'You have given me back my dog as well as the hare, and this dog is worth a great deal to me.'

'It's a fine hound.'

'The finest of any in the clan! It comes to me as soon as it hears my voice.'

'What is its name?'

'Shambhu.'[12]

'And yours, friend?'

'Rikshshrava, son of Rochna.'

'Rochna! My mother's name was Rochna too. Riksh, if you have no need to go quickly, sit down here for a while.'

Riksh laid his bow and his jacket on the snow, and sat down near the girl's feet.

'Your mother is not alive now?' he asked.

'No. She was killed in the war with the Nisha clan. She was very fond of me.'

Tears came into the girl's eyes as she spoke. Riksh brushed the tears away with his hand, saying –

'What a bad thing this fighting is!'

'Yes, when so many loved ones are taken away.'

'And still it is not finished.'

'How can it end, until one side has been wiped out? They say the Nisha people are going to make another attack. Riksh, I was thinking they must be young men like you.'

'And there must be other girls like you among the Kurus.'

'And yet we shall have to kill one another. Why is it, Riksh?'

It came into Riksh's mind that three days later his people were going to attack the Kurus. Before he could speak, the young woman added –

'But now we are not going to fight.'

'Not fight? The Kurus will not fight?'

'Our numbers have shrunk so much that we should have no hope of winning.'

'Then what will you do?'

'Leave the banks of Volga, and go far away. How dear this river is – this mother Volga! We shall never see it again. That is why I come here and sit for hours, staring at the sleeping current.'

'So you will never be able to look at the Volga again!'

'Nor to swim in it. How pleasant it is to swim in those deep waters!' Tears fell on the girl's cheeks.

'It is very hard for you,' said Riksh sadly. 'It is very cruel.'

'It is the law of the tribes, O' son of Rochna.'

'And the law of the jungle!'

1 2 **3** 4 5 6 7 8 9 10
20 19 18 17 16 15 14 13 12 11

Amritashv

Region : Central Asia – The Pamir
People : Indo-Iranian
Time : 3000 bce

This story is of an Aryan clan some 200 generations ago. It was a time when the fair-skinned races of India and Iran lived as one clan or Jan, 'Aryan' being the common name of both. Cattle rearing was their chief means of livelihood.

—1—

Those who have seen the beauty of Kashmir can form some idea of how lovely Farghana[1] was, with its green hills, wandering streams, and fountains. Winter was over and spring had come, and the radiance of spring was transforming the mountain valley into a paradise on earth. Herdsmen had abandoned their winter quarters in hill-caves or stone huts for the spacious pasture lands. From their horse-hair tents, most of them dyed red, smoke was curling upwards. Out of one of these tents a young woman emerged. With her water bag slung over one shoulder, she made her way down towards the margin of a stream roaring its way among the stones. She had not walked far from the tents when a man appeared in front of her. Like her, he wore a thick white woollen cloak, with two folds secured over the right shoulder in such a way as to cover the whole body except for the right arm, shoulder and part of his right side, and the legs below the knees. He was yellow haired, and his hair and beard were both well combed.

The handsome young woman halted as she saw him before her. The man smiled.

'Soma,' he said, 'today it is very late that you are going for water!'

'Yes, Rijrashv![2] But you – what has brought you roaming here?'

'Not roaming, my dear. I was coming to you.'

'Coming to me? It is after a very long time.'

'Today I thought of you again, Soma.'

'Well! I need to fetch the water home. Amritashv has sat down to eat.'

Talking as they went, they reached the stream, and then came back. 'Amritashv must have grown quite big,' the man remarked.

'Yes, you haven't seen him for several years, have you?'

'Not for four years.'

'He is twelve now and, really, he looks very much like you Rijrashv!'

'Why not? Wasn't I also one of your lovers at that time? Where has Amritashv been living all this time?'

'With his uncle, among the Vahliks.'

The woman went inside the tent with her water-skin and told her husband Krichhashv of the newcomer's arrival. They came out together with Amritashv behind them. Rijrashv saluted his host, and enquired –

'Well, my friend, how have you been?'

'Well enough to thank Agni! Come along, come along, we have just been fermenting *som*[3] juice and getting it ready, with honey and mare's milk!'

'Honey and *som*! What, at this time of the morning?'

'Oh! I'm just going off to my herd of horses. Didn't you see the riding horse standing ready for me out there?'

'Then don't you want to get back by this evening?'

'Maybe. Anyway, that's why I've got together this skin full of *som* and this nice soft horse-flesh.'

'Horse-flesh!'

'I can afford it. Agni has blessed our herds. I rear horses for the most part.'

'It seems your name Krichhashv[4] has lost its meaning.'

'In my parents' time we had scarcely any horses with us, that is how the name came to be given.'

'But now you ought to be called Riddhashv.'[5]

'Well! Come along inside.'

'No, why not sit on this green grass, friend, in the shade of the pine tree?'

'All right; then bring it out, Soma! Let us fill our friend with *som* and meat out here!'

'Yes, but Krichhashv you were just going to the herd.'

'Oh I will go! Not today – tomorrow. Come, sit down Rijrashv.' Soma brought the skin of *som* and *chashaks*. Amritashv had sat down between the two friends. She put the liquor and *chashaks* on the ground saying, 'Wait a little, I'll bring a rug.'

'No no,' answered Rijrashv. 'This soft green grass is better than any rug!'

'Then tell me Rijr, would you like your meat boiled with salt or roasted over the fire? It's from an eight-month-old colt, the meat is quite tender.'

'I like young horse-meat roasted, Soma. Sometimes I roast a colt whole on the fire. It takes time but it makes the meat very sweet. And look, Soma, you will have to sweeten this *chashak* of mine too with your lips.'

'Yes, yes,' cried Krichhashv, 'Rijr has come back after a very long time!'

'I'll be back quickly; the fire is hot, the meat won't take long to roast.'

'Why such haste?' Rijrashv enquired from his host, seeing him pour out *chashak* after *chashak*.

'*Som* is so delicious! *Som* from Soma's hands! It is the wine of immortality. It makes whoever drinks it immortal. Drink and live forever!'

'Live forever? At the rate you are going, one *chashak* after another, you'll be as good as dead in a very short time.'

'But you don't know how I love this drink, Rijr!'

Soma arrived at this moment, carrying three portions of roast meat on a skin platter.

'So it isn't Soma you love?' she asked.

'Soma and *som*, both!' Krichhashv replied. His voice was altered, his eyes had grown bloodshot. 'Anyway, what does it matter to you today?'

'That is true. Today I belong to my guest – to Rijr.'

'Your guest or your old friend?' said Krichhashv with an

attempt at a laugh.

Catching Soma's hand, Rijrashv pulled her down beside him, and held a *chashak* brimming with *som* to her lips. She took a sip or two, and said – 'Now you drink, Rijr. How long we have had to wait for today!'

He emptied the *chashak* in one breath, saying as he put it down – 'How sweet it tastes when your lips have touched it, Soma!'

The effects of the drink on Krichhashv were by now evident. He hastily filled up his *chashak* and stretched it out to Soma, stammering unevenly –

'S... Soma ... ! S... sweeten this t... t... too!'

She brushed it with her lips and gave it back to him. The boy, finding little of interest in the sentimental talk of his elders, ran off to find children of his own age to play with. Krichhashv, with blinking eyelids and lolling head, suggested –

'Sh... shall I s... sing, S... S... oma?'

'Of course! What singer is there like you anywhere among the Kurus!'

'Ri... right! N... no s... i... n... g... er like ... me! Th... then ... listen! D... r... ink ... in ... *som*. ...'

'That's enough, Krichhashv! Look, your music is making all the animals and birds run away from the forests!'

'All r... r... right ...'

Drinking *som* at this hour of the day was decidedly not the way to immortality. The usual time for drinking it was after sunset; but any excuse was good enough for Krichhashv. When his senses failed him and he relapsed into a stupor, the other two left their *chashaks*, and went to find a resting place on a rock overhanging the stream. Here, between the mountains the current flowed through a tract of even ground, but its channel was full of stones and pebbles of all sizes, and the water murmured as it beat against them. Here and there, sheltered among the stones, could be seen fish with glancing, darting fins. On the dry ground along the banks grew thick *sal* trees and pines and other trees. There was a charm in the lyrical warbling of the birds: and in the caressing breath of the light flower-scented breeze. In this heavenly garden the pair, separated for many years, were renewing their bygone love. Now floated back into their remembrance the days when Soma had been a golden-tressed girl of sixteen; when at the time of the spring festival Rijrashv had gone to his uncle's[6] house in the Vahlik territory. Soma was this uncle's daughter, and Rijrashv had been one of her lovers. A wager was made among her admirers, but it was Krichhashv who carried off the garland, and Rijrashv with the rest had to accept defeat. Now she was the wife of Krichhashv; but in this unrestrained age woman had not yet consented to become the movable property of man. She was still quite free to indulge in casual love affairs. And to offer one's wife to a guest or friend, by way of making him welcome, was still a respectable mode of conduct. Today, Soma did indeed belong to Rijrashv.

In the evening all the men and women of the settlement were gathered in the spacious courtyard of the Great-Father.[7] *Som*, honey-beer, and well-flavoured beef and horse-meat were continually being brought in. The Great-Father was celebrating a feast in honour of the birth of a son. Krichhashv had not recovered enough strength to bestir himself, but Rijrashv and Soma came to take his place in the festival. Till far into the night drinking, singing and dancing kept up the merriment. As had always happened, Soma's songs and Rijrashv's dances won the admiration of all the Kurus.

—2—

'You are not tired, Madhura?'

'No, I enjoy riding.'

'But those brigands had carried you off so brutally!'

'Yes. The Vahlik men had come to steal their young girls from the Pakthas,[8] as well as their cows and horses.'

'Cattle-stealing causes enmity between the two for a long time, but stealing women only creates a short-lived enmity. After all, a father-in-law has to reconcile himself to his son-in-law.'

'But tell me, I don't know what your name is yet.'

'Amritashv, son of Krichhashv, of the Kurus.'

'Oh! The Kurus are my uncle's clan.'

'Well, Madhura, you are in safety now. Where do you want to go?'

A gleam of pleasure flitted across her face, but it vanished quickly. Amritashv understood, and to turn the talk another way remarked –

'Some Paktha girls have come to our village too.'

'Were they all brought by force?'

'No, most of them are daughters of our mothers' brothers.'

'Then that is why. But I think this robbing and killing to get women is very wicked.'

'So do I, Madhura. It means that men and women don't even know whether there is any love between them.'

'It is better for a man to marry his uncle's daughter; then they have the chance to come to know each other beforehand.'

'Did you have a lover of that kind, Madhura?'

'No; my father had no sisters.'

'Then, any other lover?'

'Not a regular one.'

'Are you willing to make me happy?' The girl dropped her eyes in confusion.

'Madhura,' said Amrit, 'there is a country where the women belong to nobody else, but only to themselves.'

'I don't understand, Amritashv.'

'Nobody can carry them off, nobody can make one of them his own wife for good. Men and women are equal there.'

'And know how to use weapons equally?'

'Yes. Women are free.'

'Where is that country, Amrit ... Amritashv, I mean!'

'No, call me Amrit, Madhura! That country lies far away in the west.'

'Have you been there, Amrit?'

'Yes. A woman there, all her life, remains free; as free as the deer roaming in the forest, or the birds flying in the treetops.'

'It must be a fine country! Nobody carries off a woman as a prisoner there?'

'What living thing could hope to capture a live tigress?'

'And what are the men like?'

'They too are free.'

'And the children?'

'A family there is different from what it is among us, Madhura; all the people of a village are one family.'

'But what duties does a father have there?'

'Men are not known as fathers. A woman is not the wife of one man; she can love as she wishes.'

'So no one knows his father?'

'All the men of the family are the fathers.'

'What customs!'

'It is because of them that women are free; they go out to fight, they go out to hunt.'

'Do those people breed cows and horses?'

'Cows and horses graze in the woods there, as the deer do here.'

'Do they have sheep and goats?'

'They know nothing of herding. They live on game and fish, and fruit from the forest.'

'Nothing more! Then they get no milk?'

'Only their mother's milk, in childhood.'

'And they don't ride horses?'

'No; and they have no clothing except animal skins.'

'They must have many hardships to suffer!'

'But at least their women have the same freedom as the men; they join in gathering fruit, and hunting, and fighting enemies with stone axes and arrows.'

'I like that. I have learned to handle weapons, but to go to war as men do, where could I do that!'

'Men have taken that work on themselves here. Men do the herding of cows and horses, sheep and goats, and they have made women into house-mistresses, not animal-mistresses.'

'And they have made young women into creatures to be seized by force. Amrit, is it true that girls are never captured in that country?'

'The boys and girls of a clan always live with their own clan; there is no giving wives out of it or taking wives from outside.'

'It is a good custom!'

'It is impossible here.'

'So here young women must go on being taken by violence?'

'Yes. But, Madhura. What do you say?'

'About what?'

'About my love for you.'

'I am in your control, Amrit.'

'But I don't want to take you with me by force.'

'Will you allow me to take part in battles?'

'So far as I have the power to.'

'And to go hunting?'

'As long as I can.'

'Why only so long?'

'Because I shall have to obey the orders of the Great-Father, Madhura; so far as I am concerned, I shall always treat you as a free woman.'

'Free to make love or not, as I like?'

'It is love that makes our union firm. But, yes, free even in that!'

'Then I am ready to have your love, Amrit.'

'Shall we go to the Kurus, or to the Pakthas?'

'Whichever you choose.'

Amrit turned his horse, and following the path that Madhura pointed out they arrived at the Paktha village. In the village, in some tent-houses someone had been killed and in others they had been wounded; some had had a girl stolen. On all sides rose the noise of lamentation. Madhura's mother was in tears and her father was trying to soothe her when the horse came to a stand outside the tent of woven hair.

When Amritashv had dismounted, Madhura jumped down, and telling him to wait outside, entered the tent. At their daughter's sudden appearance, her parents at first could not believe their eyes. Then her mother folded her in her arms, and bathed her face with tears. When they had grown calmer, and her father began to question her, Madhura explained what had happened.

'The men of Vahlik were carrying off the Paktha girls they had captured. The one who had seized on me fell behind the others. As soon as I had a chance, I threw myself off the horse. He caught me, and was trying to put me on it again. Just as I was struggling with him, a young horseman rode up; he challenged the Vahlik man, wounded him and left him on the ground. The young man was a Kuru, and he has brought me back home.'

'He didn't want to treat you as his plunder, then?' asked her father.

'He didn't want me by force.'

'And yet, according to the customs of our country, you belong to him!'

'And I do love him, *tat*.'[9]

Her father came out to welcome Amritashv, and led him into the tent. The affair struck the villagers as inexplicable; but Amritashv had gained the respect and sympathy of all when he took Madhura away from his father-in-law's house.

—3—

Amritashv rose to be the Great-Father of the Kuru encampment. He owned scores of horses, besides cows and a good many sheep and goats. His four sons and Madhura saw to the work of the herds and the house. In addition, some men belonging to poor families of the village helped in the work, not as servants but like members of the household. A Kuru had to remain on a footing of equality with another Kuru. More than fifty families lived in Amritashv's nomadic camp. It was the Great-Father's duty to look into all quarrels and disputed claims. Control of water, roads, and all other matters of public concern, was likewise the Great-Father's province. And in war – that was an ever-present danger – to take command of the warriors was his paramount function. It was success in battle, in fact, that brought a man to the dignity of Great-Father.

Amritashv was a bold fighter, and had displayed his courage in many a battle with the Pakthas, the men of Vahlik and other tribes. He had kept his word to Madhura. She took part, side by side with him, not only in hunting the bear, the wolf and the tiger, but even in his battles. There were some among the clansmen who had not approved of this, it is true; their view was that a woman's business was at home.

On the day when Amritashv was first chosen as Great-Father, the Kuru camp was holding festival. On such days the youths and girls were free to form temporary attachments. As it was summer, the herds of cattle and horses had been turned loose to graze over the river valley and the hills. The clansfolk had forgotten that they had enemies; but their wealth in herds had swelled the number of their foes. While the Kurus had lived on the bank of the Volga, they had owned no animals; in those days they had had to glean a livelihood from the woods, or to go hungry if game, honey or fruit were not to be found. They had now domesticated some of the animals they once hunted – cattle, horses, sheep, goats and asses. From these they provided themselves with woollen clothes, as well as meat, milk and hides. Their women were skilled at spinning yarn and weaving blankets. But this skill did not avail to preserve their old status in society. Men, not women, ruled. Authority was vested in no chieftainess or clan council, but in a warlike leader – the Great-Father, who, though he paid some respect to the feeling of his people, often took decisions by himself. As to property, whereas in the days of matriarchy the entire clan had lived and laboured jointly, each family now owned cattle privately, and its wealth or poverty were its alone; though when adversity fell on all alike, the clan once more resumed its bygone form.

The clansfolk were too absorbed in their revelry at their great-father Amritashv's feast to spare a thought for their herds. The young men, posturing in the dance to the sound of music, could think of nothing but *som* and pretty girls. Three quarters of the night had passed, and there was still no sign of the dance coming to an end, when on all sides arose a frantic barking of dogs, which sounded as if they were dashing off towards the upper end of the valley. Amritashv was one of those men who enjoy drinking enough wine to bring a bright glow into their eyes, but not enough to make them lose control of themselves. At the clamour of the dogs, he quietly got up, seized his wooden-handled stone club and set out, following the course of the stream, in the direction of the noise. When he had gone a short distance and reached the hill behind which the sun had set, he saw a woman approaching in the moonlight. He halted, and as she came close, recognized Madhura.

She was panting for breath as she exclaimed agitatedly –

'The Purus are driving off our cattle!'

'Driving the cattle off! And all our young men are reeling drunk! How far have you been, Madhura?'

'Just far enough to make sure what was happening.'

'They are taking away all the cattle?'

'It's clear they must have been busy rounding up the scattered herds for a long time.'

'What do you think about it, Madhura?'

'There's no time to be lost.'

'But my young men are too drunk to stand!'

'You must take as many of them as can follow you, and attack the robbers.'

'Yes, that's it, but one thing, Madhura! You are not to come with me. Half the young men's drunkenness will disappear as soon as they hear the news, and as to the rest – give them curds to eat. As fast as they come to themselves, keep sending them on to me.'

'And the young women?'

'I can use my power as Great-Father and order them to take part in this fight. We shall have to revive the old forgotten custom.'

'I won't try to come into the front of the battle. Make haste – go!'

At the Great-Father's command, the music instantly ceased, and all the revellers, men and women, pressed round him. Some of them did indeed throw off their intoxication when they learned of the plundering of their cattle and horses. Instead of amorous looks their faces wore an air of stern determination.

'Men and women of the Kurus!' cried the Great-Father in thunderous tones, 'We must snatch back our wealth out of the hands of our enemies, the Purus! There is going to be a hard fight. All of you, who are fit to ride, get your arms, mount your horses, and follow me. Those who are too drunk, get curds from Madhura to eat, and as soon as you feel fresh again, come as fast as you can. Women! Tonight I give you also the order to enter the battle. Kuru women in olden times played their part in war shoulder to shoulder with their men, as we have heard from our grandparents. Tonight Amritashv, your Great-Father, commands you to follow him!'

In a moment forty horses were collected. The Purus, meanwhile, were driving all the animals they had gathered together up the valley.

The Kurus came in sight of them far away as dawn broke, after two hours of hard riding. It was no easy task to drive up the slope at gallop such a multitude of cattle and horses as the Purus had gathered together; they were cracking their leather whips in the air and against the rocks to frighten the animals forward. Amritashv saw that their numbers were about a hundred, but he was not inclined to rack his brains for long over the question of whether or not to join battle straight away with his troop of forty.

Gripping his long horn-tipped spear, he gave the order to attack. Fearlessly, the Kuru warriors, nearly half of them women, galloped their horses forward. The Purus, leaving a few men to halt the herd and hold it in check, turned and rode back downhill, and in order to have the full advantage of their mounts took up their position on level ground adjoining the stream, where they awaited the Kurus' charge. Now it was that Amritashv showed his true mettle. He and his horse, Amrit, seemed to form one single creature. No enemy, whom his spear with its sharp point of stag's horn once pierced, ever kept his saddle to face a second thrust. The Purus had made the mistake of putting too much trust in their bows and arrows and stone axes; if they had had as many horn-tipped spears as their enemies, the Kurus would never have been able to resist them. The battle had raged for an hour, and the Kurus were still standing their ground, though a third of their warriors were out of action, and they had good reason to fear the issue. At this juncture thirty whooping Kuru horsemen galloped up and threw themselves into the fray. This restored their friends' spirits and the Purus, hard pressed, began to fall fast. Seeing them in a tight corner, the horsemen whom they had left to control the herd now came to their help; but at the same time Madhura reached the scene with a band of forty more men and women. For another hour and a half the murderous fight raged on. The majority of the Purus had by then been killed or wounded; the remainder took to flight.

The Kuru forces lingered only to dispatch the enemy wounded before pressing on towards the Puru settlement, eight miles higher. At their approach the folk abandoned their tents and fled. Their cattle was grazing all round but the Kurus had first of all to deal with their foes. The Purus were hemmed in and their position was desperate; there was little chance of escaping into the hills. The valley was narrow, and the ascent from it precipitous, but still some men and women were making for it on horseback in an attempt to save their lives. They got some way up the slope on to ground where a horse could climb no further. They forced themselves on foot, but the Kurus were now close at their heels. The old men, women and children could not climb fast, so, to give them a chance of escape, some of the fighting-men made a stand in a narrow defile. Unable to make full use of their numbers, the Kurus had to spend several hours in clearing the path. Both sides were on foot now, but barely a dozen men were left of the Purus. For a few days they were able to defend what was left of their clan. Then, taking with them some few brave women, they struck off up a barely accessible track, and leaving their valley behind crossed the hills and made their way southward. The Kurus captured a number of children, women and old people hiding in odd corners and praying for their lives. To take slaves had no place in the customs of this patriarchal age; all the males, from boys to old men, were butchered. The females were carried off. All the livestock likewise became the property of the Kurus. The whole valley of the green river, from the upper end to the lower, was now the Kurus' pasture ground. The Great-Father ordered that for one generation, each man might have more than one wife. It was the first time that co-wives were seen among the Kurus.

4

Puruhut

REGION : THE OXUS VALLEY – TAJIKISTAN
PEOPLE : INDO-IRANIAN
TIME : 2500 BCE

This story is about Aryan tribes – 180 generations ago. The scions of some of these Jans were now about to emigrate to India. In this period agriculture and copper-working had come to be practised. Slavery had found its way among the Aryans, but they were now anxious to forget it.

—1—

Down the valley flowed the gurgling current of the Oxus. On the right bank, the hills rose from the water's edge; on the other side, the ground sloped more gently and the valley was broader. At a distance nothing could be seen but the dusky mass of the tall, dark green pines; from closer at hand, one could distinguish the pointed, arrow-like tips of the boughs, long near the base of the trunk and shorter and shorter above. Beneath them were growing many kinds of plants and smaller trees. It was late summer, and the rains had not yet set in – a month when on the plains of northern India people suffer acutely from the heat. But in this mountain valley, seven thousand feet up, hot weather could not intrude. Along the left bank of the river a young man was making his way. He wore a woollen tunic, with a waistband over it tied in several folds, woollen trousers, and plaited shoes. He had removed the cap from his head and put it on top of the bag hanging at his back, so that his long, gleaming yellow hair, falling loosely behind, rippled now and then in the light gusts of air. A copper sword hung at his side in a leather holder. The funnel-shaped bag at his back was woven from thin twigs, and held an unstrung bow, a quiver full of arrows, and many other things. In his hand he grasped a staff, which from time to time he propped under the bottom of the sack while standing still and resting, for the ascent was growing harder. In front of him six fat sheep moved along, carrying on their backs big horse-hair bags filled with parched grain. Behind him came a reddish, shaggy dog. The hillside re-echoed the pleasant, low notes of sparrows, which roused the youth to emulation, for he began to whistle as he walked.

Bubbling out from above a rock, water came falling in a fine silvery stream. To let it fall down, someone had cut through the rock and placed a wooden conduit there. The panting sheep began drinking under the rock; the young man noticed small clusters hanging on the grapevines that trailed near it, and sitting down and depositing his sack on the ground, he began plucking off the grapes and eating them. They were still too bitter and rather sour. It was still a month before they would be ripe, but they seemed good enough to the young traveller, and he went on slowly sucking them, one grape at a time. Perhaps he was waiting a while before drinking, because he was too thirsty, and to begin swallowing cold water at once would be harmful.

After slaking their thirst the sheep straggled off to browse on the fresh green grass. The shaggy dog, which found the warm weather very irksome, paid no attention either to its master or to the sheep, but squatted down in the pool of water below the spring. Its belly was soon distended like a blowpipe and the long red tongue hanging from its open mouth quivered. The young man now held his mouth under the trickle, and quenched his thirst in one long draught of the falling water; then he washed his face, bathing his sore eyes and drenching his front hair to the roots. A yellow moustache was beginning to grow; hair would soon overspread his tawny cheeks and red lips.

Noticing that his sheep were grazing contentedly, the youth sat down beside his sack, and interpreting the meaning in the dog's eyes, fixed on his face, and its pricked-up ears, he groped in one corner of the sack for a piece cut from a quarter of dried mutton, sliced it up with a sharp copper knife that had been hanging in a leather sheath at his belt, and began feeding both the dog and himself. At this moment he heard the clapping of a wooden bell, and he saw approaching in the distance a donkey, half concealed by the bushes; then a second, and behind them a girl of about sixteen, clothed like himself and likewise carrying a bag on her back. He whistled lightly. Whenever he was thinking about anything, to start whistling was as natural to him as breathing. The sound certainly reached the girl's ear once, and she looked in his direction, but he was screened by the foliage. Though she was still some thirty feet away from the watcher, the delicate but attractive cast of her face caught his fancy, and he waited impatiently to learn which way she was going. Upriver hereabouts, there were no settlements, as he knew, so it might be guessed that she was a traveller like himself.

Eyeing the pretty stranger, the dog began barking, but at the young man's 'Quiet!' it crouched silently in its place. The girl's donkeys put their heads down to drink, and she began to loosen her sack, on which the youth came and removed it in his muscular arms and set it down. Her smile showed her gratitude, as she said –

'It's very hot.'

'Not really hot, but coming up the slope makes you feel hot. When you have rested awhile the sweat will go off.'

'The days are good just now.'

'There's no fear of the rains for another ten or fifteen days.'

'The rains do make me afraid. The paths become so bad with all the streams and slippery mud.'

'It makes the going harder for donkeys.'

'We had no sheep with us at home, so I had to bring donkeys. Well, friend, which way have you to go?'

'To Danda.[1] Our horses and cattle and sheep are there at present.'

'Just where I'm going too! I'm taking parched grain and corn and fruit there.'

'Who is looking after your animals there?'

'My father's grandfather, and my brothers and sisters.'

'What, your father's grandfather! He must be very, very old!'

'Oh, yes, you might not find such an old man anywhere.'

'Then how does he manage to look after a herd?'

'He's still quite strong. His hair and eyebrows are all quite white, but his teeth are like new; you wouldn't say, to look at him, that he was more than fifty or fifty-five.'

'Oughtn't he to be kept at home?'

'He won't agree to it. Since before I was born, he has never been into the village.'

'Never!'

'He doesn't want to. He hates the village. He says that man was not born to be kept cooped up in one place. He tells us about very long-ago things. But what is your name, friend?'

'Puruhut, a Paurav;[2] my mother was of the Madr[3] clan. And what is yours, *svasr*?'

'Rochna, a Madr.'

'So you belong to my mother's clan, *svasr*! The upper Madrs, or the lower?'

'The upper.'

The Puru villages lay on the left bank of the Oxus, but its lower course, debouching on the plains below, was occupied by the Madrs; and of the right bank the upper part was held by the Madrs, the lower by the Parshus.[4] In point of territory and population, the Purus were not inferior to the Madrs. Those of the latter who lay downstream from the Purus were known as the lower Madrs.

After learning each other's names, the two felt a close relationship and Puruhut began again –

'I say, Rochna, we can't get as far as Danda today. How did you venture to come out alone?'

'I knew it would be difficult to keep the leopards away from the donkeys at night, but I had to bring this food for the old man. He thinks so much of me, Puruhut, and I expected to meet with someone else on the way; just now a good many people are going towards Danda. Besides, I was thinking that by lighting a fire I should get over the worst part.'

'How can you light a fire when you are on the road? Have you brought kindling with you, Rochna?'

'Yes.'

'Even then, it isn't easy to make the Fire-god reveal himself by rubbing two sticks together. Never mind, I have a sacred stick with me, it has been in our family since my grandfather's time. A great many sacrifices and prayers have been performed with fire kindled from it. I know the spells of the Fire-god by heart as well, and they make him reveal himself sooner.'

'Besides, there are two of us now, Puruhut, so the leopards won't be bold enough to come near.'

'And we have Shaggy, too.'

'Shaggy?'

'Yes, this red-haired *shvak*[5] of mine,' and as Puruhut called out to it, the dog got up and came to lick its master's hand. When Rochna also called its name, it came and sniffed at her feet, and crouched with tail wagging as she stroked its back.

'Shaggy is a very intelligent dog, Rochna,' remarked Puruhut.

'Strong as well!'

'Yes, not afraid of wolves or bears or leopards or anything.'

By now the sheep and donkeys had had their fill of grass, and recovered from their fatigue, so the two young travellers resumed their journey, the dog trotting behind them. Though their footpath wound from side to side instead of running straight up, the ascent was still arduous, and it was only cautiously that they advanced, step by step. Occasionally, Puruhut picked up some red strawberries nestling close to the ground, or *karonda* berries[6] and shared them with Rochna. But he was a good deal disappointed with them; the berries had not yet come to ripeness.

In this way they went on climbing till evening, talking as they went. The sun was sinking when they came on a spring gushing out under deep shady foliage. There was some open space near it, with the embers and ashes of a wood-fire half burned out, and horse dung. Puruhut bent down and scraped away the ash, and found there was still a glow lurking under it.

'Rochna!' he suggested, delighted with his find, 'we shan't meet with any better place than this further on for staying the night. There's water near, plenty of grass and dry wood, and the travellers who started from here this morning have left their fire still burning under the ashes!'

'Yes, Puruhut, there won't be any better place than this, let us stay the night here. It would be quite dark before we could get to the next spring.'

Puruhut knelt down, hastily slid his sack off and let it lean against a rock; then he lifted Rochna's bag off. Together they removed the donkeys' packs and unsaddled them. The animals rolled over two or three times on the ground, and then began munching grass. Unloading the sheep took some time, because they had to be caught and held by force. Then Rochna took a skin bag and went to the spring to fill it.

Puruhut got the fire going with leaves and twigs, and then piled bigger pieces of wood on and built it up to a good blaze. When the water had been brought, he placed a copper pan before him and set to work cutting up a quarter of a cow's haunch with his knife.

'By tomorrow evening,' he observed, glancing at Rochna, 'we shall have got to the top. It won't be very far then to your herding-place, right?'

'It's about six miles east from Danda.'

'My place is twelve miles east. So your great-grandfather and his herd will be on my way, Rochna?'

'Yes you will be able to see him! I was wondering how you could meet him.'

'As we only have one more day to go, a quarter of a thigh is enough. This is from a hind leg of a calf, Rochna.'

'I have got half a leg of a colt; at this time of the year, if meat is kept for a long time it begins to smell, doesn't it?'

'How would it be to cook it with salt?'

'That will be good. And I have some *gurh*-wine,[7] Puruhut; if we mix the meat and *gurh*-wine and then put in some parched grain, we can make good soup. It will be ready by the time we are going to sleep.'

'If I were by myself, I wouldn't make soup, it takes too long. But we can spend the time tying up the animals and talking.'

'Grandfather is very fond of my soup. What a fine copper pan!'

'Yes, copper is very valuable Rochna. This pan was worth as much as a horse but it's very useful on a journey.'

'Your family must own a great many animals, then?'

'Oh yes and plenty of grain. That's why I can have a pan that costs the value of a horse. Here, take this meat, I have finished cutting it up. You put it in water, with salt, and boil it while I get some wood burning over there too. Then we must cut a little grass and tether the donkeys and sheep in between here. You know donkey meat is even tastier to leopard than calf's meat to us. In the meantime, Shaggy! Take this to have a lick at' – and Puruhut threw down in front of the dog a bone with a little meat on it. The animal wagged its tail, and with the bone held down by its paws, began trying to crack it with its teeth.

Puruhut removed his outer tunic and waistband. Under a sleeveless shirt his well-formed chest and his brawny arms revealed the strength of this twenty-year-old body. The hair on his limbs quivered as he went to work. He brought out a scythe from his sack and quickly put together a heap of grass and piled it in front of the donkeys, which he dragged forward by the ears and tethered to a stake he had driven into the ground; then he did the same with the sheep.

When he was free of work he came and sat down near the fire. Rochna was lifting the pieces of boiled meat out of the pan and putting them on a square of skin. Puruhut drew a leather folder from his sack and, unwrapping it, produced a handsome wooden cup and a small wine-skin. A flute fell out on the ground with them. It was as if a delicate infant had fallen, and its mother were in terror of its being injured; Puruhut snatched the flute up, wiped it on his clothes, and replaced it in the leather wrapper. Rochna, who was watching him, interrupted –

'Puruhut! You can play on the flute?'

'This flute is very dear to me indeed, Rochna. I feel as if my whole life were bound up with it.'

'Let me hear you play.'

'Now or after we have eaten?'

'Play a little while now.'

'Very well!'

Puruhut put the pipe to his lips, and as eight fingers began to stray over its stops, amid the far-spreading hush of evening, sweet music began to steal and float magically all about from under the shade of the tall trees till it seemed to re-echo from the horizon. Rochna was carried out of herself as she sat absorbedly drinking in the notes. It was a plaintive song of some Pururava,[8] desolated by separation from Urvashi,[9] that Puruhut was playing. When it ended, Rochna felt as though she had suddenly dropped from heaven to earth.

'Puruhut,' she said, with tears of delight in her eyes, 'the music of your flute is very sweet – so sweet! I have never listened to such a flute. What a lovely tune!'

'People often tell me that, Rochna. But I never can understand it; as soon as I put the pipe to my mouth, I forget everything. As long as I have my flute with me, I don't want anything else in the world.'

'Well, come Puru, or the meat will be getting cold.'

'Yes. And see, when I was setting out my mother gave me this grape wine. There's only a little, but it will be good to drink with the meat.'

'Are you very fond of wine?'

'I can't say very fond of it. If you are very fond of it you can never have enough of it. As soon as I have drunk enough to brighten my eyes a little, I don't want to drink another mouthful.'

'I think just the same about it, Puru. I hate to see people overcome by drunkenness,' said Rochna as she brought out her own wooden cup and put it beside her.

A third of the meat was given to the dog as its share and after a while the pair finished eating and drinking. A thick cloak of darkness lay all around. Nothing was to be seen except the red light of the logs blazing on the fire, and the small circle around it; though there were sounds to be heard, which seemed to come from gnats and such tiny creatures. They went on talking together and at intervals the flute gave out its melodies. Finally, at the end of some hours the parched grain was thoroughly done and the soup was ready. They both drank it hot out of their cups. It was well into the night before they decided to sleep. Rochna arranged her bedding of skins and began to undress, while Puruhut piled fresh wood on the fire, gave the animals more grass, then recited a prayer to the spirits of the forest, threw off his clothes and fell asleep.

Next morning, when they woke up they felt as though they had found a blood-brother and sister in each other in a single night. When Rochna got up, Puruhut could not help saying –

'I should like to kiss your face, sister!'

'I want to kiss you. We have found a brother and sister for ourselves in this world.'

Puruhut smoothed Rochna's dishevelled hair away from her face and kissed her on both cheeks. Their looks expressed the happiness of both of them though their eyes were wet.

They washed, ate a little grain and dried meat, loaded the animals and set off. On the journey they stopped two or three times to rest but the time passed so quickly in conversation that they hardly knew when they had reached Danda, and when they had got to the old man's post. Rochna made her friend known and the old man welcomed him, speaking highly of the manliness of the Purus.

—2—

Here at Danda stood a small Madr village, whose dwellings were either tents or thatched cottages. On the sloping ground and in the hill country below it, nothing was visible except dense pine-forests, but further up there was no trace of any trees; the ground was more level and covered by a thick carpet of green grass. Here and there over this green plain were grazing sheep, cattle and horses, and among them young calves and colts were jumping up and frisking. It was this open country that the old man stared towards when he said – 'Man was not born to be kept cooped up in one place'. When grass became scarce he would move on to another spot. Here there was abundance of milk, curds, butter and meat, and the tent was well stored with provisions. Every fifteen or twenty days a man would come from the village and go away with butter and meat. In winter, when snow fell, the old grandfather would still have stayed where he was, if he could have pleased himself; but the herds could not feed on snow, so he took the meandering path and moved a little lower down into the forest lands, while the animals all went down to the village. At the mere suggestion of going to the village himself, the old man would look as if he could kill you.

It was still daylight when the two wayfarers reached his tent, and when they had unloaded their baggage and he had put before them wooden *chashaks* and poured out a drink of fermented mare's milk to cheer them up, they shook off all the weariness of the road in the time it took to drink three or four cupfuls. In the evening Rochna's brother and sister, and other young herdsmen from the village, arrived with their calves and colts. When Rochna began singing praises of Puruhut's flute, the old man was in far too high spirits to let Puruhut go. He and all the young folk of the herding-post were delighted with the music. At night, when there was dancing, Puruhut unfolded its magic again.

Next morning he talked of going, but the old man would not hear of his leaving so soon. After the midday meal he began talking; it was the sight of the copper pan standing near the sack that set him off!

'When I see this copper,' he said, 'or ploughed fields, my blood boils. Since such things appeared on the banks of the Oxus, wickedness and lawlessness have been spreading all round; the gods have grown angry, and there have been more epidemics, more killings.'

'Were there none of these things before, then, grandfather?' asked Puruhut.

'None of them, son. In my boyhood they were just beginning to come. My grandfather never heard even their names. In those days all the implements were made from stone, bone, horn or wood.'

'How were they able to cut timber?'

'With stone axes.'

'That must have taken a long time, and the cutting would not be so good.'

'It is this being in a hurry that has spoiled every kind of work. Nowadays you give away a horse, that would give you two months' meat or carry you half your life, to get a copper axe and then cut down whole forests and make a desert of them or attack and wipe out whole villages. But a village is not as defenceless as the forest trees are, it has the same kind of sharp axes as you have. These copper hatchets have made war more cruel. The wounds they make are venomous. Arrowheads used to be made of stone. It is true they were not so sharp, but with a good archer they were more useful. Now with these copper arrowheads, mere infants want to go and hunt tigers. Why should anyone want to be a skilful archer now?'

'Grandfather, I agree with you in one thing that men were not born to be shut up in the same place always.'

'Oh, my boy! Think how bad it is to go on defecating on the same place every day! Today our tent is here, the animals eat the grass round about, but by the time the dirt of all the people and animals here has begun to pile up, we shall be leaving this place and moving somewhere else, where fresh grass will be more plentiful, and the soil and the water and the air will be purer.'

'Yes, that is the kind of place I like too. My flute plays more sweetly there.'

'That is right, lad. Once we used to call a cluster of tents like this a village and we didn't live in them in one spot for more than three months at a time, to say nothing of a whole year; but the villages now are built to inhabit the sons and grandsons for hundreds of generations. They build up walls of stone, wood and mud, till no air can get inside. They cover them with stone, wood and thatched roofs, and how can any air come in through them? Nowadays people talk of the Fire-god and Wind-god, but it is only talk; we have no reverence for them in our hearts. That is why so many new diseases are spreading. Oh, Mitr! Nasatya! Agni![10] You are showing your anger against these people, and your anger is just!'

'But grandfather, how should we keep ourselves alive if we gave up these copper axes and swords and spears? If we gave them up our enemies would wipe us out in a day!'

'I agree with you son! Those lower Madrs and Parshus, having happily sold their horse that was two months' food or half a life's ride, have not just bought a copper sword but befouled the breast of our mother Oxus. Where the Oxus river flows to, I don't know, nobody knows. Those who are fond of gabbling such lies say that it flows into limitless waters at the end of the world. We know that beyond the boundaries of the Madrs and Parshus the river leaves the mountains and enters the plains, and beyond is the land of the lying enemies of the gods. They say there are creatures living with enormous legs, as big as small hills, what is it they call them, son? Nowadays my memory is failing me.'

'Camels, grandfather! But they are not as big as hills. Once, a man from the lower Madrs came up here with a young camel. He said it was six months old, and it was the same size as our horses.'

'Oh! People who come wandering from foreign lands learn to tell a lot of lies. They were saying ... what is it they call those things?'

'Camels.'

'Yes, that a camel's neck is so long, it could stand on this bank of the Oxus and eat grass off the other bank. That must be a lie too, son, isn't it?'

'Of course! The young camel's neck was longer than a horse's, no doubt, but that tale of eating grass is all nonsense!'

'It is these lying Madrs and Parshus who have spread the plague of copper axes and swords. The Parshus made an attack on us upper Madrs with such weapons. It was in my father's time. Our people had to buy copper axes from the lower Madrs, at two horses for each axe.'

'Stone axes must have been useless against copper axes, weren't they?'

'Yes son, they were useless. So we became weak, and we had to get metal weapons. Until then there had never been a quarrel between the upper Madrs and Purus. But the Parshus and lower Madrs have always gone in for banditry, always been deserting the old laws and wanting new things and because of them our people had to do the same, to save their lives. I know that until the lower Madrs and Parshus give up their metal weapons, for us of the upper river to abandon them would be suicide. But this spreading everywhere of copper is evil, son; no doubt of that, and it is those two peoples who have been spreading this wickedness; they will never have the blessing of the gods. They will go to the awful underworld of darkness. They will go! It is in imitation of them, and for fear of them, that we have built our villages of mud and stone. Formerly there were only camps of tent-dwellers, like ours, here today and gone tomorrow, in the valley of the Oxus. But those Madrs and Parshus have broken it all up. How could it come into their heads to tear the breast of mother earth, those people with their metal tools! Such wickedness no one had ever committed. We call the earth our mother, lad, don't we?'

'Yes, grandfather, we call the earth our mother, we call her a goddess, we pray to her.'

'And those evildoers have wounded the breast of mother earth with their own hands. What is it they have done – I am forgetting the word, my memory is getting weak now.'

'Agriculture, farming.'

'Yes, they have started cultivating, farming. Sowing wheat, and rice, and barley was never heard of before our days. Our forefathers never scratched the bosom of mother earth, they never dishonoured the goddess. The earth yielded grass for our herds, and its woods were full of sweet fruits of many kinds, which were never exhausted by our eating them. But with the Madrs' sinfulness, and the sinfulness we have fallen into by imitating them, what has become of our grass that used to grow as tall as a man? Where are those cows as big as the cows of old days, one of which would supply a whole Madr clan with a day's food? There are no such cows, no such horses, and no such sheep as we once had. Even the deer and the bears in the forest are not as big as they used to be. And men don't live so long now. All because of the anger of the Earth-goddess my son, nothing else!'

'How many winters have you seen, grandfather?'

'More than a hundred. Once there were only tents in our encampment; now there are a hundred houses with mud and stone walls in the village. When there were no ploughed fields, our dwellings moved about freely, our whole camp wandered about. After farming began, the wheat had to be protected against deer and other animals. The fields have become pegs to tether men down. But, son, man was not born to be kept cooped up in one spot. The Madrs and Parshus have brought into existence what the gods never created for men.'

'But could we give up farming now, even if we wanted to? Grain is half our food.'

'Yes, yes, I know. But our forefathers ate no grain. Fifty miles south of here is a wilderness of wheat; it grows there by itself, ripens by itself, and falls by itself. Cows eat it, and yield more milk. Horses that eat it grow big and strong. Our herds go there every year. Mother earth has not produced these grains for man's use – the seed is smaller than in the wheat grown in our fields; they were meant for animals. I am afraid of that wild wheat being destroyed somehow. For our own eating, son, we have these cows, and horses, sheep, goats, and in the woods all kinds of game – bears, deer, boars; and grapes and every other kind of fruit. Mother earth has willingly given us all this for our nourishment, but these Madrs and Parshus, ill-luck take them, have deserted down the old ways and taken a new road, and brought anger of the gods on mankind. And now, son, there is no knowing what is ordained in the destiny of the people of the Oxus. As far as I am concerned, I have not gone anywhere leaving the Danda for twenty-five years. In the winter I move to a hut a little lower down. Why should I go among people who all want to break down and abandon the customs that our ancestors have built up? The words our ancestors spoke have been so long treasured in my heart, that even now whoever wants to learn them comes here to me. But there are more and more every day who will not obey those words. Now it seems the Madrs and Parshus can't satisfy their bellies even with their fields to help them. Where are they loading away the food and clothing of the river folk, and what do we get in exchange? Look at that copper pan, bartered for a horse. If famine comes, will that pan fill any one's belly with food? You would now have the Purus without food for their bellies, or without clothes for their backs, and instead you would see their houses furnished with these pans!'

'I have heard another thing, grandfather, that the women of the lower Madrs have begun to wear white and yellow ornaments in their ears and round their necks, and a single earring is worth the price of a horse! They call them "*hiranya*",[11] not copper, and the white ones are called "*rajat*".'[12]

'And no one gives the wretches a beating! They will leave the whole valley of the Oxus people in ruin; they won't leave us even with the bit of food or clothing we may have saved for ourselves. Our own women will start imitating them and put rings worth a couple of horses in their ears. Merciful Agni! Don't leave me for many more days among these human beings; take me away to the world where my forefathers live!'

'There is something else very sinful, grandfather. The Madrs and Parshus have captured prisoners from somewhere, and they force them to make their copper swords and axes. They are very clever workmen, but their masters treat them like animals, keep them as long as they want, and then sell them. They get their farm work, and blanket-weaving and any other kind of work done by these prisoners; they call them *das*.'[13]

'Buying and selling men! We used to think even buying and

selling clothes bad enough, but our forefathers never dreamed that the villainous Madrs would fall to such a depth! When a finger begins to fester, the only remedy is to cut it off, or the whole body will be infected. My son, it is a sin to let the Madrs and Parshus go on living on the banks of our Oxus. I won't stay to watch it much longer.'

The old man's talk was impressive; nonetheless, Puruhut clung to the belief that without the new weapons that had been introduced, life in the midst of their human and animal foes would no longer be possible.

On the third day, when he took his leave, the old man touched his forehead and eyes, and gave him his blessing. Rochna went with him a long way to see him off, and when the time came for parting, they made each other's cheeks wet with their tears.

—3—

The old man's words came true, though twenty-five years later. The lower Madrs and Parshus exploited, more and more callously, the Purus and Madrs of the upper river. While among the latter the weavers of clothes and blankets were free men and women, whose own food and clothing cost a good deal and made the stuff they produced expensive, though excellent, the people downriver had slaves, whose products were not so fine, but much cheaper. When, therefore, merchants went out to neighbouring regions carrying the slave-made wares on camels and horses, they had a brisk sale. By now, also, copper articles in ever-increasing numbers had become indispensable to the upriver folk. For one thing they were becoming a little cheaper year by year, and for another they lasted longer than earthenware or wooden utensils. Whereas a quarter of a century earlier a copper pan was only to be seen in a very few homes, now only a few homes were without one. The use of gold and silver was likewise spreading. In exchange for all these goods, they had to part with food, blankets, hides, horses and cattle, with the result that their wealth was steadily being drained away.

Some upriver men made efforts to turn traders themselves, for they had begun to suspect the strangers from down the river of cheating them. But the route down the Oxus ran through the latter's territory, and they were determined to keep it closed. Occasionally, there was a more or less serious quarrel on this issue. The northern Madrs and Purus made many an attempt to find an alternative route to the outside countries, but always without success.

In this friction between the two sides, an important point was that the lower people were unable to form a strong union among themselves, while those higher up banded together and so were always ready to attack or counterattack. Puruhut, in these skirmishes, won the esteem of his people by his bravery and intelligence, and at the early age of thirty he was elected by the Puru clan as its Great-Father.

It became plain to Puruhut's mind that unless a stop could be put to the unfair trading activities of the Madrs, there was no hope for his people. The use of copper, far from diminishing, was increasing day by day, and not merely for making weapons, cooking utensils or ornaments; now for ordinary purposes of barter, men preferred to receive a copper sword or knife instead of a quantity of meat, for example, or a blanket. Puruhut assembled his clan, and put it to them that all their losses were due to the unjust trading practices of the downriver Jans. All agreed that they must sink to mere puppets on the hands of the Madrs, unless they could clear them out of their way. The day might even come when they would be virtually the slaves of the Madrs. The same conviction was expressed when a joint council of the Puru and upper Madr chiefs was held. Puruhut was chosen by both peoples as commander of their combined forces for the war, and was given the title of Indr.[14] And so, Puruhut became the first Indr in history.

He set to work with utmost energy to organize his army. As soon as he received his new title, in order to arrange for a supply of arms he took under his protection a couple of slave metalworkers. The upriver people gave them the friendliest reception, and with their help succeeded in acquiring a fair degree of skill in working copper. A number of artisans were thus trained among them. Their neighbours were prepared to use force as well as persuasion to get their slaves handed back. Their military prowess, however, had diminished as money-mindedness had taken hold in them. Having failed in the battlefield, they resolved to sell their enemies no more copper; but they quickly realized that this would spell ruin only to their own trade. The upper Madrs and Purus could supply themselves for a generation by turning into weapons the pans and other utensils they had bought earlier.

At last the Indr and his two clans resolved on the destruction of their enemies. Puruhut had himself learned metalworking, and at his suggestion some improvements were made in the swords, spears and arrowheads. He had a number of copper breastplates made, to protect his bravest and most skilful warriors against blows.

He determined to tackle only one enemy at first, and his choice fell on the Parshus. In winter most of them were usually away engaged in trading, and the Indr considered this the best opportunity. He had trained his warriors to fight craftily. Although animosity between the two sides was of such long standing, the downriver men had no notion that their enemies were about to launch so sudden and so savage an attack on them, an attack that would blot out their very names from the Oxus valley. The Indr himself began the attack with the warriors chosen for service under his personal leadership. It did not take long for the Parshus to see the meaning of this invasion, and when they grasped what was happening, and saw their lives at stake, they fought with desperate courage. But so rapid was the onslaught that they had no time to collect their forces from the different villages. The enemy captured one village after another, slaughtering thousands of inhabitants: no prisoners were taken. When tidings of the disaster reached the lower Madrs on the other bank, it was late for them to save themselves. At length only a few villages remained and, leaving enough warriors to deal with them, Indr Puruhut marched into the Kuru territory. The lower Madrs attacked, but they were under the same handicaps as the Parshus had been. Of both peoples not a single male who was captured – boy, youth or old man – was spared; the females were added to the women of the conquerors. Captured slaves who wanted to go home to their own lands were allowed to do so. Some men and women of the vanquished escaped with their lives and fleeing from the Oxus valley made their way westward. Their descendants in later years won fame in Iran, under the names of

Parshu and Madr. They could never forget what had been perpetrated against their ancestors under Indr Puruhut's leadership. Hence it was that Iranians thought of Indr as their most cruel foe. The whole of the Oxus valley had fallen into the hands of the upper Madrs and Purus, who shared the two banks of the river between them.

The valley-dwellers made a resolute attempt to banish the new ways and re-establish the old. But it was impossible to abandon copper and return to stone implements, and to obtain copper they were compelled to link their mountain valley to the outside world by means of trade.

Slavery, however, they never admitted, and they allowed no one from outside to become a permanent settler in the valley. After many centuries, when men had almost forgotten the Indr Puruhut, or had transformed him into a god, the race had multiplied so greatly that the valley could no longer support it, and many were obliged to migrate towards the south.

Once, each Jan had been independent, and even with the rise of the Great-Father to supremacy, these had had to depend on popular support. But the last war on the banks of the Oxus had given birth to a commander over more than one Jan, to an Indr.

1 2 3 4 **5** 6 7 8 9 10
20 19 18 17 16 15 14 13 12 11

Purudhan

REGION : UPPER SWAT
PEOPLE : INDO-ARYAN
TIME : 2000 BCE

This story is of a conflict between the Aryans and the Asurs[1] *belonging to a period about 170 generations ago. In the mountain life of the Aryans of that age slavery had not yet been accepted. The use of copper and brass, and the development of commerce, were on the increase.*

—1—

This part of Suvastu[2] on the left bank was a picture of beauty, with its green-clad hills, gushing springs and far-stretching fields of waving corn. But what the Aryans took the deepest pride in was their homesteads, with stone walls and roofs made of pine-boughs, and hence they had called the country Suvastu (Swat – the country of beautiful houses). When they left the banks of the Oxus these Aryans had crossed the Pamir and the almost inaccessible crags of the Hindu Kush, and made their toilsome way over rivers like the Kunar and the Panjkora. The memory of their journey lingered long in the race; so long perhaps that even today the elaborate celebration of the festival of Indr at Mangalpur (Mangalore) may be an expression of gratitude to the 'Indr' who led them safely across those precipitous tracks.

The Purus of Mangalpur had decorated their pretty houses with pine branches and many-coloured pennants. Purudhan had hung up some red flags of a peculiar kind; and his neighbour Sumedh noticed them and took hold of one.

'Friend Puru,' he remarked, 'these flags of yours are very delicate, very smooth! We don't make any such cloth here. They must be made from the wool of some new kind of sheep!'

'This is not wool from any sheep, Sumedh.'

'What then?'

'This is a kind of wool that grows on trees. Wool like ours grows on sheep, and this kind grows on trees in the forest, in the same way.'

'That is what one hears, friend, but I never saw such trees myself.'

Sumedh rubbed a spindle across his thigh and set it spinning, with a fresh hank of wool on it, remarking, 'How lucky they are, those people who find wool growing on their trees! Could such trees not be planted here?'

'I can't say. We don't know how much cold or heat they can bear. As to those people's luck, meat at any rate doesn't grow on trees, Sumedh!'

'If there is a land where wool grows on trees, there may be a land where meat does the same. What does this cloth cost?'

'Much less than woollen cloth, but it doesn't last as long.'

'Where did you buy it from?'

'From the Asur people. Their country is only fifty *kos*[3] from here, and they use this material for their clothes.'

'If it is so cheap, why should we people not wear it also?'

'It won't do for the winter.'

'Then how can the Asurs wear it?'

'Their cold weather is not as severe as ours; there is never any snowfall there.'

'Why do you go only to the south for your trade, and not to the east or the north or the west?'

'There's more profit to be had in the south, and more kinds of goods to pick up; though there is one great drawback – the heat is terrible, it makes you pant for a gulp of fresh cold water.'

'What sort of people are they, Purudhan?'

'Very short, with coppery skins; ugly devils, with hardly any noses on their faces – squat, flat things. And they have a very evil custom, buying and selling human beings.'

'What?'

'They call them *das*.'

'Is there any difference of face or figure between the *das* and their owners?'

'No, the *das* are mere wretched chattels; they belong to their masters in body and soul.'

'Indr protects us, and may I never have to set eyes on such people!'

'Well, Sumedh, your spindle is still at work, isn't it time to go to the sacrifice?'

'Why not? It is the mercy of Indr that sends fat cattle and good *som* juice. Is there any luckless fellow who will not take part in the festival of Indr?'

'And how is your good wife? Nowadays one doesn't catch even a glimpse of her in the meeting ground.'

'And you find that very unpleasant, eh?'

'Unpleasant? That is not the question. After all, Sumedh, you insisted on falling in love with a young girl in your old age!'

'A man is not so old at fifty!'

'There is a good deal of difference between fifty and twenty, all the same.'

'She could have refused at the time.'

'At that time you had curled your beard and moustaches to look like eighteen. Besides, Usha's parents had their eye on your herds, not on your age.'

'Stop talking like that, Puru! You young ones are always ...'

'All right, I won't say any more! Listen, the music has begun to play, the ceremony is beginning.'

'You will have made us late, and I'll have to listen to a lot of abuse.'

'Come on, then, and we'll take Usha along with us.'

'Is she still sitting in the house this entire time, do you think?'

'Come, put this wool and the spindle away, and let us be going.'

'These won't be in the way at the festival.'

'Oh! This is the sort of thing that keeps Usha from liking you!'

'She would like me all right, if only you young fellows of Mangalpur would let her.'

Talking as they went, the two companions walked out of the township and went to where the altar stood ready for the sacrifice. Whenever a young man or woman met Purudhan's glance, they always gave him a smile, and Purudhan turned his head towards them with a wink. Once Sumedh caught sight of a certain youth doing this and he began to growl –

'They're the disgrace of Mangalpur, those young fellows!'

'What's the matter, friend?'

'Friend – fiddlesticks! They are always laughing when they see me.'

'That one is a rogue, friend, as you know; why do you take any notice of what he says?'

'I can't see a single decent man in Mangalpur!'

There was a level expanse round the altar, with platforms and pillars draped in pine leaves here and there, hung with festive garlands. The space near the altar was thronged with crowds of men and women from the town; but the really big meeting would begin in the evening, when every man and woman of the Puru tribe would attend the great Mangalpur festival, as well as the Madrs from the other side of the Swat river.

Usha saw the two companions coming, and hurrying up to Sumedh clasped his hand, mimicking the gestures of a youthful lover, and said –

'Dear Sumedh! I have killed myself looking for you ever since morning; I couldn't find a trace of you anywhere!'

'Oh, had I gone and died somewhere?'

'Don't say such things, Sumedh! Don't go and make a widow of me while I'm still alive!'

'And have widows among the Purus a shortage of young brothers-in-law?'

'And do the women detest their husband's brothers while their husbands are alive?' asked Purudhan.

'Oh, yes, that's the question!' cried Sumedh. 'She has come to make a fool of me. She left home in the morning, and I don't know how many houses she got invitations from; and then in the evening one fellow will say "Dance with me", and another will say "No, with me". There'll be quarrelling, bloodshed, and on account of his wife, Sumedh will come in for abuse!'

Usha let go his hand, and with an altered expression in her eyes and her voice exclaimed –

'So you want to keep me shut up in a box! Go and sulk by the fireplace yourself! I'm going my own way.'

She threw Purudhan a smile meant for no one else to see, and disappeared in the crowd round the altar.

This was the one day of the year in the Swat valley when, as in old days beside the Oxus, the flesh of the biggest horse that could be found is devoted to Indr. The horse was chosen out of all those possessed by the tribe. Though horses were not eaten here, at this annual rite the remains of the offering were distributed, and piously accepted by all. All the tribal Great-Fathers, now known as the Janpati,[4] were present with all their folk to join in offering the chosen oblation. They knew by heart the ritual forms of the sacrifice, and the sacred formulas of praise with which the Oxus valley dwellers had been accustomed to perform the offering to Indr. To the accompaniment of music and the recitation of prayers, the sacrifice of the horse was completed, from the first touching and the sprinkling of holy water to the death blow. Then its skin was removed, and the carcass cut into pieces, some of which, just as they were or with condiments added, were laid on the fire as the burnt-offering. Evening fell while the remnants were being shared out. By this time the ground was packed with people, all wearing their handsomest clothes and ornaments. The women wore soft, dyed shawls held by embroidered waistbands of many colours, with pretty tunics underneath. In their ears most of them had golden earrings. Spring was drawing to a close, and the valley was full of flowers, as if specially blossomed for this day. Men and women alike had used them to decorate their flowing hair; and during this festival they were at full liberty to indulge in their amorous tastes. At night, while Usha, decked up for the occasion, was wandering about with Purudhan's hand clasped in her own, Sumedh's glance fell on them. He turned away his face. What else could he do, poor man? At the feast of Indr he could not even fly into a rage; only last year he had fallen foul of the Janpati by doing so.

Tonight the fermented milk mixed with *som*-juice was flowing in torrents. Tasty horse-meat and beef, and *som*-juice, the contribution of many villages, were brought in and piled up. Everywhere there was welcoming of young people, intoxicated with the excitement of new loves. They would stuff a morsel of meat in their mouths, swallow a cup of *som*-juice, dance to the instruments that were always playing or ready to play, and then go over to the reception place for people from another village. Preparations on a grand scale had been made by the whole tribe, and the space left open here for dancing was ample.

The Indr festival was the grand holiday of the young. For this one day and night they were set free of all restraints.

—2—

This part of upper Swat was rich in herds and grain, and its inhabitants, therefore, contented and prosperous. Of the other articles they required, the chief was copper, and, among luxuries, gold and silver and some jewels, the demand for which was daily expanding. To supply these, every year temporary Asur settlements sprang up near the junction of the Swat and Kubha (Kabul) rivers.

It seems the Aryans later gave to the Asur outpost here the name of Pushkalavati,[5] and even now we make use of the same name. In mid-winter the clans inhabiting Swat, Panjkora and other mountain valleys – the Purus, Kurus, Gandhars, Madrs, Mallas, Shivis, Ushinars, and so on – brought their horses, blankets and other wares, and pitched their tents on the plain outside Pushkalavati. The Asur merchants came with their goods to the same place, and offered the articles in demand by way of barter. This system had been flourishing for centuries.

This year the Purus' caravan had come to Pushkalavati under the leadership of Purudhan. It had been a complaint among the hill-men for some years now that the Asurs were cheating them heavily. The Asurs, as townbred traders, were undoubtedly much more astute than the hill-men; so they considered them utterly clownish barbarians, with some degree of culture. But the yellow-haired, blue-eyed Aryan horsemen would never admit themselves to be inferior to the Asur townspeople. Gradually, as many Aryans came to pick up the Asur language, like Purudhan, and to have opportunities of mixing in Asur society, they began to realize that the Asurs viewed them as mere brutes. This was the beginning of hostility between the two races.

The Asur cities were very fine. They had buildings of baked bricks, water pipes, baths, roads, wells and so on. Even the Aryans did not deny the beauty of Pushkalavati. They were also ready to admit good looks in a certain number of Asur women, though they still criticized their noses, hair, and stature; but they could never be prepared to agree that Mangalpur, in its girdle of pine-covered hills, gay with many-coloured wooden balconies and rows of neat dwelling-houses, was any whit inferior to Pushkalavati – a place where they always found it hard to stay for a month at a time, while their thoughts kept straying back to their own birthplace. The same river Swat might flow by Pushkalavati; but they found a different flavour in its water there. The touch of the Asurs was enough, they used to say, to muddy its pure stream. However that might be, the Aryans were by no means ready to recognize Asurs as even their equals, especially when they saw their hordes of male and female slaves, or their prostitutes sitting on flat roofs, offering their bodies for sale.

In private relations, however, many friendships sprang up between members of the two races. The King of the Asurs lived in a city far away from Pushkalavati, on the banks of the Sindhu;[6] so Purudhan had never seen him. But he had seen the King's local representative – a short, fat, slothful man, whose thick eyelids were perpetually blinking from the effects of drink, and whose body was loaded with dozens of gold and silver ornaments. The lobes of his ears were pierced, and hung down to his shoulders. To Purudhan's eyes this Governor was the embodiment of ugliness and stupidity; and a man like Purudhan could not form a high opinion of a King who had such a representative as this. He had heard that the Governor was a brother-in-law of the King, and had been elevated to his office on account of this sole virtue.

Many weaknesses in Asur society had become evident to Purudhan in the course of his occasional residence among them over several years. Intelligent as the Asurs of the upper class might be, most of them were also growing cowardly; they relied on the strength of armed dependants or slaves to cope with their enemies. This might, indeed, give them success against a weak foe, but such an army would not be able to stand up against a powerful opponent. Their rulers – the King and his Governors – made pleasure the single object of their lives. Each of the ruling men kept hundreds of concubines and slave-girls. All their women in fact were treated as slaves. At present the King had in his seraglio a number of Aryan women who had been carried off by their own people. Fortunately, the King's capital was far away from the frontier and no Aryan had yet made their way so far; so that people treated the sad fate of these Aryan women as mere gossip.

From the shops of Pushkalavati ornaments of many kind – cotton, cloth, weapons and other articles – had spread not only to Swat, but to the nomadic encampments on the upper spurs of Kunar. The golden-haired belles of Swat were wild for the ornaments made by the skilled hands of Asur craftsmen, so that more and more of them began going to Pushkalavati with the yearly troop of dealers. The unfortunate Sumedh had indeed made Usha a widow, and she had become the wife of her husband's cousin, Purudhan. This year she too had come to Pushkalavati. The Governor's men observed that there were a good many pretty faces in the strangers' tents; and their master, on being informed of this, resolved that the caravan should be attacked on its way home as soon as it entered the hills, and the women carried off. It was a foolish design, the mountaineers being as warlike as he well knew them to be; but his was a brain without even a spark of intelligence.

The big merchants of the town had reason to hate the Governor. He had recently taken violent possession of the handsome daughter of a merchant who was Purudhan's friend, and made the father his mortal enemy. Usha had sometimes visited this trader's house; she could not understand a word of his wife's talk, but with the help of Purudhan as interpreter, and the lady's friendly manners, a friendship had been formed between the two women.

Two days before the departure of the Aryans, this merchant held a banquet in honour of Purudhan, as a valuable customer. While it was going on, he whispered into his guest's ear the Governor's villainous scheme. The same night, Purudhan summoned all the leading men of his party and unfolded a plan. Those who lacked good weapons were to buy some. They had sold off the horses they had brought to market and their heavy bales of stuff, and were left with nothing more than their riding-horses and what they had bought – ornaments and other metal articles; so they had nothing to trouble about on this score. As to their women, although the girls of Swat were growing fonder and fonder of luxuries to adorn themselves with, to wield weapons was still part of their education along with singing and dancing. When they heard what was afoot, they too got ready their swords and shields.

Purudhan's information was that the Asur soldiers would block the way and make their attack in the steep pass leading across the frontier, while at the same time a strong band of them would come in the rear to effect encirclement. To meet this threat he took all the precautions which his early news of the scheme enabled him to take. Otherwise, the visitors from Panjkora, Kunar and Swat would have set out separately, not caring about one another's movements; as it was, all made their preparations together. So as not to give anything away to the enemy, they made their start from Pushkalavati at intervals of a day or two; but it had been arranged that all should arrive simultaneously at the entrance to the pass.

When within three or four miles of the pass, Purudhan sent twenty-five horsemen in advance. Just as these riders entered the pass and began the ascent, the Asurs opened fire on them with arrows. It was true, then, that an attack had been planned. The horsemen fell back and brought the news to their commander. Purudhan wanted first to settle with the enemies who were closing in from the rear. This was not beyond his strength; for, the Asurs, though they bought thousands of horses annually from the Aryans, had not yet trained themselves into good cavalrymen.

The cavalcade halted: a number of fighting men were left there on guard, while Purudhan took the rest and rode with them. The Asur force had no expectation of being attacked so unceremoniously. It could not hold its ground for long against the Aryans with their long spears and swords; but the latter had no intention of letting their enemies off with a mere defeat. They wanted to convince them that it was very dangerous for flat-nosed, swarthy Asurs to cast their eyes on any Aryan woman. When Purudhan saw them in flight, he sent word to his reserve, and dashed forward on Pushkalavati with his own horsemen. Like his soldiers, the Governor was taken by surprise. The Asurs had no time to bring all their forces into play, and their citadel, with the Governor, fell easily into the assailants' hands.

The Aryans had been roused to fury by the treachery of the Asurs. They massacred ruthlessly all the men they took. The Governor was dragged to the public square and hacked to pieces before the eyes of his people. Women and children, and the merchants, were spared, and perhaps so many men would not have been slaughtered if the Aryans had had at that time any desire to take slaves. Several quarters of the town were burned to the ground.

Thus fell the first stronghold of the Asurs; and thus also commenced the great struggle between the two races, which was to pass into Aryan mythology as Devasur-Sangram.[7]

Purudhan turned back home, wiping out the Asur soldiers who still held together in the pass, and then each party of the hill-men took its road to its own territory.

For some years the trade with Pushkalavati was dead. The hill-men refused to buy any goods from the Asurs. But it was not for very long that they could deny themselves copper and brass.

6

Angira

REGION : GANDHAR-TAKSHSHILA
PEOPLE : INDO-ARYANS
TIME : 1800 BCE

This story of about 152 generations ago depicts the early conflicts between the Aryans and the Asurs living in the north-west of India.

—1—

'They are useless, these cotton clothes; they neither keep the winter cold out nor protect you from the rain,' said the young man, stripping off his damp tunic and throwing a blanket round his shoulders.

'But they're good in the hot weather,' returned the second youth, spreading out his own tunic above the shutter. Evening was still far off, but in the guesthouse there were already people stretched out before the fire. The two youths, instead of sitting near the smoky fire, went and sat near the window, wrapped in their blankets to keep off the cold breeze.

First youth – 'We can still go another *yojan*[1] and get to Gandhar-town (Takshshila[2]) before the end of tomorrow morning, but facing this rain and wind is not easy.'

Second – 'These cloudy winter skies make everything worse. But when clouds don't come, our farmers deafen *Indr* with their prayers for rain, and the herdsmen grumble even more.'

First – 'Yes, friend, it's only we travellers who don't like this weather. And nobody is always travelling. What is your name?' the speaker added, noticing at the back of the other's neck the scar of a deep wound.

'Pal, of the Madrs. And yours?'

'Varun, a Sauvir. You are coming from the east, then?'

'Yes, from the Madr country; and you from the south? Is it true, as we hear, that in the south the Asurs are still fighting against the Aryans?'

'Only on the sea coast, where they still had one city left to them. You know, friend, I suppose, how our Indr Maghva[3] destroyed a hundred of their fortified towns.'

'They say those Asur fortresses were built of copper.'

'The Asurs have plenty of copper, but not enough for making fortresses out of it! I don't know how this tale got about. Their buildings are made of oblong baked bricks, and so are the walls round their towns. The bricks are reddish coloured, but there is a great difference between them and metal. It would be absurd to call bricks copper!'

'Yet we keep hearing of the Asurs and their copper fortifications, Varun!'

'Possibly the name grew up just because of the effort our Indr had to make to destroy them; they seem as strong as if they were built of metal.'

'And then we always hear great tales about the prowess of Shambar,[4] and how his house stood in the sea, and his chariot flew through the sky.'

'All that, about his chariot, is nonsense. If there is one part of warfare the Asurs are weaker in than any other, it is horsemanship. Even now, in their festivals, instead of horse-chariots they make use of ox-carts. I believe, Pal, it was on account of our horses that we conquered them; without them we could never have overcome Asur-*purs*.[5] It is two centuries now since Shambar's death, but in my opinion he can't even have had a horse-chariot, to say nothing of being able to fly through the sky!'

'Then if Shambar was only an ordinary enemy, how did our Indr gain such glory by defeating him?'

'Because Shambar was a great hero. I have seen in Sauvir-town his copper armour, inlaid with gold; it was tremendously strong and heavy. Most Asurs are quite small men, but Shambar was a huge man, tall, broad, perhaps even rather fat; while our Maghva was a slender, active young man. You can still see the ancient Asur citadels on the banks of the Sindhu. A hundred archers or so in one of them could hold off a thousand assailants. In fact, those fortresses were impregnable; and to destroy such strongholds our Indr Maghva had to be a very resolute man.'

'In the south, have the Asurs any strength left in them, Varun?'

'Didn't I tell you their last citadel on the seashore has just been conquered? I took part in the struggle myself.'

A deeper glow brightened Varun's sunburned cheeks as he said this, and he threw back his long glistening yellow hair.

'The last stronghold of the Asurs has fallen!'

'Who was your Indr?'

'We have abolished the title of Indr.'

'Abolished?'

'Yes; we southern Aryans began to grow afraid of it.'

'Why?'

'The duty of an Indr is to command in war, isn't it?'

'Yes.'

'And Aryans do not regard their military chiefs as sovereigns. In time of war we certainly pay obedience to them; but an Aryan considers his *Jan-parishad*[6] the highest authority, and every Aryan has the right to express his opinion freely in it.'

'Certainly.'

'But among the Asurs it is different; their Indr or king is all in all, he recognizes no *Jan-parishad* with higher powers than his. Whatever he says, everyone has to do unless they want to be killed.'

'An Indr of that kind can never be accepted by us!'

'Well, the Asurs had always been accepting such rulers. They regard their king as a god, not a man and you would never believe it, my friend, if you heard how they worship him even while he is alive.'

'Well, I have seen for myself how the Asur priests befool their people.'

'They treat them as if they were lower than donkeys! You may have heard that they worship the sex organs – parts that serve the happiness of men and women no doubt, and enable the race to be carried on; but worship them, either the organ themselves, or clay and stone images of them, what folly is that!'

'Of course!'

'And the Asur kings were very much devoted to that kind of worship. But it seems to me there was a good deal of pure mummery in it. After all they and their priests were no fools, they were far shrewder than us Aryans. We shall have to learn a great deal from them if we are to build cities like theirs. Their shops, their ponds dappled with lotuses, their lofty buildings, their highroads – these were things you could never find in our primitive Aryan lands. I have seen the deserted Asur cities of northern Sauvir, and this city that has just been conquered. We Aryans were not able even to repair their old cities and restore them to what they were; but this new one – they say it was founded by Shambar himself – is like "Devpur" [city of the gods]!'

'Devpur!'

'That is the truth. There is no place on earth that can be compared to it. For instance, take one of its houses meant for a single family. It will have one or two furnished sitting-rooms, a separate kitchen with a chimney, a brick well in the courtyard, a bathroom, a bedroom, and a granary. I have seen houses of ordinary citizens with two or three storeys. There is no way of describing it; I can't compare that Asur city to anything but Devpur.'

'There are Asur towns in the east also, but they lie far beyond our Madr country.'[7]

'I have seen them, friend. And we must admit that those who built them were cleverer than us. Have you ever heard about the ocean?'

'Only its name.'

'You can form no notion of it from hearing its name, or even from hearing it described. It is only when you stand at its edge and stare at it that you begin to learn what it is. In front of you the blue water runs up to the blue sky.'

'How can it run up to the sky, Varun?'

'It does, as far as your eye can see, the water spreads on and seems to rise up, as high as several palm trees, until it touches the sky. Both are almost the same colour, for seawater is bluer than the sky. And over this boundless ocean the Asurs sailed their great boats fearlessly on voyages of months or years; and they brought up gems of many kinds out of the waves. That is another example of the courage and skill of the Asurs. Besides, there is one thing you can't have heard of, friend. The Asurs can talk and converse without using their mouths.'

'What's that? Without words?'

'Yes, without words! Give him clay, stone and leather and an Asur will draw some symbols with them so that another man will understand all that he means. What we could not explain in two hours of talking, they can make clear with five or ten symbols. The Aryans never learned this. Now they are trying to learn these symbols, but even if they spend years on it, they will never master it fully.'

'There seems no doubt that the Asurs were more intelligent than we are, then!'

'Yes. We see everywhere the work of their craftsmen, porters, chariot-builders, swordsmiths, blacksmiths, weavers. How could there be any doubt of their superiority over us?'

'And the Asurs are brave as well, you say.'

'Brave, yes, but only a very few of them. Their children are not like ours, who all begin playing with swords as soon as they are weaned. Their soldiers are a separate class; so are their craftsmen, merchants and slaves. No one outside the warrior class learns to bear arms; the warriors regard all the rest with contempt, and the slaves, men and women, are worse off than animals. Their masters not only buy and sell them; their arbitrary power over them extends to life and limb.'

'How many are the soldiers amongst them?'

'The soldiers are less than one in a hundred; forty out of every hundred are slaves, another forty are in a half-servile condition, for their craftsmen and peasants are half slaves; ten will be traders, and the rest men of other professions.'

'That must be why they have been defeated by the Aryans.'

'Yes, it was one of the chief causes of their defeat, and another main reason was their deifying the king and putting him far above the people.'

'We Aryans could never do that.'

'That is why we had to abolish the rank of Indr. It was because of a certain Indr, after the time of Maghva, who wanted to be just like an Asur king.'

'To lord it at his whim over the Aryan nation?'

'Yes, and he was not the only one; after him came another,

and then some other Aryans were found helping them to gain what they wanted.'

'Helping them?'

'In the interests of their own clans or families. So the Sauvirs have determined that henceforth no one shall be made an Indr. "Indr" is also the name of the god who wields the lightning which might give rise to confusion in people's minds.'

'The Sauvirs have done well, friend!'

'But some have sprung up to disgrace the Aryans' name, who are never tired of praising everything of the Asurs. Many Asur achievements are praiseworthy: I praise them myself, and we must adopt them. We have made their implements our own. It was by copying their ox-carts that our Indr Maghva designed the horse-chariot. It is more convenient for an archer to shoot from a chariot than from horseback, because he can have as many quivers as he likes by him, and he can have a shield to protect him from enemy arrows. We have also learned much from their armour, their javelins, their maces, and so on. We are adopting many things from their cities. We must learn the art of seafaring from them, because metals like copper, and jewels, and many other articles, come from across the sea, and all the trade in them is still in the hands of Asur merchants. If we want to be independent of them, we must learn how to sail the seas. But in spite of all this, there are many Asur customs that we must recognize as dangerous for us, such as worship of phallus.'

'But what Aryan would like to worship phallus?'

'Don't be too sure, friend. There are some Aryans who are saying that we ought to set up a priesthood of our own, like what the Asurs have. At present there is no cleavage among us between warriors, priests, merchants, farmers and artisans; everyone can do every kind of work at will, whereas the Asurs have marked off each class from the other. Once let priests be set up among the Aryans, and within a few years you will see sex-worship beginning as well. The Asur priests are very artful, and ours would do the same as they do, out of greed for profits.'

'That would be a curse, Varun!'

'A great many evils have crept among the Aryans because of their contact with the Asurs in the last two hundred years. Our old men have watched it in despair. I am not hopeless. I believe that if the good old ways are properly taught to our people, they will not degenerate. They say there is a *rishi*,[8] a man of learning, in Gandhar-town named Angira. He teaches people, in order to set the Aryans again firmly on the Aryan way. I have drawn my sword to help the Aryans to victory; now I want to do something to save the Aryan way of life.'

'This is a coincidence! I, too, am on my way to Rishi Angira, to learn the art of war from him.'

'Oh! But, Pal, you have told me nothing about the state of the Aryans in the east.'

'In the east they are spreading like a forest fire. The country stretching beyond Gandhar we Madrs have occupied. Further on still the Mallas have established themselves, and in the same way the Kurus, the Panchals and others have carved out big territories for themselves.'

'The Aryans must be in great numbers there!'

'Not very great. The further they have spread, the more they are outnumbered by the Asurs and other races.'

'What other races?'

'The Asurs are of the colour of the *mangur*[9] fish, or copper. To the east are people of a different kind, called Kols – they are black as coal. Some of them live in villages, others in the forest like the deer. Most of the forest Kols' implements are made of stone.'

'I suppose there is sharp fighting between the Aryans and the others?'

'There are few pitched battles now. The natives run away at the mere sight of our horses; but they attack our settlements in the night, so we often have to give them a cruel lesson, and many of the villages of the Asurs and Kols have been left deserted; they are retreating eastwards.'

'So there is no danger of Asur customs getting a foothold among you, Pal?'

'Not among the Madrs, nor perhaps among the Mallas; I don't know about further east. Among us, in fact, the non-Aryans survive only in the forests.'

The two friends kept up their exchange of news till nightfall, and perhaps would have kept it up even later if the keeper of the guesthouse had not come to enquire about food for them. The building had been put up at the cost of the village, for all travellers – those of the yellow-haired race, needless to say – to stop at, and those who had no food with them could be provided with parched grain and beef soup. If a traveller had provisions he could give them to the keeper, who would cook them and prepare a meal; if not, some equivalent had to be given.

This guesthouse was famous for its *som* and wine. Varun and Pal cemented their friendship with roast beef and liquor.

—2—

Angira the Rishi had risen to the highest position among the Gandhar folk to the east of the Sindhu. The Asurs had begun to retreat after the first sack of Pushkalavati; and when in the next generation a branch of the Gandhar tribe came from the Kunar river to seize the western part of what became the Gandhar country, the Asurs who still survived made haste to evacuate this area. Only thirty years went by before the Gandhar and Madr tribes invaded the country east of the Sindhu, and shared it between themselves, the former taking the region between Jehlam[10] and the Sindhu rivers, and the latter the region between the Jehlam and the Ravi – the lands that in course of time were to become well known under the names of their conquerors.

In this opening contest between the Aryans and Asurs, the two sides rivalled each other in their inhuman brutality, as a result of which not a single Asur was left in Gandhar, and very few among the Madrs. But as time passed, the resistance of the Asurs in the borderlands weakened, and their enemies treated them with less brutality. Not only this, but, as Varun had said, the yellow-haired race began to feel an admiration for much of Asur culture.

Angira was not only deeply versed in the Aryan tradition that had descended from the Oxus valley; he was anxious that the Aryans should not lose the purity of their blood and their beliefs and customs. This was his motive for encouraging and reintroducing among the herdsmen the eating of horse-flesh, which for some reason had died out. So celebrated had he become for his devotion to the Aryan tradition, his learning, and his mastery of the art of war, that Aryan youths even from the remotest Aryan colonies began to come to him as students. Yet no one at that time could guess that the seed planted by Angira would one day grow into a great tree – the Takshshila academy,[11] to gather whose mellow fruit, devotees of Aryan lore would come journeying from a thousand miles away.

Angira was sixty-five years old, an impressive figure with his white hair, his gleaming white beard hanging to his waist, and his calm, meditative face. Several centuries were still to elapse before pen and ink and writing on leaves were devised; all his instruction was given orally and his pupils learned the old songs and stories by heart through repeating them over and over again. Students who came from far-off places could not bring provisions with them. Angira had to make arrangements for feeding and also for clothing them. Besides devoting his own land to this purpose, he cleared some forest tracts with the aid of his pupils, and brought new fields under the plough, where enough wheat was grown to supply food for the whole year. Orchards and fruit-gardens had not yet been planted; but at the time of year when fruit was ripening in the forest Angira used to go there with his band of disciples and gather it. Ploughing, sowing and harvesting, or collecting flowers, fruits and firewood, they would sing in chorus the songs first composed on the banks of the Oxus or the Swat. Angira's horse-breeding farm, also, was the biggest in Gandhar. He had set his students and acquaintances on the lookout, far and wide, for stallions and mares of the finest quality, and had bred from them; and it was from his stud that originated the Sindhi breed, celebrated everywhere in later times. In addition, Angira owned thousands of cattle and sheep. His students were expected to do manual work along with intellectual, the Rishi himself bearing a hand in it off and on. It was unavoidable, for only in this way could the problem of feeding and clothing them be solved.

The hills east of Takshshila were all well watered, fertile and green. Today, Varun and Pal had joined a group of youths who were with Angira, keeping an eye on the pastures. Not far from the tents, young calves with clear, reddish skins were frisking. The Rishi and his pupils were sitting out on the grass. Angira had a skein of fine wool in his left hand, and with the other was twirling a big wooden spindle. Some of the others were also spinning, some were carding the wool, and some were smoothing out fleeces with their fingers. The Rishi was explaining many things old and new, the rites and customs of Aryans and non-Aryans, what kinds of craftsmanship deserved adoption, and what ought to be rejected.

'To say that everything newfangled must be rejected, and everything ancient preserved, is ridiculous,' he was declaring, 'and to put such an opinion into practice is impossible. When copper tools, instead of stone ones, began to be known to the Aryans of the Oxus valley, no doubt many of them disliked such novelties.'

'How did they manage to do their work with stone tools?' asked Varun, who was a favourite with the Rishi.

'Today my son, work is done with copper tools, tomorrow something sharper still will be discovered, and then people will wonder how they ever managed with copper tools! A man has to get through his work with whatever implement is available at the time. When battles were fought with stone axes, both sides were armed with the same weapons; as soon as one side got hold of copper axes, the other side too was obliged to throw away its stone weapons, or it would have had no living space left in the world. That is why I said it was foolish to denounce all things new because they are new. If I had been an enemy of whatever is new, I should never have been able to breed such beautiful horses and cows. I noticed that when you have good stallions and mares, you get good foals; so I picked out some animals, and now after thirty-five years, you see how my herd has developed.

'The Asurs had a good method of irrigating their fields. They dug channels from the hill streams, and led water along them; we adopted the same method in Gandhar. They had many useful ideas in town planning and in medicine and those also we have adopted. Whatever valuable things we may come on – in the way of food, or clothing, or self-protection – we must turn to account, without considering whether they are old or new or whether their origin was Aryan or non-Aryan. When they were in Swat, and before that time, the Aryans had never even heard of cotton cloth, yet now we are all wearing it because of its comfortableness in hot weather.

'But there are many other things which we should reject as if they were poison. For us, Asurs' Phallus-worship is an abomination. Their strict division into classes is something we must not imitate, for when you have that you can no longer call on every man to bear arms for the defence of his country, and the people feel themselves divided into high and low. We must not mix our blood with Asur blood, for that would be the beginning of our turning into Asurs, and then among the Aryans too there would be a growth of higher and lower classes, representing various crafts and professions.'

'Do all the Aryans think it wrong to intermarry with the Asurs?' Pal enquired.

'Yes, but they are not careful enough about it. Are there not Aryans who have relations with Asur and Kol women?'

'Yes, on the frontiers they do it, they say, and visiting the prostitutes in the Asur cities is quite common among our warriors.'

'And what will come of it? The mixture of races will go on. Boys and girls of our blood will be born among the Asurs, and we Aryans, out of uncertainty or from being tricked will accept them as our own. What will be left of our purity of blood then? To safeguard this purity all of us, men and women, will have to be on our guard. Moreover, we must be careful not to admit the institution of slavery into our lands, because nothing is more dangerous to racial purity. I even tell you, we must see to it that not a trace of any non-Aryan is found in our country.

'The greatest danger, and the root of all evil, is the Asur institution of monarchy of which their priesthood is an offshoot. The Asur people have no rights; each Asur thinks it his religious duty to do anything the king may command. Their priests teach them that the control of all public affairs rests with the gods above and the king below, and that the people can have no freedom to speak or to act. The king himself is a god on earth. I was full of joy when I heard that the Shivi-Sauvirs had abolished the title of Indr; although among the Aryans the Indr never gained as much power as the Asur king enjoyed, for he was simply a notable warrior chosen by the people, and had no authority to establish his rule over them. Still, there was danger in the title itself, and under cover of it there were some who tried to set up an Asur monarchy among the Aryans.

'If the Aryans want to keep their own way of life safe, they must not confer royal power on any individual. Aryans detest the Asur religion, no doubt; but from the day when kings arise among them, Asur priesthood will begin to spring up too; and then the Aryan way will be as good as lost. The king will make merry at the expense of his people, and to get the assistance of the gods he will bribe the priests on to his side; and between king and priest the people will be reduced to slavery.

'We must hold fast with all our strength to the ancient Aryan ways, and if any branch of our race is seduced from them, it must be expelled from the Aryan fellowship.'

—3—

Many disturbing rumours were reaching Varun from the southern part of Sauvir. It appeared from them that, with the capture of the last Asur stronghold, bitter dissension was rearing its head within the Aryan fold. Varun often discussed the problem of Sauvir from every point of view with his teacher. Rishi Angira always said that although this quarrel had broken out first in Sauvir, it was bound to spread from there to all the Aryan lands. From the beginning, Aryans had placed the authority of the people above the individual, but the spectacle of unchecked despotism among the Asurs might well inspire many Aryan leaders with the temptations of power find self-indulgence. Between the two conceptions a mortal struggle was inevitable, and the more Asurs were left in any region the greater was the likelihood of its flaring up quickly, for the vanquished Asurs would be eager to profit by the internecine strife of the Aryans.

After staying at Gandhar-town for eight years, Varun decided to leave it because the news from Sauvir-town[12] was becoming more alarming still. Pal, his earliest friend among the Rishi's pupils accompanied him. Passing the limits of Gandhar, they entered the region where Sindhu flows by the Salt Range. Those busy in the salt-mine, merchants, and labourers were still Asurs for the most part, and this had bad effects on the Aryans, who had grown slothful and ease loving. They were too fond of getting their work done for them by the non-Aryans, and considered horsemanship and swordsmanship the only business worthy of them. Non-Aryan lands were fertile soil for the growth of Aryan monarchies as powerful as that of the Asurs. However, on crossing the Salt hills, the friends arrived at the first outpost, Moolsthan[13] of Sauvir, and there they found a somewhat better state of affairs. All the inhabitants were Aryan, and it was very much to their credit that they had made this an Aryan land in spite of the frightful heat. Varun and Pal were making their journey in mid-summer, though their hardships were lessened by the fact that they were descending the Sindhu by boat.

The heat of Sauvir-town itself was indescribable; it was a severe affliction to them. Since the Aryans had not yet devised an alphabet, the occasional news that Varun was able to send back to his friends through Sauvir travellers, could not be very full. He often thought of the Asurs and their art of writing. As soon as he reached Sauvir-town, it was clear to him that things had already gone very far. In the town itself there were few supporters of Sumitr – the commander who had destroyed the last Asur citadel – but in southern Sauvir there were many Aryans ready to take his side. At the time of the Asurs' final defeat, Sumitr had shown their townsfolk more clemency than he need have done, and Varun had warmly admired him for it. But now it was borne in upon him that it had been a piece of cunning on Sumitr's part: Sumitr knew that the Asurs would never again be able to rise against the Aryans, and that by his display of kindness he could turn to his own account the wealth and might of the Asur merchants overseas.

Sumitr was still occupying the Asur city on the coast with the army, and, on the pretext of imaginary wars, refused to think of coming back. Varun began by meeting the ordinary headmen of the people, who were in the dark as to Sumitr's intentions. They thought that some of the higher leaders were opposing Sumitr because of private hatreds. Then, when he met these important men, they explained the whole situation, but added that although Sumitr's evil purpose was clear enough to them, it was not clear to the mass of the people, who saw it in a different light.

In the attack on the Asur city, Varun had been Sumitr's second in command and though nine years had passed by, his prowess was still held in high respect by the people. Before trying to impress his views on them, he wished to go in person and glean information about Sumitr. With this object, he and his friend one day boarded a boat bound for southern Sauvir. They had equipped themselves to appear as Gandhar merchants. The Asur city looked indeed a city of Asurs rather than of Aryans. Its streets were full of palaces of Asur sea-traders, and of merchandise from many countries. Many leading Asur families were still living in their own quarters of the town, where, just as formerly, fettered slaves could be seen for sale. In fact, Varun began to wonder what had become of the Aryan conquerors. Sumitr was living in the old royal palace. One day Varun sent Pal to see him, under colour of taking him a present from the Gandhar merchants. Pal came back with the report that, except for his fair hair and skin, Sumitr had completely transformed himself into an Asur ruler. His mansion was not the unpretentious house of an Aryan leader, but an Asur Court glittering with gold and silver. There was equally little of plain living among his military attendants. As the weeks went by, it grew clear that the Aryans were only busy with dances and drinking bouts in the company of Asur girls. Many Aryan women were eager to come and join their husbands, but excuses were always found for preventing them. Sumitr himself kept sending messages to prevent his wife from coming; he had fallen in love with the daughter of an Asur priest, not to speak of the numerous Asur beauties who were inmates of his harem, and he allowed the same license to his followers. Whenever other Aryans tried to come from outside, he put a stop to it by setting slaves to assault them, which resulted in several murders.

Having gathered all the information he wanted, Varun made his departure unobtrusively, and returned to Sauvir-town with his friend. There he informed the leading men of how firmly Sumitr had established his power: so firmly that they now had to deal not only with the Aryan soldiers in the Asur city, but with the Asur forces also;

and therefore they must make preparations, and at once let the people understand how things stood.

Varun was beloved as a dancer, and when the women, who had not seen their husbands' faces for years, heard from the mouth of this handsome actor of their husbands' misdoings, they gave him their full confidence. Then the news began to fly from ear to ear. Varun was a poet also: he made into haunting songs the curses of the deserted Aryan against the Asur charmers, and the lustful, selfish life of Sumitr; and his songs spread like wildfire through all the Sauvir settlements. At last he sent the wives to their faithless husbands, a few at a time, and contemptuous dismissal established the misconduct of the husbands still more clearly. On Sumitr's refusal to return home when summoned, Varun was elected commander instead, and he set out for the Asur city with a large force. At the news of Varun's approach disagreement broke out among Sumitr's followers; a good many of them genuinely regretted their lapse into Asur habits. With his remaining troops Sumitr had no hope of waging a successful struggle; finally, he delivered up the city to Varun and expressed willingness to return to Sauvir-town.

Thus the Aryans passed through their first severe test. Varun did not molest the Asurs, who were no longer capable of taking up arms. But to remove his Aryans from their influence, he built a separate town there for his own people, and began to put into effect many of the ideas he had learned from Angira, the Rishi.

Sudas

REGION : KURU-PANCHAL (WESTERN PART OF THE UNITED PROVINCES[1])
PEOPLE : VEDIC ARYAN
TIME : 1500 BCE

This story is of the Aryans, 144 generations ago. At that time, the earliest Rishis – Vashishthh, Vishvamitr and Bhardwaj were composing the prayers of the Rig Ved; and the Aryan autocratic rulers of the Kuru-Panchal region, with the help of these Aryan priests, were dealing their final and fiercest blows against the people's civil rights.

—1—

Spring was coming to an end. The plains of the river Chandrbhaga[2] were covered with a far-stretching expanse of ripe golden wheat, rippling in the breezes; here and there groups of harvesters, men and women, were singing at their work. Herds of mares with their young ones had been turned loose to graze on the fresh grass springing up in the fields already cut.

Through the sunlight a wayfarer was moving onward with lagging step. The frayed cloth turban tied round his head left a matted lock of fair hair in view; an old cloak was thrown round his body, above a waistcloth that hung to his knees; a staff was gripped in his hand. His mouth was parched with thirst. He had gathered strength to reach the next township; but when he caught sight of a well (without brick walls) and a low *shami*[3] tree beside the track, this resolution deserted him. He pulled off his turban, next removed his waistcloth, and tying the two together attempted to let one end down into water but he could not reach it. At length he sat down, leaning against the nearby tree; it seemed to him that he would never be able to get up again.

But just now a girl appeared, with a water bag on one shoulder, a rope on the other, a skin pitcher in her hand. The traveller's dying down hope rose once more. The young woman came up to the well and put down the water bag, and was about to lower the pitcher into the well when her eyes met those of the wanderer. His face was pallid, his lips cracked, his cheek yellow, his eyes sunken, his feet caked with dust. Yet his youthfulness was apparent, despite all this.

The traveller saw her dress as plain but dignified – a girl's cap on her golden hair, a shawl, a bodice and a skirt. The hot sun had flushed her cheeks and perspiration glistened on her forehead and upper lip. She stared for a moment at the unexpected stranger, and then her pretty lips curved in the natural smile of a Madr girl as she said to him, in a pleasant voice that already half soothed his thirst –

'It seems to me that you need water, brother!'

The traveller made a brave but unavailing effort to steady his giddy brain.

'Yes. I am very thirsty.'

'I'll give you water.'

By the time she had filled her pitcher, he had got to his feet and was standing by her. His sturdy limbs and well-formed bones showed that he still retained an unusually vigorous frame. The girl handed him a leather cup attached to her water bag, and poured water into it from the pitcher. He took a big mouthful and let it trickle down his throat and then lowered his head and sat down, and emptied the cup at one draught. The cup slipped from his fingers; he struggled to pull himself together but fell backward.

The girl was struck speechless for a moment; but she quickly realized from his staring eyeballs that he had fainted. Hastily, wetting her head-cloth in water, she began pressing it on the man's mouth and forehead. A short time later he opened his eyes, and said, painfully, as though embarrassed –

'I am sorry for troubling you.'

'There is no trouble: but I was frightened. What happened to you?'

'Nothing; my stomach was empty, and I was so thirsty that I drank too much. It's all right now.'

'Your stomach empty?'

Without giving him time to answer, she ran off and in no time reappeared with a basin of curds, parched grain and honey. Catching the traveller's expression of embarrassment and hesitation, she exclaimed –

'Don't be afraid! I have a brother who left home several years ago. It reminds me of my brother to give you this little help.'

He took the basin; she poured more water for him, and he mixed the parched grain into it and swallowed it little by little. When he had drunk it, the exhaustion had begun to leave his face, and a speechless gratitude was written on it. He was searching for words, but the girl, as if guessing what was in his mind, said –

'There is no need to feel awkward, brother. You seem to have come from far away?'

'Yes. From very far in the east, from Panchal.'

'Where are you going to?'

'This way or the other way, anywhere.'

'But just now?'

'I want to find some work that I can earn food and clothing by.'

'Would you like to do farm work?'

'Why not? I know how to plough and sow and reap and thresh. I know how to look after horses and cattle. I am quite strong; it's only that just now I am worn out, after a little while I shall be fit for hard work again. I have never left a master dissatisfied.'

'Then I think my father will put you to work. Come with me, I've filled my bag.'

The youth tried his best to offer help for carrying the water bag, but she would not let him. In the fields ahead of them a red tent had been pitched and outside it some forty men and women were sitting. Which of the men was his companion's father, the youth could not guess. All had the same simple clothes, the same fair hair and skin, the same lively faces. The girl put down the water bag and pitcher on a skin spread out in the middle and then went up to one of the men, a man sixty years of age, but still hale and vigorous.

'*Pitar*,'[4] she said, 'this stranger is looking for work.'

'Farm work, *duhitar*?'[5]

'Yes, any kind.'

'Let him work here, then. He will get the same as all the other men.'

The newcomer was listening, but the old man called him and repeated his offer, which he accepted.

'Come along, then. We are just having our midday meal; take your share.'

'I have eaten some parched grain that your *duhita* gave me, O' Arya.'[6]

'Arya! No such nonsense. My name is Jeta, son of Ribhu of the Madrs. Eat and drink as much as you like. Apala! Give him some of the country liquor fermented from mare's milk. It's a good drink for hot weather. Boy, I will talk to you in the evening; all you need tell me now is your name.'

'Sudas. I am a Panchal.'

'Don't call it "Sudas"! The name should be Sudah[7] – "Giver of *daan* (alms)". People from the east can't even talk properly. So you are from the Panchal country? Well, Apala! These eastern people are always bashful. Give him enough food to make him ready for some work in the evening.'

On Apala's insistence, Sudas drank two or three cups of the liquor and forced a couple of morsels of bread down his throat. His appetite seemed dead; he had had nothing for two whole days.

As the heat of the sun diminished, he felt fresh energy coming to life in him and before the evening's labour was ended he was using his sickle being no lesser than any.

At nightfall they went away a good distance, to the threshing barns. Jeta's fields were broad, as was proved by the more than two hundred workers collected that night near the threshing floor. The cooks were busy in their huts. A fat ox had been slaughtered and its bones, entrails and part of the meat had been put on fire three hours before sunset, in big cauldrons. The rest of the meat was being boiled with salt in portions of half a *ser* weight each. Close to the buildings was a big flat plot of ground where the threshing was done with a good well and a pool of water at one end. Men and women flocked to the pool to wash – some their faces and hands, others their whole bodies.

When darkness fell they all sat down in a row with bread, meat and pots of liquor before them. Apala, remembering Sudas's shyness, made him sit next to her, though in fact what she was remembering still more was her brother who had gone away to foreign lands. After the meal singing and dancing began; and though Sudas could not join in on this first night, he was to make himself before long the favourite singer and dancer of the company.

The reaping, carting and threshing went on for a month and a half; but before two weeks were over, Sudas had altered beyond recognition. His wide blue eyes were sparkling and his cheeks had regained their natural colour. The veins and bones no longer stood out from his skin. At the end of the first week Jeta had given him a new set of clothes.

The threshing was almost completed; all those who had been working at it, except for half a dozen including Jeta and his daughter and Sudas, had taken their payment in grain and gone away. These were the folk who had little land of their own, and so had come to work in Jeta's fields after reaping their own crops. In this month and a half Jeta and Apala had come to know their young labourer well, and his pleasant, merry disposition. One evening Jeta fell into talk with him about the people of the eastern lands, while Apala sat near them listening.

'Sudah, I have never been far towards the east,' he remarked, 'but I have seen your Panchal city.[8] I used to go there in the winter to sell my horses.'

'And what did you think of the Panchal (Rohilkhand[9]), sir?'

'There's nothing wrong with the Janpad.[10] It is as well kept and rich as our Madr lands, and the fields seemed even more fertile than ours; but ...'

'But what?'

'Well, don't be angry, Sudah, there are no men living there.'

'No men? What then – gods, or demons?'

'I only say that humans do not live there.'

'I shan't be angry, master; what makes you say this?'

'Sudah, you have seen a couple of hundred men and women working in my fields, haven't you?'

'Yes.'

'Did you ever see them cringing to me because they were working on my land and taking my wages?'

'No; they all behaved as though they belonged to your family.'

'Yes, they really are human beings; they really are like a family. We were all Madrs together. That is the kind of thing one pines for in the east. Over there you find slaves and masters, but no human beings, no brotherhood.'

'What you say is true. I have only come to see what humanity is worth since I crossed the river Shatadru,[11] and especially since I came into your Madr land. Living among men is a joy; it is something to be proud of, to think oneself of being lucky for.'

'I'm glad that you are not upset by what I said, my son. Every man loves his own land.'

'But he ought not to shut his eyes to the faults of what he loves.'

'I often used to think about it in my days of travelling in those parts, and I talked about it with the learned men here. I came to understand how the evil had entered, but not the remedy for it.'

'How did the evil come?'

'The Panchal *janpad* is supposed to be the home of the Panchal people, but as a matter of fact half the inhabitants are not Panchals at all.'

'Yes, many from outside have settled there.'

'Not outsiders, son! The native inhabitants are so many. Those who form the artisan classes now, the merchants, the slaves – they were all living long before the Panchal folk ever set foot in the land. And you know what colour their skins are.'

'Yes, it is quite different from that of the Panchal folk – it is black or like copper.'

'And are the Panchal folk fair-coloured like the Madrs?'

'More or less.'

'That's it – more or less, because intermingling with the other race is altering their colour. I believe that if there were only Aryans living there, just as there are here, perhaps life there would be what human life should be. The difference of status between the two races may be the result of their having different skins.'

'And as you know, perhaps, these distinctions of high and low, master and slave, were common even in old days among the non-

Aryans – the Asurs, as our forefathers called them.'

'Yes but the Panchals were once simply Aryans, all alike, all of the same flesh and blood. Then gradually the division between high and low penetrated them. Their king, Divodas, was once buying some of my horses, and I was brought before him. He was a well-built, handsome, fair-skinned young man; but he had a heavy red and yellow crown on his head, his ears were pierced and had big rings in them, and there were all kinds of ornaments on his fingers and round his neck. I felt sorry for him when I saw all that. It was like seeing the moon hidden by an eclipse. His wife was there too. She was as pretty as a Madr girl, but the poor creature was bent under the weight of her coloured ornaments.' Sudas felt his heart beating faster. He struggled to keep his emotion from showing itself in his face, but finding this impossible, and wanting to change the subject, he said –

'So the King took your horses?'

'He took them, and paid a good price for them. I don't remember how much gold; but it used to put me in a fever, to see even the Panchals themselves coming to him, kneeling to him, saluting him, begging him. No Madr could do that, my son, not even to save his life.'

'You didn't have to behave like that, Arya?'

'Had anyone told me to do it, I should have come to blows with him. Those kings in the eastern lands never give us such orders. But among them it is a very old custom.'

'Why?'

'You want to know why? It is a long story. When the Panchal folk were migrating from the west into those parts between the Yamuna, Ganga[12] and the Himalayas, they all lived like one family, just as the Madrs do. Then they mingled with the Asurs, and in imitation of them many among the Panchals were fired with the ambition of becoming chiefs, kings or priests.'

'But what was the root of their ambition?'

'They were eager for pleasure, eager to live on the labour of others without working themselves. It was these kings and priests who spread division among the Panchals, and would not let them live like human beings anymore' – Jeta got up as he said this, and went off to some work.

—2—

Four years had passed. Sudas was still living in the Madr township (where Shakla or Sialkot now stands) with Jeta's family. Jeta's wife was dead; one or two married sisters and daughters shared the house, but permanent occupants were Jeta himself, Apala and Sudas. Apala was now twenty years old. It was clear from their behaviour that she and Sudas were in love with each other. Apala was reckoned one of the beauties of the Madr town, and had no lack of handsome young suitors while there was also no lack of pretty girls for a handsome young man like Sudas to choose from. But it was noticed that the two always chose each other for the dance. Jeta noticed it with the rest, and would have been delighted if Sudas had been prepared to settle down there for good. Sudas, however, had recurrent moods of anxiety about his parents. Jeta knew that he was their only son.

One day Apala and Sudas had gone to bathe in the Chenab, the river of lovers. Often enough before, bathing, Sudas had seen Apala's naked, sun-browned limbs; but today, seeing her among fifty naked girls and comparing her beauty with theirs, he felt as though he were fully realizing her charms for the first time. On the way home, finding him silent, Apala asked –

'Are you tired, Sudas, you are saying nothing? Swimming right across the Chenab and back twice is quite a tiring business!'

'What about you, Apala? You swam across and back, I did it twice, but I could cross the Chenab ten times if I could stay there long enough!'

'When we were coming out I noticed how much your chest had broadened, and the muscles on your arms and legs seem to have grown twice as heavy.'

'Swimming is good exercise. It makes a man's body strong and well shaped. But you Apala – how much more beautiful you have grown! There is no one else in the world so beautiful as you are now!'

'It is only your eyes that care about me, isn't it!'

'It is no silly infatuation that makes me say it.'

'Yes, you have never asked me for a kiss even, and yet the Madr girls are generous enough with such gifts.'

'You were quite generous to me with them even without my asking!'

'But then it was because I used to look at you and see my brother Shvetshrava!'

'And now you won't give me anymore?'

'Why shouldn't I kiss you, if you ask me to?'

'And if I ask you, will you be my ... ?'

'Stop Sudas! It would make me unhappy to have to say "No"!'

'But it is in your own power to prevent that unhappiness.'

'Not in my power. In yours.'

'How?'

'Are you willing to stay all your life in my father's house?'

Sudas had long been afraid of the moment when he should hear from these sweet lips these fateful words. Now, swift as lightning, they pierced his ears and reached his heart. For a while his face was clouded with perplexity. He could not let Apala see what was going on in his mind. Just the next moment he said quietly –

'Apala, how much I love you.'

'I know, and you know that I love you. I want to be yours for ever. It would please my father too. But you must turn your back on Panchal.'

'That is no hardship for me. Only my old mother and father are there. I am my mother's only son. I gave her a promise that I would see her again before she died.'

'I don't want to make you break your word. I shall always love you, Sudas! Even if you leave me. If you do, I know I shall always be weeping for you, to the end of my life. But neither of us can break the promise we have made, you to your mother, and I to my heart.'

'What promise have you made to your heart, Apala?'

'Never to go away from this country of men to that inhuman place.'

'Inhuman? The Panchal country?'

'Yes, where humanity has no value, and women have no freedom.'

'I think of it as you think.'

'That is why I give you this kiss ...'

She laid her tear-stained cheek against his lips.

'Go now,' she said, when he had kissed her. 'See your mother, come back with her blessing. I shall be waiting for you here.' Sudas, as he listened to her artless words, experienced an unconquerable self-disgust, which was never to be expelled from his heart.

On his promising to return when he had seen his parents, Jeta gave him leave to go home. Father and daughter were united in their consent.

On the day before his departure Apala clung to him more than ever. Her eyes and his, blue as the lotus, were bathed in tears, which they no longer attempted to conceal. For hours they kissed each other's lips, lay in oblivious embraces, or gazed at each other speechlessly with swimming eyes.

When it was time to go, Apala threw her arms round him for the last time saying, 'Sudas, I shall be here waiting for you.'

These words remained engraved on his heart as long as he lived.

—3—

Sudas loved his mother deeply. His father, Divodas was a powerful king in whose praise famous Rishis like Vashishthh, Vishvamitr and Bhardwaj composed verses[13] upon verses that survive in the *Rig Ved*. And just because these sayings have been collected and put in the *Rig Ved*, the sycophancy lurking in them cannot be overlooked. Sudas's love was for his mother only. As he knew too well, Divodas had many other wives like her, and numerous slave-girls. As the mother of the king's eldest son, the successor to the Panchal throne, she might be treated with a degree of respect; but Divodas, in his seraglio filled with fresh young beauties, was not likely to feel any love for a toothless old woman. And though Sudas was the only son of his mother, he was by no means the only son of his father. If he died, his brother Pratardan would inherit the throne.

As the years had gone by, Sudas's mother had despaired of seeing him again, and long hours of weeping had dimmed her sight. Then one day Sudas was standing before her. He had come quietly, not letting anyone know, not meeting his father. She stared at him with her faded eyes.

'Mother!' he said, 'I am here, your Sudas.'

Her eyes brightened, but she only answered, without stirring on the bed where she lay –

'If you are really my Sudas, why do you stand there keeping yourself out of sight? Why do you not put your arms around my neck? Why do you not lay your head in my lap?'

Sudas rested his head on his mother's lap. She touched it with her hand: it was really a head, not a fancy that would melt away into thin air. She kissed his mouth, his cheeks, his forehead, his hair over and over again, wetting them with her tears, and kept on embracing him. 'Mother,' said Sudas, when he saw her tears were flowing endlessly, 'why are you crying now, when I have come back?'

'Only this one day, my son! Only this one day! These are my last tears. Sudas dear, star of my eyes!'

From the women's apartments the news reached the King. He came in haste to embrace his son. Tears of joy trickled down his cheeks as he held him in his embrace.

Days grew into months and months slipped by until two whole years had passed. Sudas struggled to keep up a cheerful appearance in front of his parents; but in his ears, when he was alone, that poignant voice sounded – 'I shall be here waiting for you!' – and those red quivering lips floated before him and hung there until he could no longer see through the tears that filled his eyes. Two loves beset him; on one side Apala's spontaneous devotion, on the other, his old mother's deep-rooted affection. To break his mother's heart when she had no one else to turn to, seemed to him the biggest egotism. He resolved never to quit Panchal while she lived. But to accept the luxurious existence of a prince was beyond him; though he maintained a respectful bearing towards his father, and did his best to carry out his wishes.

One day the old King said to his son –

'Sudas, I am coming near the end of my life; the burden of ruling Panchal has grown too heavy for me.'

'Then why should this burden not be given over to the people of Panchal?'

'To the people! My son, I don't understand your meaning.'

'After all, the power belongs to the Panchals themselves. Our ancestors were only common men of the people. There was no king then. The people decided everything, as they do still among the Mallas, the Madrs, and the Gandhars. Then some ancestors of my grandfather Vadhyashv[14] fell prey to ambition, to desire for pleasure, for stealing the fruit of other men's labour. He must have been the headman or the war-chief of the clan, and by winning some battle for the clan he must have gained its love and confidence, and acquired wealth, and then by their means struck a treacherous blow at his people. He seized power out of their hands and set up a monarchy such as the Asurs had. He copied from them, and bribed some forgotten ancestor of Vashishthh or Vishvamitr with the office of priest, and this man, to throw dust in the people's eyes, began telling them that Indr, Agni, Som, Varun, Vishvdev and the rest of the gods had sent this king to reign over them, and they must obey his commands and make offerings to him as his due. It was all dishonesty, father, all of it, simple robbery that you forget those who gave you the all the rights and you don't even remember their name!'

'No, my son. It is the people that we recognize as the conferrer of our power. At the time of the coronation-oath it is from the people that we receive the branch of the *palas*[15] tree as a royal symbol.'

'That coronation ceremony has become a mere show. Is the people really the king's master? Not at all, as anyone can understand when he sees that the king will not sit down with other people, will not eat with them, and will not work with them. Can any headman among the Madrs or the Gandhars behave like that?'

'If we lived as they do, some enemy would assassinate us one fine day; we would be poisoned.'

'Such fears can only come to thieves and plunderers. Clan headmen are not thieves or plunderers. They think of themselves as true sons of their clan and lead their life that way, so they have no reason to be afraid. Kings are thieves, who have taken the people's power, so they live in perpetual fear. Kings get their harems, their gold and silver and jewels, their slaves, by plundering others, not by their own toil.'

'Well, my son, does this mean that you consider me a criminal?'

'Oh, no, father! When I am in your place I shall have to do the same as you have done, willingly or unwillingly. How can I call my father a criminal, then?'

'You talk of restoring the power to the people. Is it possible to restore it? You must understand, my son, that Divodas the king of the Panchals is not the sole robber of the people's food. He is only a single one among many powerful robbers. He may be strong, but in the face of their united strength he is helpless. And apart from many of his feudatories, princes of his family, and his army commanders, the strongest force is the priesthood.'

'Yes, I know the power of the priests. A king's younger sons cannot inherit the throne, so they become Brahmins.[16] I think that is what my younger brother Pratardan will do. Already there is a distinction between king and priest, government and religion, and who knows, in times to come these two – Kshatriyas[17] and Brahmins – may grow into two separate groups, two separate classes. A Madr in Gandhar, can hold a dagger and a *sruva*[18] at the same time, but here the sword belongs to you, the descendant of Vadhyashv, and praying is Vishvamitr's business. This cleavage in the ranks of our people has already broken it up into three divisions. Kings and priests may be connected by sharing power, by being the plunderers of the people, by marriage ties and blood-relationship; but the two are beginning to be counted as different groups, and their interests are already beginning to come in conflict. That is why such efforts have to be made to restore friendship between Kshatriyas and Brahmins. There is a third group outside these two groups of the same ancestry – that is the general public of the clan in huge numbers. Today the name of the Mahajan (great-clan) has been changed to Praja (subjects). What a wretched alteration! Is not the whole business a fraud?'

'And still, there are a great number you have not counted.'

'Yes, the non-Aryan multitudes, the craftsmen and traders and slaves. Perhaps it was because of them that the rulers were successful in stealing power from the people. They were glad to see their conquerors reduced by someone else to the same servitude as themselves. That is what the kings called their "justice".'

'Perhaps you are not wrong, my son; but tell me this – to whom is the power to be handed over? Apart from those who live by plunder – the rulers and the traders together – there are the common people – Aryans and non-Aryans; are *they* capable of governing? And the ruling classes, religious and military, are ready like vultures to pounce on them and devour them as soon as *I* let go of them. It's only six or seven generations since power slipped out of the hands of the people; the days when the people ruled are not yet forgotten. There was no Divodas ruling then in this country. It was called "*Panchalah*" (the land of all Panchals). But now I can see no road leading back to that age.'

'There are too many crocodiles like Vashishthh and Vishvamitr lying across the road!'

'*They* are the thing *we* are enslaved to. We cannot return to yesterday and we cannot guess where tomorrow will bring us. I am happy that I have found a son like you. There was a time when I too was young. There was not so much then of the priests' fables, and of all the tricks and illusions, of superstitions they have invented to rob the people of their wits. I thought I would lessen the royal looting of the people. I discovered that I had no power to lessen it. In those days your mother was everything to me. Afterwards, when my will was broken and I gave up hope, these priests used their daughters as well as their flattering verses as a noose to catch me in. They filled my palace with hundreds of slave-girls, comparing their beauty with Indrani.[19] Learn by your father's fall, be on your guard, strive hard; perhaps some road will open to you, and all this plundering may be brought to an end. But to rid the Panchals of a good-hearted master like Sudas, and leave them in the grip of a heartless, cunning master like Pratardan, would be no kindness to them. I shall watch your struggle, my son, from the land of the spirits, and I shall be happy.'

—4—

Divodas was gathered to his fathers, and Sudas was ruler of the Panchals. The priestly swarm hovered around him. And now Sudas understood how thoroughly those greybeards had stupefied the people on the name of Indr, Varun, Agni and Som. He found himself fast in their trap. Those whom he was eager to benefit were prompt to proclaim him an irreligious king and misunderstood his motives. Those bygone days often came back to his mind when he had wandered, barefoot and ragged, in strange lands. He had been more of a free man then. Now he had not a soul to understand his warm heart, or to sympathize with him. The priests – *rishis* – sent him their daughters and granddaughters; his feudatory chiefs sent him ladies of their families; but Sudas felt like a man sitting in a house on fire. He could never forget those blue eyes waiting for him beside the Chenab.

Sudas was bent on serving the entire people, Aryan and non-Aryan alike. But it was necessary first to convince the people bogged in the mire of superstition, that he enjoyed the favour of the gods, and of this favour, priestly praise was the only possible proof. In the end, to gain the priests' goodwill, he was compelled to fall back on presenting them with gold and silver, cattle and slaves. After that these priests, gorged with meat of the calves of healthy cows and sweet *som*-juice, came to the conclusion that Sudas was truly what his name meant, a generous giver; and numerous are the eulogies of his generosity, composed by these pious sycophants, which are still to be found in the *Rig Ved*. But who can tell with what a depth of contempt Sudas, as he listened to these panegyrics, contemplated their authors!

Sudas's enviable reputation, before long, was not confined to north-Panchal, or what is now Rohilkhand, but extended much further. Dragging on a joyless existence, he worked, as far as was possible, for the good of all his subjects.

Some years after his father's death, his mother also died. Now the pain that had festered in him night and day for years until he had grown inured to it, seemed to break out like a dangerous cancer. Every moment of the day he seemed to see Apala standing before him, with tearful eyes and trembling lips, repeating: 'I shall be here waiting for you.' And no tears of his could extinguish this burning thought. One day, on the pretext of a hunting expedition in the mountains, he left his city behind.

The old house was still standing, where he had won Apala's love; but neither Jeta nor his beloved daughter was to be seen. Both had died, Apala only one year before. Her brother, long lost and found again, and his family were living there; but Sudas could not bring himself to form any new ties with that house. He met a woman who had been Apala's friend, who shed tears as she showed him some new, bright-coloured clothes belonging to the dead girl – skirt, shawl, bodice, cap – and said, 'My friend was wearing these on her last day, and the last words she spoke were – "I gave Sudas my promise that I would be waiting for him here".'

Sudas lifted the clothes and pressed them to his heart and to his eyes. The fragrance of Apala's body was still in them.

8

Pravahan

REGION : PANCHAL (UNITED PROVINCES)
TIME : 700 BCE

This story goes back 108 generations, to the later Vedic Period, when the theology of the Upnishads[1] *was beginning to be constructed. By that time the laying out of gardens and the use of iron had become familiar in India.*

—1—

'On one side the green forest with the scent of *karonda*-fruits and the sweet trilling of birds; on the other side the Ganga flowing with its clear waves, our thousands of black and brown cows grazing along the banks, and the fine strong bulls rumbling among them – one must feast one's eyes sometimes on such sights as these, O' Pravahan! But you are always either absorbed in chanting the hymns of Udgeeth (*Sam Ved*), or busy learning the *mantras* of Vashishthh and Vishvamitr by heart.'

'Lopa, your eyes look at these sights, and I feel happy when I look at your eyes.'

'Oh! You are very clever at thinking of things to say; though when I watch you with the other students, repeating your old verses over and over like a dog howling, I think my Pravahan is going to be just like a little boy for the rest of his life.'

'Indeed! Is that your opinion about him?'

'Never mind my opinion ... but I have another opinion as well, a real one – that Pravahan will always be mine.'

'I hope and believe so, Lopa; that is what gives me strength for all my toil and studying. I am accustomed to keep my mind under this rigid control; otherwise very often it longs to run away from these old poems, old formulas and old hymns. When my head is worn out with labour, and I want to leave it all and lie down, the only consolation I have is looking forward to a few moments with you.'

'And I am always waiting for you.'

Lopa's glance strayed into the distance, while the morning breeze made ripples in her soft fair hair. She seemed far away. Pravahan stroked her hair with his fingers, and said –

'Lopa, I feel like a dwarf beside you.'

'A dwarf!' she echoed, resting her cheek against his. 'No dear Pravahan. I am proud of you. I remember the day when you came with my aunt (father's sister) and I saw you first, a youngster of eight, with my even younger eyes. I was only three or four years old; but my memory can never go wrong in showing me that picture of my childhood. I can see it all clearly – your yellow curly hair, your nose like a parrot's beak, your small red lips, your big bright blue eyes, your warm clear skin! And I remember how my mother said to me – "Lopa, this is your brother,"[2] and I felt shy; she kissed you and said – "Pravahan, your little sister Lopa is shy, make friends with her!"'

'And I went up to you, and you hid your face behind my aunt's (wife of mother's brother) scented hair.'

'But when I hid there I made a peephole to look through, and watched what you did. There had been nobody in the house except my mother and the slave-girls and their children. My father's academy[3] was not yet born. I had felt as if I were all alone in the house; so I was very happy when I saw you.'

'Yes, to have someone to play with; and yet you were hiding from me. I looked at you and saw a fair-skinned little thing with no clothes and chubby face. You seemed very pretty to my childish eyes. I came to you and put my hand on your shoulder. Do you know what our mothers said? They both smiled and said – "May Brahma[4] fulfil our wishes!" I didn't understand then what the wishes were.'

'I don't remember that. It is enough for me that I felt the touch of your soft hand on my shoulder.'

'And your face was a silly round ball, you were so bashful.'

'You took my hand in yours, but your lips were tight-shut; what was it mother said then?'

'I remember everything she said. How can I forget her? My

mother left me with my uncle Gargya[5] and went away home; but my aunt's love soon made me forget her. How could I forget my aunt?'

Pravahan's eyes filled with tears; he kissed Lopa on the lips.

'Her mouth was like yours, Lopa. We two used to sleep side by side. You slept, but often my eyes used to be wide open. But when I saw my aunt coming, I would shut them tight. She would give a soft sigh and touch my cheek with her lips. When I looked up she would say "wake up, little boy", and then give you a kiss, but you would still be fast asleep.'

There were tears in Lopa's eyes also.

'I saw so little of my mother,' she answered sadly.

'Yes; well, that day when she saw me standing near you, so dumb, she said, "This is your sister, my son. Give her a kiss and ask her to play at horses with you".'

And you did kiss me and ask me to play and I poked my head out from behind mother's hair. You were the horse and I got on your back.'

'I carried you outside.'

'How impudent I was!'

'You have never been afraid of anything, Lopa! And soon you were everything to me. I used to work hard at learning my lessons, for fear of my uncle, and when I got tired I came to you.'

'I used to sit beside you at your work, to be with you.'

'I believe, Lopa, if you had spent half as much time on it as I have, you would have been the very best of uncle's students.'

'Not better than you,' said Lopa, looking thoughtfully into his eyes. 'I should never want to outstrip you.'

'But that would please me very much.'

'Because we two have no separate selves from each other.'

'Lopa, you gave me bodily strength as well as mental. How little I used to sleep at night! Repeating lessons myself, and hearing others repeat them, I forgot even food and drink. You brought me out of the darkness of my school-room and carried me by force to the forest or the park or the banks of the Ganga. How good they were! But all the same I longed to master the three Veds and all the knowledge of the Brahmins as quickly as possible.'

'But now you have finished them all. Father says you are

his equal now.'

'I know that myself. There is not much of the Brahmins' wisdom left for me to learn. But wisdom does not come to an end with that.'

'That is what I always told you. But then, are you still going to have your *palas*-tree wand[6] and unoiled hair?'

'No, don't talk of them, Lopa! I am saying goodbye to my *palas* wand; and you will be free to rub sweet oil into this hair that has been left dry for sixteen years.'

'Pravahan, I can't understand why there should be so much fuss about unoiled hair. It is not as if you ever stopped yourself from kissing me.'

'No, but I had been used to kissing you since our childhood.'

'Do the students of other academies keep these hard rules?'

'When they are forced to; otherwise all these things are done only to win fame. The people believe them to spring from the severe austerity of the Brahmin youths.'

'And meanwhile the Kuru king gives my father villages, gold and silver, slaves and horse-chariots. I had enough slave-girls in the house already; now he has just sent three more, and there is no work for them to do.'

'Sell them, Lopa. They are young; you'll get thirty gold pieces for each.'

'Oh, no! We are Brahmins, we are wiser and more learned than other people, because we have leisure for learning. But when I think of the life our slaves have, I feel nothing but loathing for Brahma, Indr, Varun and the rest of our gods and for Vashishthh, Bhardwaj, Bhrigu, Angira and all the Rishis, and for all the rich Brahmins like father. Everywhere you see trading, bargaining, profit-making, greed! One day father sold a black slave-woman's husband to a merchant of Kosal for fifty pieces of gold. She was clinging to me, weeping and praying. I pleaded with father, but he said – "If we keep all our slaves with us there will be no room in the house and if this man is kept what benefit will it be to us?" The night before they were separated, how terribly they were weeping! They had a little girl, two years old, whose features everyone said were very much like her father's, she woke up early in the morning and kept on crying. But the husband was sold as if he had been an animal, not a man; as if Brahma had created him and all his descendants for that! I can't believe in it, Pravahan. I haven't studied the three Veds as you have, but I have listened to them and understood them; there is nothing in them except about immaterial things, worlds, forces, and their charms or their terrors.'

Pravahan rested his forehead against her flushed cheek, and said, 'Our love seems only to foster our disagreements!'

'And disagreement makes our love even stronger.'

'Yes, Lopa, yes! If anyone else were to say such things as you do, I should grow angry; but when I hear abuse of all my gods, seers and teachers falling from these lips of yours, I often feel only that I want to kiss them. Why?'

'Because even inside ourselves there are often two contradictory ideas, and we are patient with them, because they are inseparable parts of ourselves.'

'And you, Lopa – you are an inseparable part of me!'

—2—

'You have never put on these shawls from Shivi,[7] or used the sandalwood paste of Kashi,[8] or pearls from the ocean to adorn yourself with. Darling, why are you so indifferent to them?'

'Should I look any better with them?'

'For me you are always beautiful.'

'Then what is the good of loading my body with such things and torturing myself with them? To tell you the truth, Pravahan, it hurts me when you put that dead weight they call a crown on top of your head.'

'And yet other women are ready to fight for the sake of clothes and ornaments.'

'I am not a woman of that sort.'

'You are the woman who rules the heart of the ruler of Panchal.'

'I am Pravahan's wife, not the queen of Panchal.'

'Yes, dear; how could we have dreamed of this day? My uncle kept it quite hidden from us that I was the prince of Panchal.'

The Indian Caste Hierarchy
(As explained by the author)

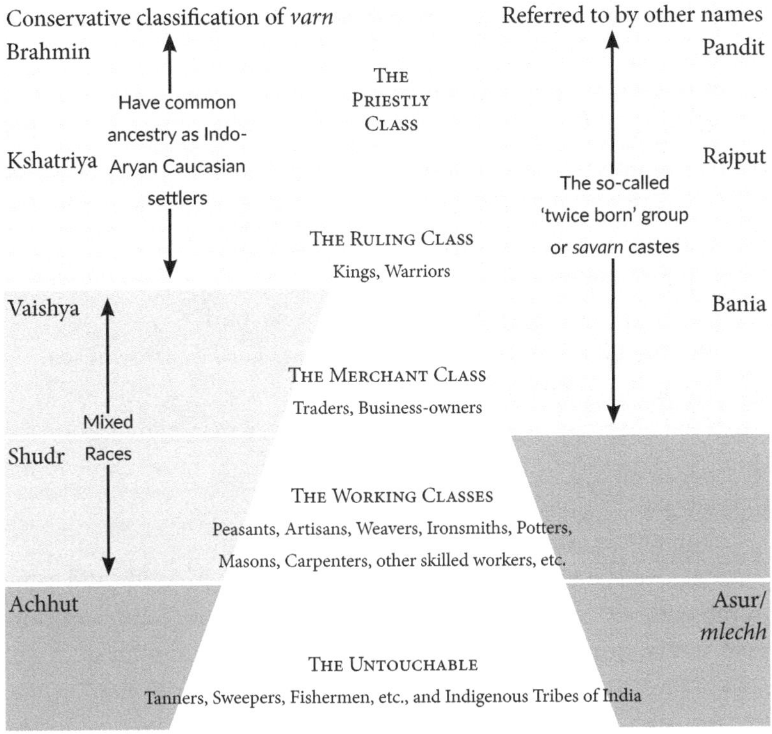

Etymology of 'caste'

Caste: *casta* (Spanish, Portuguese) – 'race', both from the feminine of *casto* (pure) from the Latin *castus*. Indo-European root: 'kes'.

Related vocabulary

varn-vyavastha (Skt.) or *jati-pratha* (Skt.): the caste system
varn (colour) + *vyavastha* (arrangement/management): colour-management (Lit.)
jati (birth/by birth) + *pratha* (tradition): a tradition based on birth (Lit.)
suvarn (Skt.): *su* (good) + *varn* (colour) – fine coloured (Lit.)

Vedic Reference

When they divided Purush how many portions did they make?
What do they call his mouth, his arms? What do they call his thighs and feet?
The Brahmin was his mouth, of both his arms was the Rajayan made.
His thighs become the Vaishya, from his feet Shudr was produced.

Rig Ved 10.90, 'Purush', Couplets 11 and 12
Early Vedic Period, approximately 1700–1100 BCE

'What else should father have done? Your mother was only one among hundreds of royal consorts, and there were a dozen princes older than you. Who could expect that one day you would inherit the throne of Panchal?'

'Well, Lopa; why are you not pleased with this palace?'

'Because I felt unhappy even in the mansion where my father taught his pupils. It was a fine mansion for us, but what was it for the slaves there? And this royal palace is a thousand times bigger. Everyone in it, except you and me is a slave. Two free souls cannot make a building filled with slaves into a place of freedom. I wonder, Pravahan, I wonder how your heart can be so hard.'

'But then it may be able to bear words as hard as arrowheads.'

'No, a man ought not to be like that.'

'I did not try to become a man merely, but a man of intellect, even though while I was training my mind the thought never came to me that one day I should set foot in this royal palace.'

'You do not regret having loved me, Pravahan?'

'To love you was as natural to me as my mother's milk, and came to me without any effort; it has become part of me. I am a worldly man, Lopa, but I know the value of your love. The mind does not always flow in one channel. Whenever weakness seizes hold of me, life for me becomes intolerable and it is only your love and your kindness that support me.'

'But I am never able to give you as much support as I want to, Pravahan! That makes me sad.'

'Because I was born to rule.'

'But once your ambition was to be a great teacher.'

'I had no notion then that I was the inheritor of the royal palace of Panchal-city (Kannauj).'

'But what need is there for the things you are attempting that have nothing to do with the business of government?'

'You mean my flight of imagination from the Brahma (Creator) to the Brahm (all-pervading spirit of the universe)! Lopa, this is not a thing separate from the business of government. It was for the sake of bolstering up their power that my royal ancestors gave so much honour to Vashishthh and Vishvamitr. Those Rishis, in the name of

Indr, Agni and Varun taught the people to obey the will of their king. In those days the rulers offered costly sacrifices, to foster faith among the common people. Nowadays we still offer sacrifices and lavish gifts on the priests, to make our subjects believe in the divine power of the gods, and fancy that it is through the favour of the gods that we enjoy the finest rice, the tenderest beef, and ornaments of pearls and other gems.'

'The old gods were enough; what need is there of your newfangled Brahm?'

'Generations have passed, yet no one has ever seen Indr or Varun or Brahma; so doubt has begun to take root in some men's minds.'

'Will they not doubt your Brahm too?'

'I have described Him in such a way that no one will expect Him to become Visible. How can there be any question of seeing one who has no more of a corporal being than the heaven itself, one who is omnipresent? Such a question was only asked about the old semi-human gods.'

'All this talk of yours about heaven is deluding not only the common folk but Brahmins like Uddalak and Aruni as well. Is it simply to throw dust in people's eyes that you have made it up?'

'You know me well, Lopa; I can hide nothing from you. To keep the power in our hands, it is necessary that a check should be given to the logic of those who are spreading doubt; because, for us today, the enemies most to be feared are the men who cast doubt on the gods and their worship.'

'But you are also talking of the existence of your Deity and its manifestation?'

'If there is an existence, it must also be perceptible. Not by the senses, for if we talk of sense-perception, the sceptics will again demand to see it. What I tell them is that there is another, more subtle sense, that makes us aware of the Deity; and to create this sense I am framing such a doctrine which will keep people wandering blindfold for scores of generations; they will never be able to shake off their belief in it. I have forged this fine weapon because I know that the crude weapons of the priests are growing useless. You have seen stone and copper tools among the Shabar,[9] Lopa?'

'Yes, when we visited the southern forests together.'

'Of course, when we crossed the Yamuna river. Well, would those stone and copper things be of any use against our weapons of pure iron?'

'No.'

'In the same way, the old gods and sacrifices that Vashishthh and Vishvamitr taught could satisfy minds as primitive as those savages but they are useless when confronted by such sharp wits as our intelligent sceptics have.'

'Your Deity will be equally useless. You are going about trying to make Brahmin scholars your pupils and teach them your theology; and here am I under your own roof, believing all your talk to be only lies and fraud.'

'Yes; because you know its real secret meaning (*upnishad*).'

'If the Brahmins are intelligent, will they not discover the secret?'

'That also you see! A few of them are able to probe the secret purpose; but they realize that this weapon of mine will be very useful to them. The people were losing faith in their priestcraft and their teachings, and that would end in their being deprived of the donations which supply them with horse-chariots to ride in, fine food to eat, beautiful houses to live in and pretty slaves to enjoy.'

'It was all money-making, then?'

'Yes, and a sort of money-making where there is no risk of loss. That is why clever Brahmins like Uddalak are coming to me as pupils carrying their *samidha*[10] with them; and I, with a great show of deference to Brahmins, make them a present of my theology, without giving any sacred thread or any instruction in rituals.'

'It is a vile plot, Pravahan.'

'Agreed; but for our purposes it is the most useful achievement. The ship that Vashishthh and Vishvamitr built has not lasted for even a thousand years; but in the ship I am building, kings, princes and those who live on the wealth of others, will still be carried in safety two thousand years from now. I saw that the old vessel – the sacrifices and rituals – had grown weak, Lopa; and I have designed this new, strong vessel to take its place, one in which Brahmins and Kshatriyas alike, if they use it well, will be able to attain power and prosperity. But besides my new heaven, or Brahm, I have another revelation to give.'

'What?'

'Return to this world after death – reincarnation.'

'The worst deception of all!'

'And the most serviceable. In proportion as we princes, priests and merchants have heaped up our boundless means of pleasure, the ordinary people have been reduced to indigence. Men have begun to appear who play upon the pauperized masses – craftsmen, peasants, and slaves – by telling them – "You give away your earnings to others and bear all the burdens. They throw dust in your eyes by filling you with lying hope that in return for your hardships, sacrifices and contributions you will go to heaven when you die. No one has ever seen those heavenly pleasures of the spirits of the dead!" Well, my reply to them is this: All the distinctions between high and low that exist in this world, between superior and inferior castes, between rich and poor – they are all due to our conduct in a previous life. In this way we reap the consequences of our good or bad behaviour before our birth.'

'Then can a thief call the wealth he gets by stealing his reward for goodness in another life?'

'No. To deal with him we already enjoy the protection of gods, holy men and popular faith, which will not allow the thief's gains to be mistaken for the reward of a previous life. We used to explain our enjoyment of wealth without labour in this life as due to the favour of the gods; but now when doubt has begun to be cast on the gods and their favour, it has become necessary for us to hit on some other expedient. Our Brahmins are no longer capable of thinking of one; forty to forty-five years of their life they spend in memorizing the verses and the sayings of the ancient sages – how can they invent any new, profound idea?'

'But you also spent a long time on the same studies, Pravahan.'

'Only sixteen years. At the age of twenty-four I left the learning of the Brahmins behind and came out into the world. There I had to learn much more. When I entered into the intricacies of government, I realized that the old ship built by the Brahmins was no longer seaworthy.'

'And so you have built your own strong ship.'

'My concern is not with the truth or untruth, but with utility, Lopa! The idea of rebirth into this world seems novel today, and you understand the selfish motive that is concealed in it. But my Brahmin disciples are already full of it and have begun to broadcast it. To learn the way of the spirits and the gods, even now men are ready to study and guard their teachers' cattle for a dozen years. You and I will not live to see it, Lopa: but the time will come when all the poor and wretched will be willing to endure all the bitterness, misery and injustice of their lives, because of their hope of reincarnation. Lopa, have I not found the shortest cut to explaining heaven and hell?'

'But for the sake of your own belly you are condemning hundreds of generations to perdition!'

'It was for the sake of their bellies that Vashishthh and Vishvamitr put together the Ved. They composed poem after poem in eulogy of Divodas, the king of upper Panchal, when he captured a few Shabar strongholds. To make provision for one's belly is no bad thing; and when we do so not only for our own, but for those of our sons and grandsons, our brothers and friends, we earn eternal fame.[11] Pravahan is accomplishing a work that was beyond the strength of the olden sages and of all the priests who live by religion.'

'You are so ruthless, Pravahan!'

'But I have performed my task.'

—3—

Pravahan was dead; but the triumphant march of his doctrines of God, rebirth, and the destiny of the soul, resounded from the Sindhu to Sadanira.[12] The practice of sacrificial rites had not fallen off; the god-men displayed particular activity in celebrating them. But the Brahmins had studied thoroughly the doctrines formulated by Pravahan – the Kshatriya. Yajnavalkya,[13] a Kuru, had earned the highest reputation by his mastery of them. The Kuru-Panchal country, which had once given birth to the Rishis who composed the sacred rules and established the old rituals, now rang with the fame of Yajnavalkya and his male and female disciples who accompanied him. There was more credit to be gained by holding assemblies of the new teachers than by offering sacrifices; so kings, along with their state ceremonies, or else separately, held meetings in the course of which thousands of cattle, horses and slave-girls were bestowed as pious tributes on the most persuasive debater; slave-girls above all, because these theologians had a special relish for slave-girls brought up in the royal harems.

Yajnavalkya had carried off the palm in several such meetings and disputations. He had just gained a signal victory in a debate held by King Janak[14] of Videh (Tirhut), and his disciple Somshrava had come into a thousand cows. It was not worth for Yajnavalkya to drive all these cattle home with him from Tirhut to Kuru. He distributed them among the neighbouring Brahmins, thus greatly enhancing his fame. He loaded his gold, silver, mule-carts and slave-men and -women in boats and brought them to his Kuru land.

Sixty years had passed since Pravahan's death. He had died before Yajnavalkya was born. Lopa, now more than a hundred years old, was still living in the royal gardens outside the Panchal capital. She liked to live amid the shade of mango, plantain and *jambu*[15] trees in those gardens. While Pravahan lived, she had steadily opposed his ideas; but in the years that had passed since then she had forgotten his faults, and remembered only his lifelong love. Even now in old age, the light was still alive in her eyes, and her mind was but little clouded. Theologians were still her abhorrence.

One day Gargi, a woman who took part in religious discussions, participated in the debate that took place in Panchalpur. She was honourably lodged in a park close to the royal pleasure-grounds. But the recollection of how unscrupulously Yajnavalkya had crushed her in King Janak's assembly would not leave her brain. 'Your head will roll in the dust, Gargi, if you argue any further' – was that a way to debate? Only assassins could behave like that, thought Gargi.

Lopa, on her father's side, was a kinswoman of Gargi's and was well known to her, though they entirely disagreed on religious questions. Now Gargi was burning with resentment at the base weapon Yajnavalkya had used against her; hence it was with distinctly altered feelings that she met her great-great-aunt. As soon as she came, Lopa kissed her forehead and eyes, embraced her, and asked about her health and whether she was happy.

'I have come from Tirhut, aunt,' answered Gargi.

'You went there for *mallyayuddh*,[16] child?'

'You may well call it that! These theological debates are no better than fights. The aim in them is to use all your tricks to throw your adversary down as the wrestlers do.'

'Were there many of the theologians of Kuru-Panchal in the arena?'

'Kuru-Panchal has become their great stronghold nowadays.'

'My Pravahan kindled the first little spark of these new ideas, under my own eyes and with no good purpose in his mind, and they have swept Kuru-Panchal like a forest fire; now they have travelled as far as Tirhut.'

'Aunt! I have begun to believe a little in the truth of what you used to say. It is true that religion is a fine highroad to prosperity. Yajnavalkya came by huge riches at Tirhut, and other Brahmins also made big profits.'

'It is a more profitable business than even the old performing of sacrifices, my child. My husband used to say that it would prove a stout ship, bringing prosperity to kings and priests. So Yajnavalkya triumphed in King Janak's assembly? And did you speak there?'

'If I had not wanted to speak, why should I have sailed down the Ganga to such a far-off place?'

'Did no robbers attack your boat?'

'No, aunt. The merchants go in strong bands protected by soldiers. We religious people are not stupid enough to travel in ones or twos and put our lives in danger.'

'Well, Yajnavalkya got the better of everyone else?'

'Got the better of them? More than that!'

'What do you mean?'

'That those who propounded questions kept silent as soon as they heard his answer.'

'Even you?'

'Yes, even me: but it was his nonsense, not his sense that silenced me.'

'Nonsense?'

'I was raising questions about the Brahm and I had driven him to a corner from which he had no escape. And then he said something I had never expected to hear.'

'What was it, child?'

'Something that stopped me from asking for an answer to my questions – "Your head will roll in the dust, Gargi, if you argue any further."'

'You had never expected to hear that? I should have expected it, Gargi! Yajnavalkya has blossomed into a true disciple of Pravahan. He has brought Pravahan's system of falsehood to perfection. It was well that you did not go on arguing, Gargi.'

'How do you know I did not, aunt?'

'I know because I can see your head still safe on your shoulders.'

'Then you really believe that if I had gone on I should have lost my life?'

'Certainly. Not through the power of Yajnavalkya's god, but just in the same way as we see other people being killed.'

'Aunt! No!'

'You are still an infant, Gargi. You think this religion of *Brahmism* is nothing but intellectual pirouetting and somersaulting. No, Gargi; there is a selfish interest of kings and priests concealed beneath it. When it was born, its creator was sleeping in my arms. It is a powerful means of making the position of kings and priests safe, as powerful as a steel sword, as powerful as a blood-stained army.'

'Aunt, I never realized that.'

'Many people do not realize it. I did not; no doubt Janak, the King of Tirhut does not. But Yajnavalkya understands it all, as well as my husband Pravahan did. Pravahan had no belief in any god or heaven or spirit or demigod or religion. He believed only in pleasure, and he dedicated every moment of his life to pleasure. Three days before his death, a golden-haired girl entered his harem, the daughter of a priest of the clan of Vishvamitr. He had no longer any hope of life, and yet he was making love to that girl of twenty.'

'Yajnavalkya gave away his cows, aunt, but he brought back with him the beautiful slave-girls King Janak gave him.'

'Didn't I tell you he was a true disciple of Pravahan? Haven't you seen what his religion is? And yet you have only had a distant glimpse of it. If you ever get a chance of viewing it from close at hand then you will see, child!'

'Then you do believe, really and truly, that if I had gone on with my questions it would have cost me my head?'

'Of course it would; and as I said, not through any supernatural force of his. In this world many lives are cut short, without any noise.'

'My head is spinning round, aunt!'

'Only today? My head has been spinning ever since I grew up enough to understand things. All hypocrisy, all impostures, all this talk of kings and priests and rituals is simply a way of getting for nothing what the people produce by their toil. No one will be able to rescue the people from the pit they are in, until they themselves learn to use their wits; which these selfish schemes do not want to let them do.'

'Will man's heart never teach him to hate this deceitfulness?'

'It will, my child. That is my sole hope.'

Bandhul the Malla

REGION : KUSINARA AND MALLAGRAM (UNITED PROVINCES)
TIME : 490 BCE

This is an historical story of a period 100 generations ago. By that time, social conflict had taken deep root. The wealthy trading class had won a high place in society; numerous teachers had arisen to show the road to the other world, or offer salvation from Hell; but men were blind to the raging hell of slavery in their own towns and villages.

—1—

The spring was in its first bloom. The trees were clothed with new leaves in place of those they had shed. The white flowers of the *sal*[1] trees breathed their perfume through the woodland. It was still long before the sun's rays would be strong. Through the thick grove came the sound of footfalls on dry leaves. A young man and a girl stood beside a big anthill, staring at it.

Long curving tresses of blue-black hair, falling carelessly round the girl's light brown face, added to its beauty.

Putting his strong arm round her shoulder, the youth said –

'Mallika, why are you so much interested in this anthill?'

'Look, it is as high as two men!'

'Yes, it is bigger than most anthills, but there are some which are bigger still. Are you wondering whether what they say is true, that when rain falls an anthill gives out flame and smoke?'

'No; perhaps that is only a silly tale. But how can creatures as small as ants, or those even tinier white insects with red heads, build such big hillocks?'

'If you compare the size of a man's body with the size of those palaces which he builds, you will find that the one is many times smaller than the other, just in the same way. This hill is not the work of one ant; hundreds and thousands of ants have joined together to build it. It is just like the way human beings work together.'

'That is why it made such an impression on me to look at them, and see how strongly they are united among themselves. We think them insignificant creatures, and yet they can work together and build such castles. What a pity that our people do not take a lesson from these insects!'

'Man is as good as any animal when he practises cooperation; in fact, it is through cooperation that he has become the highest of living creatures. That is what has made him able to build great cities, towns and villages, to cross the limitless ocean in ships and gather the treasures of its swarming islands, and to make the elephant, the rhinoceros, and the lion yield to him.'

'Yes, but his enviousness! How good he would be if he were only not jealous!'

'You are thinking of the enviousness of our Mallas?'

'Yes, because our people are so jealous of you. I have never known you to find fault with anyone; everybody knows that your kind ways make even the slaves and workpeople fond of you. And even then many of our respected Mallas are full of spite against you.'

'They know that I am the most popular man, and there are always many who hate anyone who is loved by his people; in a *Gan*[2] it is only through popularity that one becomes a leader.'

'But they ought to have seen your good qualities and been glad of them. No other Malla has ever been known to win so much honour at Takshshila. Don't they know that even now King Prasenjit of Kosal sends you message after message asking you to go to him?'

'He and I were students together at Takshshila for ten years, so he knows what qualities I have.'

'So do the Mallas of Kusinara here. How can you doubt it? When that great Head of the Lichhavis was here and stayed with you, many of our people heard him talking in praise of you.'

'But those who feel envy of me, Mallika, go on feeling it even if they do know me to have some good qualities. To have talents and popularity is an easy way to incur envy among one's people. I am not thinking of myself; I only regret it because it was to serve the Mallas that I studied the art of war at Takshshila with such labour. Today, the states of Kosal and Magadh recognize the Lichhavis of Vaishali as their equals; whereas our Kusinara accepts the king of Kosal as her superior. My plan was to bring together Pava, Anupiya, Kusinara and the rest of the nine Malla tribes in a fraternal union, and make them into one strong confederacy such as the Lichhavis have. If the nine Malla tribes stood shoulder to shoulder, Prasenjit would not dare to cast even a glance in their direction. Well, that is my only regret.'

Mallika was unhappy to see a cloud on Bandhul's fair, handsome face and to divert his thoughts she remarked –

'Your comrades will be ready waiting for you for the hunt, dear! I also want to come with you. Are you going on horseback or on foot?'

'We don't go on horseback after *nilgais*,[3] Mallika! And can you go hunting with this waistcloth hanging to your knees, and a long floating shawl and your loose hair flying in the wind like a coil of black snakes!'

'Don't you like them?'

'Not like them?' he kissed her rosy lips. 'I could not dislike anything that is merely even connected with your name. But for hunting, one must be able to run through thickets and bushes.'

'Then you'll soon see me put myself in order!' Mallika tightened her waistcloth and fastened her hair in a knot, 'Bandhul, make my shawl into a headband for me.'

He did it for her, and then asked, as he caressed the little breasts, as round as apples, peeping out from her bodice –

'What are we to do with these?'

'Why, don't all the Malla girls have breasts like these?'

'Not so lovely as these.'

'Is anyone likely to steal them, then?'

'The young men will cast evil eyes on them.'

'Everyone knows that they belong to Bandhul.'

'Still, let me tie this piece of cloth round them, Mallika, under your dress.'

'You are not satisfied with seeing them from outside my dress?'

she asked with a smile, kissing him. He removed her bodice, and wound the cloth about the well-developed, round breasts swelling like white marble globes from her bosom; and then she put her bodice on again and said –

'Now are your fears leaving you?'

'I have no fears about what belongs to me! But now they will not shake so much when you run.'

All the young men and women of the tribe, dressed in hunting clothes, were ready waiting for this pair, and, as soon as they came up, bows, swords and spears were grasped, and the band moved off. One of them knew the place where the *nilgais* rested at midday, and acted as guide while the rest followed. In the shade of the tall trees, in the thin grass, a herd of *nilgais* was reposing and chewing the cud, while its leader, with ears cocked first to one side then the other, was standing on guard. The Mallas had divided into two parties; the first, with its weapons ready, was crouching behind the trees on one side, while the second, divided again into two groups, was moving so as to take the animals in the rear. The wind was blowing from the quarter where these two latter groups would meet.

The leader of the herd was standing with its tail, as short as a deer's, twitching; the rest of the animals, before the hunters could meet, had also got to their feet, with dilated nostrils and ears pricked up, and were staring nervously in the same direction. In a second it was clear that they had detected the danger, for they set off at a gallop behind their leader in the direction from which the wind was blowing. When they were near the lurking hunters they swerved and halted to stare about them again. At that moment the twang of bowstrings was heard. Bandhul, with unerring aim, shot at the leader's heart. Mallika and several others aimed at the same mark, but it was certain that if Bandhul's arrow had missed, the animal would have escaped. It fell on the spot. The rest of the herd scattered and fled. Bandhul ran up to the leader, which was gasping its last breath. The hunters followed the bloody trail of two other wounded beasts for a mile or so, and found one of them stretched on the ground.

Joy reigned at the forest banquet that followed these successes. Some piled up wood, and made a big smokeless fire. The women got ready their pans, while men skinned the carcasses and began cutting up the meat. The feast began with the heart, roasted over the fire and cups of wine. Bandhul's two hands were busy with the work of cutting up, so Mallika put some morsels into his mouth and held a cup to his lips.

When night fell the meat was not yet cooked and ready. The blazing flames of the wood fire threw out a strong red light, and singing and dancing began in its circle. Mallika, most beautiful of the girls of Kusinara, excelled herself as she danced in her huntress's costume and displayed all her grace. Bandhul's comrades congratulated him on having won such a girl, a jewel worth all the wealth of Jambudvip.[4]

—2—

A large concourse of people was assembled in the building where the people of Kusinara met in council. Every member of the tribal assembly was seated in the hall, while onlookers stood outside in the field. At the end of the hall, on a raised platform, sat the Ganpati.[5] He ran a reflective eye over his audience, rose to his feet and began –

'Worthy folk! Listen, while I explain to the assembly the purpose of our meeting today! Ayushman[6] Bandhul, having mastered at Takshshila the art of war, returned home, adding lustre to his people's name. His skill in arms is known outside Kusinara as well as here. Four years have passed since his homecoming. From time to time I have entrusted to him many of our affairs, small or great, and he has discharged each responsibility with diligence and success. It is now proposed that he should be given a permanent post, that of second-in-command of our warriors.

'Worthy folk! Listen! Shall the post of second-in-command be conferred on the Ayushman Bandhul? Let the Ayushmans who agree remain silent, and let any who do not agree, speak!

'For the second time, worthy folk! Listen! Shall the post of second-in-command be conferred on the Ayushman Bandhul? Let those Ayushmans who agree remain silent, and let any who do not agree, speak!

'For the third time, worthy folk! Listen! Shall the post of

second-in-command be conferred on the Ayushman Bandhul? Let those Ayushmans who agree remain silent, and let any who do not agree, speak!'

At once a member of the gathering, Roj, threw off his cloak baring his right shoulder which he turned towards the platform, and stood up.

'This Ayushman wishes to speak,' cried the Ganpati. 'Let him give his opinion.'

'Worthy folk!' said Roj. 'Listen! I do not doubt the Ayushman Bandhul's skill in battle. It is for a special reason that I wish to oppose his being made second-in-command. It is the custom of our Gan that when any man is raised to a high position he must first undergo a test. My opinion is that the Ayushman Bandhul also should submit to this custom.'

When Roj had sat down, two or three others supported his view. Others warmly asserted that there was no need of a trial. Finally, the Ganpati declared –

'Worthy folk! There is some difference of opinion among us as to whether the Ayushman Bandhul should be made second-in-command or not. Therefore it is necessary to take a vote. The vote-tellers will come round to you with bamboo-splinters. Each will have in one hand a bag of red splinters, in the other of black. A red splinter stands for "Yes", a black one for "No". Those Ayushman who share the Ayushman Roj's opinion and do not agree to the proposal, will draw a black splinter. Those who agree to the proposal will draw a red one.'

The vote-tellers came to each member with their bags, and every man drew a splinter according to his opinion. When the bags were brought back to the Ganpati, the splinters remaining in them were counted. The red were more numerous than the black, which meant that the members of the assembly had drawn more of the black. The Ganpati announced –

'Worthy folk! Listen! More have been taken of the black than of the red. Therefore, I hold, that the assembly agrees with Roj. Now let the assembly decide what kind of trial Ayushman Bandhul is to undergo.'

After some time spent in discussion and voting, it was decided that Bandhul must cut through seven faggots with his sword in quick succession. The seventh day was fixed for the test, and the assembly broke up.

When the seventh day came, the open ground at Kusinara was thronged with crowds of men and women. Mallika was there among them. At a little distance from each other were placed the seven faggots of hard wood. The Ganpati gave the signal, and Bandhul grasped his sword, while the entire populace watched with bated breath, confident of his success as they eyed the long, straight blade and the muscular arms wielding it. They saw the sword flash like lightning as it rose and fell. The first faggot was shorn through, the second, the third. At the sixth stroke a metallic sound caught Bandhul's ear. His brows contracted in a frown; his ardour seemed quenched. The sword checked itself as it was about to descend in the final stroke. He threw a single hasty glance at the cut-off ends of the faggots. His frame trembled, his face reddened with anger, but he uttered not a word.

The Ganpati announced that the seventh faggot had not been cut through. There was a feeling of sympathy for Bandhul.

When they came home, and Mallika looked into his angry, frowning face, she forgot her own regret, and tried to console him.

'Mallika,' he said, 'a cunning trick was played on me. I never expected that.'

'What was it, dearest?'

'Each of the faggots had been stuck full of iron nails. As far as the fifth stroke I suspected nothing, but at the sixth I heard quite plainly the ring of metal. If I had not heard that sound, I should have cut the last faggot in two as well, but as it was, I felt disgusted.'

'What a trick! Whoever did it was a great scoundrel!'

'We can't find out who did it. I am not angry at all with Roj; after all, what he said was right enough, and the majority of the assembly agreed with his opinion. What pains me and angers me is to find that I have so few true friends in Kusinara.'

'So, Bandhul is not pleased with his Kusinara!'

'Kusinara is my mother, who has reared me up; but now I am not going to stay in Kusinara any longer.'

'You want to go away?'

'Yes. Kusinara has no need of me.'

'Then where shall you go?'

'Mallika, will you come with me?' he asked with his face full of eager animation.

'Dear Bandhul, I will go with you like your shadow.' She kissed his inflamed eyes, and immediately his wrath began to ebb away. 'Give me your hands, Mallika.' He took her hands in his own, and went on – 'A current of strength seems to flow into me from these hands of yours, they give me strength to roam the whole world without any fear.'

'Well, darling, where do you intend to go, and when?'

'Without any delay, for those nails in the faggots will soon be reported to the Ganpati, and then he will fix another day for a new trial. We should leave before they come to persuade me again.'

'Why not let their treachery be exposed?'

'Kusinara has given its opinion of me, Mallika! My work is not here. Not now, at least. When Kusinara stands in need of Bandhul, he will be here.'

The very same night, Mallika and Bandhul left Kusinara, taking with them what they needed for a journey. The next day they reached Mallagram,[7] a permanent settlement of Brahmin families, on the bank of the river Achirvati (Rapti). Throughout the Malla country the Sankritya clan of this settlement was renowned for its warlike spirit. Bandhul had friends there; however, it was not to see these that he had come, but to find a boat to carry him to Shravasti. Among the inhabitants were some employees of the big merchant Sudatt through whom it was easy to obtain a boat. The Sankritya Brahmins, faithful to the custom of their clan, killed a fat pigling in front of their door, cooked it with their own hands, and presented the travellers with the tender pork.

—3—

At Shravasti, the capital of Kosal, King Prasenjit gave his old friend and fellow student the heartiest of welcomes. Even at Takshshila he had expressed his desire that when he came to the throne Bandhul should become his commander-in-chief; and since his accession he had several times sent the same proposal to Bandhul. But the latter, instead of wanting to command the army of Kosal, the wealthiest and strongest kingdom then existing, had always preferred to be a mere second-in-command in the militia of his native Kusinara. Now that his native land had rejected him, however, he was ready to come to terms, when Prasenjit repeated his proposal.

'I am willing to accept the offer, friend; but on one condition.'

'Good, Bandhul! Tell me what it is.'

'I belong to the Malla folk.'

'I know; and I shall never order you to march against the Mallas.'

'That is all I ask.'

'My friend, I only desire to strengthen the links I have with the Mallas. You know I have no ambition to enlarge my kingdom. If I am ever forced into hostilities with them, you will be at liberty to choose sides. Is there anything else my old friend wishes from me?'

'No, Your Majesty, that is enough.'

—4—

And so Bandhul the Malla became the head of the army of Kosal. A ruler so weak and inactive as Prasenjit stood in great need of a tried and tested commander. If he had not met with Bandhul, in fact, perhaps Magadh and Vats[8] would have annexed some of his provinces.

Sometime after their arrival at Shravasti, Mallika became pregnant. One day Bandhul asked her whether she had a craving for anything (such as pregnant women feel).

'Yes, dearest; I do have craving but it is for something very difficult.'

'Nothing can be difficult for Bandhul! Tell me, what is it you long for?'

'To bathe in the sacred lake.'

'Of the Mallas?'

'No, of the Lichhavis, at Vaishali.'

'You were right, Mallika; it is something very difficult. But Bandhul will find a way to accomplish it. Tomorrow morning, get ready; we shall set out together in a chariot.'

Next day they drove on in a chariot, taking provisions, a sword, a bow and other weapons.

In several weeks they covered a great distance and then entered Vaishali by a gate whose guardian, Mahali, was an old fellow student of Bandhul; he had been blinded, through the malice of certain Lichhavis. At first Bandhul was inclined to stop and spend some time with Mahali, but as that would delay the fulfilment of his wife's longing, he abandoned his intention.

There was a guard on the shore of the sacred lake. Only once in his life was a Lichhavi allowed to bathe in it – when he was elected to fill a vacant place among the nine hundred and ninety-nine full members of the Lichhavi Gan.

When sentinels tried to stop them, Bandhul beat them off with his whip. Mallika took her bath; they jumped back into the chariot, and it rolled off at once on its way out of Vaishali. But five hundred Lichhavis, warned by their sentinels, appeared in pursuit, driving their chariots at full speed. Mahali had learned what was happening, and had forbidden the pursuit; but the haughty Lichhavis had small habit of obedience.

'Darling,' said Mallika, looking back as she heard the rattling wheels in the distance, 'there are a great many chariots behind us!'

'Wait till you see them all strung out in a line, and then tell me.' Mallika did so.

What the ancient historians tell us is that Bandhul drew an arrow and fired it, and it went straight through and under the belts of all the five hundred Lichhavis and came out at the rear of the line. The Lichhavis continued to gain ground, until they drew up and challenged Bandhul to battle.

'I don't fight with dead men like you,' returned Bandhul calmly.

'You'll see what kind of dead men we are!'

'I shan't waste one more arrow. Go back home, call together your wives and friends first, and then take off your belts.' Bandhul took the reins again out of Mallika's hands, put the chariot at full speed, and vanished.

When their belts were taken off, all the five hundred Lichhavis were, in fact, found dead.

—5—

Shravasti (now deserted Sahet-Mahet[9]) was then the biggest city of Jambudvip. Prasenjit's kingdom included two other big cities, Saket (Ayodhya) and Varanasi (Banaras). In the combined kingdom of Kashi and Kosal lived numerous opulent merchants like Sudatt (whose name meant 'Nourisher of the Destitute'), Mrigar of Shravasti, and Arjun of Saket. Their merchandise was carried not only throughout Jambudvip, but also from Tamrlipt across the Eastern Sea (Bay of Bengal), and from Bharukachh (Bharuch) and Supparak (Sopara) across the Western Sea (Arabian Sea), to remote shores. Their status was not equal to that of the dominant Brahmins and Kshatriyas, yet their place in society was high, and in wealth the ruling classes could not compare with them. Sudatt bought the Jetvan gardens from Prince Jet, paying as many coins as would be laid on the ground of the garden, and made a hermitage there for Gautam Buddh. King Prasenjit himself went with all his retinue to Saket to attend the wedding of Mrigar's son Pundravardhan, and was the guest of the bride's father, the merchant, Arjun. The bride, Vishakha, with such a father and such a father-in-law, sold a necklace and with the money built a great monastery of seven storeys and a thousand cells, which was named after Mrigar's mother Purvaram. The wealth of so many lands was being sucked into the coffers of these merchant-princes that their immense wealth was beyond computing.

Jaivali, Uddalak and Yajnavalkya had reduced sacrificial rites to the second place in religion, and had fashioned a more abstract faith as a secure ark for their worldly interests. Rulers like Janak had paid deep respect to it, and had begun the custom of holding gatherings for the discussion of theological questions, which opened the way to free speculation even beyond the limits of the Veds. It was an age when the floodgates of enquiry and discussion had been opened, and each philosopher made use of these common meetings to lay his views before the public. Sometimes their teachings were given in the ordinary form of lectures; sometimes as a challenge to disputation, they would fix a staff of *jamun*[10] wood in the ground at any place in their wanderings. Pravahan, to cloud the brains of scores of generations, had invented religious practices like monasticism, contemplation, asceticism. Now, thinkers who had abandoned the Upnishads also lent the aid of their independent theories to monasticism and austerity.

Ajit Keskambal[11] was a declared atheist; he believed in no worship, no eternal essence, no heaven or hell or rebirth, only in material substance; yet he too was a world-renouncing ascetic. To win the favour of rulers in that age or merely to escape their anger, it was necessary for thinkers to give a religious colouring even to their atheism. Lauhitya, the Brahmin chief, and princes like Payasi, were free thinkers, and became so celebrated among their people that the latter came to feel that any abandonment of atheism would be something shameful. In the atheism of such men there was nothing dangerous to society.

A spread of atheism was thus in progress, but it was Gautam Buddh who was held in the highest respect by the dominant Brahmins and Kshatriyas, and the wealthy merchants, for his teachings, in which the soul had no place. This was especially so in Kosal, partly because Gautam himself belonged to the Shakya community inhabiting Kosal. Like the atheists, he asserted that there was no soul in the universe, no god, no eternal substance, but that all elements passed from birth to speedy annihilation. The world was not an aggregation of actual bodies, but a stream of events. To intelligent men this thought was something at once rational and heart-stirring.

But such a non-spiritual philosophy might unsettle the relations between rich and poor, master and slave. For this reason the atheism of Ajit could not win great favour with the ruling and commercial classes. Gautam added other ideas to his materialism – his atheism – so as to soften its sharpness. Although, he said, there was no such thing as an eternal soul, the stream of consciousness passed, within the boundaries of heaven and hell and whatever other realms there might be, from one body to another, from one physical existence to another. In this doctrine the weapon of reincarnation forged by King Pravahan found full scope. If Gautam had preached undiluted atheism, the merchant princes of Shravasti, Saket, Kaushambi, and the capital city of Bhadrika, would certainly not have opened their money bags, and the feudal lords of Brahmin and Kshatriya castes would not have been ready to kneel at his feet.

Gautam's teachings won the devoted adherence of the upper-class women of Shravasti. Mallika Devi, the consort of Prasenjit, was a disciple of Buddhism, and her friend Vishakha, daughter-in-law of the great merchant of the city, in token of her faith built the great Purvaram monastery and presented it to Buddh. The other Mallika, wife of the commander Bandhul, was a dear friend of the queen, and under the latter's guidance she began to be interested in Buddh's teachings, until she also became a Buddhist.

This Mallika's house was now a very luxurious one. The house of a commander-in-chief, in so large a state as Kosal, was bound to be palatial. Mallika had ten sons, who held high ranks in the royal army. Bandhul had, for a long time, maintained his influence on the King; meanwhile, he had made many enemies, who were irked by the sight of a foreigner occupying so high a position. These envious souls began to poison the King's mind. The King was somewhat slow-witted; he was gulled with reports that Bandhul had described him as witless. Finally, it was asserted that the commander was ambitious of seizing the throne. To Prasenjit this seemed quite plausible. He played into the hands of his own and Bandhul's enemies.

One day, seeing Bandhul preoccupied and gloomy, Mallika said to him –

'Why are you so thoughtful, my dear?'

'Because the King has begun to suspect me.'

'Then why should you not give up your command, and let us go back to Kusinara? We have enough land there to live on.'

'That would mean leaving the King at the mercy of his enemies. Do you not understand, Mallika? The king of Magadh, Ajatshatru, has already made several attacks on Kashi. Once we took him prisoner. Our king was generous; he married his daughter Vajra to him, and released him. But Ajatshatru dreams of making himself a *Chakrvarti*[12] of all Jambudvip, Mallika. He is not going to be restrained by a marriage alliance. Our capital is swarming with his spies. And the Vats king, Udayan, the son-in-law of our other neighbour, the ruler of Avanti (Ujjain), also has no honest intentions. He, too, is making preparations on our frontier. It would be shameful cowardice, Mallika, to run away from Shravasti at a time like this.'

'Yes, and it would be treachery too.'

'It is not for myself that I am anxious. Many a time I have looked death in the face on the battlefield, and survived. It will not be astonishing if some day death catches me in its claws.'

Mallika Devi, who from being the daughter of a common labourer, a gardener, had risen by her virtues to be the King's consort, died; had she lived, she might have prevented the King from being so misled.

One day the King, on the pretext of danger to the frontier, dispatched Bandhul's sons to a certain point. When they had accomplished their mission and were returning, he treacherously sent Bandhul himself against them. The unwitting father and his ten sons perished together. When a letter reporting this event reached Mallika, she was giving Buddh and his monks a meal, which her ten young daughters-in-law had prepared. She read the letter, and a knife went through her heart; but such was her self-command that she said nothing; there was not a tear in her eyes; her face was not even pale. She tied up the letter in a fold of her dress, and gave all the company their food. After the meal she listened reverently to Buddh's homily, and then at last read the letter aloud. It was as if a thunderbolt had fallen on the family. Mallika was firm enough; but to strengthen the minds of the youthful widows was a difficult task even for Buddh.

In time, Prasenjit realized the truth, and regretted what he had done: but now it was useless. To soothe his conscience he made Bandhul's nephew, Dirghkarayan, his commander-in-chief.

—6—

It was winter, and the fields round Kapilvastu[13] were alive with green wheat and flowering mustard. Today the city was gaily decorated, with ornamental arches rising here and there. The palace was most ornate of all. A group of slaves, enjoying a short rest after three days of heavy labour, were sitting in a corner of a house. One of them, Kak by name, was saying –

'Is there any life for us slaves? It would have been better for us to be born as cattle instead of human beings; then we should not have had human minds.'

'That is the truth, Kak! Yesterday my master Dandpani heated an iron red hot and burned my wife with it.'

'What did he burn her for?'

'Who can ask him that? They think nothing of even the bond between man and wife among us slaves; and yet this Dandpani calls himself a Jain[14] – a follower of the Niganth[15] – who respects all life so much that he keeps a peacock-feather fan to prevent himself from trampling on any insects on the ground! My wife's crime was that she had come to tell me that our little girl, who had been very ill for several days, had lost consciousness. In the end the poor thing never recovered. It was a good thing for her that she died, or she would have had to live the same kind of life as we have in this world. Really, Kak! There is no life for us slaves. As if it wasn't enough already, my brute of a master is saying that he means to sell my wife as soon as these festivities are over.'

'So your Dandpani brute was not satisfied with burning her with a hot iron!'

'No, brother. He says that after twelve years my little girl would have fetched him fifty pieces of gold ... as if we had intentionally robbed him of his fifty pieces!'

'And as if we slaves had no feelings of parental-love.'

'And yet,' a third slave interjected, 'it's the son of a slave-girl that all this reception is being got ready for.'

'Who?'

'This prince of Kosal, Vidudabh.'

'A slave's son!'

'Yes. Don't you know that old woman belonging to the Shakya[16] Mahanam? She is not dark like us: some Shakya must have been her father.'

'There's no lack of slave-girls born like that!'

'No; well, from this woman, Mahanam had a daughter. Very fair, very pretty to look at; she was just like a Shakya.'

'Why shouldn't she be? And the masters are quite willing to take pains in bringing up a pretty girl, even if she is a slave's daughter.'

'Prasenjit, the king of Kosal, was eager to marry some Shakya girl, but no Shakya was ready to offer his daughter – the Shakyas consider themselves the greatest aristocrats in the universe, Kak! But the king of Kosal would have been angry with the Shakyas if they had given a flat refusal. So Mahanam pretended that this daughter of his slave-woman was a Shakya maiden, and offered her in marriage. And the son of this bride, Varshbhakshatriya, is the prince of Kosal, Vidudabh.'

'But he must treat his slaves as bloodthirstily as any Shakya.'

Trumpets sounded; the Shakyas had received the prince of Kosal and were now giving him a ceremonious welcome in the palace; though in their heart of hearts, knowing him to be the son of a slave-woman, they felt nothing but contempt for him.

Vidudabh, having enjoyed his welcome by his supposed maternal relations, and having received his grandfather Mahanam's blessing, departed from Kapilvastu. The palace had been polluted by the feet of one of servile birth; it was necessary to purify it, and numerous slaves, men and women, were employed in washing away every trace of dust from the carpets. During this labour, one slave-woman kept up a constant stream of abuse against the slave-born Vidudabh. One of the latter's soldiers had left his spear behind in the palace; he came back for it and stood listening attentively to the woman's tirade. Slowly, Vidudabh came to know the whole story. He vowed that he would not leave a single Shakya alive in Kapilvastu, and the time was to come when he would make good on his threat. He was equally enraged with Prasenjit, for having begotten him on a slave-girl.

Dirghkarayan could never forget the deaths of his uncle and his cousins. On the other hand, Prasenjit, repenting in his old age all his sins, tried to show more and more goodness and kindness. One day after the midday meal, he thought of Buddh. Learning that Buddh was at a Shakya town some miles away, he set off there with Dirghkarayan and a guard of soldiers. Before entering Buddh's cell, he put his mace, royal crown and other regalia into Dirghkarayan's hands. The commander, who had come to an understanding with Vidudabh, left one of Prasenjit's wives at the door, proclaimed Vidudabh king, and took the road back to Shravasti. After listening for some time to Buddh's words, Prasenjit came out, and his wife, half choked with sobs, told him what had happened. Prasenjit set out for the capital of his nephew[17] Ajatshatru, king of Magadh, to seek his help. Travelling on foot for weeks, in his old age, he exhausted all his strength before reaching his goal. It was evening when he reached the capital, and the city gates were already shut. Prasenjit died that night, in a cottage outside the gates. In the morning, when his wife's lamentations were heard, Ajatshatru and Vajra came in haste; but except to cremate the corpse with great pomp, there was nothing for them to do.

The death of Bandhul was avenged, and the poison of slavery had done its work.

Naagdatt

REGION : NORTHERN INDIA
TIME : 335 BCE

By now the Aryans were completely settled in India and had accepted many of the concepts and traditions of the Asurs. This story brings us to the eve of the concept of an all-powerful monarch, an emperor; and to the eve of foreign invasions.

—1—

'We must think what is appropriate, Vishnugupt! As human beings we have some duties, and we must fix our minds on doing what is right.'

'Duty means religion?'

'I consider religion a fraud. It is nothing but a device to allow those who live by robbing others to enjoy their wealth in peace and comfort. Has religion ever thought of the poor and helpless? There is no race in the world which does not believe in some religion, but has it ever made people remember that a slave is a human being? Let alone slavery, think of women, even free women: has religion ever done them justice? If you have money, you can marry two wives, four wives, ten, a hundred; they will be no better than slaves, and religion has nothing to say against it! My conception of "appropriate" is not a religious one; I mean by it whatever a healthy human conscience supports.'

'Well, then I say that whatever is necessary is right.'

'Then there is no distinction of right and wrong.'

'Of course there is, my friend. When I speak of what is necessary, I don't mean what is necessary only for the individual.'

'Try to explain it more clearly, Vishnugupt.'

'Take this country of ours, Takshshila-Gandhar. Now, to us our independence is very dear, and that is rightfully so. But our land is too small to stand up to an attack by a strong enemy. So long as our neighbours were small republics, like western Gandhar or the Madrs, we could live at peace; there might have been occasional wars, but they cost us nothing more than a few lives. Our independence was not at stake, because nobody would find it easy to digest Takshshila's crops, full of thistles as they are. But when the Parshavs (Iranians) became our neighbours on the west, our independence was at their mercy. What is necessary to save our independence then? That we should make ourselves as strong as the Persians.'

'And what are we to do to make ourselves strong?'

'Nothing can be done with a tiny republic. Instead of all these petty states we must bring into existence a big empire.'

'What position would the small states have inside it?'

'They could keep their sense of individuality.'

'That is a foolish notion, Vishnugupt! Does a slave ever keep a sense of individuality under his master?'

'Naagdatt, it is not through thinking or wishing that one gets a good place; that depends on ability. If Takshshila knows how to act, she will be able to capture a strong position inside a big empire; if not, she will have to take a lower rank.'

'A servile rank?'

'Even that would be better for her than what has become of western Gandhar in the empire of Darius. But very well! Leave my prescription alone, and tell me what you think we should do to safeguard our independence. This much is certain, remember, that with the resources of our wretched little country we can never safeguard our existence.'

'Yes, I will tell you Vishnugupt. We have to maintain our national independence, without putting ourselves under the despotism of a monarch. I admit that, as a single wretched little country, we cannot do it. Therefore, we must unite all the republics of Uttarapath[1] into a federation.'

'In which every republic will still be free? Or will the federation be supreme?'

'I think the federation must be accepted as something higher than Gandhar, or the Madrs, the Mallas, the Shivis, or any other member; just as we accept our Republic as something higher than the individuals living in it.'

'How are the members to be convinced of that? After all, in any republic we have to keep up an army for defence against foreign enemies. Your federation will have to collect taxes.'

'The members of the federation will have to be treated just as individuals are inside the Republic.'

'Inside the Republic, we have a long tradition of living as a single great family, united by common blood and ancestry, and this family has been in the habit of obeying its native laws since time immemorial. But your federation of republics will be something new with no ties of blood to strengthen it; on the contrary, blood feuds and disputes have divided the members since time immemorial. How are we to enforce the laws of the federation, then? If you would only think about it like a practical man, my friend, you would not talk of such schemes. The republics will only obey the federation when they are compelled to do so. And where is the power that will compel them?'

'I believe that it must grow up from within them.'

'I say that if that happened, it would be very good; but we have already felt the weight of the Persians' fists once, and we know from experience that it cannot grow up from within. Therefore, we have to create it, somehow or other.'

'At the cost of submitting to a monarchy?'

'Even if it were not Takshshila alone, but all the individual republics like Takshshila that had to submit to a king – a paramount sovereign – we should be none the worse.'

'Why not accept Darius of Persia as our ruler, then?'

'Darius, the Persian, is not of our race, as you know very well, we belong to Jambudvip.'

'Then – Nand?'

'If we cannot build a federation of all the northern republics we should not refuse to become Nand's subjects. Which is better: to be enslaved by Darius, as western Gandhar has been, or to live under the rule of a sovereign who is an Indian like ourselves?'

'Oh, Vishnugupt! You have never seen a country ruled by a monarch. To see one is to realize that the condition of the common folk there is no better than slavery.'

'I admit I have never set foot in a country ruled by a king, except western Gandhar; but I feel in my heart the longing to wander and see many lands. Unlike you, instead of travelling occasionally while living a stick-in-the-mud life at home, I mean to roam about once my studies are finished. But it can make no difference to my conviction that if we are to escape a shameful subjugation to foreigners, our petty frontiers must be wiped out. We must use the same key to success as Cyrus and Darius used.'

'I want to take a close view and see for myself how much success they had.'

'A close view?'

'Yes. In the east I have been as far as Magadh, and I have seen Nand's kingdom, which, compared with our eastern Gandhar, is a hell. It is certainly strong, strong enough to grind the faces of the poor, but as to the labouring classes, peasants, artisans and slaves, their misery is beyond description.'

'This happened because in Nand's empire no self-respecting, freedom-loving republic like Takshshila had a place.'

'Oh, no, Vishnugupt! The Lichhavi republic was more warlike than our Gandhar, yet today, Vaishali is the bond servant of Magadh, and the Lichhavis are just big strong hunting-dogs for their masters, nothing better. Go to Vaishali, look at it, all in ruins; its population has fallen to barely one third of what it was a century and a half ago. All its spirit of pride and independence, that it had taken hundreds of years to foster, serves now only to provide the king of Magadh with brave soldiers. Wherever a people have once given itself into the clutches of a great empire, it can hardly hope ever to escape from them again.'

'Naagdatt, my friend, there was a time when I used to think as you do, but I know now that the day of the small republics has passed, and that the creation of a big republic or federation is a mere dream, I bow to the necessity of the times and admit its justice. But tell me: are you making preparations to travel towards the west?'

'Yes, to see the land of the Persians first and then if possible I want to see Yavans[2] as well. The Yavans have republics like ours: what I want to find out is how they were able to frustrate the ambitions of

Darius the Great and his descendants. I want to see with my own eyes.'

'I am going away too, friend. Let me find out by travelling eastward whether Magadh has strength enough to unite all Jambudvip or not. Yes, this is the task for us to undertake when our studies are over, instead of collecting wealth or bringing up families. I only regret that I have not learned the art of medicine as you have done along with your other studies. You did well; it is a very profitable art for those who go travelling.'

'But you have learned even more profitable arts, astrology, fortune-telling and magic charms.'

'They are mere trickery as you know very well.'

'What has Vishnugupt Chanakya to do with truth or falsehood? For you, whatever is necessary is right!'

Naagdatt Kashya and Vishnugupt Chanakya had reached the end of their student days, and this was the last talk between the two young men of Takshshila who had played together and worked together since boyhood. They were going out, each guided by his own ideas, to search for a way of protecting the freedom of Takshshila, which had already more than once been invaded by the Persians.

—2—

There were hills on every side, low hills bare of trees or grass; the eye ached for a glimpse of greenery. Between the hills stretched a valley of some breadth in which one might have some hope of finding a trace of water and vegetation. A caravan route threaded this valley; travellers were constantly moving along it, and rest houses had been built for them and their beasts to halt at. Viewing the country round about, it was difficult to believe that so much comfort could be found in these inns, or to understand how so many furnishings and provisions could have been collected in such a wilderness.

At halting places the rest houses were of more than one type; some were meant for ordinary government officials or soldiers, some for merchants, and one at least at each stage was a royal mansion where the king, when on progress, or his Satraps,[3] would repose. Today, at this halting place, someone was stopping in the royal building; horses were in the stables, and numerous slave-attendants could be seen in the courtyard. Every face wore a downcast expression. In spite of the bustling throng, a strange hush seemed to spread over the place.

Three anxious looking officers emerged from the gate, and moved towards the plebeian rest houses. Those whom they passed stood aside timidly and respectfully at the sight of their expensive clothes and impressive faces. They were making enquiries whether there was any doctor to be found. At length, in the inn reserved for common wayfarers, they were informed that a Hindu physician was staying there. It was a region of scanty rainfall, and the rainy season had ended some time before. Apples, grapes, melons and such fruits were cheap enough to be on sale at the inn. When one of the officers came face to face with the physician, he was eating slices of a big melon; a number of Persians, similarly dressed in beggars' rags, were sitting and eating melons near him.

At sight of the officer, the mendicants jumped up in a fright and fell back on all sides. Someone pointed to the man standing in the middle, and said –

'This is the Hindu doctor, master.'

The officer glanced first at his dirty clothes with an air of contempt; then he looked at the man's face. It was not what might be expected in a wearer of such rags. There was no trace of fear or of servility in it. There was a light in those eyes that made an impression on the officer; his frown vanished and he began, with something of respect in his tone –

'You are a physician?'

'Yes.'

'Where from?'

'Takshshila.'

At the sound of this name the officer grew still more respectful, and said –

'The wife of our Satrap, the Satrap of the provinces of Oxiana and Sogdiana,[4] is very ill. She is the sister of the *King of Kings*.[5] Can you give her any treatment?'

'Why not, seeing that I am a physician?'

'But these clothes of yours ...'

'It is I who am to give the treatment, not my clothes.'

'But they are so very dirty!'

'I was going to change them today. Wait a moment.'

He put on a somewhat cleaner woollen cloak, took up a leather bag stuffed with bundles of medicines, and set off with the officer.

The royal building might be known as a rest house, but no donkeys had littered its courtyard with dung, no beggars had rid their bedding of vermin here. Every corner was spotless. Rugs of many coloured embroidery were spread on the staircase, flanked with handsome carved balustrades. There were valuable carpets also on the floor in each room; soft silk curtains hung in the doorways, where beautiful girls stood motionless like marble statues.

The officer approached a door, signing to the physician to wait, and whispered something in the ear of the girl in waiting. She opened the door noiselessly; nothing inside could be seen through the hanging curtain. The girl went in, and returning in a few moments, told the physician to follow her.

As he entered, he noticed that the room was pervaded with some sweet perfume; then he darted a rapid glance about him. A miracle had been performed in the decorating of this chamber. Carpets, curtains, cushions, lamps, paintings, sculptures, all were of an excellence he had never seen before. In front of him was a luxurious divan, with two or three cushions resting on it near the wall. Leaning on one of these sat a corpulent middle-aged man, with some streaks of grey in the brown moustaches that curled up towards his ears. An impression of sleepless nights and grave sadness was obvious in his wide tawny eyes. At his side sat a girl of incomparable beauty. Her skin was as white as milk; or rather, it reminded one of something even softer and purer, except that there was a faint flush, fainter than ever now, in her pale cheeks. The scarlet of her thin lips couldn't be compared with the red of a parrot's beak. Her light eyebrows were soft, delicately arched lines; the extraordinarily wide eyes below them, blue and long-lashed, were flushed and swollen. Her head was adorned with a net of woven silk that looked like gold thread. She wore a green silk vest with long sleeves, and red silk trousers. On so pure and exquisite a form, her pearl-studded ornaments seemed a useless burden.

Apart from these two figures, there were several young women in the room; the physician was not long in guessing, from their faces and their submissive bearing, that they were attendants of the Satrap's harem.

The man – it was the Satrap himself – looked him up and down from head to foot as he entered; but his glance was soon arrested by the blue eyes that met his, and the thought passed through his mind that if he gave this man his clothes to wear, the stranger might pass for one of the handsomest youths of Persepolis.

'You are a physician of Takshshila?' asked the Satrap courteously.

'Yes, O' Great Satrap.'

'My wife is very ill. Since yesterday her condition has become serious. The medicines my own two doctors have given her are having no effect.'

'After I have seen your lady I should like to talk with your doctors.'

'They will be ready here. Come, let us go in.'

A snowy curtain was drawn aside from the spotlessly white wall, disclosing an inner door. The Satrap and his sixteen-year-old daughter led the way; the physician followed. In the room within stood a bed, with legs of ivory; on the soft mattress, as white as sea foam, lay sleeping the sick woman. She was wrapped in an upper garment of white antelope's skin, and only her face above the chin was visible.

The attendants stepped back as the Satrap appeared. The physician drew close and gazed at the patient. Her face bore a close resemblance to that of the young girl but instead of the latter's fresh young beauty the effects of advancing years could be seen, and the ravaging marks of long illness. The once rosy lips had turned yellowish; the once plump cheeks were wrinkled and hollow. Her eyes were closed and sunken; the fair arching brows were still contracted; the shining white of the forehead had turned dry and lifeless.

'Afsha!' said the Satrap, bending over her. The patient's eyes half opened then closed once more.

'She is unconscious,' said the physician, 'semi-unconscious.'

He drew her hands out and felt the pulse, which could only faintly be distinguished. A chill had spread almost throughout her body. The Satrap saw that the physician's face was grave. After some reflection the physician said –

'A little grape wine – the older the better.'

There was no lack of wine in the Satrap's establishment, even now when he was on tour. A shining glass flagon filled with blood-red wine and a golden cup inlaid with jewels were brought. The physician unwrapped one of his bundles, measured out with the long nail of his right hand's little finger one *ratti*[6] of some medicine, and asked for the patient's mouth to be opened. The Satrap had no difficulty in holding it open. The doctor poured into it the medicine, and a drop of wine, and watched with satisfaction as the patient swallowed them. 'Now,' he said to the Satrap, 'I shall go out and talk to the Great-Satrap's doctors. Before long the Lady-Satrap will open her eyes: then I must be called.'

They retired into the other room and he consulted with the Persian doctors who gave him a full account of how, from an ordinary fever contracted at the time of their departure from Sogdiana, the patient had fallen into her present condition. An attendant then brought word that the Lady-Satrap was asking for her husband. The Satrap's face lit up as he hurried in again with the physician. His wife's eyes were now wide open, and life had come back to her features.

'They tell me,' she began, in a low but self-possessed voice, 'that you have been very anxious. I have called you to tell you that I shall soon be better. My mind is coming back, I feel I am stronger now.'

'That is just what this Hindu physician was telling me,' returned the Satrap.

Her face brightened as she said –

'The Hindu physician understands my disease. It is over now, doctor, is it not?'

'Yes, the illness is over, but you will have to rest for some time. I am thinking of how to give you enough strength to go on to Persepolis as quickly as possible. I have with me some wonderful drugs made from certain minerals. I shall give some drugs that Hindus use; and you must drink a little grape juice and pomegranate juice.'

'You understand my disease, doctor! The others are fools, fools. I will do whatever you tell me. Roshna! ...'

The young girl came forward, exclaiming – 'Mother!'

'My child, your eyes are wet. Those other doctors were killing me, but now you need not be anxious. Ahura-Mazda[7] have sent this Hindu physician to me. See that he is well taken care of, and whatever he tells me to eat or drink, you must give it me yourself.' The physician gave Roshna some instructions, and went out. He entrusted to the Satrap, whose face was beaming with joy, some medicines wrapped up in beech leaves, and was about to return to his own lodging when the Satrap said –

'You must stay here, with us!'

'I am not used to court manners.'

'You know very well how a man should behave. As to manners, each nation has its own.'

'My staying with you would be troublesome to your servants.'

'I will give you a separate room to yourself, near ours. It will be a great satisfaction to us to have you close at hand.'

'There is no cause for anxiety now about your lady. Your doctors had not diagnosed the disease correctly. If I had come two hours later, there would have been no hope. But now you can consider the danger over.'

On the Satrap's insistence, he consented to occupy one of the royal apartments.

On the fourth day, the Satrap's wife began to sit up, and the deep lines on her face were soon fading away. Of all those about her, the most delighted was Roshna. On the very day after their first meeting, she brought in her own arms and gave to the physician a cloak made out of two valuable pieces of cloth, a present from the Satrap. With this cloak, a gilded belt, and gold-clasped shoes, he was a very different figure from the man who had sat eating his melon among the beggars.

The patient was soon able to begin eating light food. On the sixth day, in the evening, she sent for the physician. He appeared before her a new man; it might have been a nephew of hers who was approaching. She made him sit down near her, and then said –

'I am very grateful to you, doctor. Mazda sent you to save my life in the middle of this lifeless wilderness. What is your native town?'

'Takshshila.'

'Takshshila! It is a very famous city, known everywhere for its learning. And you are its jewel!'

'Oh no, I am only an ordinary doctor, a beginner.'

'You are young, no doubt, but there is no contradiction between youth and wisdom. What is your name, my honoured physician?'

'Naagdatt Kashya.'

'It would be hard for me to pronounce your name in full! Is it enough if I call you "Naag"?'

'Quite enough, O' Great Lady-Satrap.'

'Where are you travelling to?'

'At present, to Persepolis.'

'And after that?'

'I left home simply because I had a longing to wander about.'

'We, too, are on our way to Persepolis; you must come with us. We shall take every care of you. Roshna, you must see to it yourself that our honoured physician is made comfortable; the slaves will be too careless.'

'I am seeing to it already, mother. I have made Sophia responsible for it.'

'The Greek girl my brother sent here for me?'

'Yes mother. You had no work for her to do, and she seems a very intelligent girl, so I have given her this work.'

'Then, doctor, you will come to Persepolis with us. I will do nothing to oppose your own wishes, but if you will stay in my household as our physician, I shall be happy.'

Naagdatt remained there for some time and then returned to his own room.

—3—

Naagdatt had not dreamed that the capital of one of the great kingdoms of the earth would be set among such bare, treeless hills, in such a 'poor' landscape. Persepolis was a great city. The royal palace, with its massive pillars of shining marble and its pinnacles that seemed to kiss the sky, gave the beholder some understanding of the wealth of the *King of Kings*. The opulence of the city corresponded with that of the palace; yet all this was the fruit of human labour. Nature, for her part, had been niggardly of her gifts.

There was no better illustration of the wealth of Persepolis and its ruler than the mansion of the king's sister, Afsha. When they reached the capital, she took pains to satisfy all Naagdatt's wants. Since she insisted on rewarding him, he asked for Sophia, and she was given to him. Even though it was difficult to follow her broken Persian, he could see at least that a living flame lurked in her bright eyes. After she became his, his slave that is to say, Naagdatt never treated her as a slave, and little by little her knowledge of the language improved. Naagdatt on his part, learned the Greek alphabet, and Sophia began the laborious task of teaching him her Attic[8] dialect. In the course of a year he grew quite well versed in it.

One day Sophia showed her gratitude to the young doctor by saying –

'How strange a thing destiny or fate is! I never hoped that I would fall into the hands of a master with such a kind nature as yours.'

'Oh, no, Sophia; if you had stayed with the Satrap's wife, perhaps you would have had an easier life still. But don't call me your master! The very name of slavery makes me feel ill.'

'But I am your slave.'

'You are not a slave. I have told the Satrap and his wife that. I have set you free from slavery.'

'Then I am not a slave now!'

'No; you are as free now as I am, and I will try and help you to go wherever you choose.'

'But if I want to go on staying with you, you will not send me away?'

'To go or to stay is at your own choice.'

'How deeply slavery degrades a human being! I used to see our own slaves in my father's house; I saw them laugh and enjoy their amusements; I never guessed how much anguish was hidden under that laughter. It was only when I became a slave myself that I discovered what a hell this bondage is.'

'Tell me, Sophia, if it is not too painful for you – how did you come to be a slave?'

'My father was a leading citizen of Athens. When King Philip of Macedonia conquered our city, he took his family with him and escaped to Asia by ship. We expected to find shelter there, but the town where we disembarked was besieged a few months later by the Persians. The city was sacked, and in the panic people fled in every direction; some of them were caught by the Persians. I was one of the captives, and because I was young and pretty I was sent to the general. The general sent me to the King. The King already possessed hundreds of Greek girls like me. He heard that his sister was coming, and sent me to her. Although I was a slave, my looks gave me a privileged position, so my experience has not been the same as what ordinary slave-women go through. All the same I know what torture it is. I felt that I was no longer a human being.'

'Then you never saw your father again, Sophia?'

'I do not believe that he can have escaped alive. Now we are all just dead leaves blown by the winds. Our dear Athens has been conquered. Even if he were still alive, what place is left for us to meet in?'

'Athens must be a great city, Sophia?'

'It was once, master!'

'Not master, Sophia! Call me Naag.'

'Naag, then! It was so once! Now it has fallen in ruins. Our republic, that clipped the great Darius's claws, has been broken to pieces by a petty king like Philip.'

'How did it happen, Sophia?'

'Even though we had repelled several Persian invasions, the belief rooted itself in the minds of many Athenian leaders that there could be no salvation for us until we too had built up a kingdom powerful enough to counterbalance the Persian monarchy. Philip would never have triumphed if he had not gained support from inside Athens.'

'Ah, Takshshila! You also have given birth to a Vishnugupt!'

'What are Takshshila and Vishnugupt?'

'Proud Takshshila, my birthplace, the Athens of the east. Our republic several times, like yours, put to flight Darius the Great and his successors; but now my old fellow student Vishnugupt is saying the same thing as your Athenians who supported Philip said.'

'So Takshshila is a republic, as Athens was?'

'Yes; and in our Takshshila there are no slaves. Any slave who sets foot on its soil becomes a free man.'

'Oh, Takshshila is a merciful land! But I could see from the beginning, Naag, that you did not know how to behave with slaves.'

'And I shall never let myself learn it. I told Vishnugupt that if we let the Magadh men into our famous land of Takshshila, the curse of slavery was certain to enter it with them.'

'Who are the Magadh men?'

'The Philips of India; a big Hindu kingdom to the east of Takshshila. We have been hard pressed by the Persian onslaughts, and year by year we have grown more weak and exhausted. It is true that Takshshila cannot hope to resist the *King of Kings* single-handed; but the remedy I believe in is to band together our various republics into a league.'

'But Naag, we have seen that tried in my own country. A great many of the republics of Hellas united in a league to resist the Persians but the league could not make itself permanent. Every republic is so determined to retain its own independence that they refuse to give enough power to the federation.'

'Perhaps my opinion will turn out to be wrong then, and Vishnugupt's right.'

'Vishnugupt sees no chance of success for a federation?'

'He says our enemies are so strong that no league of republics could resist them; that if several of them were to abolish their frontiers and unite in one big republic, there might be some hope, but that they will never agree to do.'

'Your friend may be right, Naag, but to the very end we never let the thought of voluntarily surrendering the independence of Athens enter our minds.'

'Then how did Athens, being a republic, come to admit slavery into its territory?'

'It did so as if to hasten its own ruin. The interests of the rich made slavery widespread and little by little the slaves multiplied until they were more numerous than their masters.'

'What struck you as the worst customs among the Persians?'

'Slavery, which existed in my country also; and then the seraglios kept by the King and the rich men.'

'Are there no seraglios in your country?'

'No. There even King Philip of Macedonia cannot marry more

than one wife. Here even minor officials marry several times.'

'In my country a man with several wives can be seen occasionally: it is rare, but I felt that it pointed the way towards the enslavement of women. Athens may have introduced slavery, but Takshshila has laid the foundation for it by admitting polygamy.'

'And for the accumulation of wealth in a few families.'

'I told Vishnugupt that in a republic anyone might amass as much wealth as he liked, but they could not pour it out like water, as kings do. You see for yourself, Sophia, what kind of manners are spreading here along with costly deer skins, silk, pearls and gems and such luxuries. Their rose-cheeked, coral-lipped owners never think how many millions must starve to provide them with their luxuries.'

'The little rain that falls on our poor houses is all sucked away into their brimming ocean!'

'Those who turn dross to gold die hungry and naked, while those who turn gold to dross wallow in pleasure. I have been in the King's presence three times, and each time I came back with my brain burning. In all his magnificence I saw the misery of the toilers who die under the frosts of winter and the burning suns of summer. His red wine looked like blood from the veins of his oppressed people. Persepolis suffocates me; I want to make haste and escape from it!'

'Where do you want to go, Naag?'

'First I want to know about you?'

'What place can I think of?'

'Greece!'

'I should be happy there.'

'Then let us go to Greece!'

'But on the way somebody may capture me again, and this time I shall not find another protector like Naag.'

Her voice fell to a whisper, and her fine wide eyes had a look of terror in them. He stroked the golden hair that fell over her ear, saying –

'I have thought of a plan to prevent that, but first I must have your consent to it.'

'What?'

'I shall get the Satrap and his wife and the King to give me a letter, declaring that I am the King's honoured Hindu physician.'

'Yes, then nobody will molest you!'

'And if you are willing to appear to the world as the physician's wife. I will have your name too put in the letters.'

Tears started into her eyes; she clasped Naagdatt's hands in her own.

'You are so kind, Naag,' she exclaimed, 'and yet you are perfectly unconscious of it! You are so handsome, and yet you have never noticed glances stolen at you from "topaz-sapphire" eyes! Naag! Roshna has confessed to me a hundred times that she loves you. There is some sickly cousin of hers to whom her parents want to marry her; but it is you she loves.'

'It was a good thing I did not know it, or I should have had to make her a refusal. Sophia! I was not born for any of these palace creatures. Perhaps I was not born for any woman, for there will be no easy life to dream away for the woman who loves a man like me. However, if you are willing, I will have you described everywhere in the King's letters as my wife. Perhaps in Greece you will find someone you love; if so, you will be free to go wherever you want.'

—4—

Everywhere Naagdatt the physician met with respectful treatment: he was a Hindu physician, he had been in attendance on King Darius of Persia, and he possessed a wonderful mastery of the art of healing. He had learned Greek while he was in Persepolis, and he had Sophia as his companion. He visited Macedonia, and met Aristotle, the tutor of Philip's son Alexander. Naagdatt was himself versed in philosophy – that is, in the philosophy of India. Naagdatt did not like Aristotle's love for monarchy, yet when he left Macedonia he had developed a great respect for him. What pleased him most of all in Aristotle was that the latter made Nature, experimental science, and not abstract thought, the touchstone of truth. Aristotle assigned a very high place to action and experience. Naagdatt regretted that the philosophers of his own country were bent on excogitating all truth from their inner consciousness alone. He heard much praise of Aristotle's intelligent pupil from the tutor's mouth, and himself had several conversations with him. He observed in the youth, besides exceptional vigour, an exceptional strength of judgment.

Naagdatt obtained Aristotle's permission to return and meet him again after visiting Athens; he little knew that this was fated to be his last meeting with the Greek philosopher.

He entered the city of Athens, nursery of heroes and standard bearer of democracy, with the same sensations of love and reverence as he felt towards Takshshila. The city was now again inhabited, but Sophia told him that it was no longer the Athens of old. The temples of Zeus and Aphrodite were still adorned with the beautiful creations of immortal sculptors; but the Athenians had lost the intellectual quickness, the pulsing life, that Sophia had once seen in them.

The present owner of her father's house, or rather of a new house built on its site, was a trader from Macedon. The sight of this house made her so dispirited that for a whole day and night she had to struggle against her natural melancholy, though she said little. Sometimes a shower of tears fell from her eyes; sometimes she sat as motionless as a marble statue. Naagdatt divined that it was this altered aspect of the loved home of her childhood that had plunged her in such a sorrowful mood. But it was difficult for him, since no opportunity of consoling her offered itself, and the grief that had pierced Sophia's heart made its impression, before it passed away, on Naagdatt as well.

When Sophia came to herself again, she seemed quite changed. She had never thought much of adorning herself; but now she bound her loose golden hair with a chaplet of fresh flowers, in the style of the maidens of republican Athens. She wore the handsome Greek tunic, falling in several pleats to the feet, and ornamented sandals. There was a dazzling combination of youth, beauty and health in her well-shaped forehead, her rosy cheeks, and her firm mouth. A smile of joy played all the time on her lips.

Naagdatt was not surprised at this, but was very glad.

'Dear Naag!' said Sophia, when he questioned her, 'I always believed until now that life contained nothing but sorrow and trouble, but now I am seeing that I was wrong in thinking so. To have such a one-sided opinion of life takes away from the value of living, and weakens one's strength for performing its tasks. After all, Naag, you have just as much to grieve, when you think of the future of Takshshila; but you keep your brain calm and use all your energy to think of plans for it.'

'Sophia, I am very glad to see you so happy.'

'Why should I not be happy? I have come home to Athens and found my beloved here.'

'That is something to give you even more joy,' answered Naagdatt, with a keen thrill of satisfaction, 'to have found the one you love after so many days.'

'I see you are more than a man, Naag, you are above the gods themselves! There is not even a spark of jealousy in you.'

'Jealousy! Why should there be any jealousy? Didn't I undertake to bring you safe to Greece, Sophie? Didn't I tell you that you could look for your beloved there?'

'Yes, you told me that.'

'As soon as I saw you looking so much more cheerful, I began to think that you must have found something very dear to you.'

'You guessed right, Naag.'

'Well, let me invite him here, or if he can't come here let me go and see him.'

'But why are you so impatient?'

'Am I really impatient? Yes, what you say is true.'

He tried to control himself. Sophia began to be afraid that she would not be able to hold her tears back. She turned her face away as she said –

'You can see him: but you must have an Athenian young man's costume, it is better than this.'

'I'll get that new cloak and the new sandals you bought yesterday and put them on.'

'Go and put them on, and I'll get a garland that Lydia is making for my lover.'

'Good,' said Naagdatt, going into the next room. Sophia stood in front of the big mirror in the sitting room, and quickly smoothed down her dress and her flower ornaments; then she hung a garland behind the mirror, went softly to the door and called –

'Naag! It is getting late; I don't want my lover to have gone out in search of pleasure.'

'I'm coming quickly! What kind of a cloak is this you have got me; its fold doesn't hang properly!'

'I'll arrange it for you.'

'Thank you!'

It was easy to put the disorderly fold straight. Then Naagdatt put on his new sandals. Sophia could not bring herself to look at his bright face. She caught him by the hand, exclaiming –

'First come and look at your new clothes in the mirror!'

'You have seen them, Sophia, isn't that enough? My clothes must be quite respectable.'

'Yes, I know they are respectable, but it won't do you any harm to take one look at them.'

She made him stand in front of the mirror; he began to stare at his costume. Sophia drew out the garland.

'I have made this for my love,' she said.

'It is a very pretty garland, Sophia.'

'But I can't tell how it will look on him.'

'Oh, it will look very well!'

'His hair is yellow, and this chaplet is all roses.'

'It will go quite well.'

'Just put it over your head and let me look.'

'If you like. My hair is yellow too.'

'That is why I want to make certain.'

She slipped it over his head and looked at it from the front, and then asking him to turn away from the mirror, added – 'So today you will see my love, Naag. Just now – look at this!'

Naagdatt turned his head; she was pointing her finger at his reflection in the mirror.

'This is my love!' she whispered with swimming eyes.

And the next moment she had caught him in her arms and pressed her lips to his. Naagdatt was silent. Sophia released his lips, and laying her cheek against his, said –

'My dearest! How fine he is, Naag!'

'Sophia, how can I think myself worthy of you?'

'I know I am worthy of you dear Naag! Now we shall be with each other until we die.'

Naagdatt could not restrain his tears – 'Until we die,' he repeated.

—5—

Naagdatt had a great desire to see the Bay of Salamis, where the Greek navy had inflicted a crushing defeat on the Persians. He and Sophia were on their way together to visit it. He had discovered a new energy in himself and his thoughts were turning continually to Takshshila. On the way they stopped to rest under a tree and Sophia remarked –

'You must have heard, Naag, that Philip is dead, and that Alexander has become king of Macedonia and is collecting a very strong army.'

'Yes. His ambition is to make himself master of all the Aegean coasts. But its eastern and southern coasts are in the hands of the Persians.'

'Which means that he intends to declare war on Persia.'

'And therefore he wants to enlist the support of democratic Greece in building up his empire. His plan is to kill two birds with the same stone, Sophia: to expel the *King of Kings* from the Aegean, if not drive him even further back, and to inspire the proud Greek republics with enthusiasm for a monarch.'

'That is the counsel Aristotle gave him; Aristotle has fanned the flame of his ambition.'

'Aristotle, the philosopher?'

'Yes. His master Plato drew up a scheme of a model republic; but he also wanted to make the common people mere ploughmen or the like. Aristotle, instead of a perfect republic, conceived of a perfect ruler, a universal monarch. Who knows how far this Greek world-conqueror may march and drive back the *King of Kings*!'

'Once he sets out, Sophia, it will not be in his own power to call a halt. And away in India my old comrade Vishnugupt Chanakya has gone to Magadh to look for a universal monarch!'

'Perhaps the Greek conqueror and the Indian conqueror will come face to face on the banks of the Indus!'

'If not in this generation, then in the next, Sophia! But how small the world will have grown then!'

From the coast they embarked on a ship for Salamis. The sea was calm, there was hardly any wind blowing. Sophia and Naagdatt gazed with gratitude at these waves which, two centuries before, had lent their aid to the destruction of the Persian fleet.

When they had sailed far out from land, a violent storm broke on them. It seemed to them as if they were experiencing the very storm that had broken long ago on the Persians. Just then they noticed that the faces of the crew were full of terror, and realized that the sail had carried away. The ship swung sideways. What was about to happen was only too clear. Sophia put her arms round Naagdatt and drew him to her breast. There was a smile on her lips as she murmured –

'Until we die ...'

'Yes! Until we die.'

He pressed his lips against hers, and they lay locked in each other's arms. Another moment and the vessel foundered. They had, indeed, stayed together until death.

1 2 3 4 5 6 7 8 9 10
20 19 18 17 16 15 14 13 12 **11**

Prabha

REGION : NORTH INDIA
TIME : 50 CE

With this story we enter the period of the more familiar history of India.

—1—

Saket had never formerly become the capital of any ruler. King Prasenjit of Kosal, the contemporary of Buddh, had indeed possessed a palace there; but his capital had been Shravasti, some fifty miles away. His son-in-law Ajatshatru destroyed the independence of Kosal, and from that moment the fortunes of Shravasti decayed. Saket, standing on the river Saryu, had been from the first a great centre of waterborne traffic, and also, since it was on the caravan route between the east (Prachi) and the Uttarapath (Panjab), a centre of commercial movements by road, it retained this position for a long time.

Chandrgupt Maurya, the pupil of Vishnugupt Chanakya, extended the kingdom of Magadh, first up to Takshshila, and then, after defeating the Greek ruler Seleucus, as far as Herat and the Amu Darya, well to the west of the Hindu Kush range. Under Chandrgupt and the Maurya dynasty, Saket continued to be no more than a commercial centre. It was Pushyamitr, the general who overthrew the Maurya dynasty, who first conferred on this city the status of a capital; though without, perhaps, abolishing the preeminence of Patliputr (Patna). The new name – Ayodhya – was popularized by Valmiki, when he wrote his *Ramayan*[1] in the reign of Pushyamitr or some later king of the Shung dynasty. There can be no doubt that Ashvghosh had a keen appreciation of the fascinating poetry of Valmiki; and it is not to be wondered that Valmiki sought the patronage of the Shung rulers

– just as Kalidas sought that of Chandrgupt Vikramaditya – or that, in order to magnify the glory of the Shung capital, he changed the setting of the Jatak (Buddhist) legends from Varanasi,[2] the capital of King Dashrath, to Saket or Ayodhya. He extolled the Shung emperor, Pushyamitr or Agnimitr in his poem, under the figure of Ram; just as Kalidas extolled Chandrgupt Vikramaditya under the figure of Raghu in his *Raghuvamsh*[3] and his son Kumargupt under that of Kumar in *Kumarsambhav*.[4]

When the commander Pushyamitr put his master to death, he failed to gain control of the entire Mauryan Empire. The whole of the Panjab fell into the hands of the Greek ruler Menander, who once even laid siege to Saket, according to the account left by the Brahmin Patanjali, the household priest of Pushyamitr. We learn from the same source that in the early days of Pushyamitr's reign Saket had a position of special importance, and that at that period its name had not yet changed to Ayodhya.

Coming down now to two centuries later, we still find Saket as the home of opulent merchants. Where Lakshmi – the Goddess of Wealth – had her seat, Sarasvati – the Goddess of Learning – could not lack some measure of respect, and that religion and Brahmins should abound there was as natural as that flies should be drawn to honey. Among these Brahmins was one clan, distinguished for its wealth and scholarship, the name of whose senior member time has buried in oblivion, while his wife's name was immortalized by her son. This lady was Suvarnakshi;[5] she owed this name to her eyes, which had a touch of golden in them. In that age blue and golden eyes were not uncommon in Brahmin or Kshatriya families, and a yellowish eye was considered no blemish. Suvarnakshi had one son, who possessed, like herself, a pair of golden eyes, yellow hair, and fair complexion.

—2—

It was springtime. Everywhere mango blossoms breathed their perfume on the air. The trees had shed their old leaves and clothed themselves afresh. Today was the ninth day of the moon of the month of Chaitr.[6] The people of Saket, men and women, were gathered on the bank of the river Saryu, ready to go swimming. Swimming in the river was their way of celebrating the spring festival. Young men and women took part equally in the competition, swimming naked from the same landing steps. Among the girls were numerous Greeks with skins white as snow; their lovely bodies were as perfect as the marble statues of the Greek sculptors, and they had wonderful golden or auburn tresses. There were just as many Brahmin maidens, with ebony or yellow hair and golden eyes, not inferior to any of the Greeks in beauty. Nor was there less charm in the transient, youthful bloom of the dark-haired, wheat-coloured girls of Vaishyas.[7]

On this day all the virgin beauty of Saket, from every corner of the city, was gathered on the bank. Young men of the same diverse stocks were throwing off their clothes and preparing to dive into the river; men with bodies hardened by exercise, well rounded and handsome, of every shade of colour from pure white to wheat-yellow. Their hair, faces and noses bore the distinguishing marks of their origin. No better opportunity than this swimming festival could be afforded for scrutinizing the person of any youth or maiden. It was an occasion when a number of *svayamvars*[8] were performed every year. Parents encouraged their children to make use of it in this way, which was quite proper to the occasion.

The competitors went across the river in boats, and then dived in to swim back. Tresses of golden, auburn, pale yellow or reddish hair gleamed on the blue water, while blue-black tresses lost themselves in its colour, as the swimmers forced themselves across the current with threshing arms. A flotilla of small boats kept pace with them, the people in them urging on the swimmers or pulling out of the water those who became exhausted, for some mishaps were possible among thousands of competitors. Every swimmer was putting out all his strength in the effort to forge ahead. By the time two thirds of the river's breadth had been crossed, a great many of those in the race were exhausted. Just then two swimmers were seen pressing forward, ahead of the others. The point reached by them was marked by two floating masses of hair; one yellow, the other auburn. As the bank drew close their exertions became still more violent, while the onlookers in the boats held their breath with excitement: the two heads far ahead of all rivals were exactly abreast of each other. The goal was now very near. Everyone was hoping to see one of the two take the lead, but neither seemed able to shake the other off. It even appeared that someone in the boats heard them encouraging each other to win.

They reached the bank simultaneously. One was a young man, the other a girl. The crowd applauded them while they put on their clothes and then they were carried off in open palanquins under a rain of flowers from the onlookers. They were now able to take a closer view of each other. Not only their good swimming, but their good looks as well were the object of the bystanders' admiration.

'I know the maiden,' one of these remarked; 'but who is the young man, *saumya*?'[9]

'Have you never heard of Ashvghosh, the son of Suvarnakshi?'

'No, I only know the Brahmins related to my own family priest, we merchants have no leisure for hearing things.'

'Oh, but Ashvghosh's reputation for learning has spread far beyond Saket,' exclaimed a third. 'He is an expert master of all the Veds and all learned subjects.'

'But he can't be more than twenty-four years old,' observed the first speaker.

'Yes, he is just twenty-four, and people read his songs and sing them in raptures.'

'So this is the poet Ashvghosh, whose love songs are on the lips of all our young people!'

'The same man. And what is the girl's name, *saumya*?'

'Prabha; her father, Dattmitr belongs to a distinguished family in our Greek community here, and he is a merchant well known all over Kosal.'

'Oh, that explains it; we seldom see such beauty in any other community. How soft her body is to look at! And yet what a strong swimmer!'

'Her parents are both unusually healthy and strong.'

The crowds which thronged the city park to pay their warm tribute to the two swimmers learned all about them; and the bashful pair were making each other's acquaintance.

—3—

The flower gardens of Saket were a memorial of the reign of the General Pushyamitr. The latter had expended much money and labour in laying them out; and though his dynasty ruled no longer, and Saket was not now the capital of any other royal family, the townspeople regarded them as a valuable possession of Saket, and still maintained them in as good order as in the days when Pushyamitr was on the throne. In the centre of the park was a handsome lake on whose clear blue water floated lotus plants of many species, such as *padm*, *saroj*, and *pundrik* in full bloom, and a pair of swans. It was terraced all round with steps of white stone leading down into the water, and gleaming like crystal. A wide grass border stretched round the margin of the pool. Scattered beds were bright with roses, jasmine and many other flowers; elsewhere stretched rows of *ashok* plants and other shrubs. There were arbours, big and small, overhung with trailing creepers and floored with stone; there were fields where boys and girls played at ball; there were little ornamental hills of rock or earth, covered with green foliage; there were fountains whose falling spray seemed to mimic showers of rain.

In the afternoons a throng of young people of Saket was often to be seen about one of the arbours; they were people who could not find room inside it. Today, there was a crowd of this sort, but it stood all round in silence. All seemed to be listening intently to something from the arbour. Inside, on the stone-flagged floor, sat the same youth who, a month before, had purposely failed to win the swimming race. He wore a tunic of smooth, soft silk; his long, fair hair was gathered up on top of his head. He held a stringed instrument, the Mukhar Veena,[10] from which the effortless play of his fingers drew forth a bewitching melody. He was singing to his instrument, with eyes half closed, lost in his music; not another poet's song, but his own. He had just finished his Sanskrit poem – '*Vasant Kokila*' ('Spring Cuckoo') – and after Sanskrit he must sing something in Prakrit, for the poet-musician knew that Prakrit was the better-loved language of his audience. He sang his recent composition, '*Urvashi Viyog*' ('Separation from Urvashi'): the dancing girl of heaven has been stolen away, and

Pururava, who calls her his *apsara* (water-nymph), is searching for her, calling her name, among hills, streams, lakes, woods, thickets, everywhere; he cannot find her, but he hears her words echoing in the wind. The singer's own eyes filled with tears as he sang of the tears of Pururava, and all his hearers wept with him.

At the conclusion of the music, the crowd broke up and dispersed. When Ashvghosh emerged, a group of young folk, who had lingered, surrounded him. Among them, with flushed and swollen eyes, stood Prabha.

'What a great poet you are!' cried a youth, coming up to him.

'A great poet? I am not even a poet, *saumya*.'

'Let me say what I think! Listen; we Greeks here in Saket have a small theatre.'

'For dances? I am very fond of dancing, too.'

'Not only for that; we often have some acting there as well.'

'Acting?'

'Yes; it has a very honoured place among Greek customs. We have painted scenery to call up different ages and countries, and we try to represent all the episodes in a realistic manner.'

'I am very sorry to think that though I was born in Saket, I have never seen any of this acting.'

'Our audience is confined to the Greek families of Saket and a few of their close friends, so that there are many people in Saket to whom Greek acting ...'

'Acting – that is, performing plays?'

'Yes, plays. Well, we are going to perform one today, and we should like you to see it.'

'Very gladly! It is very kind of you and your friends to invite me.' Ashvghosh went away with them, and a place was given him in the theatre, near the stage. The performance was of a Greek tragic drama, translated into Prakrit. All the roles were taken by young men and women of Greek descent, and all the actors and actresses wore Greek costumes. The various scenes had likewise been painted in the Greek style. The heroine was Ashvghosh's acquaintance, Prabha, and her brilliant acting carried him away. During an interval, the Greek youth who was previously known to Ashvghosh, seized the opportunity of begging him to sing '*Urvashi Viyog*' again. He picked up his *veena* without hesitation, and went up to the stage. Once more his music drew forth his own tears and those of his hearers. Once as he sang, his glance met the grieved eyes of Prabha.

When the play was over, all those who had taken part in it were introduced to the poet in their dressing room.

'In spite of living in Saket,' he said, 'I have been quite ignorant of this beautiful art. I am very grateful to you for giving me a view of a *prabhalok*[11] (bright world) I have never known.'

At the word 'Prabha' some of the girls looked at Prabha with a smile.

'An idea has come to me,' Ashvghosh went on, 'just as you have performed today a Greek play in a Prakrit translation, it seems to me that we might treat our own country's legends in the same form and put together some good plays ourselves.'

'We are quite confident that if a poet like you were to take it up, he could compose dramas even better than these Greek originals.'

'That is too much to expect! I am only fit to be an apprentice to your Greek playwrights. Well, shall I write a play on the story of Urvashi?'

'We shall be very glad to perform it! But you will have to take the part of Pururava.'

'I have no objection and I think with a little practice I shall not do it too badly.'

'We must get some scenery ready as well.'

'For the scenery we must have views of Pururava's country. I can paint a little myself and I shall be able to lend some help with it if I am needed.'

'It will be very good if we have the scenes painted under your direction. And you will have to give us instructions about the actors' costumes and ornaments. What other parts will there be?'

'We can't decide all the characters on the spot, friend. But we should keep the number small. How many should we have?'

'We can easily fill up sixteen parts or, say, twenty.'

'I shall try to limit the number to sixteen.'

'Well then, you yourself are to be Pururava, and as for Urvashi, how would our Prabha here do? You have seen her acting today.'

'To my inexperienced eyes she seemed quite perfect.'

'Very good: we decide on her for Urvashi. In our club nobody can refuse to take on any work he is given.'

A slight frown crept into Prabha's eyes, but when the leading youth turned to her, saying 'Well, Prabha?' she gave a hesitant assent.

—4—

Ashvghosh read through some Prakrit translations of Greek plays with the handsome young Greek, whose name was Buddhpriya, and discussed with him ideas about the scenery and so on. He borrowed Greek terms to describe stage settings, to commemorate the art of Hellas. He wrote a play in a mixture of Sanskrit and Prakrit, prose and verse. In that period the Prakrit vernacular was still so close to the literary Sanskrit that the play was understood quite easily in families familiar with either language. This *Urvashi Viyog* was the first Indian drama, and Ashvghosh the first Indian playwright. Though it was his first attempt, *Urvashi Viyog* was not less beautiful than his later plays, such as *Rashtrpal* ('Protector of the Nation'), or *Sariputr* ('Son of Sari').

While the scenery was being got ready and the performance rehearsed, the young poet forgot everything else, even food and drink. He felt that he was living through the most wonderful hours of his life. He and Prabha worked together for hours every day. Now the seeds of love sown in their hearts on the day of the race began to sprout. The young Greeks were anxious to see Ashvghosh linked to them as a kinsman, and therefore felt that they had an interest in encouraging the connection.

One day, after hours of labour with the brush, Ashvghosh came out of the theatre and sat down on a chair in the small garden adjoining it. A moment later Prabha also came out.

'What had you in your mind,' she asked in her natural, pleasant tone, 'while you were composing your "*Urvashi Viyog*"?'

'The tale of Urvashi and Pururava.'

'Of course, the story I know. You turned Urvashi into a water-nymph and kept calling her a nymph, didn't you?'

'Urvashi was a water-nymph.'

'Then in the poem you described Pururava, separated from

Urvashi, seeking her distractedly through streams and pools, hills and woods, and so on.'

'It was natural for Pururava to behave like that in his situation.'

'And then the singer of "*Urvashi Viyog*" let his own tears falling in the arbour make another accompaniment to his song, as well as the *veena*.'

'A singer or an actor must be absorbed in his theme, Prabha.'

'No! You don't want to tell me the truth.'

'What are you thinking?'

'I think that it was not the song of separation of any ancient Urvashi that you were singing.'

'What then?'

'Your real Urvashi was in fact Ur-basi,[12] who was an *apsara*[13] – a swimmer in the Saryu river.'

'Well?'

'This nymph's real Pururava was not wandering in search of her through any Himalayan hills or forests or streams or lakes or thickets, but near the Saryu, the flower-garden pool, the artificial hills and pleasure-groves and creepers of Saket.'

'Well?'

'His tears were not flowing in sympathy with any ancient Pururava, but to quench the fire that was burning his own heart.'

'Prabha, let me tell you something else.'

'Tell me! All this time I have been talking more than you.'

'That day, when I came out of the arbour, I saw that your sweet blue eyes were swollen and inflamed.'

'You had been making me cry with your music.'

'That music spoke to you of your own separation from a lover.'

'But the Urvashi in your poem had a heart of stone; at least that is how you had portrayed her.'

'Because I was troubled and helpless.'

'Why? What were you thinking?'

'... that she had shone only for a moment, like lightning, and I should never be able to enjoy the sight of her again; that she must have forgotten me long since.'

'Were you so insignificant – you, a poet?'

'When a man has nothing to give him self-confidence, what can he think of himself apart from being insignificant?'

'You are the great poet not only of Saket but of all our wide land. You are the winner of Saket's swimming race. Everyone in Saket is loud in praise of your learning; and as for the women, the most beautiful girls of Saket are ready to make you the light of their eyes ...'

'What use that? For me, my Urvashi alone mattered. When I went for two weeks without seeing her, life seemed hollow. I am telling the truth, Prabha. I never found my mind so weak as then. Had I not seen you for another week, I don't know what I should have done.'

'My poet, you should not be so selfish. You are our country's immortal singer. What great hopes she has of you! Do you know how highly your *Urvashi Viyog* is being praised?'

'I have heard nothing.'

'Last week a relation of mine, a Greek merchant, came here from Bharukachh. There is a big Greek settlement there. In Saket we Greeks have turned into Hindus,[14] but over there they have not forgotten their own language. Many traders and scholars come to Bharukachh from Greece. This relation of mine is very well read in Greek literature. He compared your play with the compositions of the great Greek dramatist Euripides and made a copy of it to take away with him. He said he would translate it into Greek and send it to King Ptolemy of Egypt, who is a great lover of the theatre. There are always ships sailing between Bharukachh and Egypt. While I listened to him talking, my heart was bursting with pride.'

'Your heart's pride is everything for me, Prabha.'

'You don't know your own worth.'

'I know it now. Prabha, you have been its touchstone.'

'No, you must not feel like that. Ashvghosh the lover of Prabha, and Ashvghosh the great poet of the age are two individuals; you must keep them apart. The lover may say and do what he likes, but the great poet is more important and you must regard him as belonging to the whole world.'

'I will do whatever you tell me.'

'I never hoped that I should have such good fortune.'

'Why?'

'I was thinking that you must have forgotten me.'

'You were so insignificant!'

'Before you I was, I still am.'

'You have given me a new gift of poetry. I am finding a fresh purpose, a fresh inspiration, in my poems. My *Urvashi Viyog* was inspired by you, the song as well as the play. I am naturalizing the art of drama in our country, Prabha! But how could you imagine that I would forget you?'

'How could I ever dream of being able to reach you! When I came to learn all your qualities, one by one, I felt nothing but despair. And then I saw all the young beauties of Saket infatuated with you, one after the other; that was enough to deprive me of hope. Besides, I heard that you belonged to a very high Brahmin family, and although I may belong to a Greek family which is included in the Rajput[15] caste, the highest after the Brahmins, how could my love be accepted by one of you Brahmin aristocrats, who never marry without investigating the bride's ancestry on both sides for seven generations?'

'I am sorry to think that is how I appeared to you, Prabha.'

'So you ... ,' her tongue faltered.

'Prabha!' he exclaimed, kissing her wet eyes and pressing her to his breast, 'Ashvghosh will always be yours. Even death cannot take him from you.'

Tears were pouring from her eyes, and he wiped them away as he held her clasped in his arms.

His play was performed excellently, several times over, and was seen by all the wonderstruck citizens of Saket, who had never suspected that dramatic art could be so rich and lofty. After the final curtain Ashvghosh repeatedly declared that he had done nothing but borrow from the Greek stage; but his play was so distinct in its style that no one could trace any element of foreign influence in it.

His songs and poems in Sanskrit and Prakrit had spread beyond the limits of Saket and even of Kosal; his plays attained an even wider celebrity. They speedily found their way on to the stage in cities like Ujjain, Dashpur, Supparak, Bharukachh, Shakla, Takshshila and Patliputr, where there were Greek colonies and theatres, and became popular with the entire aristocracy and commercial class.

—5—

That Ashvghosh was appearing on the stage and was in love with a Greek girl could not be kept hidden from his parents. His father was particularly disturbed by the news, and got Suvarnakshi to try and make him understand his position. When his mother told him that such a marriage, for such a family as theirs, was forbidden by religion, Ashvghosh drew on his Vedic lore and placed before her a mass of evidence compiled from the precepts of the Rishis. (Some of these he later collected in his *Vajrchhedika*, which is still to be found included among the texts of the Upnishads.) But his mother only replied –

'That is all very well, my son, but we Brahmins today do not follow those antiquated customs.'

'Then I shall introduce a new standard of good conduct for Brahmins.'

His mother could not be reassured with his arguments but when he told her that he could not live without Prabha, she came over to his side, saying, 'My son, you are all I have.'

One day Ashvghosh sent Prabha to visit his mother. When the latter saw that Prabha's virtue and sweetness of temper equalled her beauty, she gave the girl her blessing.

But the father could not give way. He said plainly to Ashvghosh one day –

'Our family holds a very high position in the Brahmin community. For many generations, only brides of the highest Brahmin families have entered our house. If you stoop now to this marriage you desire, we and our descendants for ever will be polluted. All our rank and dignity will be lost.'

But for Ashvghosh, to renounce Prabha was unthinkable.

His father then made ingratiating approaches to Prabha's parents, but it was of no avail. Finally, he went to Prabha herself and threw his turban at her feet[16] in token of appeal. Her only answer was that she would talk to Ashvghosh about what he had said.

—6—

Prabha and Ashvghosh became inseparable companions. If one of them visited the river bank, the park, the pilgrims' fair-ground, the dance theatre, the playhouse, or any other spot, the other was sure to be there too. His heart expanded in her presence like a flower in sunlight. In the radiance of the milk-white moon, the pair would often stroll beside the river, and there pass their time not only in love-play but in discussion of the serious matters of life too.

One moonlit night, beside the dark flood of the Saryu, Ashvghosh was drawing in his mind a picture of Prabha's beauty as she sat on the glimmering sand. Suddenly and impulsively he exclaimed –

'Prabha, you are my music! It was your inspiration that made me write my "*Urvashi Viyog*", and your beauty will help me to create so much beauty in poetry. Poetry is not an externalization of inner feeling, but an inward expression of things around us. You have taught me the truth of that, love.'

As he spoke, Prabha stretched herself out on the cold sand. Ashvghosh looked at her long fresh tresses, floating on the sand, and took her head on to his lap. She gazed up at the outline of his face and when he had finished speaking she said –

'I agree with all that you say. Yes, indeed, poetry cannot fulfil itself without the inspiration of sensuous beauty. I should have liked to make a picture of you in poetical words, though all I can make is a silent portrait, poetry is not mine to command. I told you that day that you must think of yourself as a double individual, and that you must think chiefly of the immortal Ashvghosh, the great poet of the age, because he is not one person's treasure, but the world's treasure. You remember the words of that learned monk, whom we went to see two days ago from the Kalkaram monastery?'

'He seemed remarkably intelligent.'

'Yes, and he has travelled very widely. He was born in Egypt at Alexandria.'

'So I heard. There is one thing I can't understand, dearest. Why do all the Greeks have such a respect for Buddhism?'

'Because it seems to harmonize with their character and their independent nature.'

'But Buddhism tries to make everyone passionless, ascetic, and monkish.'

'Among Buddhists the monks are very few compared with the number of those living with their households, and they are second to none in recognizing the blessings of family life.'

'After all, there are so many other religions in this country; why should the Greeks admire Buddhism in particular?'

'It is the most liberal of all these religions. When our ancestors entered India, everyone called us *mlechhs*[17] and looked down on us. I am not speaking only of the invading Greek armies; the same treatment was given to Greeks who came to settle here or for such purposes as trade. But Buddhists showed no contempt for them. Of course, the Greeks had got to know of Buddhism in their own country.'

'In Greece itself?'

'In the time of Ashok, the grandson of Chandrgupt Maurya, a good many Buddhist monks made their way into Greek territories. The monk we met, Dharmrakshit,[18] did not become a monk after coming to India; he was already a monk in a monastery at Alexandria.'

'I want to meet him again, Prabha.'

'You must certainly meet him. He will talk to you about other deep problems. Only, darling, don't let hearing this Buddhist turn you into an ascetic and make you give me up!' She folded him in her arms, as if someone were trying to pull him away.

'There were some things about Kalkaram that seemed to me very attractive. The thought came into my head: what if all our country could be made like it?'

'No, darling!' exclaimed Prabha, sitting up. 'You mustn't think of going into the monastery and leaving me!'

'Leaving you, as long as I live! Impossible! I was just thinking about the absence of distinctions and divisions there. Imagine, there are learned monks of many lands, like the Greek Dharmrakshit or the Persian Suman, and along with them monks of our country, of every class from Brahmins to Chandals[19] (menials), all of them living together, eating and drinking together, studying together. What is the name of that old dark-skinned monk at Kalkaram?'

'*Mahasthavir*[20] Dharmsen. He is the head of all the monks of the Saket monasteries.'

'I have heard that he was born in the Chandal lineage. My uncle, the monk Shubhgupt, bows before him when he greets him. Look at the difference: one is a rich Brahmin of a prestigious Shrotriya family and the other – a son of the Chandals – Dharmsen!'

'But Mahasthavir Dharmsen is also a very wise man.'

'I am saying it from the religious point of view of the Brahmins, Prabha! If it were in their power, would Dharmsen be even considered human, to say nothing of worshipping him like a deity?'

'Buddh has named his Sangh[21] an ocean. Whoever enters that ocean, just like rivers, abandoning their identity, becomes a part of it.'

'But dearest! Why do the Buddhist family men not do the same?'

'In a country of family men, Buddhists can't live by segregating themselves from the rest. After all they too have responsibilities towards their families.'

'I think it would be very good if all the people of town and countryside abolished their differences as the monks of Kalkaram have done, and had no caste divisions or racial divisions.'

'There is one thing I have not told you, dearest. One day your father came and threw his turban at my feet, and begged me to set you free.'

'As if your setting me free would give him back his son! What did you say to him, Prabha?'

'I only said I would talk to you about it.'

'Well, you have talked to me. I feel a bottomless disgust at the hypocrisy of our Brahmins. I feel all my body on fire with that disgust: First they say that they believe in their holy scriptures; well, I read through all their books, laboriously and zealously. But what they really believe, I can't discover. Perhaps they really only believe in their own self-interest. When you confront them with a quotation from one of their ancient sages, they only say – "Our customs nowadays are different". They should follow either custom, or the precepts of the sages, one or the other. Isn't it only when someone has destroyed the old dispensation that a new practice can come into existence? They deserve to be known as a timid, cowardly, selfish lot. All they want is beef of the fat calves to eat and hefty endowments to enjoy. In return they are ready to do anything in the world to please the kings, feudal lords who are their patrons.'

'There is no place in their religion for the poor – and the low castes, as they call them, are always poor.'

'Yes. They have recognized invading races like the Greeks, Shakas and Abhirs, as Kshatriya-Rajput because these people had power and wealth, and handsome donations could be extracted from them! But the menials, scavengers and slaves of our own country these Brahmins have doomed to remain forever in the dust. I think any religion a disgrace to humanity which does not elevate man's heart, which classifies men according to the size of their purse or their stick. The world changes; I have studied the rules and practices laid down in Brahman scriptures, from the most ancient to the newest, and I have seen a complete revolution taking place in them.

'But if you say as much today to the Brahmins, they want to persuade you that all those things are eternal and fixed. What stupidity it all is, darling!'

'I have not become the cause of all these fiery ideas, Ashvghosh?'

'Yes, you have, and I am grateful for it my darling! You have given new vitality and inspiration to my poetry and you are helping me very greatly by doing the same to my power of insight. I used to fancy that I had already drained the cup of knowledge. That is a false conceit that a Brahmin falls victim to easily. But now I realize that knowledge is not limited to the Brahmins' *shrutis*[22] and their palm- and birch-leaf[23] volumes; it is vaster than all of them.'

'I am only a woman.'

'I look upon with disgust anyone who considers someone inferior merely for being a woman.'

'Still, among the Greeks women are respected more than among others. Even if it means dying without children, a man can never remarry while his first wife is alive.'

'And these Brahmins keep on marrying hundreds of women, simply to get money. Shameful! I am glad that no Greeks follow the Brahmin religion.'

'Even though we are Buddhists, Brahmins come to our house to perform ceremonies.'

'When they have admitted the Greeks as Kshatriyas, for their own benefit, why should they hesitate to do that – it is a question of their fees.'

'So it is not I who has dispelled your pride in your Brahminism?'

'No harm if you had. If Brahmin pride tries to come between me and you, I consider it a worthless, despicable thing.'

'It makes me so happy to know that you love me so much, Ashvghosh!'

'From the core of my heart, dearest! If I lost your love, all my roots would wither.'

'Then do you want to honour my love by making me a gift?'

'I will give away anything except that love!'

'If my love ever does the least harm to my immortal Ashvghosh, the great poet of the age, then it should be cursed.'

'What do you mean my beloved?'

'I don't want to put any obstacle in the way of our love, but I want it to help you in creating immortal things, and if I were to die ...' Ashvghosh sprang up as though suddenly beside himself, lifted Prabha, and strained her to his heart in a bear's hug. She saw that his cheeks were wet. Over and over again she kissed him and repeated –

'My Ghosh,' and then, when he grew calmer, she said, 'Listen, dearest, I want you to give something very big in return for my love, and you must give it.'

'There is nothing I cannot give you, Prabha.'

'But you didn't even let me finish what I was going to say.'

'You were trying to say something terrible.'

'But I am forced to say this terrible thing, if I am to be a true friend to my immortal Ashvghosh. My love wants my great poet to think of it as something immortal, as his own verses, and not to measure it by Prabha's body. The Prabha who belongs to the immortal part of Ashvghosh will have eternal youth and beauty. That is all I wanted to make you believe, from your heart.'

'You want to put an ideal Prabha in front of me instead of my living Prabha?'

'I think them equally real, darling. It is only this, that one of them will live for fifty years or a hundred years, and the other will live forever. Your Prabha will be immortal in your *Urvashi Viyog*, and to make my love immortal you must think of the immortal part of yourself. It has grown very late now, the river bank seems to have fallen asleep, we should go home.'

'I have been drawing a picture in my memory of the immortal Prabha.'

'Dearest! That is all I wanted to ask!' She pressed her silken hair over his cheeks and stood there silently.

—7—

It was a big courtyard with a colonnade running all round, and behind it the rooms of a three-storeyed building. In the colonnade some yellow clothes were drying on clotheslines. In one corner of the courtyard was a well, with a bathing place next to it. In the rest of the area were several trees, among them a *peepal*.[24] Round the latter was built a platform, and a bit further, a stone balustrade with niches for hundreds of small clay lamps.

Prabha knelt in prayer before this beautiful tree and then said –

'Dearest, it was a tree of this kind that the inspired Gautam was sitting under when by toilsome meditation he threw off all the perplexities of the soul and gained enlightenment and came to be known as Buddh (the wise). It is simply for the sake of this sweet memory that we always bend our heads when we pass a *peepal* tree.'

'By toilsome meditation he gained enlightenment! Such a living embodiment of wisdom deserves worship, Prabha; to worship such an embodiment of wisdom is to revere one's own struggle towards the soul's triumph.'

They both went up to the *Bhadant*[25] Dharmrakshit. He was sitting just now under a *bakul*[26] tree in the courtyard, where fresh flowers spread their sweet perfume. Prabha, like a Buddhist nun, saluted him by kneeling and putting her palms and forehead to the ground, Ashvghosh greeted him respectfully, but remained standing. Then they took some skin rugs that were lying on the ground and sat down. The Bhadant's disciples, seeing that Ashvghosh had come to hold a discussion with him, withdrew from there. After some ordinary talk that decorum required, Ashvghosh broached the question of philosophy.

'Noble Brahmin,' said the Bhadant, 'in the religion of the Buddhists, that is of the scholars, philosophy itself has been called a chain, and a very heavy chain.'

'Then, is there no place for philosophy in Buddhism?'

'Why no place? Buddhism is a philosophical religion. Only Buddh said that philosophy should be like a raft to ferry one to the other side of the river, not a burden to carry on one's head.'

'What did he mean? Raft?'

'Yes, when people come to a river and there is no boat, they build a raft to carry them across, but when they have got over they do not think themselves obliged by gratitude to lift up the logs and carry them on their shoulders.'

'A man who was bold enough to say that even for the sake of his religion must certainly have seen the truth and felt its force. Bhadant! Explain to us what it is in Buddh's philosophy that would enable us by knowledge of it to grasp wisdom with our own minds.'

'Disbelief in the soul, my son. The Brahmins believe that the soul is the eternal polestar, the imperishable essence. In the Buddhist universe no such imperishable element exists; hence this philosophy may be defined as one that dispenses with the soul, that sees everything as ephemeral, born one moment and vanishing the next.'

'This idea by itself is enough for me. I honour the Enlightened One most fervently for proclaiming this religion, built like a raft, and this denial of the soul. I have found what I was seeking. I felt already inside myself some stirrings of the same thought, but I was never able to define them. If men today would only guide themselves aright by the teachings of Buddh, the world would be a different place.'

'True, my son, true. In our homeland, Greece, profound philosophers arose; Pythagoras and Heraclitus among them, who lived at the same time as Buddh. Democritus, Plato, Aristotle came a little later. Those Greek philosophers thought deeply; but, except for Heraclitus, none of them could get beyond the notion of immortality. Existence had an unbounded fascination for them and, therefore, they wanted to impose its shackles on all futurity. Heraclitus indeed thought of the universe as something which is in constant flux – never the same for two consecutive moments, in the same way as Buddh; but there was an element of self-interest in his idea.'

'How can self-interest enter into philosophical speculation?'

'The belly plays its part in everything, my son! At that time our city of Athens was a republic, there was no kingship. At first political power was in the hands of aristocrats belonging to families like that of Heraclitus; later on the merchant class pushed them aside and took the power into its own hands. Heraclitus was dissatisfied with this state of affairs. He longed for a revolution – not to carry progress further, but to put the clock back.'

'We also need a revolution; one that will carry us forward, not push us back. I think the past is dead, honoured monk!'

'What you say is right, noble youth. Buddh wanted a revolution, one that would make the world a better place. He organized his Bhikshu-Sangh[27] as a kind of model for a world of tomorrow.'

'Where there would be no division of classes, no high or low.'

'Where happiness and labour would be equal for all. You might have seen Mahasthavir Dharmsen outside with his broom, sweeping?'

'That very dark man?'

'Yes. He is the loftiest of us all. Every day we kneel down before him in reverence. He is the head of all the monasteries of Kosal.'

'Is it true that he comes from the Chandal caste?'

'A monastery takes no account of caste, my son. It regards only a man's qualities. He is our head because of his learning and his virtue. He is our father. When he goes begging for alms, if he gets only just enough of something to grease his bowl, so to say, he will never eat without giving a share to his companions. That is what Buddh taught. All our property belongs to us in common except for three robes, a clay begging-bowl, a needle, drinking-pot, a comb and a girdle. All the rest – house, garden, benches, stools – all belong to our community. Some of our monasteries also own land. We examine a man thoroughly before admitting him, but once he has become a monk, a member of the community, he is the equal of all.'

'What if such a community were organized to include the entire nation?'

'How could that be, my son? When will kings and rich men submit to equality with others? Some monks admitted a slave into their fellowship. As a member, he ceased to be a slave and was the equal of his brethren. But his owner began to raise an outcry, and the other slave-owners supported him. The king himself is master of thousands of slaves. How could he tolerate such a blow at his property? What could Buddh do? He had to lay down that henceforth no slave was to be admitted into the community. Our community is a little island in an ocean full of classes and inequalities; it cannot be secure so long as poverty and slavery exist in the world.'

—8—

It was a full-moon night in autumn. Since early evening the white saucer of the moon had been afloat over the eastern horizon, and as the sun's last red rays, glowing on the horizon, faded from the sky, the cold white moonbeams flowed over it. Ashvghosh spent most of his time now at Prabha's house. The pair was sitting on the flat roof. 'Dearest,' said Prabha, 'the waves of the Saryu are calling me, those waves that first brought me in contact with you, that bound us together in love. Two years have gone by since then, but it seems as if it happened only today. How many moonlit nights we have passed on the river bank, and how sweet they always are! Tonight the spring moon is here again. Come, let us go to the river!'

They went off together. The river flowed at some distance from the city. They walked a long way on white sand gleaming in the moonlight. Prabha was carrying her slippers in her hand; it was pleasant to feel the sand crushing under her feet.

'How delightful it is, the touch of this river-sand!' she exclaimed, putting her arms round Ashvghosh.

'It tickles one's feet.'

'An exquisite feeling, it makes all one's hair prickle! Dear River Saryu!'

'I have thought sometimes, darling, that we ought to run away together. Run away to a country where there will be no one to spite our love, where you can inspire me and I can make songs for us to sing together to the *veena*. Here I can't bring my *veena* out to the sands on nights like this. People would come, and some of them would have eyes, black with spite.'

'Don't take it ill, but it seems to me sometimes that if I were to die ...'

Ashvghosh held her tightly in his arms as he cried – 'No, darling! Never! We shall go on as we are!'

'I mean something different. Just think if you were to die, I should be left all alone. That does happen in the world, doesn't it?'

'Yes, it happens.'

'You were not upset at the thought of your own death, Ashvghosh! And why? Because if I lost you, all the mountain of grief would fall on me alone!'

'It is a very cruel way of treating me to say such things, Prabha.' Prabha kissed him on the lips and comforted him.

'Life has many faces,' she said. 'It is not always full moon: there are also moonless nights. I was only saying: if one of us were lost, what ought the other to do? Do you know what I should do if I lost you?'

His head sank and he gave a long sigh. 'Tell me.'

'I should never put an end to my own life. The divine Buddh said that suicide was a foolish and blameworthy act. You know I have made myself quite skilful with the *veena*.'

'Very. How often I have given you the *veena* and gone on singing to it forgetting everything else.'

'Well, if that happens, my mortal Ashvghosh will have been taken away from me, but I can still give myself up to the immortal Ashvghosh, the poet of the ages. I will play your *veena* and sing your songs, through all India and in foreign lands; all my life, until the streams of our existences are reborn in another clime, another age, and reunited with one another. And what will you do, dearest, if I die?'

At these words Ashvghosh trembled in every limb, in every fibre: Prabha could feel his body shaking. He struggled to speak, but his throat was constricted, his eyes were bursting with tears. After wrestling with himself for some moments he said, brokenly –

'It will be a terrible hour! But I too, Prabha, will not kill myself. I will sing whatever song the spark of your love kindles in my heart, to the end of my life. Your immortal Ashvghosh.'

He stopped, unable to bring out another word.

'The river has gone to sleep, dearest. Let us go back.'

—9—

During the hot season, Suvarnakshi fell ill. Ashvghosh was at his mother's bedside day and night, and Prabha also stayed there all through the day. Medicines had no effect, the patient only grew worse. The full-moon night came, and shed its milky whiteness. Suvarnakshi asked them to carry her up into the moonlight. Her bed was made for her on the roof. By now she was mere skin and bone; her son's heart ached as he sat by her.

'How beautiful the moonlight is!' said the sick woman, in feeble but clear tones. As she spoke he seemed to hear Prabha's words again – 'The waves of the Saryu are calling me', and a shiver ran through him.

'Where is Prabha?' asked his mother.

'She has gone home, mother. She was here until evening.'

'Prabha ... daughter ... my son, ... never leave her ...'

Before she could finish, a fit of coughing came on, and after two spasms her body lay cold and motionless.

Suvarnakshi was gone, and her son's heart was breaking. All night long he wept.

Next day until noon he was busy with his mother's funeral rites. Then he thought of Prabha. He went to Dattmitr's house. Prabha's parents were under the impression that she had been with him. Ashvghosh's mind was still in a fever from the blow that had fallen on him the night before; now he grew more agitated still. He went into Prabha's bedroom. Everything was in order. He lifted the white sheet from the bed, and under it was a painting of himself. Prabha had had it made by a Greek artist who happened to come that way, and the reluctant Ashvghosh had had to spend hours sitting to him. On the picture lay a garland of fresh jasmine. Underneath was a folded palm-leaf letter in Prabha's handwriting. Ashvghosh picked it up; the dark clay seal on the string round it was still damp. He cut the string and kept the seal. When he unfolded the long sheet, he found only a few lines of Prabha's fine writing.

'Dearest, Prabha is taking leave of you. The Saryu's waves have called me, and I am going away. You gave me a promise in return for my love, do you remember? I am going away, leaving you my immortal youth and my unchanging beauty. Now you will never have to look at a Prabha with grey hair, decayed teeth and sagging hips. My love and my eternal youth will remain to inspire you. Never close your eyes to their messages. Do not think, dearest, that I am putting an end to my life because of the scolding of your family; I am only offering you my youth, still unblemished, to inspire your poetry. Dearest, Prabha embraces you and kisses you with her spirit, for the last time.'

Ashvghosh had to wipe the tears from his eyes several times before he could finish the letter. The letter fell from his hands and he sat down on the bed: his heart was numbed, and he sat plunged in abstraction, as if waiting for its beating to end altogether, gazing before him with empty eyes like a clay figure. Prabha's parents, after waiting for him for some time, entered the room, and were alarmed to find him in this condition. They saw the letter lying near him and read it. The mother gave a stifled cry like an animal, and slipped to the floor. Dattmitr was speechless, tears flowed from his eyes. Ashvghosh was still staring with the same fixed look. Seeing him like this, the others after a long time went out silently. Evening came, night fell. Ashvghosh was still sitting there. His eyes were dry, his heart seemed frozen. Late in the night he dropped off to sleep where he sat.

In the morning Prabha's mother came and found him composedly sitting and thinking. She asked him how he felt.

'I am quite well now mother. I shall do the work that Prabha entrusted to me. I did not understand; but she knew. She has shown me my duty. She has given me life, not death. I might turn this gift of life into suicide, but I cannot be guilty of such ingratitude.'

The mother understood what he was feeling.

'Where are you going, my son?' she asked as he stood up.

'I want to meet the Buddhist Bhadant and look at the Saryu.' A lump came into his throat as he answered.

'Bhadant Dharmrakshit is waiting for you below, and to look at the Saryu, I myself will come with you.'

She could not utter a single word more.

Ashvghosh went down and knelt respectfully in front of the Bhadant Dharmrakshit, saying, 'Bhadant! Admit me into your Sangh.'

'Son, your sorrow is great.'

'It is great; but it is not that that makes me speak. Prabha has made me ready for this. I am not hurrying into it blindly.'

'Still, you will have to wait for some days, the Sangh will not admit you hastily.'

'I will wait, Bhadant; but let me stay under the protection of the monastery.'

'First you must take your father's permission. No one is accepted as a monk without his parents' consent.'

'Then I shall go and take permission.'

Ashvghosh left the building. Prabha's mother, who was uneasy in her mind even at hearing his apparently sane words, had followed him. They took a boat together and spent all day searching the river downstream. The next day they descended the river still further, but not a trace was to be found.

Ashvghosh went home and asked his father's permission to become a monk; but his father was naturally unwilling to give up his only son. Then Ashvghosh said –

'It is not because I am overwhelmed with grief for my mother and Prabha that I am doing this, father. This is the road by which I can fulfil the task I have chosen in life. You can see that there is no sign of mental derangement in my voice and my behaviour. I have only to tell you this, father, that if you want me to go on living, you must give me the permission I ask for.'

Next day, in the evening, with tear-filled eyes, his father consented. The community of the noble Sarvastivad[28] sect of Saket admitted Ashvghosh as a monk. Mahasthavir Dharmsen himself became his preceptor, and Dharmrakshit his guide. The latter was then about to go by boat to Patliputr. Ashvghosh left Saket with him.

—10—

In the monastery at Patliputr, the monk Ashvghosh passed ten years.

Along with the Buddhist religion, he acquired a profound knowledge of Buddhist and Greek philosophy. He won a high place among the learned men of the religious fraternity in Magadh. It was at this time that the Shaka king Kanishk, advancing victoriously from the west, reached Patliputr. Patliputr and Magadh were distinguished centres of Buddhism, for which Kanishk had a deep respect. He wanted to find some able and learned monk to accompany him to Gandhar. The Sangh presented him Ashvghosh!

Upon arriving at the capital, Purushpur,[29] Ashvghosh found himself in a place where Shaka, Yavan, Turushk,[30] Persian and Indian cultures mingled with one another. Ashvghosh had formerly introduced the Greek drama into Indian literature. Now, after mature examination of Greek philosophy, he took many of its peculiar features, its analytical method and cognate elements, and with these borrowings enriched the philosophy of India, or rather of Buddhism. It was he who opened a new road forward for the Buddhists from Greek speculation. Then other Indian thinkers were forced to follow suit. The Vaisheshik and Nyaya[31] schools were those which made most progress. The atomic theory, concepts such as identity and universality, ontology, syllogistic logic, and so on, were among their borrowings from Greek philosophy.

Prabha had widened his mind, and the Buddhist Ashvghosh had no thought of self-isolation. Inspired by her memory he wrote various poems, plays and stories, some of which were later lost. Yet Nature seems to have watched over him with special care: seventeen hundred years later the great Gobi desert of Central Asia yielded up his play *Sariputr*.[32] His *Buddhcharit* ('Life of Buddh') and *Saundaranand* are immortal poems. They were a splendid fulfilment of his promise to Prabha and her unfaded beauty, and to his poetry its highest graces. His works immortalized his native Saket and his mother Suvarnakshi; he always signed his works as 'Ashvghosh, son of the noble Suvarnakshi of Saket'.

12

Suparn the Yaudheya

TIME : 420 CE

—1—

Mine has been a stormy destiny! I have never been able to halt for long at one place. Restless and adventurous, I have been tossed on all the billows of life. There have been hours of bliss in my existence, though not so many as the hours of bitterness. Looking back on its vicissitudes, I see mingled rainstorm and sunshine, as one does among the clouds at the end of the monsoon. And why the cycle of change continues to revolve, I do not know. Even today, in western Uttarapath-Gandhar, beef is served in the Madhupark[1] but in central India it is sin even to speak of beef; over there, to protect 'cows and Brahmins' is the holiest of religions. How there can be such contradiction in religion passes my understanding. Can a thing be proper in one place and improper in another, or must a change that has come about in one place be imitated sooner or later in the other also?

I was born in a village of Avanti (Malwa)[2] on the bank of the Kshipra river. My people regarded themselves as travellers, staying there temporarily, though they possessed fields and houses, things which they could not carry away with them on their backs. They differed somewhat in build and complexion from the other villagers. They were taller, broader and fairer, and with this they could not bear any assumption of superiority in others. My mother was the handsomest woman of the village; her brown hair fell charmingly round the light oval of her face.

Those of my family called themselves Brahmins, but I could see that the villagers had their doubts about this. And there was room for doubt. Brahmins in that part of the country considered wine-drinking a heinous sin, but in our house wine was made and drunk regularly.

In other respectable families it was unheard of that men and women should dance together, whereas in the seven households related to us, all of common descent, couples went out to dance in the open space as soon as evening fell.

When I was young I fancied that things were the same everywhere as at home; but when I began to understand the covert remarks of the other boys I played with in the village, I realized that they regarded us as a very odd people, and that even when they admitted our respectable status they were dubious about our being Brahmins. Ours was a large village; there were shops in it, and houses belonging to merchants. Among the inhabitants were some Naagar families, who were treated as Banias (trading caste), though they called themselves Brahmins, just as we did. Some Naagar girls had intermarried with us, which was one reason why folk did not recognize our Brahminhood. We could not be Brahmins, in their opinion, if we ignored the Brahmin rules of food and marriage. Whenever my playmates quarrelled with me, they used to sneer at me and call me a *jujhva*.[3] I often asked my mother why, but she evaded my question.

I grew up a little, and reached the age of ten. I was studying in the village school, kept by a Brahmin teacher. Nearly all my class-fellows were Brahmins, genuine Brahmins according to public opinion, while I and two Naagar boys were called by the rest 'Half-Brahmins'. I was quick at learning, and won the teacher's special affection. I had an independent temper, like all my family, and would fight rather than knuckle under to anybody. One day a boy at the school was taunting me – 'So you have become a Brahmin, you bloody *jujhva*!' The son of my uncle's brother-in-law tried to take my side, but came in for the same abuse – 'This Greek fellow has turned into a Naagar Brahmin!' Ever since my childhood I had heard such insults from the little boys, but never before had they stung so sharply or risen to such a flight of fancy. In the school, apart from my group of three there were thirty pupils, besides four girls. They were neither so fair nor so tall as we were, yet we saw all 'three worlds'[4] were ready to bow before them!

When I got home I was looking miserable. My mother noticed my quivering lips, and gave me a kiss.

'Why are you feeling so wretched today?' she asked.

At first I pretended there was nothing wrong, but when she pressed me, I said –

'Mother, there is something about our family that makes people say we are not Brahmins.'

'We are Brahmins from another province, my son, that is why they think what they do.'

'It is not only the Brahmins who show that they doubt us, mother, all the rest of the people say the same.'

'Only because the Brahmins have made them say it.'

'No one employs us to offer prayers for them. The other Brahmins work as priests. They attend the feasts given to Brahmins, which none of our relations do. And the other Brahmins will not even let us eat with them. Mother, if you know what it all means, tell me.'

She tried for a long time to cheer me up, but I would not be comforted.

When I was upset by such things my Naagar class-fellows and relatives sympathized with me, or rather we all sympathized with one another.

—2—

Time passed. My studies at the school were about to come to an end when I was thirteen. I had read my Veds – the *Rig Ved*, the *Aitreya Brahman*, books on Grammar and Nirukt[5] and some poems. My teacher had grown fonder and fonder of me. His daughter Vidya was four years younger than me and I used to help her learn her lessons. And she, seeing how her parents treated me, also had a warm regard for me, and called me her brother. I could never have a bad moment with this family; the teacher's wife loved me as if she had been my mother.

About this time, once more a schoolfellow threw at me the word '*jujhva*' without provocation, for in those days I was careful to keep to myself. His only motive was jealousy, because I was so quick at reading and writing. But my character was now growing more steady; not that my mind was less excitable, but I was gradually learning self-restraint.

My grandfather was over seventy years of age. I had listened to many a tale from him of lands far and near, of battle and strife. I had also heard that he and his brothers had been the first of our family to settle in this village. I was determined to seek from him the truth about our origin. East of the village we owned a mango orchard. The fruit was doing well, though still far from ripe, and our slave-woman Sona had taken up her quarters in a hut there to watch over it. I knew that when my grandfather first came to the village he had bought Sona from a southern trader for forty silver coins; many traders used to come from the south in those days to sell their slaves. Sona must have been young then, or she would not have fetched such a high price. Now her dark skin was loose and wrinkled, twisted furrows lined her face, though it was said that she had once been handsome. Grandfather treated her like a favourite, especially when the two were alone together. People explained their intimacy in different ways; he was a hale old fellow, without a wife, and it was natural that a certain conjecture should arise.

My grandfather used to visit this orchard every evening. One day I accompanied him. He was very fond of his bright young grandson. We were talking of various things and I said –

'I want to know the truth from you about our family. Why do people not consider us real Brahmins, and why do they insult us by calling us "*jujhva*"! I have asked mother many times, but she does not want to give me a clear answer.'

'Why must you ask about this?'

'I must, grandfather! As soon as I know the truth properly, I shall know what is to be done when our family is insulted. I have read a great deal about Brahmins now. I have gained enough learning to make our family respected.'

'I believe you have, my boy. But your mother herself, poor thing, does not know the truth about it, so you must not think that she is trying to avoid telling it to you. As regards our family's status in the world, it is now determined by our connection with the Naagars, with whom we intermarry. There are great numbers of them in Avanti and Lat (Gujrat) too, so we are bound to sink or swim with them. But in fact your generation is closer to the Naagars than to the Yaudheyas.'[6]

'What is Yaudheya, grandfather?'

'It is the name of our people. That is why folk call us *jujhvas*.'

'Were the Yaudheyas Brahmins?'

'They were purer Aryans than the Brahmins themselves.'

'But they were not Brahmins, then?'

'Instead of giving you an answer in one word, Yes or No, I had better explain to you what sort of people they were. The Yaudheyas lived in the country between the Satluj and the Yamuna from the Himalayas as far as the desert, and they were all its masters.'

'All of them?'

'Yes; they had no king over them; their government was known as a republic. All public business was managed by the public, or a council. They had a great hatred of rule by one man – monarchy.'

'I have never even heard of such a government, grandfather.'

'But that is how it was. I still have three Yaudheya silver coins that came to me from my father, part of the money he had with him when we fled from the country.'

'Then you were not born in that country yourself?'

'I was ten years old when my parents had to escape. I had two older brothers, whose families you see here now.'

'Why did they have to escape?'

'That land had belonged to the Yaudheyas since ancient times. Great and illustrious emperors were born in India – Mauryas, Greeks, Shakyas – but none of them molested us except for levying some small tribute. It was the Gupt dynasty – the ancestors of the Chandrgupt who calls himself *Vikramaditya*,[7] and who sometimes holds his court at Ujjain – it was one of them who rose to supreme power and destroyed the Yaudheyas.

'They were already paying some tax to the powerful emperor, but he was not satisfied with that. He said he must appoint his own governor and have commissioners of his own living there; he must have the same power there as he had throughout his dominions. Our leaders tried hard to convince him that from time immemorial the Yaudheyas had known no other kind of government than republican. But how should he care about that, drunk with power as he was?

'At last the Yaudheyas took an oath in the presence of the goddess whom they worshipped, and drew the sword. In repeated encounters they routed the Gupt army, and if it had been only four or five times their strength, it would not have been able to withstand them. But the Yaudheyas could not defend themselves for ever against the whole strength of a great empire stretching from the Lauhitya (Brahmputr) river to the Rajputana desert. Even though they won battles, their resources were wasting away, so heavy were their casualties. The Gupts sacked all our towns and villages, and made a terrible slaughter of men and women alike. Our people kept up the struggle for thirty years. They were willing to pay a heavier tribute, but not to allow the tradition of republican rule in their land to be subverted.'

'What did republican rule mean, grandfather?'

'Every Yaudheya held his head high; no one dreamed of abasing himself before another man. War to them was sport, that is why their race had acquired its name.'

'Then, grandfather, are there other Yaudheyas left besides ourselves?'

'There are, child, but like dry leaves before the wind, they have all been scattered.'

'And will they have intermixed with Naagar families as we have done, and forgotten their origin? Why do we call ourselves Brahmins, grandfather?'

'That is also a very long story. In ancient times, instead of monarchy everywhere, there was republicanism, and there was then no distinction between Brahmins and Kshatriyas.'

'They were all one caste?'

'Yes, any man of them could either perform worship or handle a sword as the need might arise. But later on Vishvamitr and Vashishthh arose and began to divide them into groups.'

'So if a man had two sons, one of them might become a Kshatriya like Rantidev and the other a Brahmin teacher, like Gauriviti!'

'Does it say that in the books, child?'

'Yes, grandfather. In the Veds and in history it is like that. Those two were the sons of the Rishi Sankriti. There are a great many odd things besides that in the old books, things which people today will not believe. You have seen Dashpur, grandfather, on the bank of the Charmanvati[8] (River Chambal)?'

'Yes, child, often; it is in Avanti. I have often gone there to attend weddings. There are many Naagar families there, including a good many big merchants.'

'Well, that same Dashpur was the capital of Rantidev. And how the Charmanvati came to get its name is a real marvel.'

'How was it?'

'Rantidev, who was the son of the Brahmin Sankriti but a Kshatriya by his own choice, was famous for his hospitality. Two thousand cows were slaughtered every day for his kitchen. Their dripping hides were stored in the kitchen, and the liquid that ran down from them formed a river. So it came to be called the River Charmanvati.'

'Does it really say that in the old books?'

'Yes. It is all written in the *Mahabharat*.'[9]

'What, beef-eating, in the *Mahabharat* – the Fifth Ved, as they call it!'

'There were two thousand cooks to get the beef ready for Rantidev's guests! And all the same the number of Brahmin guests increased so much that there was a shortage of meat, and the cooks had to ask for more soup to be served out.'

'What are you saying child! Brahmins eating beef!'

'Can the *Mahabharat*,[10] the Fifth Ved, tell a lie?'

'How the world has changed!'

'It keeps on changing, grandfather. And still these owlish folk who call themselves true Brahmins want to throw dust in everyone else's eyes. I believe our Yaudheya ancestors must have followed the customs and religious practices of the days before the Brahmins spread everywhere with their trickery.'

'Yes, and they never regarded Brahmins as superior to themselves.'

'When you came here, grandfather, why did you marry your sons and nephews to Naagars, instead of to Brahmins of Avanti?'

'There were two reasons. One was that the Brahmins had suspicions about our descent; but that would not have mattered, we could have married true Brahmin girls if we had wished. We began to intermarry with the Naagars because they, like ourselves, had unusually fair skins, and called themselves Brahmins, although they were not recognized by the other Brahmins.'

'Who are they, the Naagars?'

'The Brahmins do not accept a man as a Brahmin just because he calls himself that: they ask what province is he a Brahmin of, which stock he belongs to. These people with whom we intermarried were living in towns[11] and so they began to call themselves Naagar Brahmins, just as we call ourselves Yaudheya Brahmins.'

'But what are they in fact, grandfather?'

'They are Greeks from the coast. Many of them follow the Buddhist religion instead of Brahminism. You will see that, if you go to Ujjain. There are still a large number of them who simply call themselves Greeks. The Brahmins are insisting that they ought to be classed as Kshatriyas.'

'So the races and castes are being defined as one wishes to or is made to accept, grandfather?'

'That seems to be happening, child!'

—3—

I grew up to be a good-looking, well-built youth of twenty. As I had finished my studies at home, I went to Ujjain to become a pupil of the great scholars there. My maternal great-grandfather's family were wealthy Naagars of Ujjain, and they welcomed me and made me live with them. To students from the countryside, like me, Ujjain was like a window opening on the great world. I had already heard of Kalidas, and read some of his poems, but here, on certain days, I had the opportunity of reading with the great poet himself. He enjoyed a high status in the court of Chandrgupt Vikramaditya, and hence was often absent from Ujjain. I was proud of having him as my teacher, but disgusted by his servile pride in his relations with the King. He was engaged at that time in writing *Kumarsambhav*, and he explained to me that his intention was to shed undying lustre on Vikramaditya's son Kumargupt, whom he introduced under the name of Prince Kartikeya, the son of Shankar.[12] My unabashed sarcasms at the expense of this scheme, bitter though they were, did not cause the poet to take offence. One day I said –

'Master,[13] you have an imperishable empire in your literary fame, while Chandrgupt and Kumargupt are emperors only so long as they live. Why do you reckon yourself so insignificant compared with them?'

'But Vikramaditya is truly the preserver of our religion, Suparn. Has he not liberated India from the Huns?'

'The Huns are still there in the north, Master, and in Kashmir.'

'They have been expelled from many regions.'

'Well, rulers always drive one another out, and take each other's places.'

'Yes, but the Gupt family stands in defence of cows and Brahmins.'

'Master, I did not expect to hear you say things that are only meant to deceive fools. You know very well that the Rishis, our ancestors, "protected" cows only in order to eat them. In your *Meghdoot* you yourself have called the Chambal river the Charmanvati which commemorates the fame Rantidev won by slaughtering cows.'

'You are very presumptuous, my dear pupil!'

'I was prepared to hear you say that; what I cannot bear is to see my immortal king of poets fawning on the Gupts, these perverters of religion.'

'You call them perverters of religion, Suparn?'

'Certainly. They have committed a crime that the Nands, the Mauryas, the Greeks, the Shakas, even the Huns, left undone. They have obliterated republicanism from the soil of India.'

'Republics were not suited to this age. If Samudrgupt had left them in existence, he would not have been able to defeat the Huns and other such powerful enemies.'

'What was his success? He founded an empire for himself and became another Chandrgupt Maurya. But the empire that was founded and organized by the matchless wisdom of Chanakya, did not last long. And the family of Vikramaditya and Kumargupt is not going to outlast the sun and the moon. What service did they do to religion by wiping out the last trace of popular government? Was it not a sin against religion to destroy the popular rule of the republics that had come down from antiquity?'

'But the king is a portion of the god Vishnu.'[14]

'Yes, and Kumargupt in his turn will have a peacock painted as his emblem, and tomorrow some poet will represent him as an incarnation of Kumar.[15] What is the motive for such impostures and perversions? To let them have fine rice and savoury meat-soup, to let them drive the beautiful girls of the whole land into their harems, to let them spend like water on their own pleasure the hard-earned gains of the people who toil until they die at the plough or the anvil! And for that you call the Gupts the royal preservers of religion! Yes, the Gupts are playing a fine trick by calling themselves what the Brahmins are turning them into, incarnations of Vishnu, and the image of his wife, the goddess Lakshmi, is being stamped on their coins. Vast sums are being extorted from the starving people, to be spent on images and temples of Vishnu, and all so that the Gupt dynasty and its empire may survive to the end of time!'

'Do you know what you are doing, Suparn? These are harsh words to use against the King.'

'Today, Master, I speak them only to you; but the day will come when I shall say them to the face of *Parambhattarak*[16] Kumargupt! I can never bring myself as long as I live to stomach these deceits. But that is for the future, perhaps a distant future. What I have at heart today is that you should tread in the footsteps of Ashvghosh.'

'But, my dear son, I am only a poet, and Ashvghosh was both a great poet and a great man. For him the pleasures of the world had no value; but I need women as beautiful as those in Vikramaditya's harem, and crimson wine, and a fine mansion, and attendants. How can I turn myself into an Ashvghosh?

'I embellished the divine descent of the Gupts, under the disguise of other names in my *Raghuvamsh*, and Vikramaditya was delighted and gave me this palace, and presented me with my lovely Greek girl, Kanchanmala. She has been living with me for fifteen years, and still holds me in the chains of her golden hair. Now I have planned this new poem, *Kumarsambhav*, and you will see what new gifts it will bring me.'

'I don't believe, Master, that if you had written *Buddhcharit* or *Saundaranand* only as Ashvghosh did, you would have found yourself very hungry or deprived of all enjoyments. But you live under the delusion that you can find no pleasure in life without flattering kings. You have set a bad example to future poets; they will excuse their faults by pointing to what you did.'

'I will write poems of another kind as well.'

'But you will not write any poems where all the curses the Gupts have brought on the world are attacked!'

'That is no work for me, Suparn. I have grown too soft.'

'And you will throw a religious cloak over every royal crime?'

'That must be done. Without it the royal power cannot be firm. Vashishthh and Vishvamitr themselves saw the necessity of it.'

'Vashishthh and Vishvamitr were given to deeds of such wickedness for the sake of fine houses and women, just like the poet Kalidas.'

'Suparn, I hear that you are studying the art of war, as well as book-learning. If you agree, I will speak to Parambhattarak; I should be very happy to see you made a counsellor or an army officer, and the King too would be pleased.'

'I will not sell my body to anyone, Master.'

'Then how would you like a place among the royal priests?'

'I have too much detestation for the selfishness of the Brahmins.'

'What do you intend to do?'

'At present, to go on with my studies.'

—4—

Living at Ujjain, I had the opportunity not only to quench my thirst for learning, but also, as I said before, to get to know something about the great world. I could see there very easily how completely the Brahmins had sold themselves to the kings. There had been a time when I was very proud of being a Brahmin, even though I was not accepted as such by the others, but that pride had begun to melt away already before I left my village. After exchanging the village for the city, I met many pure Greeks, who often used to come to Ujjain from Bharukachh, and who had many big shops there. I came in contact with many Shaka and Abhir families, whose ancestors, a century before, had been governors of Ujjain, Lat and Saurashtr (Kathiawad). I saw Huns, too, with their round eyes and their faces the colour of a ripe orange. They were proficient at fighting, but otherwise showed no remarkable talent. I studied all these different kinds of people, but what I admired most were the Buddhist monasteries, several of which were to be found on the outskirts of Ujjain. Families from my mother's side were Buddhists and there were many Naagar monks in those monasteries, so I often had to visit them.

When I had completed my studies I desired to extend my knowledge by travel. I learned at this time that there was a very celebrated monastery in Vidarbh, called Achintya,[17] where monks from every land were living. I went to see it.

Hitherto, wherever I went, I had travelled with plenty of provisions, and in the company of others. Now, for the first time, I set off alone and unprovided. There was no risk of meeting robbers on the way; one must give credit to the Gupts for ensuring this. But was it because their regime had made every family in the country so prosperous that all temptation to highway robbery was removed? No. The Gupts had outstripped all previous rulers in collecting taxes. Never before had so much treasure been expended on the building of palaces, and in furnishing them there was still greater profusion. They tried to transplant hills, rivers, lakes and seas, and surround their beautiful palaces with them. Their pleasure-parks were really like forests, where wild beasts were kept in cages while deer and *nilgai* roamed free. On their garden-hills, trees of the kind found in mountains grew, and cascades of water were made to play. There were pools linked by small canals, crossed by bridges and covered with boats. Inside, the palaces were crammed with ivory, gold, silver, gems of many sorts, silks, and precious carpets. In adorning them, painters had lavished all the skill of their brushes, and sculptors had set up in fitting places their statues of stone or metal. I had heard from travellers and ambassadors the loudest praises of these paintings and sculptures, which had certainly filled me with rapture, but when I saw the state of the hovels in the wretched villages, my blood boiled at the thought of Ujjain and its palaces. I felt that the poverty of the one was caused by the wealth of the other, just as the walls and mounds of a town are bordered by pits which show where the material for them has been dug from.

Not only in the towns and cities, but in the villages themselves skilled craftsmen were making articles of many kinds. Women spun fine threads and weavers turned it into delicate cloth; goldsmiths, blacksmiths, leather-workers were all accomplished in their crafts; those who created the artistic furnishings for the royal palaces were the kith and kin of the artisans here. Yet when I saw the physical condition of these people, and the houses they lived in, I realized that they gained no more from the exquisite work of their hands than from the illusions of a dream. Their manufactures disappeared from the villages to the towns, to city mansions, palaces or markets. A great part of them were carried thence, by way of Bharuch and other western ports, to Persia or Egypt, or by way of Tamrlipt (Tamluk) on the eastern coast to Yavdvip (Java) or Suvarndvip (Sumatra). India's overseas trade had never been so flourishing; foreign wealth had never flowed in so abundantly in exchange for her wares. But who profited by this? First of all the Gupt government, which levied a heavy impost on all sales. Next the feudatory chiefs, lords of large principalities or estates, who had their fingers in the pockets of both craftsmen and traders. The merchants and traders came last, but their share of the spoils was no mean one. Seeing all this I understood clearly enough why the peasants and village craftsmen were so poor, and why the government was so attentive to the upkeep of roads and highways.

Yes, the villages are squalid, but there is one heart-rending sight that rarely meets the eye there – the sight of markets where human beings are sold like cattle, the sight of the whip falling on their backs. My teacher Kalidas on one occasion had said that men owe their slavery to their misdeeds in a previous life. My belief in a previous existence ceased from the moment when I heard him say this. Such doubt might naturally enter any thinking man's head, from the mere haste shown by the Gupts in utilizing religion in every way to bolster up their own power. But when I studied the ordinary people, they seemed quite apathetic. Why? Perhaps they felt helpless. The villagers knew nothing of any world but their little village. For a single inch of its fields they would fight more stubbornly than perhaps Kumargupt would have fought for a whole province. But they were indifferent to anything outside the boundaries of their village.

I remember an occurrence in one village. It contained about

forty houses, all of them with thatched roofs. It was summer, and one house caught fire from a spark from the hearth. The whole population rushed to the scene with buckets, except for one couple, who were sitting with their water pots near their own house. Fortunately, in the whole village these were the only ones who did not help; otherwise not a single house would have escaped! The incident made me think of the old Yaudheya republic where every household in the country was willing to live or die for the sake of the rest. Myriads of men, indeed, gave their lives to aid the conquests of Samudrgupt, Chandrgupt and Kumargupt, but they perished like slaves, for the benefit of another, not like free men in defence of themselves and their families. It made me shiver to contemplate the effect on the people of a single century of Gupt rule. I felt that if this regime lasted for centuries longer, the land would be a land of nothing but slaves, born only to fight and die for their rulers, and absolutely ignorant of the idea that a human being has any rights.

The monastery at Achintya was most charming. There was a green hill valley, intersected by a stream flowing in a half-moon curve. On the left bank of this small but perennial river, artisans had hewn out of the living rock a row of caves, serving as chapels, living rooms, and places of assembly. They were adorned like so many palaces with paintings and sculptures, though here these had been created by the work of generations, to last for perhaps hundreds of generations. Beautiful as the wall paintings and stone statues of Achintya were, they could not rival the Gupt palaces, and therefore did not attract me so much. What attracted me was the community of monks, in which men of many lands were living together like a single affectionate family. There I met monks from distant China, Persians and Greeks, men from Sinhal, from Java, from Sumatra; I heard the names of Champadvip and Kambojdvip, and saw their representatives in flesh and blood. There I met the yellow people,[18] wearing red robes of monks from Kapisha, Udyan, Tushar and Kucha.

I was very eager to acquire information about foreign countries, and if I had encountered these foreign monks singly, I would have been glad to spend a whole year with each of them. Meeting them all together in such numbers, I was ready to jump out of my skin with excitement, like a pauper who has come into a fortune. I had heard the name of the poet Dingnag from my teacher. Kalidas was a resolute supporter of the Gupts, of monarchy, and of the Brahminical religion which formed its main bulwark. I have already explained his motives for being so. He knew that Dingnag was a vigorous opponent of his ideals, and used to say, 'The thrones not of Vishnu alone, but of all the three hundred and thirty million gods tremble before this Dravidian atheist; he knows the secret of all the false teachings we give in the name of religion to serve the interests of the king and the Brahmins. The trouble with him is that he had old Vasubandhu for his teacher.' Kalidas used to call Vasubandhu an ocean of learning. He was a Buddhist scholar who spent some years at Ayodhya, the capital of Chandrgupt Vikramaditya II, not as a courtier, but as an independent and respected teacher. Later, disgusted by the mean ambitions of the Gupts, he returned to his native place, Purushpur. Dingnag had vowed to give to the world not iron arrowheads, or swords, but the even sharper weapons of knowledge and reason. In a mere half-hour's discussion with him, all the Brahminical hocus-pocus could collapse like a house of cards.

I stayed at the Achintya monastery for six months, and listened daily to Dingnag's luminous addresses. I am proud to have had such a teacher. His knowledge was extremely profound; his words were living flames. Like myself, he had seen the hypocrisy and superstitions of the world and come to loathe them. One day he said –

'Suparn, it was possible to accomplish something through the strength of the people, but now the people have been led far astray. Buddh made great efforts to abolish distinctions of race and caste and up to a point he succeeded; when foreign races like the Greeks, Shakas, Gurjars and Abhirs came, the Brahmins called them *mlechhs* and looked down on them; but the Buddhist community admitted them to equal rights with all men. For a few centuries it seemed likely that all caste divisions would vanish from India. But then, to India's misfortune, the Gupt power came to the rescue of the Brahmins. When the Gupts themselves had first appeared, the Brahmins had called them *mlechhs*. It was to raise their prestige that Kalidas wrote his *Raghuvamsh* and *Kumarsambhav*. The Gupts are crazy enough to think of establishing a dynasty that will last forever; the Brahmins encourage them in such hopes. Our teacher Vasubandhu could not hold out any such hopes to them. He was a devoted believer in the monastic fraternity that had been organized on the model of the Lichhavi republican system. The Brahmins know that Buddhists are their bitter enemies. They know that Buddhists of all countries eat beef, and will not give it up; so they have begun to preach abstinence from beef throughout India as a religious principle – what they call "protection of the cow and the Brahmin". Buddhists want to abolish race and caste distinctions, so now the Brahmins have begun to give a high place in the caste system to Greeks and Shakas and others of foreign origin. This is a dangerous snare in which many even of our secular Buddhists are being entrapped. By sowing dissension like this, the Brahmins hope to weaken the strength of the people and increase their own strength and that of the rulers. But the consequences will be perilous for our country, Suparn, for no country can be strong that relies on the strength of slaves.'

My teacher was deeply moved when I related to him the story of the Yaudheyas and their heroic sacrifice. When I told him of my ardent hope for a resurrection of the Yaudheya republic, he said – 'My hopes and blessings go with you. A resolute hero must fear no obstacles.'

Carrying his blessings with me I am journeying towards the land of the Yaudheyas, to bring my murdered country back to life, or to vanish like a footprint on the sand.

1 2 3 4 5 6 7 8 9 10
20 19 18 17 16 15 14 **13** 12 11

Durmukh

TIME : 630 CE

—1—

My name is Harshvardhan, with the honorific title of Shiladitya, or 'Sun of Righteousness'. Chandrgupt II gratified himself with the title Vikramaditya, the 'Sun of Valour'; this milder attribution pleased me better. In heroism lurks the craving to overcome and subjugate others, but virtue brings with it no desire to get the better of one's neighbour by violence. The Gupts called themselves divine incarnations of Vishnu; my elder brother, Rajyavardhan, who was treacherously murdered in youth by Gaud Shashank, and whose memory saddens my heart even now, was very much a Buddhist; and like the Great Buddh, he was merciful himself. I have always thought of myself as his disciple; and though it has pleased me to style myself a follower of the god Shiv, I have retained a heartfelt devotion to Buddh, as not only India, but the outer world also knows. I have paid respect to all the religions of my country; not merely for the sake of pleasing the people, but also in order to preserve my righteousness. Every fifth year, the surplus of my treasury has been distributed among Brahmins and Buddhist monks, near Prayag,[1] at the confluence of the Ganga and the Yamuna rivers. This will make manifest my desire to further the prosperity of each religion alike. True it is that I, like Samudrgupt, once marched out in search of conquest, but that was before I earned the name of 'Sun of Righteousness'. Do not think that, if I had not failed against the southern king Pulkeshin, I should have adopted a title more like that of Vikramaditya. Even if I had become emperor of all India, I should have conquered men's hearts by my justice, not like Chandrgupt, but like Ashok repenting his subjugation of Kaling. Mine is a temper formed for mild rule.

I refused for long to accept the crown, for as the son of Prabhakarvardhan, Maharaj of Sthanvishvar (Thanesar), and younger brother of the Parambhattarak, excellent king Rajyavardhan of Kanyakubj, I knew from experience, not from observation, how tasteless were the sweets of power. After my brother's murder, I was unwilling to mount the throne, and if the true Kshatriya thought of avenging his death had not sprung up in my mind, I would never have sat on the throne of Kanyakubj, and it would have passed to the Maukhari clan, into which my sister Rajyashri had married, and which in fact had held power before my brother's time, when the Gupts disappeared. I am saying all this to make those who come after me understand that it was with no thought of selfish interest that I placed the crown on my head. I lament that my crafty courtiers have tried to paint me in the same colours as Samudrgupt and Chandrgupt Vikramaditya. A ruler cannot get rid of the flatterers, that is the difficulty. But by their eulogies they are not doing me justice, they do me a great injustice.

I accepted the throne only that I might defend justice and religion, out of love for all mankind. I understood that charity bestowed on learning is true charity. The wealth of the Nalanda[2] monastery, which had been growing since the Gupt times, I added to still further, until it enabled ten thousand Indian and foreign scholars and students to follow one's own religion. This fills the world with peace and prosperity. To honour scholars was my highest pleasure; that is why I welcomed so warmly the Chinese Buddhist monk, Ven Chang.[3] Discerning the remarkable poetical talent of Baan,[4] I tried to rescue him from his vicious pleasures and set him on the right road, though he proved unable to rise very far, but trod in the footsteps of Kalidas and filled his poems with flattery. At any rate, my taking him out of a little village of Magadh and trying to bring him to the notice of the world testified to my love of literature.

I wanted all men to be faithful to their own religion. It is right to follow one's own religion. This fills the world with peace and prosperity, and builds heaven. I always laboured to induce each *varn*[5] group to observe the religious rules of their own *varn*, all *ashrams*[6] be dutiful to their principles, every sect to worship according to its honest faith.

From Kamrup (Assam) to Saurashtr, from the Vindhya hills to the

Himalayas, I established the reign of justice over my vast dominions. To prevent my officers from misbehaving, I myself went on tours from time to time. It was during one of these tours that the Brahmin Baan appeared before me in answer to my summons. His avowed wish was to eulogize me; but I believe that the descriptions he wrote, even when I was on campaign, of my royal pomp and splendour may really be descriptions not of my court, but of Vikramaditya's. He began writing his *Harshcharit*, his biography of me, secretly; when I heard of it one day, I asked him about it. He showed me the part he had composed. I was very much displeased with it, and took him to task; of which one result was that he was certainly unable to proceed with the same warmth. I was better pleased with his *Kadambari*, except that he painted such a picture in it of court life, harems, attendants, palaces, luxury and so on, that people must inevitably imagine that all these descriptions apply to my own court.

I am very fond of my Persian wife. Not only is she a daughter of Naushervan, but her virtues and charms would be enough to captivate any man. Baan drew her portrait under the name of Mahashveta. Another wife, from Saurashtr, was verging on the decline of her youth. To please her, I made special efforts in furnishing her residence. Baan has described this in his account of Kadambari and her mansion. No descriptions in Baan's works, apart from these two pieces, are to be considered as relating to me, or at least any others must be considered very hyperbolic.

Now, in my latter days, I am fearful that Baan will not prove to have done me any good service. The account given in his *Harshcharit* and even in his *Kadambari* of the king and his magnificence will be regarded by the public as a portrait of myself. Besides, he made the confusion worse by writing his plays *Naaganand*, *Ratnavali*, and *Priyadarshika* in my name. People will think that out of thirst for fame, I bought another man's works from him and put them out as my own. I am telling the truth when I say that I did not learn what he had done till long after, when thousands of students had already read these plays with my name on them, and they had been many times performed.

I wanted to see my people contented; my wish was fulfilled. I wanted to see my realm at peace and free from calamity. In the end this aim also was achieved, and a man laden with gold could travel from place to place in safety.

Behind my back, folk have already begun to say that my family is sprung from the plebeian caste of Banias.[7] This is quite false. We are Vaishya-Kshatriyas, not Vaishya-Banias. At one time the power of my clan, the Shatvahan, extended all over India. After the passing of the Shatvahan Empire, my ancestors migrated from Pratishthanpur (Paithan), on the Godavari river, to Sthanvishvar. It was never a Bania stock, as the entire world knows, though it intermarried with the Shaka Kshatriyas, as royal blood properly may. And my beloved Mahashveta is of the royal line of Persia.

—2—

My name is Baan. I have written many romantic plays, and people will want to measure me by the standard of these works alone, so I wish to write this also and leave it behind me. I know very well that what I am now setting down will not become known as long as the present ruling family is on the throne. I have arranged for it to be kept safely. Posterity will be saved from false ideas about me, if it reads these words before reading my celebrated works.

King Harsh called me, in public, a libertine, and what he said may well mislead people about me. I was the favourite son of a rich father. Undoubtedly, it was from reading the works of Bhas and Kalidas that I acquired a romantic disposition. I had good looks, and youth. I longed to travel. I wanted to enjoy my youth, and had I wished I could have led a life of indulgence at home, as my father did; but it seemed to me hypocritical, to be inwardly sensual and self-indulgent, and outwardly appear ascetic, virtuous, devout and spiritual. All my life I have never liked such hypocrisy. Whatever I have done, I have done openly. My father only once had courage to recognize as his own a son born as *asavarn*;[8] and that could be counted as a piece of youthful folly. I realized that I could not enjoy my youth as I wished to while I remained at home. All my relatives would be outraged and I should have to forfeit my wealth. I thought of a good scheme.

I formed a dramatic troupe, outside Magadh of course. I had for my friends only clever and artistic young people. I have never been fond of mean, flattering, stupid friends. I admitted a good many pretty girls to my band, not all of them prostitutes. It was for performance on this tour that I wrote my *Ratnavali* ('Necklace'), my *Priyadarshika* ('Sight of the Beloved') and other dramas and comedies. Art was for me a part of the enjoyment of youth, and men of good taste will always give me credit for my services to art. I have enjoyed my life, but I have also presented the world with my compositions, whereas some men of pleasure think only of their own pleasures. People may say that in order to win King Harsh's favour I published my plays under his name. They are not aware that at the time when I wrote these plays, away from home, I knew nothing of Harsh except his name. I never dreamed that he would one day send for me and make me his court poet. I published my plays in his name merely in order to conceal my own identity. All who read them know their merit. They were quite original. There were plenty of connoisseurs in my audiences. Scholars, princes, and artists especially flocked to watch my plays. If they had got to know who I was, I should not have been able to remain manager of a company of actors; crowds of people would have been running after the famous Baan. I exhibited my plays at the court not only of Harsh, but of rulers from Kamrup to Sindhu, from the Himalayas to the capital of the Sinhals – Anuradhapur. You can easily imagine what would have become of my roving, joyous existence if these rulers of Kamrup and of Sinhal and Kuntal had known me, Baanbhatt, to be the author of these plays. I had no desire to become a court poet. I would not have let Harsh make me one if I had not been living in his dominions. From my father I had as much money as I needed.

You may be reflecting that, according to Harsh, I was a mere pimp. As a matter of fact, there were few courtesans among my actresses and those I had were chosen for their proficiency in dancing, singing, acting or art. The stars of my artistic firmament came to me in another way. What will be the state of affairs in times to come, I cannot say, but in this age all the girls in the land are considered the property of the rulers and their subordinate feudal lords, even the daughters of

Brahmins and Kshatriyas. An aunt of mine was forcibly carried off by a Maukhari chief of Magadh. When he died she was past her prime and she came to live at our home. She was fonder of me than anyone else. It never occurred to me to think about her past connection with the feudal lord. What fault was it of hers, after all, poor creature? Pretty girls are scarce but when those who have the first right on them are just a few petty nobles, you can understand how many girls fall to the lot of each aristocrat! Officials and their masters found various pretexts for obtaining women. Some considered that they had a right to the first night with a bride before she went to her husband. People began to treat this as a religious obligation and send their daughters, wives and sisters in sedan chairs to pass a night in some great man's harem. Not to send such a sedan meant running a grave risk. Those who found favour were kept in the harem not as consorts, but as handmaidens, for only the daughters of kings or princes could aspire to become queens. The majority of the thousands of harem inmates enjoyed no more than a single night with their master. Imagine how their youthful cravings must have devoured them! Most of my actresses came from such harems, and not by any stealthy escape. Whether you admire me for it or not, I had the gift of winning favour with the rich and powerful easily. I don't mean in politics, for I had nothing to do with that. In proof of what I say are the hundreds of flattering letters I received from kings and their ministers. When they talked in praise of art, I would lament the trials of an artiste's life and exclaim –

'What am I to do, Your Majesty, there are talented young women, but I cannot get hold of them!'

'How is that?'

'Where are talented actresses to be got from, when hundreds of thousands of girls are kept locked up in harems, where their only function is to be kissed or embraced or slept with for a single day?'

'That is true, my good sir, I quite admit it, but when we have once taken them into our harems, how can we let them go?'

Then I would show them a way. Nowadays it is indispensable for daughters of kings and nobles, harem women, to learn dancing and singing. It is like meat and drink to them. I sent my experienced women, and the king would tell his females to learn the arts from them. When we found one suitable for us, we impressed on her mind the miseries of harem life and the joys of life in the world of art; we also impressed on her that just as the king had now given an honourable reception in his harem to a skilled actress of our troupe, so she also might at some future time meet with similar luck. Naturally such talk had its effect on some of the girls, though we only took the most talented ones. When kings kept thousands of young girls cooped up merely for the sake of one night with each of them, making rigid rules to prevent men from entering the harem can have no effect. The old Brahmin chamberlains cannot keep these girls from the pleasures of youth.

When I opposed the burning alive of widows, hypocrites (there can be no greater hypocrites in the world than Brahmins and kings) and conservatives raised a great outcry. They accused me of wanting to encourage abortions and the remarriage of widows. I did not want to encourage abortions, but I have no hesitation in admitting that I approve of the remarriage of widows. Since the Gupt Empire, our ancient religion has changed beyond recognition. Our old exponents of the Veds would never welcome a guest without giving him beef; today beef-eating is considered contrary to religion. The Rishis of old thought it quite proper for widows to make a second marriage with their *devars*[9] (husband's younger brothers), and in fact believed that no young Brahmin or Kshatriya widow should remain without a husband for longer than six months or a year. Today this is coming to be thought irreligious. In the Gupt family itself, the fountainhead of all this rubbish of the new Hindu religion, Vikramaditya, chose as his consort, not a widow, but the wife of Ramgupt while her husband was still living. Even the gods Brahma, Vishnu and Maheshvar would never be able to impose chastity on young widows; and indeed, with what face could they attempt it, when they themselves, with their own consorts living, were never weary of chasing other people's wives? Abortions are the inevitable result of keeping young widows unmarried; to let them bear children and bring them up would involve letting them remarry, which is what people now want to avoid. For fear of this, the Brahmins and rulers have found a new way of protecting the purity of their families, that is, to burn widows alive. They reckon it a most virtuous custom, and by no means a sin. Any of the gods whose hearts do not melt as they witness, year by year, the compulsory burning alive of hundreds of thousands of young widows, must be merely stone idols or they don't exist at all. They say that a woman is burned of her own free will. Scoundrels! Hypocrites, caitiffs – how can they utter such lies! Among the hundreds of inmates of a royal harem, who have been used for one night and whom you cast in the flames, how many will there be who can feel the slightest affection for their royal stallion? If there is an occasional woman distracted by her loss and willing to jump into the fire, two or three days would easily cool her fevered mind. A religion of suicide! Ill luck befall these lying priests and kings! They have made it a religious act to leap from the Akshayavat[10] banyan tree at Prayag, into the river Yamuna and drown there, and every year thousands of deluded wretches find their way to 'Heaven' by this leap. They have made it a religious act to climb the Satpath ('Path of Truth') on Mount Kedar and freeze in the snow, and every year thousands of souls set out for 'Heaven' by these 'Paths'. I could not raise my voice against all these modes of self-destruction, because I had to rely on royal protection against the Brahmins.

I still rely on it, but it was not of my own will that I sought this protection. I had enough property of my own to enable me to lead a modest but comfortable life, and I could exercise much more self-restraint than the kings and priests of my time who used religion as their cloak. I had no desire to become a *lakhchumbi*[11] like Harsh and other royal sages. At the most there may be a hundred girls with whom I have been in love at any time. But my home, my property, all I had, were in Harsh's dominions. When he sent one emissary after another to call me, how could I refuse to go to his court? Of course, if I had been another Ashvghosh, indifferent to hearth and home, I might have cared nothing for Harsh.

If you ask my secret opinion of Harsh, I reply that he was not, for his time, a bad man or a bad ruler. He had great reverence for his brother Rajyavardhan, and if religious custom had made it a duty to burn oneself with one's dead brother or even suggested it, he would readily have complied. But along with this he had certain faults, of which the worst was hypocrisy; he tried to show himself above ambition while really craving flattery; he paraded himself as a man free from passion, while in reality avid for beautiful girls; he laboured to appear far removed from all thoughts of fame, while secretly longing for it. I have already explained how I came to issue my plays under the name of 'the brilliant poet Harsh', without consulting him. But after he had come to know me, and I had been in his company day and night, he never said to me, 'Now, Baan, let these plays appear in your own name,' as I could very easily have done. It was merely a question of having them performed once before his obsequious courtiers with my name announced instead of his.

It was my earnest wish to portray the world as it really is. If I had not spent twelve years in my wanderings, perhaps I should not have experienced this wish, or might have lacked power to accomplish it. When I described the lake of Achhod, I had before my mind a lovely Himalayan mountain landscape. I was thinking of another Himalayan view when I described the house of Kadambari. In my *Vindhyatavi*, I placed my old Dravidian monk in a setting I had once seen myself. But I did not want to content myself merely with descriptive work of this kind. In my writings I depicted the palaces, seraglio and riches of Harsh and other kings whom I knew intimately, but I was not free to describe the cabins of the poor and their miserable life, whose conditions are consequences of the palaces and harems of the rich. Had I portrayed these things, it would have cast such a reflection on all royal palaces and royal pleasures that Harsh, with his five-yearly distribution of the royal treasure, or rather the surplus of it, at Prayag, would not have been satisfied with classing me merely as a libertine!

—3—

They call me Durmukh[12] (foul-mouthed) because of my habit of telling unpleasant truths. In our time some with this habit are occasionally met with, but they indulge in it under the pretence of being insane, so that many take them to be insane in fact, while others take them for wonderful seers straight from Shriparvat (Holy Hill). I also, in this age of belief in the sacred Hill, could have passed for a fine seer, but then my name would not have been Durmukh. I have no taste for this sort of fraud. It was because of it that I left Nalanda; had I stayed there I could have been one of its leading *pandits*.[13] I saw there one man who flashed a light through its thick shadows, but I also saw how hotly he was denounced by friend and foe. You may be curious to hear about this man. He was a philosopher of preeminent wisdom, the only lion among a crowd of sheep. His name was Dharmkirti. He spoke in Nalanda with a trumpet-voice –

'To set books above wisdom, to think of some god as the creator of Heaven; to try and make religion consist in taking baths; to take pride in being born into a certain caste; to defeat sin by mortifying the body – these are the surest signs of a mind numbed and lost to reason.'[14]

'Master,' I said to him, 'your doctrine is sharp, but it has grown too subtle to make any impression on these people.'

Dharmkirti replied –

'I know well how ineffective it is; to destroy what I want to destroy, I should have to throw off all armour and seize up the strongest weapons that would glitter in all men's eyes. Already the sages of Nalanda, great and small, are displeased with me. Do you think I should be left with a single disciple, if I began saying – Nalanda is all a show, a place where the kind of students come who can never embrace the great world in their view, who can do nothing but use their knowledge to dazzle others who have little knowledge or none! When men are receiving scented rice, condiments, butter and sweetmeats from the estates bestowed by Shiladitya, how can they teach the word rebellion to the poor people who have been squeezed to provide Shiladitya with his pleasures?'

'Then, is there no road of escape, Master, from this darkness?'

'Escape? There is a medicine for every disease, there is some way out of every calamity; but even in many generations, my friend, you cannot build a road out of this dark night, a bridge over this Vaitarni.[15] The hands of the builders are few, and the power of the darkness is great.'

'We can do nothing but sit down in despair?'

'To sit still is at least better than to practise deception. Do you not see what frauds are the men who ought to be pointing out the road to us? And this is not happening in one country alone, it is seen all over the world. Sinhal, Suvarndvip, Kambojdvip, Champadvip, Cheen, Tushar, Parasya[16] – there are learned scholars from all these countries in Nalanda and when you talk to them you realize that the world has gone blind. *Curse on this universal darkness!*'[17]

This holy man endeavoured by scattering abroad his fiery words to dispel the shadows of superstition, but if they had any effect at that time, I could not see it. I resolved to carry forward the blazing torch myself. One consequence of my resolve was that I have become 'Durmukh'. One thing I must explain, that while I use my tongue, I am compelled to avoid any direct attack on the royal power, or my life would not be safe for a week. Still, I sometimes, in a guarded manner, go far enough.

What does it mean, after all, that you talk of bestowing freedom and Nirvan[18] after death, while here on earth myriads of slaves are being sold into captivity like animals, and you make no effort to give them freedom? Once, at the festival at Prayag, I put this question to King Shiladitya (Harsh) also – 'Your Majesty, if you had spent on freeing slaves the treasure which you divide every fifth year among the already wealthy monasteries and Brahmins, would it have been any less meritorious an act?'

Shiladitya evaded the issue, saying he would discuss it some other time, but I found another occasion, and it was the King's sister, the Buddhist nun Rajyashri, who intervened to gain it for me. I drew a picture for her of the hellish misery of a slave's life, and it melted her heart; and when I added that the most meritorious of all deeds was to give money and bestow freedom on human beings chained to this ancient bondage, that went on for generation to generation, the thought stuck in her mind. How could that poor simple woman understand all the selfish interests that are bound up with slavery? How could she understand that on the day when this earth is transformed into a heaven, the heaven beyond the clouds will fade away? To establish a heaven above and hell below the world and reap a profit by talking of them – for this we need a heaven and hell in human life, kings and beggars, masters and slaves.

The King discussed it with me in private. His first remark was that he could no doubt set slaves free once, by spending a great deal of money, but that poverty would soon oblige them to sell themselves again.

'Then make the sale and purchase of these human beings a punishable offence for the future.'

He became thoughtful and silent. I suggested to him the example of Naag, in the *Naaganand*, who was willing to sacrifice his own life to save that of another. The play, *Naaganand*, was supposed to be the work of King Harsh, so he could find nothing to say to this. But in the end he reflected that he could not hope to gain as much glory by freeing slaves as by filling the begging-bowls of Buddhist monks and Brahmins, or by building great temples. I realized that day that Harsh was not the 'Shiladitya' (Sun of Righteousness) but 'Shilandhkar' (Darkness of Righteousness).

But why should I blame only poor Harsh? Nowadays it is the mark of distinguished and civilized people to be always cheating one another. From studying the rites and customs of the Buddhist times, in the old Buddhist writings, I know that wine-drinking was formerly as much a matter of course as drinking water. Not to drink it was then regarded as a special austerity. Today the Brahmins prohibit wine, and to drink it publicly is to risk persecution. But what is the result of all this? Under the cover of deity-worship and asceticism the Bhairvichakr[19] is secretly being practised. There is loud talk about chastity, but what happens? During these Bhairvichakr practices, all women – ones' own and those of other men – are accessible; not only this, but under the cloak of acts of religious devotion even a man's very mother, sister, and daughter are accessible to him. The monasteries of these ascetics and monks have been turned into places of unnatural debauchery. If there were, in truth, anyone watching and hearing this world of men, He would not tolerate it for a moment.

I visited Kamrup once. Its king was a great admirer of Nalanda, and a devotee of the Mahayan[20] sect of Buddhism. I said to him –

'Mahayanis believe in the promise of Bodhisattv,[21] according to which it is said that "so long as a single living thing is in captivity, Nirvan is not for me". In your kingdom are numerous untouchables;

when they enter a town, they walk along banging a stick on the ground, so that passers-by may be on their guard and not be polluted by contact with them. They must carry a bowl with them, so that their impure spittle may not fall on the pure ground of the town. A man is not contaminated by contact with a dog, a dog's dirt does not pollute a town; are untouchables worse than dogs?'

'No, they are not. They have the same source, the same life-current as other men, and as it broadens it can bring them one day to Enlightenment.'

'Then why should you not proclaim by beat of drum that from today these people need not carry their sticks and spitting bowls?'

'To do that is beyond my power.'

'Beyond your power?'

'Yes, because the rule has become a religious observance.'

'Is it the observance laid down by the religion of the Bodhisattvs; does Mahayan work like this?'

'But the people here are not all followers of the Mahayan.'

'I hear the victory drums of *Tri-Ratn*[22] beating everywhere in town and village.'

'That is only a pretension, but the day I proclaim that openly, my enemies will raise a storm against me, and accuse me of breaking the law that has come down to us from antiquity.'

'Does no light at all fall on anyone's mind from all the preaching that goes on day and night about the Bodhisattvs and their great lives? I believe that they must have some effect. Your Majesty, and if you are ready like a Bodhisattv to renounce everything, many will be found ready to follow you.'

'It is not a question of my own kingdom only. Our Parambhattarak king will also be displeased.'

'Harsh, the "Sun of Righteousness", the man who has painted such a glowing picture of saintly life in his play *Naaganand*?'

'Yes! To break down that ancient law is beyond the power of any man.'

'What would Tathagat[23] have done if he had believed that? Or the noble Ashvghosh, or the noble Naagarjun?'

'Those men had courage. Yet even they could not get very far in demolishing the old law.'

'If you cannot go far, Your Majesty, go at least a little way! Do something, and those who come after you, will do more.'

'Are you determined to make me confess myself a coward?'

'Not a coward; but certainly religion for us is a great snare.'

'If I answer you from my heart, I shall say yes but if I am to answer only with my tongue, I shall either give you a plain no, or say nothing at all.'

The Brahminical religion is hateful to me. It bears the guilt of having made cowards of many men good at heart, like the king of Kamrup. When the burden of this religion is lifted from the country, a dark stain will be removed from the earth. From foreign monks who came to Nalanda, I have learned that among them there is no dominant class of religious leaders like our Brahmins. When I heard this I understood why among them there is also no class of untouchables who have to go about with stick and earthen bowl. In our country the Brahmins have divided humanity into higher and lower castes in such a way that nobody will have anything to do with those below him. Their religion and their wisdom are nothing but a dark shadow caused by Rahu-Ketu.[24]

At Nalanda one always hears varied news from many countries, so when I have spent a year or two in travelling, I go back there for six months. Once a Persian monk told me that in his country, sometime before, there had been a wise man named Mazdak, who had spread a sort of communism. Buddh also prescribed a form of communism for his monks and nuns, in all matters of ownership, but that is only a thing to be read about in Vinay Pitak.[25] Today there are monks of enormous private wealth. This teacher Mazdak was not in favour of celibacy and mendicancy. He believed only in natural human life, family life, but he said that the root of all evil was egotism and the sense of possession. Property should not be individual, he said, we should produce and consume collectively. Marriage should not be exclusive, love should be free, and children should belong to the community. He also taught kindliness to all living things, and self-restraint. These ideas seemed to me very fine. When I learned that a Persian king, Naushervan, had slaughtered Mazdak and his numerous followers, and set himself up as the embodiment of justice on the strength of his exploits, it became clear to me that so long as kings remain, the begging-Brahmins who live by religion and its endowments remain, this earth can never be made a paradise.

1 2 3 4 5 6 7 8 9 10
20 19 18 17 16 15 **14** 13 12 11

14

Chakrpani

TIME : 1200 CE

—1—

Kannauj was now the biggest and richest city of India. Its markets and squares were always thronged. It was famous throughout India for its sweets, perfumes, oils, drinking vessels, ornaments and many other articles. People felt for it a respect of another kind also, because it had been for six hundred years the capital of dynasties like the Maukhari, Bais, Pratihar and Gahadwar, in their times the most powerful in the country. In addition, some caste-groups had given its name to their offshoots: hence today we have Kanyakubj (Kannauj) Brahmins, Kanyakubj Ahirs, and so forth, among many of our castes. The name of Kannauj acquired in people's minds the same association as the name of the Hindu religion. Many revolutions had taken place in the world since the time of Harsh, but India's mind had become narrow and limited, like that of a frog in a well.

It was in the time of Harshvardhan that a new religion of Islam had been born in Arabia. No one contemplating it then would have prophesied that within a century of its founder's death (622 CE) it would spread everywhere from Sindh to Spain. Hitherto conquest had been connected with the names of nations or kings: now for the first time men heard of a crusade of conquest, in the name of religion. It gave its victims no chance to prepare for defence, but swept over them in a moment. The powerful Persian empire of the Sassanids fell instantly like a house of cards at the first touch of the Arabs; and before two centuries had passed since the founder of Islam's death, the flag of the kingdom of Islam was waving over the Pamir.[1]

At first Islam tried to organize the whole world on the model of its Arab tribes, and at the same time to inspire its followers with the simple, democratic, brotherly feeling of the tribesmen. The ancestors of the Vedic Aryans had passed through this stage of development three thousand years before. It was impossible to resurrect that dead epoch. Therefore, as Islam came in contact with peoples that had evolved beyond the tribal stage and lived under monarchies, the political independence of these peoples collapsed before its sword; this same contact brought to an end the tribal structure of Islamic society. For some time the paramount leaders of Islam were known merely as the Khalifas – successors of the Prophet, though in fact they were Sultans – autocratic monarchs. But by now there had been several who were called Sultans, and who had no interest in the pure Islamic tribalism or the old simplicity, equality and fraternity. But for the conquest of new lands they needed warriors, and it was now no longer the Arabs, but men of other races, who yielded the sword for them. These soldiers could not be expected to show the old enthusiasm now that they were fighting for a Sultan, so along with the lure of the joys of paradise, they had to be given a share in the earthly joys also! They had a right to the plunder and prisoners taken, they were at liberty to colonize newly conquered territory and they were entitled to freedom from their former tyrants and masters and could even put these to the sword. No one had ever before gathered so many soldiers from among the people he conquered, men ready to embrace the banner of their conqueror as their own; and it was no easy task to encounter such an enemy, capable of creating within the borders of a foreign land a fresh army ready to fight on its side.

Harsh had not been dead a hundred years when Sindh passed under Muslim sway. India, as far away as Banaras and Somnath[2] had already felt the sword of Islam. If the peril was to be averted, new modes of action had to be found, yet even now the Hindus could not rouse themselves to abandon their ancient ways. Instead of the entire nation being ready for self-defence, the only warriors of India were the handful of Rajputs, that is the Kshatriyas of old and the Shakas, Greeks, Gurjars and others who had joined their ranks by intermarriage; and these were distracted by internecine rivalries.

To the very end, the feuds, old and new, among the ruling families prevented them from cooperating with one another.

—2—

'Have no anxiety, Your Majesty: the holy seer has begun to devise means by which the Turks will be scattered like dead leaves before the wind.'

'How bountiful our Priest Mitrpad[3] is to me! Whenever misfortune has threatened me or my family he has saved me by his divine power!'

'Your Majesty, the holy priest has seen the danger menacing Kannauj from the Bhot[4] country beyond the Himalayas. That is why he has sent me to you.'

'He is so generous!'

'He says that Tarini[5] (Taradevi) will help Your Majesty. Have no fear of the Turks.'

'I have all faith in our Mother Taradevi! O' Tarini! Refuge of those in trouble! Help us against these *mlechhs*, Mother!'

The old King Jaichandr was seated on a soft mattress, which was white as camphor, in his royal palace that rivalled the heavenly halls of Indr. Close beside him sat four young consorts of surpassing beauty, whose raven-black hair, drawn back from their fair faces, was gathered up in heavy knots. They were loaded with ornaments that must have weighed more than their own bodies – aigrettes, earrings, amulets, bracelets, necklaces of precious metals and gems, girdles sewn with bells, toe rings, and many more trappings of gold and jewellery. They wore soft robes and bodices, but these were evidently meant not to hide their limbs, but to reveal their charms. Each bodice seductively displayed the swelling breasts and the delicate brown skin. Below it, the body was bare to the navel. The shape and tint of the thigh and calf were plainly visible. The fragrant oil in their hair, and their garlands of newly opened jasmine, filled the chamber with perfume. Besides the queen-consorts there were more than fifty young female attendants. Some were waving fly-whisks, peacock-plumes, or fans, some held trays of betel nut, some mirrors or combs, some bowls of scented water, some wine-glasses and golden cups, some stood ready with napkins soft and white as the sloughed skin of a snake. Others sat with musical instruments, the *mridang*, the *muraj*, the *veena*, the *venu*, and many more. Yet others stood or walked about carrying golden wands. Except for King Jaichandr and his visitor – Mitrpad's disciple, the monk Shubhakar – all those present were queens, all lovely young women.

The monk took his leave, the King and his consorts standing up to salute him. Now the King was alone with his crowd of females. He was an old man, but from the manner in which his long, greying hair, parted in the middle, was drawn back, his carefully trimmed bushy moustaches, and the ornaments and rich clothes in which he was arrayed, it was clear that he regarded his youth as by no means at an end. At a sign from him, an attendant bent before him with a goblet. One of the queens took it and offered him the brimming cup. He put it to her lips, saying, 'Rajalla (Rajalakshmi), my brightest one! How can I drink this before you have tasted it?'

She moistened her lips and tongue, and then the King drank off the thus 'consecrated beverage'. Each of his favourites in turn touched a cup and presented it. His eyes began to glow. The lines of anxiety drawn there by the Turks fled from his face, and a smile played over it instead. His fat body reclined there, supported by the cushions; he pulled one of his queens down by him on each side, rested his head on the lap of a third, and put his arms across the bosom of a fourth.

The wine-cups circulated among them and he exchanged salacious jests with the women. Now the King gave orders for dancing. Dressed in skirts, with bells tied round their ankles, some of the girls stood up ready, round-breasted, slender-waisted, and heavy-hipped. The *veena* and the *mridang* began to sound, and to the accompaniment of soft singing the dance opened. After one song, the King found all this insipid, and ordered them to dance naked. The dancing girls threw off all their clothes and ornaments except the bell-hung girdles. The consorts and attendants sat at the side of the room, the King among them exchanging embraces and jokes; the nude dancing went on in the middle of the room. When a girl's bare limbs attracted the King, she was called to him, while another took her place. His potations had affected his speech as he stammered out – 'D... d... d... a... m... n yo... u T... Tu... r... ks! No ru... f... fi... an can set fo... ot in my h... ar... em! A... ll of y... o... u d... an... ce na... ked!'

All the women in the chamber removed their dresses and

ornaments. But the King was not pleased with the heavy knots of hair that loaded the heads above their beautiful, fair-coloured young bodies, and he told them to let their hair down. Long snaky tresses of dark hair floated from every head down to the hips. Seeing the King himself pull off his tunic, the girls helped him to remove his clothes and ornaments. No ordinary woman could have beheld without contempt his wobbling chins, his gross cheeks, his bushy whiskers, his breasts sagging like a mother's, his belly swollen like a water pot, his fat soft thighs and calves and his thick hairy arms. But he held the lives of all these girls in the hollow of his old hand. One surrendered her lips to his toothless mouth, while another pressed her bosom against his side, and a third took his hairy arm round her shoulders and cheek. The dance began again, to the sound of voluptuous music. The King began to dance himself with his pot belly in the midst of his consorts and concubines.

—3—

'Come, my prince of poets!' said the King, as he motioned the middle-aged man to a seat, and then presented him respectfully with two betel leaves. The 'prince of poets' was above fifty, but his fair-complexioned, handsome face still retained some traces of his lost youth, and his moustache was still black. Besides his white robe and shawl he wore a *rudraksh*[6] necklace, and three crescent-shaped lines were smeared on his forehead with ashes. The poet put into his mouth the scented betel, wrapped in gold leaf, saying –

'My lord, was your journey a good one? Did you enjoy good health? Do you enjoy comfortable sleep at night?'

'My manhood is growing exhausted, O' *Pungav*-poet!'

'Your Majesty! You like to make fun of your poet Shriharsh?'

'I call you "*pungav*" as a term of praise, not of ridicule.'

'It is also the word for an ox.'

'I know, but it is also used for distinguished men.'

'I take it in the animal sense.'

'And I, in the honourable sense. Well, my poet and friend, whom can I make fun of, if not of a dear old companion like you!'

'But not inside the court,' said Shriharsh in a low voice.

Jaichandr took the poet by the hand and drew him out of the hall of audience into the pleasure-garden. Summer was now just beginning and it was delightful to feel the breeze that gently stirred the green trees. The King seated his companion on a white marble bench, with arms set above the terraced steps of a pool, and then began –

'You ask me about my nights ... I have begun to feel that I am indeed growing old.'

'Why?'

'Even naked girls cannot arouse my desire.'

'Then you have become a true ascetic, Your Majesty.'

'And what are the sixteen thousand women of this ascetic to do?'

'Give them away. There are many who would be glad to have them or you could distribute them to the Brahmins on the Ganga, in return for the sacred water and grass;[7] you know the saying[8] – "The greatest of all charities is to give away your wife".'

'That is what I shall have to do. The aphrodisiacs of my chief physician Chakrpani have lost their power. Now my only hope of pleasure lies in enjoying your poetry.'

'What can poetry do, when naked beauty has lost its darts? After all, Your Majesty has passed sixty.'

'But a "*sathha* (sixty-year-old) is a *pathha* (bull)", as they say!'

'What! A bull that has been enjoying itself for so long with sixteen thousand heifers!'

'Well, you have not shown yourself at Banaras till now, and it is two months since I came from Kannauj!'

'During the sacred nine days of the month of Chaitr I went to visit the shrine of the goddess Vindhyavasini.'

'My boat passed it on its way. If I had known I would have called for you.'

'Or you might have landed and taken part in the worship of the local beauties!'

'Then had you also gone there just for that?'

'I am a follower and worshipper of the goddess Bhagvati.'

'But you write in praise of Ram and Sita, as if you were a true Vaishnav.'[9]

'Well, you know the saying – "A worshipper of Shakti in his heart, of Shiv in his mouth, of Vishnu in public".'[10]

'So you are a Vaishnav in public, eh!'

'I have to be, Your Majesty; we fellows can't order our critics' tongues to be pulled out as you can.'

'You blessed chameleon!'

'Your Majesty, I have gone further still. I have admitted Buddh too among my objects of worship.'

'What! Even Sugat, the Enlightened One!'

'Yes.'

'Buddh! Confound it, I am ashamed of myself whenever I say the words.'

'Your Majesty, Vajryan has simplified the worship of Sugat for us, the followers of Shakti.'

'Yes, indeed, my friend. That is why they call it the "Sahajyan" (Easy Path).'

'I see very little poetry in the verses and songs composed by the exponent of this form of Buddhism, but I am pleased with the spread of its principle of Panchmakar (five 'M's[11]). It has done the people a lot of good. But for me it would be difficult to follow these heretical Tantr rites now, I think.'

'And if you take the Vajryan form of Buddhism and add a dash of Naagarjun's Madhyamik[12] (middle path) philosophy – it is really painting the lily.'

'I can enjoy the flavour of your poetry, though sometimes it makes my head spin, but philosophy begins to feel like a leaden weight on my head.'

'Even so, Your Majesty, Naagarjun's philosophy is very useful. It drives away a great many false opinions.'

'But you are celebrated as a Vedantist.'[13]

'I have made my books celebrated, by calling them Vedants.[14] But the book *Khandan-Khand-Khadya* ['the Sweets of Refutation'] gives us only Naagarjun's less important ideas.'

'I shall never be able to remember it, still, tell me what is remarkable in Naagarjun.'

'Your peerless prophet Mitrpad believes in his philosophy.'

'What, my own family priest?'

'Yes, Naagarjun says that vice and virtue, good conduct and bad conduct are mere abstractions. The existence or non-existence of the world cannot be proved. Heaven and hell, freedom and bondage are old wives' tales. Prayer and worship are only meant to amuse fools. The superstitious notion of gods and goddesses is false.'

'Then, my dear poet, I have spent my whole life in agreeing with this philosophy.'

'So does everyone, Your Majesty. Only idiots throw away solid cash to chase after debts.'

'But now all I can do with my "solid cash" is to sit and stare at it impotently! But you don't look as if you would ever age.'

'Well, I am eight years younger than you; besides, I have never married more than one wife.'

'What question is there of marriage! If a man were to marry all the women he needs, he would die of exhaustion just from having to walk round the sacred fire so often.'

'There is only one single Brahmin-woman in my house, Your Majesty.'

'And you expect the world to believe that the poet Shriharsh is living faithfully with one toothless old woman all the time!'

'The world will believe it, does believe it. I put in my books even such things as accounts of how I have trances and come in touch with God.'

'Then there is room in your Madhyamik philosophy for God and knowledge of God!'

'There is room in it for everything, Your Majesty.'

'In short, the people must be kept blind so that we can put any sort of idea into their head.'

'Then, Your Majesty, your own faith in religion has left you?'

'I don't know. I can scarcely distinguish at what point faith begins or ends. When I listen to the sermons of your pious Brahmins, and look at their practices, it is hard to make up my mind. All I believe is this: one should give alms, and build temples and monasteries, and do whatever religion prescribes, but as long as one lives one should hold fast to the wealth of life.'

From love and religion, the conversation drifted to politics. 'Is it true,' enquired Shriharsh, 'that Your Majesty has refused to come to the support of Prithviraj?'

'What reasons have I for supporting him? He has roused the tempest himself, let him weather it himself.'

'That is what I think too. Chakrpani is just raising a false alarm.'

'His business is to mix medicines, and even there he can do nothing. Three times he has made aphrodisiacs for me, but they were all useless and now he wants to thrust his oar into politics!'

'He is a fool, Your Majesty. The prince has unnecessarily made him conceited.'

—4—

'You are right, Physician. Shriharsh is the canker at the root of the royal line of Gahadwar. He has reduced my father to a blind mania for women.'

'Prince, I have been physician to the court of Kannauj for twenty years, and there is some virtue in my herbs.'

'All the world knows that!'

'But the King is angry about his aphrodisiacs. How long can a man, consumed by such lust, hope to prolong his youth? The books tell us to practise moderation in our diet and our pleasures. Let me go and live quietly at Mallagram, I keep begging him. But he will not agree to that either.'

'Physician, you must not go away and leave me because of my father's faults! You are the only hope left to the Gahadwars now.'

'Not me, but you, Prince Harishchandr, are their hope. How much better it would have been if Harishchandr instead of Jaichandr had been head of the House of Gahadwar! It was you whom the throne of Chandrdev required!'

'And how much better if the great physician Chakrpani had been the King's bosom friend, instead of Shriharsh! But you must stay with us until the sun of our dynasty has set.'

'May my own life fade with its setting, Prince! But it will be the twilight of the Hindus, not of your dynasty alone. Of all the Brahmins, we alone of Mallagram are good at holding swords as well as at scriptures and rituals. We too want to fight against the Turks!'

'And yet my father will not help his own son-in-law against them. Prithviraj is my brother-in-law. My sister Sanyukta loved him; she married him of her own free will. What ground has my father to be dissatisfied?'

'Prithviraj is a hero, Prince.'

'No one can doubt that. It is his heroism that has made him brave the Turkish Sultan; his kingdom is nothing compared with ours of Kannauj. If he had merely left the way open to the Turks their Sultan would have treated him with favour. They have their eyes on Kannauj, not on Delhi. Kannauj has ruled over the biggest kingdom in India for six centuries. But who is to make my father understand? He has sapped his own power of understanding anything.'

'If only he would hand over the government to his son!'

'Physician, the thought did come to me once that I ought to remove my father from the throne. But then I remembered what you had taught me. All these twenty years I have found all your counsels good. I cannot go against them now.'

'The throne of Kannauj has grown old and feeble, Prince. One false step now and this edifice of power will lie in ruins. This is no time for strife between father and son.'

'But what can be done, Physician! All our generals and officers are cowardly and unwarlike. There are a few brave and skilful men among the junior officers, perhaps, but the old ones stand in their way. The ministers are irresponsible; they consider intrigue their only duty.'

'Yes, the men who earn their posts by sending their sisters and daughters to the royal harem. But it is the future we must think about anxiously, not the past.'

'If it were left to me today, I should arm the entire Hindu youth.'

'But the evil custom of many generations, Prince, has entrusted the sword to the Rajput caste alone. In the *Mahabharat* we hear of Brahmins like Dron and Kripa fighting; but since that time only a single caste ...'

'Yes, I understand, this caste system is a very great stumbling block in our way.'

'The greatest of all stumbling blocks, Prince! It is very well to take pride in the high deeds of one's ancestors, but this perpetual division of the Hindus into a thousand fragments is a wicked thing.'

'And now we are made to taste its evil fruit. Kabul no more belongs to the Hindus; Lahore is gone, now it is Delhi's turn.'

'But even now, if only we could fight along with Pithauras!'[15]

'Oh! What calamity we are facing now instead!'

'Calamity? The ship of state is being swamped by its load of calamities! Yet we are still sunk in our infatuation, and unwilling to lighten the ship by throwing a single thing overboard!'

'Physician, it is religion that has choked us.'

'Religion is a cancer. What tyrannies we have been guilty of! Every year myriads of widows perish in the flames, men and women are bought and sold like cattle, gold and silver and pearls and gems are piled up in temples and monasteries to rouse the cupidity of barbarian robbers, and when the time comes to resist them sword in hand we are absorbed in petty wrangling. Our ruler is sunk in self-indulgence, and to supply him we pitilessly plunder the people of the fruits of their toil.'

'It is not self-indulgence, it is madness. One loving wife is enough to satisfy his needs, yet fifty thousand women are not enough for his royal madness. There can be no love there. At the time of the last Sankranti festival, when my father gave away many of his women to the Brahmins, none of them wept, they were quite happy in their hearts. My dear Bhama told me this.'

'In the houses of the Brahmins they were given to, they would have one or two co-wives at the most, there would be no army of sixteen thousand women. That harem life is no better than slavery. And is woman mere chattel, to be given away?'

'At any rate, we must make an effort here as well to rally our forces against the Turks.'

'It is for the King to do that, and the wretched Shriharsh rules his mind.'

—5—

It was the eighth night of the month. The moon had just begun to rise above the eastern horizon, but it would still be long before the whole earth was bathed in its light. Silence reigned everywhere, except that somewhere in the distance could be heard the ill-omened hooting of an owl.

Through this stillness, two men appeared from above the bank and made their way swiftly down to the channel. They put their fingers to their mouths and whistled three times. A boat came in sight, moving from the opposite bank. The boat, of fair size, made a faint splashing in the sluggish current as it reached the shore. The two men, making no sound, jumped aboard. Someone in the boat asked –

'The commander Madhav?'

'Yes sir! And Alhan has also come with me. How is the prince?'

'He is still unconscious, but I have given him some medicine to keep him so, lest he return to the battlefield!'

'But he cannot disobey your order.'

'So I believe, but this way is better and he will suffer less pain from the wound.'

'Then the wound is not dangerous?'

'No, commander; I have stitched up the wound, and the bleeding has stopped. He is very weak, of course, but there is no fear of anything worse. Tell me, what have you done? Have you sent the King's body to the harem?'

'Yes.'

'So now the harem women will take the body and burn themselves with it?'

'Those who have to do so, will do it.'

'And the commander-in-chief?'

'The old man only woke up at the last moment, at the fatal moment. Many of the officers took to flight when they saw how things were going, but they were no good even at running away. I have no hope of any of them being left alive.'

'Alas, if only it had all happened three years ago, and with Harishchandr as our king and you, Madhav, as our commander-in-chief!'

Madhav sighed as he answered –

'My honourable sir, all your warnings were crystal clear. You did your best to persuade the King to unite with Pithaura and resist the Turks, but yours was a voice crying in the wilderness.'

'It is no use lamenting it now. Tell me, what other measures have you taken?'

'Five hundred boats are on their way now, filled with soldiers in squadrons of fifty each. I have divided them under the command of Gaga, Moga and Salkhu, and have instructed these forces to withdraw eastward from Chandawar (Etawa) and engage the Turks, a few frontally, the rest from ambush; and when they see the situation turning against them, to retreat still further east.'

'And the royal palace of Kannauj?'

'I have removed from it whatever I could bring away. A good many boats have gone down the Ganga and made their escape already two days ago.'

'That is why I rescued you from the commander-in-chief's anger, Madhav, and I was happy when I found that you and the prince were still alive. Now there is some hope left for the Hindus. Whatever happens, we must struggle to the end, and use every atom of strength that we have.'

'Other boats seem to be approaching.'

'Commander Alhan, soon as they are here, give word for every boat to move on,' said Chakrpani.

'Very good, honourable sir,' replied Alhan in a respectful tone.

'Well, Madhav, come down into the cabin. But it's dark in there. I put out the lamp on purpose. ... Wait a moment,' he added a little later – 'Radha! ...'

'Yes, *Baba*?'[16] was heard in a young female voice.

'Strike the flint and light the lamp; you have kept the steel carefully?'

'All right.'

'Friend,' he remarked, turning to Madhav, 'some call me physician, some call me honourable sir, some call me Baba, it is hard for me to remember all these names. You should all call me by my childhood name – Chakku.'

'No! It is hard to change the habit of women. Instead of calling you Baba Chakrpani Pandeya, we shall all simply call you Baba.'

'Very well. Come, the lamp is lit.'

Both men descended the steps. Two-thirds of the boat was covered with a deck under which, one behind the other, were a few cabins. They entered one of these. In the yellow light of the lamp could be seen a camp bed; on this a man was sleeping, covered up to the throat with a white shawl. A girl rose from a stool placed at the corner of the bed.

'Well, Bhama,' said Chakrpani, 'the prince has not stirred, then?'

'No, Baba; his breathing is still the same.'

'You are not frightened, child?'

'Frightened, under your protection? Oh! If only the House of Gahadwar had recognized you earlier as its guide, its Dron!'[17]

'See, here is Madhav, the chief officer of King Harishchandr, our leader and our supreme hope.'

'Princess Bhama, your servant Madhav has come to serve you,' said the officer, saluting her.

'I know Madhav already,' she answered. 'Can I ever forget the sight of him and the prince playing together as children?'

'And Madhav's arm,' said Chakrpani, 'has strength enough to restore the fallen fortunes of your line, Bhama.'

'Oh, Baba, how fine it is to hear you call me Bhama!'

'You must be thinking of your father.'

'No, no. Our family must set its course on a new track now. What an illusion, what a fraud it has all been! We must build a simple, united human society. Let the old royal caste vanish with my royal father-in-law.'

'It has vanished, daughter, long since. Have you seen the prince's harem?'

Bhama wiped a tear from her eye.

'You have brought me back to mortality,' she said.

'No, child. If it were anyone other than Harishchandr, I should be beating the air for nothing. All this is due to Harishchandr ...'

'Baba! ...'

The prince's eyes had half opened; they all stared at him. Bhama ran to his side, exclaiming, 'My *chandr*,[18] my *chandr*, you have returned safe from the mouth of Rahu!'[19]

'Yes, dear Bhama. ... Was it not Baba's voice I heard just now?'

'Your Baba's!'

'Not my real Baba, who has brought the sun of our line to its setting, but the man you call "Baba", I shall also call him the same.'

'Prince,' said Chakrpani, holding the lamp so that he could examine the young man's pallid face, and laying a hand on his forehead –

'How are you feeling?'

'I feel as if I had been wounded on the battlefield and were still lying there.'

'It was a deep wound, Prince.'

'Perhaps, but you were there to save me.'

'Don't talk too much.'

'Very well. To me every word from Chakrpani is a voice from heaven!'

'Don't say that, you will not be much use to me if you think like that.'

'Baba, it is a question of my faith in you. Whenever there is a question of having to think, I will not believe even the word of God without trying it on the touchstone.'

'Prince! All Hindustan,[20] not your dynasty alone, is fortunate in possessing you.'

'In possessing you, Baba Chakrpani. ... Some water.' Bhama at once filled a glass and gave it him. Chakrpani felt the boat getting under way, and explained –

'We are making for Banaras, our second capital. Madhav, your commander, has given orders to the army. It will halt the Turks here, while we at Banaras collect more troops to restore the fortunes of the Gahadwars.'

'No, Baba, as you used to say in other days, let us make ready to restore the fortunes of the Hindu race, restore them with victory won by the strength of the Hindu sword.'

'Then we must abolish the difference between Brahmin and Chandal.'

'Yes, my Guru Dron, we must.'

15

Baba Noordin

TIME : 1300 CE

—1—

'The days have gone when we regarded India as no more than a cow for us to milk, when we extorted wealth from the peasants, artisans, traders and princes, and either sent it to Ghor[1] or squandered it on our own pleasures. We are not the slaves[2] of Ghor anymore; we are the Khiljis,[3] independent rulers of India.'

It was a slim young man who spoke, running his fingers along the trim moustache that surmounted his black beard. In front of him knelt another man, with a long white beard and face alternately tranquil and excited, who wore a heavy turban and a white coat.

'Yes,' said the old man, 'but *Refuge of the World*![4] If the interests of the headmen and chiefs and feudatories are interfered with, they will grow disaffected, and we shall not be able to send our detachments through all the villages of the empire to collect our revenue.'

'First you must make up your mind on this question: do you want us to become Indians and settle down as rulers of India, or do you want us to remain plunderers from Ghazni[5] and Ghor, coming here only to carry off camel-loads and mule-loads of diamonds and pearls?'

'The time has come for us to settle down in India, *Refuge of the World*.'

'Yes. Our roots are not in Ghor, as those of the Slave Dynasty were, but in Delhi. If we are faced with any menace, any disturbance, there will be no Arab army coming to help us from Afghanistan; and if we have to flee, there will be no place of safety for us to go to.'

'Yes, that is true.'

'So we must stay where we are, and therefore we must put our house in order, so that the inhabitants will be contented and peaceful.

How many of the ordinary people here are Muslims? In a century we have not been able to convert even the districts round Delhi to Islam. Tell me, Mullah Abu Muhammad, how long do you expect it will be before all Delhi and this entire province has been converted?'

'I do not despair, *Monarch of the Age*!'[6] said another old man, smoothing the white beard that fell to his waist as he opened his toothless mouth with its sunken lips. 'But I have lived for eighty years, and the lesson of my experience is that there is no hope of full success if we try to make converts by force.'

'Then we Muslims who are settling down in India cannot afford to sit waiting for the day when all India will turn Muslim. We have wasted a century already in doing that, and meanwhile we have not given a single thought to our people, but have only tried to extort the heaviest possible land revenue and imposts and taxes. What is the result? For every rupee that enters the royal treasury, five are swallowed up by the revenue collectors. Is there any other country in the world where village officials ride out in silken clothes to indulge in sport with Persian bows and arrows? No, Vazir-ul-mulk,[7] in my dominions this kind of robbery must be brought to an end.'

'Your Majesty,' objected the Mullah, 'many Hindus have turned Muslim out of ambition for such posts, and now even this means of conversion will be lost.'

'If Islam sanctions this kind of robbery and bribery, then the royal treasury and the royal property are not safe either. Besides, what hope can there be for a government that employs such servants?'

'They cannot be strong pillars to the State,' said the Vazir, 'that I admit. I was only thinking of the danger of rebellion.'

'The officials in the countryside will be ripe for that, if their power is taken away. But which are more numerous in the villages, the officials or the peasants?'

'The peasants – they must be a hundred to one.'

'The one man, by sucking the blood of the hundred, is able to ride on horseback and dress in silk and shoot with a Persian bow. By stopping this bloodsucking we shall improve the condition of the cultivators and gain their loyalty to the government. Surely, it is good policy to make a hundred contented and prosperous at the expense of offending one individual!'

'Certainly, Your Majesty. I have no doubt now that although you will be the first of the Muslim rulers of India to embark on such a policy, it will prove advantageous. We shall only be alienating a few people of the rural bureaucracy.'

'Rural or urban, it is a matter of indifference whether we alienate them. Today we have to lay the foundations of a strong building, instead of treating our government as a temporary lodging place.'

The Mullah had been deep in thought.

'Your Majesty,' he now observed, stroking his beard, 'I too have realized that it will prove advantageous to the government to think of the well-being of the peasant masses instead of that of the village officials. We have given some attention to the cloth workers of the villages and cities. We helped them strengthen their *panchayats*[8] so as to save them from being fleeced by the traders and moneylenders. Every official used to get his clothes made, or his cotton carded, by forced labour. We stopped that, and today, as a consequence, we find that scarcely any of the spinners, weavers or tailors have failed to embrace Islam.'

'So you have seen for yourself, Mullah, that what is good for the State is also good for Islam.'

'But there is one request I have to make, *Refuge of the World*! You are also Amir-ul-mominin.[9] ...'

'I am also the Sultan of the Hindus. The number of Muslims in India is very small; they are scarcely one in a thousand.'

'The Hindus are continually insulting Islam. In the future their insolence may go even further. It must be repressed.'

'Insulting Islam? Do they trample on the Holy Quran?'

'They would never venture to do that!'

'Well, do they desecrate our mosques?'

'No, no; that is out of the question.'

'Do they vent abuse in the streets against the Holy Prophet?'

'No, *Refuge of the World*; indeed, those who have come in contact with our Sufis[10] revere the Holy Prophet as another Rishi. What I meant was that they carry out their infidel rites in front of our faces.'

'Since you consider them infidels, why object to their infidel practices? My uncle, Sultan Jalal-ud-din, had not made up his mind as I have done, to consider himself the permanent ruler of India, or as its temporary ruler until the time when all India should be converted. But he once gave a good answer to someone who was raising the same question as you. Have you heard it?'

'No, Your Majesty.'

'He said – "*Fool, do you not see how every day the Hindus pass in front of my palace, blowing their conch-shells and beating their drums, on their way to worship their idols on the banks of the Yamuna? They carry out their heathen rites before my own eyes. They affront me and my royal dignity. They are enemies of my religion, who in my own capital, under my nose, pass their lives in luxury and pomp, and puffed up with their wealth and prosperity, flaunt their conceit among the Muslims. Shame on me! I have left them their pomp and pride, and contented myself with the few straws they give me by way of charity!*" I think I can give you no better answer than this.'

'But, *Monarch of the Age*! The Sultan has a duty also towards Islam.'

'When a man has committed a capital offence, and seeks sanctuary in Islam, I can spare his life. When a slave embraces Islam, I can order his release from slavery, but only if I pay his price from the royal treasury, for there are many millions of rupees invested in slaves in this country, and you cannot think of liberating all slaves.'

'No, *Refuge of the World*! Allah himself sanctioned slave-owning.'

'Well, if you give the word I am ready to decree the liberation of all slaves, Muslim and non-Muslim, male and female, even at the risk of my throne.'

'No, that would be contrary to Islamic law.'

'Let us leave that question on one side, Mullah. You must be thinking just now of someone like Amina, your favourite slave-girl. The greatest number of slaves is to be found in the houses of the Muslims.'

'Allah has permitted it to the Faithful.'

'But what if the slaves also belong to the ranks of the Faithful? Even then, I think, you wish to deny them the breath of freedom in this world, and fix their hopes only on Paradise.'

'I have no more to say. In a Muslim State, Islamic law ought to be enforced, that is all I have to say.'

'But that is no small thing to ask for. It is necessary first that in your Muslim State the majority of the people should be Muslims. I want to make my views clear to you both, to you also, Vazir. A foreign ruler like Sultan Mahmud, with a powerful foreign army, could sack peaceful cities and carry off his plunder on mules and camels. But that is not in the power of a man like me, who has come to settle down in Delhi with his family. The revenue paid by the Hindu population and the army of Hindu soldiers and officers are the basis of my government. Malik himself, my commander-in-chief, is a Hindu, and the Raja[11] of Chittaur is a commander of five thousand soldiers in my army.'

'Even the Slave-rulers lived in Delhi, *Refuge of the World*. ...'

'Yes, speak your mind out! They call me restless and short-tempered, but they cannot prevent me from listening to criticism. The Slave-government was like a bird's one-night roosting-place. In India, Muslim power was sheltered from the Mongol tempest. The Hindus did not know that the Muslims had never faced such enemies as the Mongols; otherwise, if they had given the slightest encouragement to the Mongols, the seedling of Islam, newly planted in the Indian soil, would never have survived. You know, of course, that the dynasty of Changez is ruling over China, the greatest empire in the world.'

'I know, Your Majesty,' said the Mullah.

'And that that dynasty follows the Samaniya (Buddhist) religion.'

'Buddhism! That religion is the quintessence of infidelity, and yet it has not been extirpated from this land, in spite of so many of its monasteries and temples being burned or razed to the ground!'

'Why do you call it the quintessence of infidelity?'

'*Refuge of the World*! In the religion of the Hindus or the Brahmins, there is some notion of God, the Creator, but Buddhism denies Him altogether.'

'The family of Changez has been faithful to Buddhism ever since the time of his grandson Kublai Khan. Among the Mongols, in the army of Changez himself, there were many Buddhist warriors and leaders. They rooted out and destroyed every trace of Muslim civilization from Bukhara, Samarqand, Balkh, and many other cities of Islam. They reduced all our women indiscriminately to slavery, caring nothing for their high or low birth. They massacred our children without mercy. It was those same Buddhist Mongols who instigated all these atrocities. They said that the Arabs had destroyed their monasteries, burned their cities, slaughtered their children, and that they must take revenge. Imagine what would have become of Islam here if the Mongols had joined hands with the Buddhists in India and succeeded in winning over the Hindus!'

'It would have been wiped out.'

'That is the reason why we must not build our kingdom on sand; we must not imitate the Slave Dynasty.'

'But Your Majesty,' said the Vazir, breaking his silence, 'if we weaken the authority of the officials in the villages, how shall we exercise our power there?'

'You ought to know how it was done when there were no big men wearing silk and riding on horseback there.'

'I have never enquired into the question.'

'I have enquired into it. It was while our rulers regarded themselves as plunderers that they appointed these plundering officials. Before that time, every village had a *panchayat*. It managed by itself the village irrigation system, everything – from fights and quarrels to payment of the government revenue. The king had no need of a single official in the village. He concerned himself only with the council, which he recognized as the connecting link between himself and the peasants who paid his revenue.'

'Then we must revive these village councils which have been dead for a century.'

'There is no other way. If we wish to make Muslim power in this country strong, we must try by every means to make the common people happy and contented. And to do so we must respect the customs and laws of our Hindu subjects, and in our kingdom of Delhi we must enforce royal law, not Islamic law. To spread Islam is the task of our *mullahs*, and to them we can give stipends. It is the task of Sufis, who are performing it very well; we can make grants of money to their institutions, or can grant amnesty on the tax they owe.'

—2—

The rainy season had passed, but pools and ponds were still swollen with rainwater, the rice fields within their big embankments were flooded, and the green rice shoots glimmered on the surface. The big township of Hilsa[12] (Patna) lay amid Magadh's green expanses, which stretched away on all sides. It contained some brick-built houses belonging to merchants, the rest of its dwellings were the thatched or tiled huts of peasants and artisans, and some Brahmin houses in a somewhat better condition. Hilsa's temples had been destroyed a century earlier by the army of Muhammad-bin-Bakhtiyar Khilji, though Hindus still carried on their worship here and there in the ruins. On the western edge of the town lay a Buddhist monastery. The chamber housing the idol of Buddh was in ruins, but the building was still inhabited, and no one who made his way inside and saw its denizens would be likely to say that the Buddhist monks had deserted it.

That evening, on the small stone platform outside the monastery sat a middle-aged man. He wore a *kashaya*,[13] his head was shaved, his eyebrows also, and his beard and moustaches were very short, a growth of one week. He held a wooden rosary. It was the full-moon night of the seventh Hindu month, and men and women from the township were laying gifts of food, clothing and other things in front of the brown-robed figure, and saluting him with joined hands. He lifted one hand, smiled, and gave his blessing to each.

What was it, then? The ancient Buddhist monastery of Hilsa was indeed no more than a ruin; yet a feeling of reverence still seized on the hearts of worshippers when they passed such buildings. How could they think of this brown-robed old man of Hilsa, except as a Buddhist monk? He was a celibate, and, the four preachers who had preceded him had likewise been celibates and worn the brown robe. In the very few households of Hindu or Buddhist craftsmen converted to Islam, this place was regarded as a *khanqah*.[14] All the other townsfolk, except the Brahmins and some in the Bania caste, called it a *math* or *vihar* (monastery). Its former monks had had no caste divisions in their ranks, and these new preachers also were of no caste, did not marry, and wore *kashayas*. They exorcised evil spirits from sick people, when death or misfortune came they offered consolation with their teaching of an impalpable, formless Nirvan. And so even now, on the festival of the Pravaran[15] at the autumn full moon, people paid reverence in the same spirit as of old to these Muslim friars; and the Muslim workers whose forefathers had looked up to Buddhist monks as their holy teachers now looked up to these good old men and their brown-robed disciples.

The townsfolk, having paid their respects at the tombs of the old *pirs*[16] of the shrine, gradually dispersed. As the night fell, milk-white moonlight flooded the world. Someone approached the outer courtyard from the direction of the workers' dwellings, accompanied by two other men. As he came close, the Baba[17] recognized him as Maulvi[18] Abul Alai. He wore a white turban and a long gown over his trousers and shoes, his dark beard quivered in the light breeze.

Baba rose, stretching out both arms, and said in friendly tones –

'Come, Maulana Abul Alai! *Salaam-Aleikum!*'[19]

Baba grasped the scholar's rigid hand and embraced him.

'*Wa-Aleikum-Salaam*,' returned the Maulana reluctantly. The Baba led him to the bare platform, saying –

'This bare stone is my throne; please be seated.'

The Maulana sat down, and the Baba resumed his seat. It was the former who opened the conversation –

'Dear Sir, I stopped to watch the spectacle, when that crowd of heathens was here.'

'Well, let us call it a "spectacle", Maulana. Only let us not speak of "heathens", that word pricks my heart.'

'If they are not heathen Hindus, what else are they?'

'All men are blessed by the same divine light; enlightenment and paganism cannot exist in the same place just as daylight and night's darkness can't do.'

'All this Tasavvuf[20] (Vedant) of yours is not Islam, it is hocus-pocus.'

'We do not call your ideas hocus-pocus. We are ready to admit that "the river is one, but the bathing-stairs on its banks are many". Do you regard all human beings as God's children, or not?'

'Certainly.'

'And you believe that God is the omnipotent Lord of all?'

'Yes.'

'Then, Maulana, if a single leaf cannot be shaken without the will of this omnipotent Lord, who are you and I to call all these children of Allah "heathen"? If Allah had wished, He would have made all to follow the same path. He does not wish it; which means that all paths are pleasing to Him.'

'My friend, do not make me listen to these falsehoods of your Tasavvuf.'

'I was speaking from the viewpoint of Islam itself, Maulana. We Sufis recognize no difference between God and human being. Our formulas are "An-ul-haq"[21] (I am the truth), and "Ham-o-sta"[22] (All is God).'

'That is Kufr.'[23]

'So you think, and so many others have thought before you, but we Sufis have established this truth with our blood, and will do so again in days to come, if need be.'

'Because of you people and your way of thinking, Islam cannot spread here.'

'It is true that we abominated your way of spreading it by fire and sword, but we used no force to stop you, and how much success did you have?'

'You call the religion of the people here a true religion.'

'Yes, for we do not fancy ourselves strong enough to confine universal truth in one clay pot. If Islam is true for its martyrs, if Sufism is proved true for the martyrdom of Shams and Mansur,[24] the Hindus also have shown that their path is a true path when they happily presented their necks for your swords!'

'Hinduism – a true path! It is as far away from ours as east from west.'

'If it is so far away, why did these peasants come this evening to worship at a Muslim monastery? Or don't you want to see even the slightest trace of contact with Hinduism among the Muslims, Maulana?'

'No, we must get rid of it.'

'Then you had better go and tell people to wash off the vermilion[25] that our Muslim women put on their foreheads while their husbands are alive.'

'I shall tell them to wash it off!'

'You can go on trying that all your life,' returned the Baba with a laugh. 'Jumman, tell me, my son: will your Salima obey this rule?'

'No, Baba. The Maulvi here doesn't understand, it is only widows who wash the vermilion off,' answered Jumman, coming up to them.

'Forgive me, Maulvi Abul Alai,' continued the Baba, 'we Sufis have not settled here on the alms of any Sultan, or on charity from any Amir.[26] We have come in a loincloth and a beggar's robe. No Hindu has drawn a sword against us. Look at this shrine. It was once a monastery of the Buddhists. The fifth preacher before me here had been a disciple of Buddhist mendicants. It was no mere pretence on his part. He had come from Bukhara; he was attracted by their preaching and joined them. The life of a mendicant preacher is the same everywhere; it is not a question of outward garb which may be that of a Buddhist, or a Hindu or a Muslim. Since the time of that leader of ours, this shrine has belonged to monks who bear Muslim names. We did not insist on any change of dress; we taught the gospel of love, and today you see its fruit – there are very few in the villages nearby who dislike us. The Hindu *pandits* have watched us with a jaundiced eye; they could not recognize the way of love, any more than men like you can recognize it. That is why Jumman's father and grandfather had to call themselves by Muslim names instead of Hindu, and that's why you too have a welcome now among their people.'

—3—

The month of Chait (April) was well advanced, and the trees which had been awaiting their new leaves had begun to turn green. This year the mango trees had done well, and their old leaves had not yet fallen. Below was a threshing floor where two peasants were treading out the grain, despite the heat and the wind of the afternoon. A traveller, fatigued and sweating from the hot sun, came and sat down under a tree next to this threshing floor. Mangal the Chaudhari,[27] seeing from his face and appearance that he was a traveller from far-away parts, approached him, saying –

'Ram-Ram,[28] friend. You must have plenty of courage to be going about in this heat.'

'Ram-Ram, brother.[29] Well, when a man has to travel, he can't afford to care about heat or cold.'

'Have a drink of water. Your mouth must be parched. There is cold water in that pitcher.'

'What community (caste) do you belong to?'

'I am an Ahir, my name is Mangal Chaudhari.'

'I have a jug and a bucket-rope with me, show me where the well is. ... I am a Brahmin.'

'I will send my lad, Panditji,[30] if you like.'

'Do send him, Chaudhari, I am tired out.'

'Here Ghisa, lad,' called out Mangal, breaking in on his son's work with the grain, and asked him to bring a lump of molasses and some fresh water from the well.

The traveller enquired how far it was to Delhi, and learned that it was still nearly twenty *kos*, too far to be reached by nightfall.

Mangal was a jolly, good-humoured fellow; the hardest thing in the world for him was to keep quiet.

'This year, by God's blessing,' he remarked, 'the crops round here have been very good. We shall have hard work carrying in the harvest next month. What sort of crops have you had in your parts, Panditji?'

'Not bad, Chaudhari.'

'When the king is good, God also is pleased. Ever since the new Sultan came to the throne, the people have been prosperous.'

'Is that what you find, Chaudhari?'

'Well, you can see for yourself what a good haul is lying on this very threshing floor. If you had come and looked here a couple of years ago, you would not have seen a quarter of this.'

'So things have improved, Chaudhari.'

'Yes, but all these blessings we owe to the Sultan. We peasants used to go hungry and naked, while those damned scoundrels dressed in silk and muslin clothes and rode on horseback. As soon as the wheat had grown a few inches above the ground, their horses would be turned into our fields. Who could have thought it! They were really the Sultans of our little villages.'

'Yes,' struck in the other Chaudhari, who like Mangal wore a waistcloth hanging to his knees, a dirty jacket with four tie-straps, and a crumpled white cap.

'And you see what has become of their high and mighty ways now! That Brahmin fellow was saying to me, that ... what's his name? ...'

'Sibba.'

'Yes – only now you dare to call him Sibba, but he used to be addressed as *Pandit* Shivram! He was saying to me –

'"Chaudhari Chheda Ram, let me have a couple of bushels of wheat, I'll pay you the moment I have some cash." It isn't easy to refuse a man to his face; but I can remember when that Brahmin could never keep a civil tongue in his head; I never got anything from him but "*Hey, Chhidde!*"'

'And now you are "*Chaudhari* Chheda Ram", and I am "*Chaudhari* Mangal Ram"! We've come a long way in two and a half years from being "Chhidda" and "Manga"!'

'It's all due to the Sultan's kindness, I say. Otherwise we all would have remained "Chhiddas" and "Mangas".'

'That is just what I was telling this Panditji here.'

'Without that we should never have got our *panchayat* back and our better days would never have returned.'

'Chaudhari Mangal Ram, you don't know how to hold a pen, and yet you are the headman of the village council, how do you manage affairs? To say nothing of the officials, your trader used to pay one rupee and carry off two rupees worth of your grain. June was scarcely over before the rats were camping in your houses.'

'What we say is, may this Sultan of ours live for a thousand years.'

The Brahmin traveller had listened to the tale of these ignorant Ahirs with growing disgust, and was looking for an opportunity to put his oar in. By the time he had swallowed some molasses and drunk his water, his impatience had mounted, and, as the two Chaudharis still kept up their chatter, he interrupted –

'Sultan Ala-ud-Din has restored your *panchayat*? ...'

'Yes, O' Pandit! You have uttered the sweetest words, but I don't know who has given our king this name "Alabhdin";[31] in our village we call him "Labhdin"!'

'Call him what you like, Chaudhari, but don't you know how he has been oppressing us Hindus?'

'Our Ahir women go about in the fields and meadows, day or night, without even a shawl, proud as a peacock, and no one tries to carry them off.'

'The honour of our honourable families is being ruined.'

'Well, Pandit, if ours are not "honourable families", who are the damned honourable, then?'

'You are trying to be offensive, Chaudhari Mangal Ram!'

'The thing is, Pandit, what you ought to understand is, that our honour came back to us when our *panchayats* were given back to us. We know now how the officials and bigwigs came to be so "honourable". People talk of Hindus, or Muslims, but those bigwigs of ours were all tarred with the same brush, though in fact most of them were Hindus.'

'And they tell us,' struck in Chheda Ram, as an overlooked point occurred to him, 'that Hindus and Muslims are quite different, but these men who call themselves Hindu-Brahmins are turning their women into *begums*[32] with seven veils!'

'Yes, though my grandfather used to say he had seen the princesses of Kannauj and Delhi riding out on horseback with their faces uncovered.'

'But, Chaudhari,' protested the Brahmin, 'there were no Muslims in those days to rob them of their honour.'

'Our women do not cover themselves with any veil and go about in their fields even today. No one touches their honour.'

'No, and if ever they were molested, it was while that Brahmin fellow, that Sibba, was ruling the roost!'

'What should those who eat without working do, except steal one another's honour? It isn't a question of Hindus and Muslims, Panditji. It is all due to those who eat the bread of idleness. We are good Hindus, we shall never wrap our women up in seven veils.'

The Brahmin made one more effort.

'Chaudhari,' he said, 'don't you know that the Sultan's general, Malik Kafur, had marched into the south and destroyed our temples and trampled on the images of our gods?'

'We have heard a lot about it, we have been told not once but a thousand times that under Muslim rule there is no place for the Hindu religion. But we live very close to Delhi; otherwise we might have believed it. No temple has been destroyed in these forty miles; no image has been trampled underfoot here.'

'Ah!' exclaimed the other peasant, 'it's all a lie! You go to Delhi oftener than I do, but I have gone there many a time to see the Dassehra[33] festival. A tremendous big fair it is, and more than half the folk there are women. A Hindu festival, most of the people who attend it are Hindus. They decorate the images and carry them past the Sultan's own window, playing on conch-shells and drums and horns.'

'Yes, it's all a lie,' agreed Mangal Ram. 'Nikka Mall, the merchant, is building a big temple within a hundred yards of the palace. There's no knowing how many thousands he means to spend on it. Last time I was there I saw the foundation stone laid, and this time I saw the wall was waist-high. If the Sultan had wanted to break it down, why should he have let a temple be put up right in front of his eyes?'

'That is right. Kings fight wars with each other, and in wars anything may happen. No doubt something did happen and now they are seizing on it and making a fuss about it. Such things happened in our neighbourhood a hundred years ago, but you never hear of them nowadays.'

'I remember,' Mangal Ram added, 'when the Governor came near here and some of us from several villages went to his camp, he told us that the old Sultans were only like birds roosting here for a night, but our Sultan Labhdin has come to live with us in our house, in good times or bad, so instead of wanting to plunder the people he wishes them to be prosperous.'

'And it's not only a matter of wishing, the people everywhere round are visibly prosperous!'

—4—

Outside Delhi there was a lonely cemetery with *neem*[34] and tamarind trees growing about it. The late autumn nights were cold. Two *fakirs*[35] were sitting at a wood fire; one was our old friend Baba Noordin.

'Baba,' said the other, passing both hands through his long beard and moustache, 'five years are gone, and Haryana[36] is flowing with milk and honey again.'

'True, Baba Gyandin, true! The peasants' faces are full of smiles now.'

'When there are smiling fields you will always see smiling faces.'

'The officials and gentry have disappeared, and if the traders and moneylenders had perished with them, there would have been perfect peace.'

'They are great thieves – these men, and it's the wealth they steal that keeps their big monasteries and temples and endowments going.'

'They say religion could not live if there were no rich men. What I say is that so long as there are rich men, irreligion will always weigh down the scales.'

'Who can do more for religion than the sages and prophets and saints! And what wealth had they, more than a shirt and a blanket?'

'Men will never learn to be brothers so long as there are rich and wealthy, living on the labour of the poor, including the Sultans, O' friend Gyandin! Together they are responsible for creating a rift between man and man, for there would be an end of their pomp, if they stopped snatching away the product of the people's toil.'

'Let us hope for a day when this labyrinth of evil will have been got rid of, and the kingdom of love founded on earth.'

16

Suraiya

TIME : 1600 CE

—1—

On all sides the earth was drenched with the muddy rainwater brought by the monsoon. It oozed sluggishly over level ground, hurried down slopes, and foamed along in streams and rivers, giving them the appearance of swollen hill-torrents. Big drops were still falling incessantly from the trees as if these had rain clouds hidden in them. Otherwise, the rains had dwindled to a mere drizzle.

A little distance away from a *chhonkra* (*shami*)[1] tree, growing by itself, stood a girl in a white dress. A white shawl had slipped back from her head, and her raven hair, parted in the middle and falling on each side, showed the silver line of the parting like the Ganga flowing between Himalayan valleys. Raindrops were still dripping from the curling ringlets round her ears. Her big dark eyes on her snow-white pensive face seemed to be dwelling on some far-off, imaginary picture. Her long silk tunic was soaked, and clung to her bosom; under a red bodice her breasts swelled entrancingly like two oranges. Below the waist, over which hung the pleats of her tunic, she wore trousers, whose close-fitting lower parts revealed the fine curve of her calves. She had red shoes over her white mud-stained socks; they were wet through and sodden, and seemed useless for further walking.

A young man appeared close by. His turban, standing out over his forehead, his coat and trousers, were all white, and were as soaked with rain as the girl's clothes. He came up and watched her; she was not looking in his direction. Moving without a sound, he stood a couple of feet from her side. She was gazing fixedly at the muddy current of a stream a short distance away. Now, he thought, his companion would look towards him, but minutes, that seemed ages, passed by and still she stood motionless, not even wiping away from her forehead the drops of moisture left there by the drizzling rain. Unable to wait any longer, the youth gently put one hand on her shoulder. She turned her head; the far-away look vanished, and her big dark eyes shone. A smile touched her fine red lips and showed a sparkling row of delicate teeth. She took his hand, saying –

'Kamal, how long have you been standing here?'

'For ages, I think ever since the time when Almighty began to create the world out of the waters, the time when it was still dripping wet and not firm enough to bear the weight of hills and trees and living things!'

'Oh, stop, Kamal. You are always talking poetry!'

'I only wish that what you say were true, Suraiya, but I am afraid the gift of poetry has not fallen to my lot.'

'Well, Suraiya will not tolerate any rival. She will not let anyone else come near you.'

'And there is no one else I should like. But what were you thinking about so deeply, Suraiya?'

'I was thinking of something far off, far off ... how far away is the sea, Kamal?'

'The nearest point is at Surat, and that is a month's journey away.'

'And where does this water flow away to?'

'Towards Bengal, still further away, perhaps two months' journey.'

'What a long journey this poor muddy rainwater will have to make! Have you seen the ocean, Kamal?'

'I have been to Orissa, with my father, dear, I saw the ocean then.'

'What is it like?'

'A dark undulating cloud, stretching in front of you till it meets the sky.'

'And that ocean is this rainwater's destiny! Will it still be muddy there?'

'No, darling, the ocean is all one colour, deep blue or almost black.'

'I shall go and see the ocean someday, if you will take me.'

'I am ready to accompany this water on its journey, dear Suraiya, if you command me.'

She put her arms round his neck and laid her wet cheek against his, and then looking into his sparkling eyes, she said –

'Yes we shall go to the sea, but not in company with this water.'

'Not with this muddy water, dearest?'

'Don't call it muddy, Kamal! It is only muddy here on the ground. Was it dirty when it fell from the sky?'

'No, it was more stainless then than the sun or the moon. See how it has made these pretty curls of yours glisten, and how beautiful it has made these snowy cheeks! Wherever it has fallen straight from heaven it has only brightened your beauty.'

'So its muddiness is not part of itself; it has been given to it by the touch of all that stands between it and its union with the sea. When raindrops fall straight into the sea, do they become muddy, Kamal?'

'No, darling.'

'Well, I think the mud stains in the water are an ornament, they don't make it ugly. What do you think, Kamal?'

'Suraiya, you have said with these lips what I feel with this heart.'

—2—

The blue of the blue sky above was reflected in the deep waters of the pool and intensified the whiteness of the tiers of steps, of spotless marble, that stretched round its banks. Cypress trees made a lovely sight with their green spires soaring above the carpet of green grass round the pool, especially in this spring noontide. As far as the eye could roam, the gardens were adorned with avenues, creeper-hung arbours, and gushing fountains. Today, because of the spring festival, the royal gardens had been thrown open to the young folk, who were wandering about enjoying its bountiful freedom like creatures in paradise.

Outside a red stone pavilion, on the edge of the park far away from the pool, four men were standing. All wore the same style of turbans projecting a little in front, the same tunics buttoned at the throat and falling in pleated folds to the knee, the same white waistbands; all had the same moustaches, in which most of the hairs had already turned grey. They stood for some time surveying the park and then sat down on the rugs and pillows spread out in the pavilion, which was open on all four sides. It was quiet here; there was no one else but these four old men.

At length one of them broke the silence by saying – 'Your Majesty ...'

'What, Fazal are we sitting in the Hall of Audience now? Can human beings never be content to be simple human beings?'

'I was forgetting ...'

'Call me Jalal[2] or Akbar – or friend.'

'It is very hard, friend Jalal; we have to lead a double life.'

'Not double,' said another – 'quadruple!'

'You deserve praise, Biru,[3] you seem always ready for anything at any moment, but the rest of us need some time to get our minds in order when we step out of one world into another. Don't you agree, brother Todu?'

'Yes, indeed, Fazlu, I too am astonished at how our Biru manages; he must have a splendid brain. ...'

'Isn't it Birbal that everybody believes is the one who has measured[4] every farmland in the country?'

'But brother Biru, even Todar Mall hasn't measured every farmland in the country.'

'Whether he has measured them or not, the world at least thinks its me who did. And as for my intelligence, even Jallu would appreciate it.'

'Certainly,' responded Akbar, 'and it's not one of the tales that have grown so famous about the Emperor Jalal-ud-din Akbar roaming the villages in disguise.'

'This is something interesting that brother Jalua (Jalal) has reminded me of,' said Birbal, 'and I suffer with you in these tales. It has become a popular custom to invent some sort of story about Akbar and Birbal, and circulate it. I have made quite a collection of them; I pay one piece of gold for each tale.'

'Oh!' said Akbar. 'I hope they are not being made up on the spot just for the sake of your money!'

'That may be,' returned Birbal, 'but it makes no difference: even then we can see from these anecdotes what kind of nonsense is being invented about the pair of us. Don't look annoyed, Fazla. I'm not a miser, like the merchant Chhadamimall.'

'Not at all,' Abul Fazal assured him, 'don't get angry with me for nothing. As to your stories, I am quite frightened of them.'

'I haven't composed a magnum opus like your *Ain-i-Akbari*,'[5] said Birbal.

'Ah! Todu,' exclaimed Abul Fazal. 'How many readers will the *Ain-i-Akbari* find, tell me your sincere opinion! And how many people will go on repeating Birbal's stories!'

'Biru knows very well,' answered Todar Mall.

'Well,' said Abul Fazal, 'tell us one of the tales you have paid a gold piece for, Bira.'

'But if I tell you one, you will all make up your minds from the start that I have got it out of my own head, not out of my purse.'

'Never mind,' remarked Akbar, 'we can distinguish the genuine coin from the counterfeit without your telling us.'

'As if there were a special stamp on all my own tales! Very well, as you please; I will tell you a story, only shortening it to give you the gist –

'*Once upon a time, Akbar had a great fancy to convert himself into a Hindu. He told Birbal, who was very upset. He could not refuse the Emperor his help, but how on earth could he transform him into a Hindu?*

'*He lay low for a few days and then one evening near the palace window was heard a loud cry of "hichh-chho-hichh-cho-o ..." The Emperor had never heard a washerman's cry*[6] *in such a place or at such a time. His curiosity was roused. He put on a workman's dress and went down to the bank of the Yamuna. There, thoroughly as the latter had changed his appearance, he could not help recognizing Birbal. Birbal, instead of pounding dirty clothes on a washerman's board, was busy washing a fine big donkey, scrubbing it with alkali and soap. The Emperor hid his smile, and enquired in an assumed voice –*

'*"What are you doing there, Chaudhari?"*

'*"Doing my work, what do you think?"*

'*"You are shivering out here in the cold weather at a very odd hour."*

'*"I've got to turn this animal into a horse and give it to the Emperor by tomorrow, even if it kills me."*

'*"Turn a donkey into a horse?"*

'*"What can I do? That's the Emperor's order!"*

'*The Emperor laughed, and said in his natural voice – "Come along,*

Bira, I understand now that a Muslim can no more become a Hindu than a donkey a horse!"'

'Well, Fazal, when I heard this story, it made me feel very sorry.'

'And we are hearing it now,' commented Akbar, 'in the evening of our lives. Is this all that has come of our lifelong efforts!'

'Jalal,' answered Fazal, 'we can undertake the work only of one generation. Whether our efforts are to prove successful or not depends on those people out there in the gardens, celebrating the spring festival.'

'Yes, though it was not our object,' Todar Mall remarked, 'to turn Muslims into Hindus or Hindus into Muslims.'

'Our object was to see them both united,' said Fazal, 'as a single people, a single community.'

'Unfortunately,' said Birbal, 'the Muslim *mullahs* and the Hindu *pandits* did not see eye to eye with us. Our ambition is to make India strong. India's swords are keen, her brain is active, her young men are brave. But what disgraces and enfeebles India is her lack of unity, her being divided into so many communities. If only all her swords could be rallied under one banner!'

'Oh, my dear comrades,' cried Akbar, 'that has been my sole desire! That is what we have struggled towards for so long! When we began, it was dark all round us, but now that is no longer true. We have done all that could be accomplished in one generation; but this notion of horse-and-donkey is a heavy load on my mind.'

'We must not despair,' said Fazal. 'Just compare these times with the days of Bairam Khan-i-Khana![7] Could Jodha Bai have married you then and worshipped Vishnu in the royal harem?'

'Yes, there is a difference,' replied Akbar, 'but how far away our goal still is! I once heard from the European missionaries that in their land even the greatest king cannot marry more than one wife. Todar, you must remember from what I said at the time what a splendid custom I thought it. If only I could follow it myself! But it is a mortifying fact that a ruler has far less freedom to do good than to do evil. Had it been possible, I would not have kept in my harem a single woman except the mother of my Salim; and I wish it were possible for Salim to do the same in his turn.'

'There can be love only between two individuals,' observed Birbal. 'When I watch the swans living in happy couples, I feel how beautiful their lives are. They are partners in good fortune, and in bad fortune.'

'I remember a day,' said Akbar, 'when I could not help shedding tears. I had gone to Gujrat for a lion-hunt. There is no bravery, I admit, in riding on an elephant and killing a lion with your matchlock. A man has no claws and jaws like a lion's, so he may fairly use a shield and sword to be equal with it, but to use anything more is no sign of courage. Well, I killed the lion with my matchlock; the ball entered its head, and it gave one bound and fell in its tracks. The next moment a lioness sprang out of the thicket, she glared furiously at me, and then turned her back on me and began licking the lion's head. I at once ordered the huntsmen not to fire and turned my elephant away. It had been such a shock to me; if the lioness had attacked I should not have been able to strike a blow. I felt melancholy for days afterwards, and I reflected that if that lion had had fifteen hundred mates, they would not have come to lick its dead face.'

'Our country has a long way to go,' said Abul Fazal, 'and our pace is very slow and we do not even know whether there will be anyone to take over our burden, when our feet can go no further.'

'I hoped,' Akbar went on, 'to see a blood-brotherhood between the two fighting races of the Muslims and Hindus! I was thinking of such a union when I built a fort at Triveni, at the confluence of the rivers, that meeting of the Ganga and the Yamuna that put into my mind the idea of a universal coming-together. But now I see how little success I have had. It is true that the work of many generations cannot be performed by one generation. Still, I shall always be proud of having found such noble fellow workers as have fallen to the lot of very few men. I hoped to see in every home a mixed marriage like mine with Jodha Bai, but I could not bring it about.'

'It is the Hindus who have proved more backward in this respect,' remarked Todar Mall.

'And now they make up tales about scrubbing a donkey to turn it into a horse,' said Birbal.

'But if there is really such a gulf between Hindus and Muslims, how is it that the horse can turn itself into a donkey? Do we not see thousands of Hindus turning Muslim?'

'I have always longed to see Hindu youths marrying Muslim girls,' said Akbar, 'without changing their name or their faith.'

'Then let me give you some good news, Jalal!' exclaimed Abul Fazal. 'What we failed to bring about, my daughter Suraiya has brought about.'

They all stared at him with eager curiosity.

'You are longing to hear more,' he said. 'Just let me go outside for a moment,' and he went out and stood at the balustrade. 'Seeing is better than hearing,' he continued, coming back – 'step outside with me.'

They all went and stood at the balustrade. Abul Fazal pointed to two youthful figures sitting on a stone bench under a green *ashok*[8] tree.

'Look, there is my Suraiya!'

'And my son Kamal,' cried Todar Mall. 'Oh, my dear Fazal, the world is not dark for us now!'

He threw his arms round his old friend and embraced him. When they released each other, there were tears in the eyes of all four men. 'I have held this spring festival for the young people for many years now,' said Akbar, breaking the silence, 'but only today, after so long, it is a true festival of spring. I long to call them both and kiss them on the forehead. How fine it would be for them to know how delighted we are at this confluence of the two rivers!'

'Suraiya does not know,' said Abul Fazal, 'that her parents will approve of her love.'

'Nor does Kamal,' added Todar Mall. 'But you are fortunate, Fazal, in having your wife on your side. She and my wife are good friends, but still my wife has some old-fashioned leanings. Never mind, Suraiya and Kamal shall have my blessing.'

'I must have the privilege of giving the first blessing!' said Akbar.

'With me at your side, Jalal!' cried Birbal.

'Of course, where shall we find a better washerman than you?'

'Or a better donkey, trying to become a horse, than you!'

'What a happy meeting we have had today!' concluded Akbar. 'If only we could have such happiness for one day in every month!'

—3—

On the first floor was an ornamental room, with doors on four sides. Red, green and white chandeliers hung from the ceiling, and double curtains covered the doors, the inner curtain being of flowered, rose-coloured silk. Fine Persian rugs were spread on the floor. In the middle of the room a heap of cushions was scattered on a white divan, where two girls sat playing chess. One of them was Suraiya, whom we have met already, and the other the thirteen-year-old daughter of Birbal, dressed in a red petticoat, a green bodice, and a yellow shawl: she was called Phoolmati. They were both so much engrossed, in their moves, that they failed to hear newcomers approaching the divan. It was only when they heard an exclamation – 'Suraiya!' – that they looked up, and then rose to their feet. 'Aunt!' cried Suraiya as Kamal's mother embraced and kissed her. Suraiya's mother said – 'Run, daughter! Kamal has brought some goldfish for you, to put in the pond. I'll play chess with Munni until you come back.'

'Munni is very clever, mother! She has checkmated me twice; don't imagine you are playing with a child!'

Suraiya put her shawl right and ran out of the room. Kamal was standing near the pond at the back of the palace, with a fresh earthenware pot beside him. Suraiya came up and took his hand exclaiming –

'You have brought me the pink and yellow fish, Kamal dear!'

'Yes, and gold-coloured ones too.'

'Let me see them,' said Suraiya, peering into the jar.

'I'll throw them in the pond, they will look prettier there: just watch them in the bright surface of the water, it is so crystal clear, Suraiya!'

She stood at the edge of the pond, her eyes and teeth sparkling as she laughed. Kamal upturned the jar of fish over the water. Their pink, rosy or golden hues were certainly lovely as they fell into the crystal-clear water.

'They are still young,' Kamal explained seriously, 'but even when they grow up they will be hardly six inches long.'

'They are very pretty as they are now, Kamal!'

'Look at that one, Suraiya! What colour would you call it?'

'Rose colour.'

'Just like your cheeks.'

'You were always telling me that even when we were children, Kamal.'

'Because your cheeks were rosy even then.'

'You were so sweet even then, Kamal.'

'And now?'

'Now – oh, very sweet.'

'More than then? Why?'

'I don't know why. I think love began to sink into my heart from the time when your voice changed, and this line of soft dark hair began to grow on your lips.'

'Just the time when you began to keep me at a distance!'

'Keep you at a distance?'

'Yes! Until then you would jump up and hang on my shoulders and clasp hands with me. ...'

'Don't start giving me a catalogue of complaints! Tell me something new.'

'There is some news, Suraiya. Our love has become known.'

'To whom?'

'To both our families; even to His Imperial Majesty.'

'Even His Majesty!'

'Don't you feel frightened, Suraiya?'

'No. Our love was bound to become known some day or other. But what has happened?'

'I can't tell you all about it myself, but I hear that your parents were the first to welcome it, then father and His Majesty, and last of all, my mother.'

'Your mother?'

'She was afraid of what people would say. Don't you know she is a woman of very old-fashioned ideas?'

'But I can still feel her kiss on my cheek at this moment!'

'Yes, our fears turned out wrong, for as soon as father spoke to her she was quite pleased.'

'So our love has been approved!'

'In all our friends' families; but the outside world is not ready to accept it.'

'Do you care about the outside world, Kamal?'

'Not in the least, Suraiya. I care about the future world, for whose benefit we are leading the way on this path.'

'My sister-in-law must know all about it too, Kamal! I see it now. Last night I went to her room, and she said, jokingly, "Sister-in-law, I have been longing to see you married, and now my wish is going to be fulfilled" – though she never mentioned your name.'

'That means that your brother must have told her, and both of them are happy at our love.'

'Then all my family are in favour of you, Kamal!'

'And you have succeeded in getting my mother on your side!'

'You people were thinking about her religious ideas, Kamal; if you had only known how fond she is of me, perhaps you would not have been so doubtful about her.'

'Oh, we knew it. Father was going to use you as his trump card against her, but before he had time to play it, the game was already won. Well! Now we are going to be married.'

'How?'

'Neither by a *mullah* nor by a *pandit*.'

'No, by our own prophet, who is building in India a new fortress of a new unity!'

'The man who is trying to unite pools and ponds, rivers and streams into one unbroken sea.'

'When, Kamal?'

'On Sunday, the day after tomorrow.'

'So soon!' Tears stood in Suraiya's eyes like dew drops in a narcissus. Kamal wiped them away, but his own eyes were wet. Neither of them guessed that two other pairs of eyes were watching them from hiding, and were filled with the same tears of joy.

—4—

The bay made a lovely spectacle, on fire with the red light of the sinking sun, as it lay under the cool, rosy sky of a spring evening.

Two young hearts were enjoying the scene from the sea shore. One of them, carried away by the happiness of the moment, exclaimed –

'The sea, our deity! How lovely it is!'

'We are children of the sea, can we doubt that any longer, darling?'

'No, my lotus-like Kamal![9] And did we ever dream that the ocean was hiding such a heavenly land as this in his bosom?'

'It may not be a perfect one, but men have made a heaven of this Venice; one cannot deny that.'

'I could not believe Sadhuni[10] when she used to say that in her land the young women of the highest families went about with their faces as open and uncovered as the men. And now we have been living in this paradise for two years. Just compare Venice with Delhi!'

'Could we have believed it, Suraiya, if anyone had told us that a State as strong as Florence could exist without a monarch!'

'Or that there could be a "princess of cities" – Venice!'

'Darling, could we walk about openly like this in Delhi!'

'Without a veil! No, there I have to move about caged up inside a palanquin. Here people see us strolling about hand in hand and never give us a second glance.'

'Still, in Gujrat we saw respectable women with their faces uncovered, and one hears that in South India too there are no veils worn.'

'That shows that at some time or other all Indian women must have been free from veils. Will it ever be like that again in our land, Kamal?'

'Our fathers have struggled for it all their lives. Look at the tiny State of Florence, Suraiya, that you can walk from end to end in three days. How proudly the people hold their heads up! They never think of bowing and scraping before any man. They spit at the very sound of monarchy; to them a king is no better than a devil, or a dragon breathing out fire.'

'And is there not some truth in their opinion, Kamal? Compare the farmers of Florence with our peasants at home. Do you ever see them looking like dry skeletons here?'

'No, darling, and it is because there are no millions squandered on royal pomp and show.'

'There are rich men in Venice, whose treasures exceed those of many of our *Jagat Seths*.'[11]

'Our great merchants put one red pennant[12] up for every hundred thousand rupees they amass. I used to wonder, what was the use of those hoards of gold and silver, buried away in the dark! They ought to be circulating, passing from hand to hand. If money doesn't circulate, the sweetmeats dry up in the shops, the fruit rots on the trees, the cloth is devoured in the warehouses by insects. Our merchants bury their hoards and hoist red pennants over them. People count them and say – a hundred pennants, so-and-so must be worth ten millions.'

The sun had been set for some time now, and shadows were spreading all round, but the young couple were still unwilling to leave the beach. They thought of the sea, indeed, as a loved companion. Although they themselves had travelled by land, they knew that one corner of the ocean that stretched before them touched India, and they would sometimes wonder, could not the two shores be linked.

It was late at night when they turned their steps homeward. Suraiya was gazing into this shadowy night and into her own thoughts.

'Our Emperor,' she remarked, 'has made great efforts to establish peace in his territory, and he has had a good deal of success in his work. But we could not wander about so carelessly there on a dark night. Why?'

'Here all the people are prosperous. The peasants' farms are full of vineyards and orchards and cornfields.'

'Do our farms at home not yield wealth?'

'There are too many robbers waiting to carry off the wealth, Suraiya, in our country.'

'And have you noticed how when anyone goes into a house here, bottles and glasses are put on the table as a matter of course?'

'In India my father was abused merely for drinking water with the Emperor.'

'My nurses used to teach me that Rajput-women are very dirty people, because they have pig-meat cooked in their houses. I wish those blind fools in India could come and see life here, in this continent, where there are no superior and inferior castes.'

'And where no one is afraid of polluting himself by eating or drinking what he likes.'

'Florence is united; one day India must be united too, Kamal!'

'That day will come when we become the rulers of the ocean, when we have achieved victory at sea.'

'Victory at sea?'

'Venice is a city that lives by sea-power, Suraiya. Its canals and its fine palaces are the gifts of sea-power. Now Venice is no longer alone, she has many competitors, but I can see very clearly that world power will belong to those who achieve sea-power. I consider myself fortunate for having had my mind turned in this direction.'

'What books you keep reading every night, dear! And how easy it is to get books here!'

'We have lead in our own country, and paper, and skilled metal workers, but we have not yet learned printing. If printing presses were opened there, how quick the spread of knowledge would be! And these books I am reading and the weeks I spent going about among sailors have convinced me that the country with sea-power will also attain to world power. Our people call these *Firangis*[13] dirty barbarians because they are careless about washing and bathing; but when one considers their inventive spirit one can't help admiring them. They have not merely made up fables about the globe; they have explored and studied every corner of it. I showed you some of their maps, Suraiya.'

'How I love the sea, Kamal!'

'Love – yes, but more than that, the sea controls the lives of nations. You have seen the guns mounted on these wooden ships. They are floating forts, these ships. The Mongols owed their conquests to their horses and to gunpowder. Today, success in the world will go to those who possess such warships. That is why I have made up my mind to study naval warfare, Suraiya.'

But their hopes were not to be fulfilled. They set sail for India: but it was an age of piracy, and two days before they could reach Surat, pirates attacked their ship. Kamal joined the crew in keeping up fire on them from cannon and muskets. But the defenders were outnumbered. Their ship was raked with cannon-shot and began to founder. Suraiya was standing beside Kamal, and her last words, uttered with her last smile, were – 'Victory at sea!'

17

Rekha Bhagat

TIME : 1800 CE

—1—

It was the full-moon night of the eighth month, and multitudes had assembled to bathe in the Gandak[1] and worship Hariharnath.[2] Countryfolk, men and women, had come from miles around to Hariharkshetr[3] with money laboriously saved and rations of parched grains and rice. But none at that time, seeing the number of oxen, horses and elephants tethered in a small enclosure, could have foreseen that in days to come this would grow into the biggest fair in the world.

Rekha Bhagat and his four companions were squatting on a blanket under a mango tree, eating salted grain, green pepper and radishes out of a coarse napkin with the greatest relish. Rekha had sold his buffalo, and he still kept feeling at the corner of his dress tied up round the twenty rupees he had got. It was well known that nowadays a great many thieves came to the fair, who could steal away one's money as if by magic. His hand was at his tied up money once more as he began complacently –

'We have sold our buffalo. I have been fattening her up properly these three months, brother Bholu. Twenty rupees isn't a bad price for an animal like that. But in these days money melts away before you know it.'

Bhola – 'It does indeed and money is scarce everywhere brother Rekha. Under this Company's[4] rule, there is no luck in anything. We kill ourselves ploughing and ploughing, and we don't get enough to give our children one evening's square meal.'

Rekha – 'In the old days we were bled by presents and forced labour for the governor and bribes to the officials, but at least the land was our own.'

Maula – 'We cut down the jungle seven generations ago and cleared the land for ourselves.'

Sobaran – 'You know the "Tiger-field" brother Bholu? It used to be thick jungle, and a tiger carried off our Baba Mooris Ghinavan[5] there. Ever since then the place has been known as the "Tiger-field". Yes, we cleared the land at the cost of our lives.'

'Bhola Pandit,' interjected Rekha, looking towards the dark-skinned half-naked figure which was wrapping its head in a turban of thin cloth, 'you know all about everything right back to the *Satyug*,[6] have the people ever been in such misery before?'

Maula – 'Yes, it was we who cleared the fields, we plough them and sow them, but the Rampur's *munshiji*[7] is the master of our village now.'

Bhola Pandit – 'It is against religion Rekha Bhagat, against religion. This Company is a worse oppressor than Ravan or Kans.[8] In the old religious books it says, let the king take one tenth of the peasants' crop.'

Maula – 'I can't understand at all why the Company has appointed this Rampur *munshi* as our master and landlord.'

Sighed Bhola Pandit – 'Everything has been turned upside down, Maulu! Once, the people had a king over them. The peasant knew of only one king, who lived far away in his capital, and was only concerned with getting his one-tenth share and that only when there was a harvest. But now, whether there is any harvest or not, the landlord has to be paid his rent, even if we have to sell our flesh and blood, our daughters and sisters.'

Rekha – 'And the rent is not even fixed. It keeps going up year by year, and there is no one to ask why such unbridled extortion goes on!'

Sadasukhlal, a *patwari*,[9] had come to bathe at Hariharkshetr, and, if he could pick one up cheap, to buy a cow, but when he found how high prices were this year, it made him positively shiver. He wore a cap and dirty jacket with loose sleeves and had his reed pen still behind his ear, as if he had revenue-accounts to write even here. As Patwari to a landlord of Mashrakh, he was wondering whether he should take part in this conversation or not, but it is hard for anyone with a tongue and a pair of ears to hold his tongue when village politics are touched upon. Besides, Dyalpur was not a village belonging to his employer, so he felt there could be no harm in his joining in the talk of these Dyalpur peasants. He rolled his pen between his fingers and observed –

'No one to ask, you say Pandit! Who is there to ask? Everyone is a robber, and as Kabir[10] says – "*Everybody's wealth is being stolen: Whoever can steal, let him.*" There is no king. My cousin has her son-in-law at the Nazim[11] Sahib,[12] and he knows many secrets. There is no king, a couple of hundred *Firangi*-robbers have formed a band and they call this band the "Company".'

Rekha – 'You are right Munshiji, when we kept hearing "*Company bahadur*",[13] we used to think it was the name of a king, but now we know the truth.'

Maula – 'That is why, wherever you look, you find robbery going on. Is there no one to take account of justice and injustice? Did this Munshiji of Rampur have any connection with Dyalpur in the last seven of his generations even?'

Sobaran – 'I can't get it into my head, Maulu brother, how Rampur's Munshi ever came to be the master in our village. The Company gave battle to the Emperor of Delhi. ...'

Munshi – 'Not to the Emperor of Delhi, Sobaran Raut, it gave battle to the Nawab[14] of Maksudabad (Murshidabad) instead. Maksudabad had torn our province away from the government at Delhi!'

Sobaran – 'We folk haven't got such long memories Munshiji. We used to know only about Delhi. Well, even when the Nawab of Murshidabad got the power, there still was a single government, wasn't there? We had to pay the revenue, with whatever we could scrape up. But now – are there two separate rulers, or what?'

Rekha – 'Sobaran brother, of course there are two powers over us. The power of the Company and the power of Rampur's Munshi. When you are being crushed on one grindstone, there is some hope of escaping with your life, but not when you are between two grindstones. And that is what we have come to. You tell us, Patwari – we are rustic folk, stupid and ignorant, you are the only learned man of us, you or Bhola Pandit.'

Munshi – 'You are quite right, Rekha Bhagat. A landlord is an upper millstone, and he is no less powerful than a king.'

Rekha – 'Why less? He is rather more powerful, Munshiji. What is left now of our *panchayat*? We keep up the custom, we choose the five headmen, but what is there for them to do? The landlord and his hangers-on do everything. When there is a quarrel they squeeze money out of the plaintiff and the defendant, both. It is less than fifteen years since the *panchayat* collapsed, Sobaran; before that did you ever see a family then having to sell off its buffalo, because of a mere quarrel between man and wife?'

Sobaran – 'In the old days the *panchayat* settled everything, it never allowed a family to ruin itself, it patched up an agreement even in cases of murder, Rekha Bhagat. And then you see the state of our dykes and irrigation channels. It seems that they have no one to take care of them now. Would this ever have happened if the *panchayat* was still working?'

Rekha – 'No it wouldn't, Sobaran Raut. Who would fill his own children's mouths with grass? When there is too much rain, there are no channels kept open to drain off the water, and when the rain is too little, there are no embankments to keep the crop from drying up.'

Munshi – 'The Company has destroyed the *panchayat* and handed over its work to the landlord.'

Rekha – 'And we can see what the landlords are doing!'

Munshi – 'I myself am eating a landlord's salt. You know, I am in service with the landlord of Mashrakh. But one pays for doing injustice. Look at me! I had seven children as strong as bulls, all abounded me!' There were tears in his eyes, and the others looked at him with sympathy. 'Yes, Rekha, all abounded me. Now there is not even one little girl left in my house to bring me a drink of water. As to my master, you know the state he has been in since he met that prostitute at Chhapra? His male-organ has fallen off;[15] and the *khvas*[16] is the real father of the two lads in his house!'

Rekha – 'That happens with a lot of the gentry, nowadays.'

Sobaran – 'Our land has gone, the village has fallen to pieces, and bandits from across the seven seas have set up thieves in the midst of us; the *panchayat* is gone, and whatever little grain we can grow is taken away. If ever we get good rains, and have a little food in hand, we can't keep it out of the clutches of the landlord and his troop of watchmen and clerks and overseers.'

Munshi – 'I am aware of the *patwari*'s loot, I admit. But you know very well, the landlord only pays him eight *annas*[17] a month, and just tell me, with eight *annas* a month, can we even moisten our tongues? The landlord knows very well that we can't.'

Rekha – 'Oh, the landlords know it Munshiji. They see it all, they aren't blind. King *Company bahadur* is a robber; he has put the landlord on our backs as another robber, and the landlord sets a bucketful of smaller robbers on us. How can we go on living under them all!'

Sobaran – 'Do you call this living, Rekha? Is there anyone to be seen in Dyalpur with food for his belly and clothes to his back?'

Munshi – 'What does the Company care about that, Sobaran Raut? It has fixed the rate of its revenue; on the settlement day the landlord goes to Chhapra and pays up in cash. The Company gets its last farthing, whether the peasants of Dyalpur live or starve, and the landlord will beat you black and blue if you don't pay up his rent in full. He takes five rupees from you and gives one rupee to the Company – the other four go to stuff his own belly.'

Rekha – 'O' God! Have you gone to sleep, or abandoned us! Why don't you see justice done? We are all ruined.'

Sobaran Raut – 'Ruined! Have you heard how the people in the Twelve Parganas district joined together and refused to have the landlord as their master? They went to Chhapra and told the Company *Sahib*[18]: "Our *panchayat* will pay you your revenue; we won't have anything to do with a landlord." And do you know what the *Sahib* answered? He said, "Will you pay the revenue even when there is a drought or flood?" When droughts or floods come, it is hard enough just to keep one's children alive. That *Firangi* seemed to have no fear of God, and he said those words quite indifferently. And Rekha, then he said – "You people are poor; if you don't pay the revenue, what have you for the Company to confiscate? We are making rich, respectable men into landlords, who will be afraid of having their households sold up and losing their social position if they get into arrears with their payments to us."'

Rekha – 'That is why they have leprosy all over their bodies, those *Firangis*. They are so merciless.'

Sobaran – 'There was no help for the Twelve Parganas people, but they were ready to stake their lives. If the Company had really been brave, it would have fought like a brave man, it would have fought with someone who could fight back. Those peasants had some muskets; the Company's men had cannons. And from here, there and everywhere their troops, white skins and brown skins, descended on the district. They burned village after village, sparing neither woman nor child. What could the poor people do?'

Maula – 'Well, this is the way agriculture has been ruined, and our weavers too have begun to starve. *Company bahadur* is bringing cloth for sale now from abroad,[19] Sobaran.'

Munshi – 'Yes, cloth spun and woven by machines. See, my jacket is made of it. You can't make such cheap cloth with spindle and handloom, so for the sake of being decently dressed one has to wear it. It's a question of respectability, Rekha Bhagat. Why are you smiling? When you have to attend at official houses and sit on the reception carpet, then you know!'

Rekha – 'I wasn't laughing at your respectability, Munshiji. I was just thinking – this *Company bahadur* is a ruler and a trader at the same time! What a government!'

Bhola Pandit – 'The age of *Satyug, Tretyug, Dvapar Yug* has gone by and the five thousand years of *Kalyug*[20] too, and in all this long time such a government has never been heard of before.'

Munshi – 'A *munshi* at the Nazim's court said that the Company were just *Firangi* bandits, and another man said that the Company was only a collection of *Firangi* merchants, who left their own country only for trade. At first they got goods from here and sold them over there, but now they have started big factories in England where they get goods made for them and then come and sell them here.'

Maula – 'So now it is plain that the lives of our weavers are at stake too!'

—2—

The Ganga looks green in the cold season, and its usual leisurely flow becomes still more languid. There is very little danger to boats, so the merchants considered it an excellent time to carry on trade. If you sat for four hours or so, on the bank, you would see hundreds of big boats going by. Most of them would be loaded with the Company's goods. Largely, goods from England are being carried upriver. And if you looked out from the wharves of commercial towns like Patna, Ghazipur, or Mirzapur, the whole breadth of the Ganga would appear covered with big boats.

One such boat was dropping downriver from Patna, freighted with saltpetre, carpets and many other articles, destined for England. It was more than a week's journey from Patna to Kolkata, so Teenkaudi[21] De[22] and Coleman gradually came to know each other well, although at first each of them shrank from the other's company. To Teenkaudi De, the other's overhanging wig, tight-fitting trousers, buttons hanging on threads, black coat and white face, were very impressive and frightening things. But Coleman took the lead in initiating conversation, and little by little Teenkaudi gained confidence. From their talk, he gathered that Coleman was a sworn enemy to the Company and did not hesitate to abuse any of its representatives, high or low, including the Governor.

Teenkaudi likewise detested the Company's agents; he had spent twenty years working as a clerk in its offices. He came of a poor family, but he was one of those men whose ambition is limited and held in check by self-respect. He had earned enough to live on for the rest of his life; by the favour of some old Company man, in the days of unrestricted plunder, he had been given an estate of four villages in the Twenty-four Parganas district with a government revenue impost, very low considering its rental. Yes, this estate was a favour from a *Sahib*; but to obtain it, Teenkaudi De had done something so sinful that he could not hope even in many reincarnations to wipe away the stain. To please the *Sahib* he had put into his clutches a handsome young Brahmin girl of his village. The *Sahibs* had very few of their own women with them, for the six months' voyage with all its risks was not easily undertaken. Teenkaudi was forty-five years old, and his dark, well-built frame was perfectly healthy; nonetheless, every morning when he got up he stared at his face in the mirror and examined his hands. He was expecting from day to day to find his skin broken out in leprosy, which, in his fancy, would be his punishment for robbing a Brahmin woman of her virtue. He had grown weary of putting up with the *Sahibs* and their grumblings, insults and kicks; and all his family had died, so although he was still young enough for service, he had resigned and was returning to his village. Resentment burned in his mind at the humiliation he had borne silently for twenty years; and when he found that Coleman was an even fiercer enemy than himself of the Company and its servants, little by little they began to open their hearts to each other.

'The East India Company was founded to carry on trade,' Coleman remarked one day, 'but since then it has turned its hand to robbery. The *Sahibs* come here in swarms, each hoping to make a fortune and get home again as quickly as possible. That is the case with all of them, from top to bottom. Clive did the same, and there was no one to stop him. Warren Hastings was so rapacious that he did not think twice about letting Chait Singh's wives starve to death, or ruining the Begums of Awadh.[23] But our people at home did not let him go off scot-free. He saved himself from condemnation, but several years of prosecution cost him the fortune he had made.'

'Who prosecuted him, Sahib?'

'Parliament. In our country the king is not free to do as he likes. We once cut the king's head off with an axe because he wanted to rule according to his own will, and we have still kept that axe. Parliament is a council De, the *panchayat*. Most of its members are chosen by the rich people of the country and some big landlords have a family right to be in it.'

'How long have these landlords been there?'

'The big estates in India have been created in imitation of ours. Over there they have been expanding for about a hundred years and there too the peasants have been forcibly deprived of their right to the land. You know the name of the Governor who introduced big estates here?'

'Yes – Cornwallis.'

'Well, he is a first-class tyrant of a landlord himself in England. When he came here he saw that so long as the land belonged to the peasants, it would be impossible to collect the revenue in full in times of drought or river-floods or too much rain. He also realized that the English, coming across the seas to a strange country, must make some friends here, friends whose interests would be bound up with those of the English. The landlords are the creation of the English, and whatever danger may threaten the English power from the opposition of the peasants also threatens the landlords with the loss of their estates, wealth, and rank. So to set up big landlords, with fifty villages apiece, instead of recognizing the small cultivators as proprietors, is useful to us both in good times and in bad times. That is why that unscrupulous Cornwallis came from England and ground the peasants of India into the dust.'

'He ground them down all right,' said Teenkaudi, thinking of the peasants on his own estate.

'All over the world the people have been exploited by such feudal landowners; but now their days are numbered.'

'How, Sahib?'

'A few years ago the people of France executed their king and queen and a great many feudal landowners were wiped out by the same revolution. Landowning as an institution was put an end to. The people treated everyone as a plain human being and proclaimed the principles of liberty, equality and fraternity. I was in France at the time, De, and I saw with my own eyes the people of France hoist their three-coloured flag over the royal palaces. Now the king and the landowning nobles of England are shaking in their shoes. And the same would have happened in England as in France but for one thing that came to their rescue – more's the pity.'

'What thing?'

'You know what heaps of merchandise from English factories are pouring into the Indian markets. Your weavers and spinners are falling out of employment, while at home our businessmen have given employment in their new factories to the people who were left to starve by the cruelty of the landlords. The goods they produce are coming here. Formerly in our country all the work was done by hand, but now steam engines are being made, and the cloth made by the looms they drive is growing cheaper. The artisans of this country are ruined! So are the handicraftsmen in England, but they can earn something to keep themselves alive by working in the factories. If those factories had not been started, England would have gone the same way as France. A human being ought to live like a human being, De! And whoever regards his fellow beings as animal, he and his family too have to become animals.'

'That is true, Sahib. I never used to think of my slaves and servants as human beings, but when the *Sahibs* treat me in the same fashion, I feel how beastly it is to degrade a fellow creature.'

'Great efforts are being made in England to get slavery abolished.'

'Is slavery practised in England too?'

'The ill-fated men and women are being bought and sold all over the world, but I hope that in England a law will be made against it before long.'

'Then what will become of the rich people who own the slaves?'

'The rich are against it, and there are many of them in our Parliament, but even some of them have begun to think slavery wicked. And what a beastly thing this traffic in human flesh is! You can see that for yourself, De. But many of those who support the abolition of slavery are not doing so because they think slavery sinful, but because slaves cannot take proper care of the expensive iron machines that are being installed in factories nowadays. You know yourself that fine work is not entrusted to slaves. When you make a man's life and death your plaything all the time, he will be quite ready to take his revenge by doing you a serious injury.'

'When I see a slave-woman and her children sold separately, as they often are, it strikes me as something intolerable.'

'Anyone who doesn't think it intolerable, De, is less than a man.'

'I was thinking about France, without a king,' resumed De. 'What do they call a government like that?'

'A republic.'

'Is a republic better than a monarchy?'

'It is the best of all governments! Kings, princes, and princesses and ladies swallow up too much of the national income. A representative government will show more justice, impartiality and benevolence than any king.'

'Yes, I used to see the *panchayat* working in my own village, and it certainly gave better justice, and nobody was ruined by legal expenses. But since Cornwallis's landlords appeared and suppressed the *panchayat*, the people have been ruined.'

'Quite right, De. But the French people set themselves an even higher aim than republicanism, when they tried to establish the rule of liberty, equality and fraternity for all human beings.'

'For this land too?'

'Are you people men or not?'

'In the *Sahibs'* eyes we were not born to be men.'

'Men cannot be men until the rule of liberty, equality and fraternity has been set up all over the world, among all men, black or white. The tyrant Cornwallis never thought of his own white-skinned peasants as human beings. And in France, the king and the landowners were got rid of; but then the businessmen, kindred spirits to the East India Company men, got the power in their hands, so that the old three-coloured flag of liberty, equality and fraternity could not float freely.'

'So France has a government of merchants in place of its royal family?'

'Yes, and the merchants in England too are making a stir. They say that if they were able to cross the ocean and rule India, why cannot they rule at home? So they are trying to get political power into their own hands, though without getting rid of the king.'

'In England, you say, the king has to share his power with them?'

'Yes, and I have seen the tricks these white merchants play here. I wanted to see the country, and to get an opportunity I joined the Company's service. If I had not been in their service, these money-grabbers would have viewed me with suspicion and it would have become difficult for me to travel about. So for two years I have stayed in their employment, and it's like being in hell.'

'It is a hell, Sahib, for a decent man. No one can stand it unless he is ready and willing to commit every crime and endure every indignity for the sake of amassing wealth. By the favour of one of Cornwallis's officials, as the price of my sins, I was given an estate of four villages. But I have reaped my reward; my wife and children have died of cholera. It makes me shudder to think of that estate. I am of your opinion, that only through the reign of liberty, equality and fraternity can earth be turned into heaven and humanity be rescued from degradation.'

'But that will not come our way merely by our agreeing with it or hoping for it, De! Thousands will have to sacrifice themselves, as they did in France, and silent sacrifices will not accomplish it. Thousands of Indian *sipahis*[24] are sacrificing themselves for the good of the English. Instead, they must learn to do the same for their own good, and to do it with their eyes and ears open.'

'How do you mean?'

'I mean that Indians must learn about the world. Science is conferring power on mankind. By knowledge of science man has made gunpowder and guns and made himself strong. This science has laid your cities waste, but in England it is building new cities and new machine factories. You too must learn to take advantage of it.'

'And then?'

'And then get rid of India's system of "untouchability" and caste divisions and the gulf between Hindus and Muslims. We don't consider ourselves polluted by accepting food from any other man, do we?'

'No.'

'And is there any caste division among us English, except between rich and poor?'

'No. ... What else must we do?'

'Abolish the burning of widows. Do you think God will forgive this burning of thousands of women every year?'

When Teenkaudi De and Coleman were separating at Kolkata, each of them regretted the parting. Coleman's last words were –

'My friend, we are entering the nineteenth century. The world is being turned upside down. We have to take our part in this upheaval and the first thing to do is to set up printing presses and newspapers so as to let the people know about the great changes going on in the great world.'

—3—

This year no rain had fallen. The pools were still as dry as they had been in May. There had not been one handful of rice from the spring crop or the summer crop. Family after family had perished or fled from the misery of drought. When the big lake of Dhuradeh dried up, corpses of people from twenty-five *kos* around were found lying in its parched bed. They had come to dig up lotus-roots and stalks, and often fights had broken out among them.

Next year, when monsoons came and Rekha was harvesting the first crop of *mandua* (*ragi*)[25] he would gaze with astonishment at Mangri when she came near. In this past year, the world seemed to have grown incomprehensible. In many families most of the people had died; many other households were scattered far and wide. What astonished Rekha was the thought of how he and his wife had been able to keep body and soul together, and to remain with each other. He felt very grateful to the Dhuradeh lake.

There had been famines in other years, from want of rain, but never, perhaps, before Rekha's time had the peasants endured such torment as this. Formerly, there had been a government which contented itself with lower revenue at such times; but now, under the Company's government, there was the tyrannous rule of the landlords from whose watchmen and bailiffs not even pumpkins grown on a cottage roof were safe. A peasant could not keep enough from each crop to live on for a month and a half; how could he save anything to meet a famine?

When Mangri, in the month of Agahan,[26] gave birth to a child, Rekha was still more astonished. Not because he was fifty years old, for Mangri was only thirty and had had other children who had died, but because she had been able to nourish another life during the famine, when it was hard enough even to keep any flesh on one's own bones. He gave the boy the name Sukhari,[27] because it had been born during a drought.

In the month of Magh,[28] the landlord came to Dyalpur from Rampur, with his horses and elephants, his bodyguard and bailiffs. In his house, Rekha heard, not a single child had grown thin, even in the midst of the famine: they were eating seven-year-old rice. His court-house at Dyalpur was on the edge of the village. In front of it was being laid out a mango orchard of twenty-five acres, and the work of watering it and digging it over was done by the villagers' compulsory labour. The landlord had put each household in charge of fifty seedlings and for each seedling allowed to wither a penalty of one rupee and a quarter had to be paid.

People younger than Rekha were beginning to think of the landlords and their self-indulgence as things that had always existed, and what he and Sobaran used to say about the days before landlords existed, when the *panchayat* ruled, was beginning to sound like a fairy tale. Since the famine, the bailiffs had grown still more arrogant. They looked on the famine as something sent to break the spirit of the peasants and exalt the power of their master. Ever since the month of Agahan, when the pumpkin-creeper on Rekha's roof had begun to sprout, the bailiffs had begun to hang about. Since the famine, the villagers were saying, Rekha had grown hot-tempered. This seemed to him odd, but it was true; for the rest of the villagers were only shadows of their old selves since the famine, while Rekha remained comparatively vigorous, so his temper seemed irascible. When he saw the watchmen and bailiffs hanging about his cottage, he grew angry, though he did not betray his feelings.

But one day a watchman climbed up on the roof to pick a pumpkin for the Patwari. Rekha happened to be inside his house, fondling his Sukhari on his lap. At the first sound of the roof creaking and shaking, he laid Sukhari down on a mat and went out. He saw the watchman on the roof gathering pumpkins; three had been picked already and the fourth was about to be attacked. A thrill of rage ran through Rekha. He shouted out in threatening tones that could be heard over half the village –

'Who is that!'

'Don't you see?' returned the watchman, not turning his head – 'I am collecting pumpkins for the Patwari.'

'If you want to keep your skin whole, come down quietly!' said Rekha menacingly. 'Do you hear!'

'Do you know you're talking to the master's watchman?'

'I know all about that. You better leave the pumpkins and come down!'

Silently, the watchman descended. On hearing his tale, the Patwari curbed his wrath for the time being; he reserved the case until the landlord's coming in the month of Magh.

When the landlord arrived, the same watchman presented

himself at Rekha Bhagat's house and said –

'From tomorrow you have to give the master two *ser* of milk in the morning.'

'I have no cow and no buffalo. Where am I to get milk from?'

'Wherever you like. That is the master's order.'

The Patwari knew very well that Rekha had no cow, but this was his chance to put Rekha in his place. That very evening he unfolded to the landlord the story of Rekha's mutinous conduct, and added that the whole village was being infected by it. The landlord came to a decision the same night.

In the morning there was no milk from Rekha. When a bailiff came to him he repeated that he owned neither a cow nor a buffalo. The landlord chose five ruffians and gave the order –

'Go and milk that bastard's wife instead.'

Several villagers were present, but they only thought that the men were going to arrest Rekha. The five men seized Rekha without a word, and tied him up. Then two of them entered the house and got hold of Mangri. The helpless Rekha looked on with bloodshot eyes while they held his screaming wife's breasts and actually forced a trickle of milk into a cup. After this they went away, leaving him still bound.

Mangri sat still covering her face in shame. At last Rekha found his tongue and said –

'Don't feel shame, Mangri. If our village *panchayat* was still alive, the Emperor himself would not have dared to do this. But they shall pay for this insult. If the true blood of the Ahirs is in my veins, there will be no one left alive in the families of the Patwari and the Rampur's Munshi to weep for them. I shall avenge this humiliation with my own hands, Mangri. Come, untie my hands.'

With her eyes swimming with tears, Mangri unfastened his bonds. He went inside and took Sukhari on his lap, kissing him and then said to his wife –

'Take everything you want out of here and go straight to your mother's; I am going to burn this house.'

She knew by his voice what he meant. She took the child and a few clothes outside and then fell at his feet.

'There must be revenge,' said Rekha, in an unusually gentle tone, 'not only for your honour, but for the honour of the whole village. Go now, and you can tell Sukhari what kind of man his father was. Don't delay; I'm going to rake out the fire from the hearth.'

Mangri watched from a distance until she saw the flames going up from the roof. All the people who occupied cottages at the edge of the village came running towards Rekha's house, while he, grasping a sword, made for the landlord's court-house. Afraid for their lives, the guards took to flight. Rekha hacked the landlord and the Patwari to death, shouting as he struck – 'No one will be left behind to mourn you, villains!'

He fulfilled his vow, and more than fulfilled it.

How many Rekhas the tyrant Cornwallis stirred up!

18

Mangal Singh

TIME : 1857 CE

—1—

The two of them had gone to see the Tower. They saw the cells in which enemies of the throne had rotted in lifelong captivity. They saw the rack, and the axes and other weapons, emblems of the fact that the kings had been masters of life and death, and were in truth God's governors or executioners on earth. But what attracted them most of all was the spot where the heads of a king and several queens of England had rolled in the dust.

As usual, Annie Russell's soft hand lay in his, but today its softness seemed to have a new quality. It was as if some emanation were running from her hand through his frame, something like the electricity which the scientist Faraday had discovered eleven years before (1845).

'Annie,' said Mangal Singh, 'are you an electric battery?'

'Why do you say that, Mangi?'

'That is how I feel. Sixteen years ago, when I first set foot in England, I felt as if I had stepped out of darkness into bright sunlight; I saw a great new world in front of me. I don't mean great in square miles, but a scene stretching away into the far future. There were many novel and astonishing things to see: beet-sugar (1808), steam-boats (1712), railways (1725), telegraphs (1833), matches (1835), photography (1839), electric light (1844); but when I got to Cambridge and was able to study them and see them by laboratory experiments, I began to realize what a great future is awaiting the world.'

'You really felt that coming to England was like coming from darkness into light?'

'In the sense I have been talking about; otherwise I had only two ideas in leaving India – to see the land of worshippers of the Lord Jesus, whom I also worshipped, and to try and recover the royal treasures my family had been deprived of.'

'I have often wanted to ask you about yourself, but I always forget. Tell me your story now, Mangi.'

'I can't have any objection to talking about something which has changed the course of my life! Come along here to the peaceful Thames, Annie dear. The Thames is neither so big nor so beautiful as our Ganga, but often while I am watching it I have pleasant memories of the Ganga. You know that Christians regard all other religions as paganism, and view them with contempt; but this Thames once turned me back into a pagan instead of a Christian. It made me think of my mother, a "pagan" Hindu, offering flowers so readily to the Ganga.'

They reached the river bank and sat down on a stone bench facing the water. Annie's golden locks escaping from her white bonnet fell over her cheeks and quivered in the breeze. Mangal kissed them as he began to speak.

'How often I have stood on this bank of the Thames and offered imaginary flowers to my own Ganga!'

'Your mother used to offer flowers to the Ganga?'

'Yes, with as much devotion as Christians praying to their Lord Jesus. At first when I became a Christian it seemed to me a disgusting custom, but many a time since then I have felt contrition for the dishonour I had done to our Ganga in my heart.'

'Our poets have brought back to life the feelings that Christianity tried to suppress. We call this river Father Thames, you know.'

'And we talk of Mother Ganga.'

'Yours is a sweeter fancy, Mangi. Tell me about yourself.'

'Well, Banaras and Ramnagar are two towns a little apart, on opposite sides of the Ganga. I had sixteen years to look at the river. My home in Banaras was right on the bank, and below it a flight of sixty steps led down to the water. Perhaps when I first opened my eyes my mother held me on her lap to show me to the Ganga. At any rate, in some strange way the river seems to be in my blood. At Ramnagar stands my grandfather's castle, but I have only seen it two or three times, from a boat on the river. I had no desire to see it oftener, or to enter it. My mother had no wish to go there either. You can imagine, Annie, a woman who had lived in that castle as a princess, and now was dragging out her life in Banaras, under a false name for fear of the English, could hardly bear to fix her eyes on it again. My grandfather was Chait Singh, who was stripped of his possessions so unjustly by that robber Warren Hastings. In England, Hastings was brought to book for his misdeeds, partly at least, but no justice was ever done to my grandfather. It would have been an expensive kind of justice to restore a stolen kingdom, Annie.'

'Is your mother still living?'

'I get a letter now and then from my old Padre at Banaras, and I write to her through him. She was still living five months ago, at least.'

'You were not a Christian at first, then?'

'No, and she is a Hindu still. I used to want to convert her, but now ...'

'Now you want to offer flowers to Mother Ganga beside her?'

'If I do, the missionaries will say I have abandoned the Christian religion.'

'How did you become a Christian?'

'It wasn't a question of any inner guidance. There are missionaries at Banaras as elsewhere, preaching Christianity – both men and women; but Banaras is the Hindu Rome, so they cannot have very much success. Once a medical missionary came to attend to my mother, and after that his wife began visiting our house. A close acquaintance grew between her and my mother. I was still a child, and she often used to take me into her lap ...'

'You must have been very nice-looking even as a child, Mangi! Who wouldn't have liked to hold you?'

'Well, then she advised my mother to have me taught English, and when I was five or six her husband began to teach me. My mother was always thinking about the lost glories of her family, and she nursed a secret hope that if her son learned English he might perhaps be able to do something to restore the family fortunes. My father had died when I was three, so she had to manage everything by herself. Our wealth had disappeared with our kingdom, but she had a good deal of jewellery that her mother-in-law had given her, and her brother helped to take care of her. When I was eight I began to spend half my time in the home of this missionary and his wife. I had no chance to learn much of the Hindu religion, and what I learned was from that lady. She used to tell me I was very lucky that my mother had escaped, for when my father died people wanted her to commit "*sati*"[1] and be burned alive. I thought the Hindu religion meant the same thing as my mother being burned alive, so you can guess whether I felt anything for such a religion except the bitterest hatred. It was still two years before the suppression of *sati* (1829).

'Thinking of my welfare, my mother took the lady's advice, and sent me to school at Kolkata. While I was studying there, she began to suspect that they had done all this for me in order to turn me into a Christian. It was lucky that this had not struck her earlier, or I should never have had the opportunity of getting my mind woken up.'

'Is there no idea of educating children in India?'

'I should have been given an education, but only of the kind that would have been useful thirteen centuries ago.'

'How did you get your mother's leave to come to England?'

'Her leave? I came without asking for it. The missionary helped me; he arranged for me to study at Cambridge. When I sent news to my mother from here that I was well and happy, she sent me her blessing. She is over fifty-five now, and in every letter she tells me to come home.'

'And what do you tell her?'

'I can only make excuses. She believes that here in the capital I am meeting the Queen of England and one day I will come home to take my seat on the throne of Chait Singh.'

'Poor Ganga-worshipper! She little dreams that instead of Queen Victoria you are meeting those terrible enemies of all crowned heads in the world, Karl Marx and Friedrich Engels!'

'How could India understand Marx's communism, when it doesn't even know anything yet about the capitalist world and its power!'

'Has Marx ever talked to you about India?'

'Many times, and it astonishes me to find how much he, living here, has been able to learn about India's development. But it is no conjuring trick. Here in London is to be found all the information about India that various Englishmen have collected and written down in the last three centuries. Marx has gone through these dusty volumes very carefully, and whenever he meets an Indian here he questions him and tests the conclusions he has come to.'

'What does he think about India's future?'

'He has a high respect for the bravery of Indian soldiers, and he admires our intelligence; but he thinks our belief in the ancient superstitious scriptures to be India's greatest enemy, and regards our villages as little self-contained republics.'

'Republics?'

'Yes, it is not a question of the whole country or even of two combined villages in the same district, but of each individual village. Not everywhere. Self-government has perished in the areas where Lord Cornwallis founded landownership on the English model. Under this self-government all the people appoint five or more headmen to manage their affairs. They look after policing, justice, irrigation, education, worship and all other activities, and they are conscientious and sensible, fair and impartial. Everyone in the village, young or old, is ready to give his life when the *panchayat* calls on him, in defence of any patch of land belonging to the village or the honour of its meanest inhabitant. The Muslim rulers originally tried, while they only controlled a small area round Delhi, and regarded themselves as temporary lodgers, to undermine the *panchayat* system, but later on they recognized the *panchayats* as organs of self-government. But our English rulers, especially the English landlord Cornwallis, have set about destroying village autonomy, and to a great extent they have succeeded, though perhaps if it had been left to them the old system would not have collapsed so quickly. The most mortal blow at self-rule and economic self-sufficiency of the village has been the influx of English goods, such as Lancashire cloth and Sheffield ironware and so on. The first steamboat was launched at Kolkata in 1822, on the 10th of July. The knocking away of what was still left of village self-sufficiency has been the consequence. Dhaka, the great emporium of India's fine muslin, is now two thirds deserted, Annie, and the country weavers are in a horrible condition. An Indian village used to reckon itself independent in iron-work, pottery, spinning and weaving. Today its artisans are sitting with folded hands, starving to death, and its supplies come from Manchester, Birmingham and Sheffield. Take cloth alone; in 1814 there was 18,66,608 *thaan*[2] of cloth exported from India to Britain, and in 1835 it was 3,76,083 *thaans*. But in these same years enormous quantities of English cloth have poured into India. Today, India, which was able to make that Dhaka's muslin, is sending its raw cotton to England and getting its cloth made there. Just think of the latest figures: in 1846, cotton worth £10,75,309 came to England.'

'How cruel it all was, how bad!'

'Still, as my teacher says, we may shed tears over this foreign exploitation, but as rational men we must be pleased at the collapse of the stronghold of conservatism.'

'Then there are two ways of looking at it.'

'Certainly. Just as a mother suffers pangs in giving birth, but also feels joy in having a child; there is no creation without destruction. We cannot establish a powerful self-governing nation without breaking down the little separate autonomous units. As long as Indian patriotism is limited to the village republic, there can be no wider patriotism, no devotion to India as a whole. At present the English are introducing into India only such inventions as to assist their commerce, like their ships and railways, but Marx is right in saying that when the English capitalists are forced to use Indian coal and iron in building and repairing their railways, they will not be able to refrain for long from utilizing these materials, because of their cheapness. And the Indian mind will not remain asleep for long when it has the wonders of science before it.'

'In short, industrialization and capitalism are bound to grow in India too.'

'Yes, of course. In England today power has passed out of the hands of the landowning aristocracy, hasn't it?'

'Yes.'

'The Reform Bill of 1832 has put the reins of power in the hands of the capitalists.'

'At least, it is a sign that they are taking over power.'

'Quite right. Did the meetings and newspapers of the Chartists make any impression on you, Annie?'

'During their days my mind was still scarcely awake, I have only a hazy recollection of them. My uncle Russell, you know, was the Chartists' bitterest enemy in the Cabinet. I have often heard him talk of it as a dangerous agitation.'

'Did he look such a bold orator then as he did when Parliament was rejecting the modest petitions of the workers with their twelve hundred thousand signatures?'

'No, dear. Even now he is nervous, in spite of the fact that in this year of our Lord 1856, there is nothing to be seen of any Chartists.'

'He may well be nervous, Annie. In the same way as the capitalists have broken the power of the nobles and set up their own, the workers in their turn will overthrow the rule of gold, and bring humanity to power; they will abolish all distinctions of rich and poor, high and low, white and black ...'

'And the distinction of man and woman, Mangi?'

'Yes, women too are victims of men's oppression. Our feudal rulers, up to our own days, have been burning thousands of women alive every year in the name of *sati*, and it is still a disgrace to humanity the way they are shut up in *purdah*[3] and cheated out of any control over their property and made to bear men's tyranny.'

'You may fancy that women in this country are free, because we are not shut up in *purdah*.'

'I don't say you are free, Annie, I only say that you are better off than your sisters in India.'

'How can there be any better or worse in slavery, Mangi! We have not even the right of voting for Parliament. We are not allowed to cross the threshold of a university. We tighten our waists till you could put your fingers round them and drag skirts with sixty yards of cloth in them along the ground, just to make ourselves dolls for men to play with. So the prospect Marx holds out is of a growth of industrialization and capitalism in India, which will give the people more and more energy, and at the same time bring together in factories the unemployed peasants and artisans now scattered among the villages. Then they will learn to form trade unions and struggle, and then raise the flag of socialism and march shoulder to shoulder with the English workers for the deliverance of humanity, until the world is freed of its slavery to gold, and liberty, equality and fraternity have been established. But all this will take centuries, Mangi.'

'Marx also says that while England has deprived India of the gifts of science – machines – she has put into the hands of Indian soldiers other gifts of science, new weapons. The Indian army will give powerful help in the restoration of India's independence.'

'But can it come in any near future?'

'No question of future, the time has come, Annie! Haven't you read in the papers of the British annexation of Awadh on February the seventh?'

'Yes, and it was unjustified.'

'We are not arguing about right or wrong. The Company has always acted from self-interest, but unwittingly it has done us many services. By breaking down village self-sufficiency it has shown us all India as our motherland; with its railways and telegraphs and steamers it has broken down our mental barriers and brought us into contact with the greater world. This annexation of Awadh will bring about a change, and I have been waiting for it.'

'What else is to be expected from a disciple of Marx!'

—2—

The peaceful banks of the Ganga were about to lose their tranquillity once more. In the massive palace of Bithoor, Nana Sahib, heir of the Peshwas,[4] who had lost not only his throne but even his pension, had grown more active since Awadh had become the newest capture of the English. His agents were busy day and night getting in touch with other feudal chiefs who like him had fallen from high estate. To his good fortune, the English committed another mistake; it was more than a mistake, for in such a constantly changing situation it involved a mortal risk; instead of the old ball-muskets, they issued a new and more powerful type of cartridge-gun to their troops. When these cartridges were inserted, the cap had to be bitten off. Far-sighted enemies of the English knew how to turn this to advantage. They raised a cry that the cartridges were greased with the fat of cows and pigs, and that the English were intentionally forcing their soldiers to bite them so as to destroy the Hindu and Muslim religions in India, and Christianize everyone.

Mangal Singh, as grandson of Chait Singh, the old ruler of Banaras, was well aware that his name would have spread like wildfire among the soldiers; but he never allowed his identity to be divulged. Nana and the other rebel leaders knew only this much about him, that he was vigorously opposed to the foreign rule, and that having been in England he had a good knowledge of European science and politics. He had lost his religion by living in England, though he was not now a follower of Christianity.

It did not take him long to fathom the cherished aspirations of the rebel leaders. He saw that these fallen feudalists were each hoping to recover their power, and, to this end, aimed at uniting and expelling their only common enemy, the English. To them, the soldiers whose lives they were about to sacrifice had no more importance than pawns on the chessboard. As to the soldiers, what spurred them on was the fear of losing their religion: had they been spared the need to bite those greased cartridges they might have gone on for ever applauding *Company the great* and sacrificing their lives for it. The gulf between Hindus and Muslims, moreover, had not been narrowed in the least. Had the rebellion ended in success, their thirst for the favour of their respective gods might have hurried the inflamed and ignorant soldiers into an even more merciless fanaticism against one another. If there was any other impulse at work in their hearts, it was the desire to plunder towns and villages in their way. Those infected with this craving might be few in number, and the places sacked by them might be few, but it caused such an outcry that the countryfolk came to dread soldiers as much as bandits.

This was an unfortunate impression to attach itself to an army that was to liberate its country. When he learned of it, Mangal Singh was at first in despair. He had not come to fight for his grandfather's throne, but to work for the realization of liberty, equality and fraternity, against caste and religious divisions as well as against the domination of English capital. He had not come to restore the gloom of medievalism, but to break down India's age-old barriers and bring her into the comity of nations. For him, the removal of exploitation by English capital was only a first step towards developing friendly relations between a free Indian people and the peoples of other lands, for the building of a better world. He could not approve of the dissemination of the lie about the greased cartridges, nor of the opportunity it gave superstition to strengthen its hold on India. Nana and other rebel leaders themselves guzzled the most expensive European liquors. They were quite ready when they got the chance to swallow wine or pork or kiss the adulterated[5] lips of white women, but at present their game was to pose before the soldiers as leaders devoted to the defence of religion.

But with all the blemishes of the cause, Mangal Singh did not hesitate in seeing the path of duty, for he saw that India was being crushed by a double tyranny of English capitalists and Indian feudalists, the former being the stronger and more wily. When the foreigners had been expelled, there would remain only the native feudalists to be dealt with, and the Indian people would find its task easy.

It was January, and the nights were cold, though far less so than in London. All was silent in Bithoor, but the guards at the Peshwa's palace were all ready at their posts. They saw a stranger slip into the palace with a trustworthy agent of their master, but this was happening every night now.

This was not Mangal Singh's first meeting with Nana; they had come to know each other well enough. Besides himself, Mangal found assembled agents of the puppet king of Delhi, the Nawab of Awadh, Kunwar Singh of Jagdishpur, and many other magnates. Reports were being made of how far the revolutionary spirit had infected the soldiers in cantonments such as Barrackpur (Kolkata), Danapur, Kanpur, Lucknow, Agra and Meerut. The astonishing thing was that these chieftains, with no forces of their own, were pinning all their hopes on an army of mutineers, in the face of so formidable an antagonist. As to military science, nearly all the leaders were quite ignorant of it, though they were quite willing to officiate as generals.

'English rule in India rests on Indian regiments,' remarked Nana hopefully, 'and now they are coming over to our side.'

'But they are not all doing so, Nana Sahib!' returned Mangal. 'There is no news yet of the Panjab Sikhs breaking out; on the contrary, they remember how the other Indian troops helped the English to conquer the Panjab and will try to take their revenge. The English are intelligent, Nana Sahib. If they had kept Dalip Singh[6] somewhere in India under lock and key, along with the Peshwa and the Nawab of Awadh, it would have been very easy for us today to win over all the Sikh regiments. At any rate, we must bear in mind that the Sikhs and Gurkhas and the States'[7] troops are not with us, and whoever is not with us in a national war like this, we must consider against us.'

'You are right,' said Nana, 'but if we are successful at the outset, no enemy of the country will venture to oppose us.'

'There is another weapon we ought to make use of; when the struggle has begun we shall have to use it, but we ought to begin training men for the purpose now. We must explain to the people that we are fighting for national liberation.'

'We shall be challenging the English, will not that be enough?' put an envoy from the east.

Mangal Singh – 'Our swords will not be clashing all the time everywhere. There are plenty of cowards and selfish people in our country who believe the English invincible. They will spread all kinds of tales. In my opinion we ought to mark out three regions – eastern, central and western, and publish a newspaper in each of them in Hindi and Urdu.'

Nana Sahib – 'You are too fond of English methods! But you know how many people we have reached with our cartridge story, without the help of any newspaper.'

Mangal Singh – 'But when we are in the thick of the struggle we shall have to cope with stories against us spread by the hangers-on of the English. It is impossible for us to seize on all their machinery of administration in a single day. Suppose they spread a rumour that the mutineers – and I tell you, that is the name we shall be remembered by – are looting towns and villages and murdering children?'

Nana Sahib – 'Will people believe that?'

Mangal Singh – 'Whatever is repeated often enough and goes uncontradicted, will begin to be believed.'

Nana Sahib – 'I should think we have given the English such a bad name with our talk of the cartridges, and "religion in danger", that nothing they say will be credited.'

Mangal Singh – 'We can't trust to that forever. Well, another thing: the English will call this struggle of ours mere mutiny and give it that name all over the world. But we have many friends in the world, and the English have many enemies who will wish to see us independent, especially among the European nations. Therefore, we must not make our fight a crusade against all *Firangis* alike; and in fighting we must not touch any English women or children or old men. That would not help us in the war; on the contrary, it would unnecessarily give Hindustan a bad name in the world.'

Nana Sahib – 'It is for our commanders to think about that, and I think they themselves can decide what ought to be done at any particular time.'

Mangal Singh – 'The last thing I have to say is that greased cartridges are not sufficient grounds for a war in which our soldiers are to stake their lives, and in which we hope for the support of the ordinary people. We must explain what kind of a government we want to set up after the English have gone away, and how that government will benefit the soldiers who have done the fighting and the peasantry, from which they come.'

Nana Sahib – 'Surely the removal of a government that threatens their religion will be enough to satisfy them.'

Mangal Singh – 'What would you say if someone suggested that to you? Is your heart not full of the desire to return to Pune, the capital of the Peshwas? Has the throne of Lucknow no charms for our Nawab? If you, the leaders have other ambitions besides getting rid of greased cartridges and English rule, to make you willing to risk your lives, I think it will be good to let the common people, too, see some prospect of benefit for themselves.'

'How?'

'We should set up a *panchayat* in every village to give the people cheap justice. We should set up a *panchayat* of the whole nation, to be chosen by the whole people, and to have power even over the king. We should abolish big landownership and not let there be any master between the peasant and the government; if an estate is granted to anyone in return for service, he should merely have a right to appropriate the land revenue from it. We should develop factories and find employment in them for all our workers, so as not to leave anyone idle. We should improve irrigation by making canals, reservoirs and dams; this would provide work for millions, double or treble the nation's food supply, and make plenty of fresh land available for the cultivators.'

Nobody was prepared to give serious consideration to Mangal Singh's proposals. They all brushed them aside by saying that they could be considered after power had been won.

He lay awake on his bed for a long time, unable to sleep. This, he reflected, was the age of science. These people could see for themselves the wonders of railways, telegraphs, steamships. The age of matches, cameras, electric lights, had opened; yet they were still living in the dreams of a bygone age. Still, amid these dark shadows one thing stood out clearly. This war could be won only by the strength of the people, and through it the people would realize its own strength. Just as the English capitalists, backed by the energy of their workers had been able to defeat their rivals, and then treat the workers with contempt, these Indian magnates might succeed with the help of the Indian people – soldiers and peasants – and then betray them. But they would not be able to rob the people of its faith in itself, nor could they help adopting the new discoveries of science in order to safeguard themselves from foreign enemies. Railway lines, telegraph lines, the steamships built at Kolkata, could not vanish from India now. It was not in these out-of-date feudalists that Mangal Singh put his trust, but in the revolutionary strength of humanity, in the people.

—3—

On 10 May 1857, Mangal Singh was near Meerut when the Sepoys there hoisted the flag of mutiny. It fell to his lot to take one detachment under his command, in the name of Bahadur Shah.[8] The feudal magnates did not doubt his ability, but they also knew that his goal was very different from theirs, and so instead of sending him in the direction of Delhi they told him to march eastward. Who could guess, that in this war for Indian freedom the roads east and west from Meerut led equally to disaster. The army marching on Delhi in fact needed a leader like Mangal Singh, who could make full use of Delhi's ancient fame to secure victory.

There were a thousand men in Mangal Singh's detachment. At the outset of the Mutiny they were all inclined to look upon themselves as generals. It took him a week to convince them that a regiment of nothing but generals could never hope to win battles. There was no one besides himself with any advanced knowledge of military science, and the same was true of all the rebel forces. He could not afford to wait and train his men; the urgent task was to overthrow the government's authority promptly in as many districts as possible. After crossing the Ganga and entering Rohilkhand, he began making it his practice to explain his political ideas every night to his soldiers. The latter were some time in understanding them; many questions arose in their minds, and Mangal Singh answered them. Then he gave an account of the two French revolutions of 1789 and 1848, and of how workmen in Wales had struggled against these English merchants who had been building up their power in India, and showed the greatest courage; the merchants by force of numbers were able to overcome them, but they could never deprive them of their rights as long as there was breath in their bodies.

When the *sipahis* heard these things, their behaviour changed radically. Each of them became a missionary of the war of liberation, going into villages, towns, and cities, and by his words and conduct inspiring in the public mind confidence and respect. The fact that they expended with proper accounting the money found in government treasures; that they collected taxes, when necessary, only in accordance with public desire and sanction, after re-establishing the local *panchayat* and explaining the situation; that they never took anything without payment; and that Mangal Singh explained his plans to the crowds of thousands everywhere he went – this very quickly began to have its effect. Crowds of young men began to enrol themselves in the army of liberation. Mangal Singh organized instruction in military drill, and also in surprise attacks, commissariat arrangements and so on. He took with him a squad of Muslim and Hindu physicians.

To cleanse the Aegean stables[9] of feudal extortion and corruption, a strong infusion of selfless patriotism into the educated classes was required, and it was not easy to inspire this at such a time. Still, no one could spend a couple of days with Mangal Singh without gaining in enlightenment. No one watching him as he joked and chatted with his soldiers could have guessed that he was the commander of a force which before the end swelled to two thousand men. Yet every man of them was ready to lay down his life at the commander's bidding. He always shared with the soldiers their meal of unleavened bread, he slept like them rolled up in a blanket, he was foremost at the post of danger. He treated captured English folk with humanity. They were astonished at his clemency, for in Europe itself, at that time, such treatment of prisoners was unheard of. He entered four districts of Rohilkhand, and organized them all excellently.

Nana Sahib drew his sword against the English on 5 June 1857, but he was defeated by them within a month and a half, on 18 July. Mangal Singh was not slow to realize that the tide had turned but so long as life remained he never let the banner of freedom fall. The English commenced general reprisals against the unarmed population of Awadh; women were robbed of honour and life. Even at this news, Mangal Singh and his comrades did not molest any captive Englishman.

By the end of the rains, the resistance of the mutineers was being broken everywhere, but he was still in arms in Rohilkhand and western Awadh, assailed from all sides by English, Gurkha and Sikh troops. Day by day the numbers of the soldiers of freedom dwindled. Mangal Singh, thinking of the future, sent many of them back to their homes; but of the thousand who had marched out with him from Meerut, not one would consent to abandon him. Towards the end he saw something that robbed death of its bitterness: Brahmins and Rajputs, Jats and Gurjars, Hindus and Muslims, in the small band of doomed men, were losing all sense of communal differences. They cooked their food together, ate it together, and offered in this way a model of a united Indian nationality.

Five soldiers of Meerut city – Binda Singh, Devram, Sadafal

Pandey, Raheem Khan and Ghulam Hussain – were with him when finally, as he rowed for the last time over the Ganga, he was attacked from both sides. At the request of the English men and women who had been Mangal Singh's prisoners, the English commander had offered him a pardon and hoped that he would give himself up. He had always refused. The offer was repeated now; he gave his answer with a bullet. He was captured at last when his boat was drifting down the Ganga, manned by six dead bodies. The English paid homage to Indian valour.

19

Safdar

TIME : 1921–22 CE

—1—

It was a small but handsome bungalow. On one side of the large compound was a rose bed, bright with scarlet and pink blossoms. Another side was laid out as a small badminton court, covered with green grass which it was pleasant simply to feel under one's feet. At another corner stood a summer house overgrown with creepers, while at the back of the bungalow was an open verandah[1] where Safdar Jang, the barrister, often sat in the evenings.

Green creepers clung to the walls. Safdar had seen houses at Oxford with creeper-hung walls like these, and he had been very particular about having creepers hung here. There was a garage for two cars in the compound. Safdar Jang's mode of living, and the atmosphere of his bungalow, was an exact copy of the English style. His half dozen servants were trained on precisely the same lines as if they had been employed by some English official. They wore the same red waistband, the same stiffly tied turban with their master's monogram on a metal badge. Safdar preferred European food to any other, and had three cooks to provide him with it.

Just as Safdar lived like a *Sahib*, an English gentleman, his wife Sakina was always addressed by the servants as 'Mem-Sahib'.[2] Her eyebrows, with all unnecessary hairs plucked out, were thin curving lines, darkened still further by pencilling. She was in the habit of using lipstick every quarter of an hour. But she never acquired a taste for European dress.

Last year, in 1920, when Safdar had visited England with his wife for the first time, he had wanted Sakina to wear a frock, but she would not consent. Those they met in England, however, both men and women, admired her *saree*,[3] as well as her looks, so much that Safdar did not regret her refusal. The couple were both so light in complexion that in Europe they were always taken for Italians.

It was now the cold season of 1921. Like all other towns of upper India, Lucknow found this the pleasantest time of the year. Today, on his return from the Courts, Safdar took his seat on a cane chair in the verandah at the back of the house. His looks were unusually grave as he sat with a small table before him on which lay two or three books and a notebook. Three other chairs stood vacant near him. He wore a well-pressed English suit of the finest quality. The expression on his clean-shaven face made it clear that the Sahib was occupied with serious thoughts today, and at such times his servants took care not to come near him. He seldom lost his temper, but he had made his servants understand that on such occasions he preferred to be left alone.

Evening drew on, but Safdar remained seated. A servant brought a table lamp with a long wire and put it beside him. A voice could be heard at the house, and, at Safdar's enquiry the man told him that Master[4] Shankar Singh had called but was going away. Safdar at once ordered him to run and bring the visitor.

Shankar Singh was a man of thirty or thirty-two, but marks of old age were already visible in his face. He wore a black coat buttoned up to the neck, black trousers, and a round felt cap; his dark moustache was thick and drooping. There was nothing to suggest that he was in the prime of his youth, though his flashing eyes revealed a vigorous mind.

As soon as *Masterji* appeared, Safdar got up to shake hands. 'Shankar,' he exclaimed, giving him a chair, 'you were going away without seeing me?'

'Excuse me, dear *brother*,[5] I thought you must be sitting alone because you were buried in some work.'

'Even when I am buried in my law files I can always find a few minutes for you, and today you see there are no files in front of me.'

Safdar had the deepest affection for Shankar Singh. There was no one whom he considered a closer friend. From the time when they entered the fourth class in the school at Saudapur to the day when they took their B.A. at Lucknow, they had always been fellow students. Both had been bright students: sometimes one got a few marks more in an examination, sometimes the other, but this close rivalry had never bred ill-feeling or estrangement between them. Their friendship was aided by the fact that both were Gautam Rajputs, though one of their families had remained Hindu while the other had turned Muslim. Ten generations ago both had been Hindu, and they had, moreover, a common ancestor. Their families still met in the clan reunions held on special occasions.

Safdar was the only son of his father, and Shankar had helped him to forget that he had no brother. Shankar was the younger by six months. These were natural factors, but in addition to them Shankar possessed qualities which explained the love and respect felt by the 'real gentleman' Safdar for his plain, simple friend. The latter was good-humoured, but did not know how to flatter. The result was that in spite of his first-class M.A. degree he had become a mere assistant master in a government school. Had he given them the slightest encouragement, others would have pulled strings for him, and he would by now have been headmaster of a high school. It seemed as if he was quite willing to remain an assistant master for the rest of his life. Only once had he called on his friends for assistance: when he was being transferred away from Lucknow. With all his gentleness, he had a strong sense of self-respect, which Safdar appreciated. The intimacy that had begun when they were twelve years old was as firm as ever now when twenty years had gone by.

They had discussed a few casual topics when Sakina joined them, wearing a light green dress with a red bodice. Shankar got up, saying, 'Good evening, sister-in-law.'

'Good evening,' returned Sakina with a smile. There had been a time when she, the well-educated daughter of a wealthy knight, had disapproved of her husband's friendship with this rustic-looking schoolteacher. She had been free of *purdah* even in her father's house, so there was no obstacle to her meeting Shankar. But for the first six months she used to frown when she saw Shankar intimately working side by side with Safdar. In the end, however, she had to own to her husband that Shankar was well worthy of their affection and esteem.

By now she had come to feel quite like a real sister-in-law towards him. She had chosen to avoid having children, but from time to time she had Shankar's children to stay with her. For his part, Shankar had experienced in the past six years the favour of the god Shankar whose name he bore: there was always some new infant in his family. Observing her husband's thoughtfulness during the past week, Sakina had grown rather nervous, and she was very glad of Shankar's visit, for she knew that he was the very man to cheer Safdar up. She glanced at the visitor, remarking –

'You can't be in any hurry tonight. How would you like some chocolate pudding I have made myself?'

'No need to ask!' said Safdar.

'First I must know whether you're staying, one never knows when you may vanish.'

'That isn't fair! Can you think of any time when I haven't obeyed your command!'

'I'm not talking about disobedience. But keeping away, so as to escape getting any commands, is also an offence!'

'Well, here I am, ready to listen to orders from my commander.'

'All right,' said Sakina. 'I'm leaving you now; you must stay for dinner and eat the pudding.'

She ran away, and the two men's conversation took a graver turn. 'Shankar,' said Safdar, 'we are positively entering on a new revolutionary period. I think this is the first time since 1857 that Hindustan has begun to shake to her foundations.'

'You mean this political agitation, brother Saffu?'

'That is a very mild phrase, Shankar. When Congress[6] was founded in 1885, and it was only a doll for retired English Civil Servants to play with, even then its Christmas entertainment lectures and bottle parties were dubbed "agitation". If you want to call that agitation, I should say that we are passing now from agitation to revolution.'

'This is because Gandhiji has collected ten million rupees for Tilak's "Swarajya[7] Fund" and so the great clamour for self-rule has been raised further.'

'No single individual can give birth to a revolution, or a revolutionary agitation. Such a tremendous upheaval as it brings is beyond the power of a great man, or half a dozen great men, to stir up. When I think about the origin of this unrest that we see, this is the conclusion I come to: You know the leaders of the 1857 rebellion were broken-down feudal lords. By the way, our Lucknow was one of its centres; in fact, the English annexation of Lucknow was one of its immediate causes. But the struggle was waged at the cost of the common people's lives. It failed because of certain weaknesses on our side, and after its suppression the English carried out severe reprisals. Well, what I mean to say is that since 1857 this is the first time that the common people are joining in the struggle for independence. Tell me yourself, as a student of Indian history, can you think of any other agitation in which the people have taken part like this?'

'Brother Saffu! We have had the Nagpur session of Congress, and the Kolkata session, and I have seen for myself the excitement you speak of in the villages. It is quite astounding, I agree. But even after such a storm, when here in Lucknow there have been so many bonfires of foreign cloth, you have not been affected in the least, and now you talk as if you were a man in the thick of a revolutionary outburst!'

'You're right, Shankar, my younger brother! Yes, the flood is trying to wash my feet away from under me. I don't consider it any small, local affair; it is obviously linked with a very widespread upheaval. In any epoch the strongest revolutionary force appears only through the general public!'

'You start from 1857, Saffu brother! You are making a thorough job of it!'

'Shall I go on, Shankar?'

'I'd like to listen. The pudding is getting ready, and tomorrow is Sunday. Very well, let someone be sent to let my family know that I'm staying here in Lucknow, eating Sakina's pudding and snoring. Now I'm at your disposal, I can listen all night.'

'Shankar, Oxford would have been twice as pleasant for me if only you had been there too! Well, all foreign students of politics would agree with me that in this and the last century all the transformations in English politics were brought about by the international situation, by the circumstances of the other nations of the world; and when we look into the causes of this world situation, they are mainly economic. After the thrashing we got in 1857, our country went to sleep, or at any rate the pace of its development was so sluggish that it was as good as asleep. But other nations were undergoing great changes. Italy achieved her national union in 1860 (2 April), after being broken into fragments ever since the Roman Empire; and in Mazzini and Garibaldi she gave our own young men models to imitate. The Germans, who were able to destroy the Roman Empire but unable to unite among themselves, succeeded in forming a united state under Prussia's leadership partially in 1866, and almost completely in 1871 (18 January) after defeating France. The events of 1866 were of world importance, and when Germany went on to crush such a strong power as France in 1870 and plant her banners at Paris and Versailles, England and Russia began to watch Berlin with alarm. And that is only the fear from outside; there was still more alarm at the Commune set up by the Paris workers and kept going for a little more than six weeks (2 April – 21 May 1871); that proved that workmen as well as aristocrats or businessmen could run a government.'

'You think all this has a connection with political events in India?'

'Yes, and besides, it has a marked effect on whatever policies our English rulers adopt in India. When such a formidable state as Germany arose in Europe, France's enmity with England faded away, because she was in danger from Germany. Needless to say, our capitalist rulers were gravely alarmed by the Paris Commune, dead though it soon was, and by the federation of all the German states (1861) except Austria into a nation that was far from dead. And now other changes are taking place. The English evolved after 1672 from merchants into big capitalists, and made a monopoly of competitive trade by seizing every opportunity of making profit in everything from buying raw material to working it up and reselling it. Merchant capital makes only a single profit, by taking manufactured goods from one place and selling them in another, but industrial capital makes a profit at every stage – profit in buying cotton, profit in cleaning and packing it, profit in railing and shipping it, profit in spinning and weaving it into cloth in Manchester mills, profit in shipping and railing the cloth back. Just compare all that with the profit of a merchant selling handmade goods.'

'The profits of industrial capitalism are much desirable.'

'In 1871, at Versailles, victorious Germany proclaimed William I, King of Prussia, as German Emperor. Next year, the grasping English, the Tories, proclaimed an imperialism of their own, through capitalists. It was no mere verbal declaration by the Jewish Premier Disraeli, but an announcement of something very real. Factories had grown so huge that they needed a protected market, a market where there could be no fear of competition from French or German goods, because it would be a strict monopoly. Also, capital accumulation had gone so far that it needed a protected field of investment. And all this meant that England must exert close control over other lands. This was the real meaning of Disraeli's word "Imperialism". India answered both needs. The shortest and cheapest route from Europe to India was the Suez Canal, opened in 1869. In 1875 Disraeli bought by telegraph, from the Khedive of Egypt, 177,000 shares worth four million pounds. This was the next step in the policy of imperialism. Then in 1877, on the first of January, a *Durbar*[8] was held at Delhi, and Queen Victoria was proclaimed Empress. In this way Disraeli's government carried imperialism so far that even when Gladstone, the father of the Liberal Party, took office, he could not alter the policy laid down by Disraeli.'

'We are still teaching our students that Queen Victoria conferred a great favour on India by accepting the title of Empress, or Kaiser-i-Hind.'[9]

'And that was just the same title as the King of Prussia had accepted six years before, remember, the name of "Kaiser" had come into demand. It was a word that had lost its value since the fall of Rome, and now suddenly its market value had gone up again!'

'I wonder if there is some significance in the Latin word Caesar[10] being employed only for India, and the word Empress being used in English instead.'

'Maybe. Well, with that word, in 1871, we entered the epoch of imperialism. England came first; then defeated France, now a republic, began to recover, and in 1881 occupied Tunis (Africa) and set to work at empire-building. And Germany too, in 1884, full of its new factories and capitalists, was ready to demand colonies and attempt to found an empire.'

'How is this connected with the development of British policy in India, then?'

'When new inventions are always being improved upon and factories expanding and creating fresh capital, there must be leadership to enable them to make profits. Disraeli's cabinet provided it between 1874 and 1880 and from then till 1892 there were Gladstone's liberal governments which could not get away from the path Disraeli had marked out. Of course, some fig leaf had to be found to hide the naked tyranny of capitalist imperialism, so that the public should not take alarm. So Disraeli played his "Empress of India" comedy. Now the liberals had to show some better liberality. They did it with their Irish Home Rule Bill, but the Irish question remains in the same state to this day. We took advantage of this liberalism, when we, *Hindustani Sahibs*, started our Congress movement in 1885. Congress was born, in fact, as the godchild of the Liberal Party, and it cherished the same faith for a whole generation. But between 1895 and 1905 the Tories enjoyed another decade of power in England, and sent out worthy sons of Toryism like Elgin[11] and Curzon. They tried to strengthen the bonds of imperialism, though the result was contrary to what was expected.'

'You are thinking of the movement led by "Lal, Bal and Pal",[12] then?'

'They and their movements were only reflections of what was happening. When Japan defeated Russia (8 February 1904 – September 1905) she enrolled herself among the Great Powers and brought a new awakening to Asia. Curzon's Partition of Bengal and the Japanese victory combined incited the Indian youth to go far beyond the vague speeches from Congress platforms. Indians learned again, after half a century, how to die for India. We were helped a great deal by the example of the martyrs of Ireland and Russia. So it would be a mistake to seek only inside India the causes of what is happening.'

'Yes, no doubt, all parts of the world are interlinked, of course.'

'Well, Shankar! The strength of any revolutionary agitation depends on two factors – how much guidance is provided by international circumstances and precedents, and how far the most revolutionary class in the country takes part in it. I have said something about the first of these dynamic factors. The other is the banding together of the workers and peasants. Only men who have the least to lose can take part in a revolutionary struggle. A man who has to fear the loss of Sakina's lips or a house like this or a family estate, cannot be a soldier of the revolution. So I say it is only the common people who can carry it out.'

'I agree.'

'You know what ferment is working among these common people now. Just think what direction the international situation is pushing them in. The Great War kindled a huge conflagration. It was the outcome of imperialism; it arose from the holding or seizing of reserved markets for capital and manufactures. Germany wanted new colonies, but the world had already been shared out; so she came into collision with the colony-owners, England and France. Germany failed but at the same time a new enemy arose to break in on the dreams of imperialism: communism, the idea of producing goods not for profit but to bless and enrich humanity. Machines are improved, factories expanded, more goods are produced, requiring wider markets. Besides, people must have money in their pockets to buy those goods, which means that all employees must be drawing regular wages. When there is too little money in their pockets, some of the goods cannot be sold, they pile up in shops and warehouses; the market is dull. Then production has to be curtailed, factories have to be closed, workers thrown out of work and there is even less money available for buying goods. Then how can people buy anything, how can the factories be kept running? Communism tells us to give up the idea of profit, treat the whole country or the whole world as one family, and produce whatever it requires. Let each individual work in proportion to his strength and be given the means of subsistence according to his needs; except that pay should be by work so long as there are not enough machines and skilled workers to produce as much as is wanted. All this can only be done when land and factories cease to be owned by private wealth and all the means of production are owned by the public as if by one big family.'

'It's a beautiful theory!'

'No mere theory any longer, Shankar! In November 1917 a Communist government was set up in Russia over one sixth of the earth. The capitalist world is still trying to extinguish that sole hope of humanity, but Soviet rule has withstood its first bloody test. In Hungary, Soviet rule was overthrown after six months, with the help of French and American capital, in 1919. But the workers' and peasants' government in Russia has given a great lead to the world today and the same forces that created it are at work in every country. As soon as the war was over, why were the British in such a hurry to pass the Rowlatt Act? They wanted to damp down the revolutionary energy that was filling the world. Think, if that energy had not been rolling into every nook and corner threatening to transform the world, the British would not have passed the Rowlatt Act; if there had been no Act, Gandhi would not have given a call to the people to rise against it; if there had been no call, the fires that have been damped down since 1857 would not have blazed up again today. You see what I meant by saying that we are definitely entering a new epoch of revolutions?'

'Then you consider Gandhi a revolutionary leader? How can you think that of a man who follows in the steps of *Naram Dal*[13] leaders like Gokhale, brother Saffu?'

'I don't call every action or idea of Gandhi revolutionary. I call his work revolutionary in so far as he has tried to rouse the ordinary people, who form the potential revolutionary force. His religious vapourings – especially about the Khilafat[14] movement – I regard as counter-revolutionary humbug. I think his notion of abandoning machinery and returning to the past is also an effort to put the clock back and the same applies to his talk of closing down schools and colleges.'

'God bless you, Safdar! I was beginning to hold my breath, when you went on praising Gandhi! I was wondering whether you too were going to tell me that schools and colleges are the Devil's workshops!'

'Our methods of teaching may have many faults; but our modern schools and colleges put us in touch with science, and without science human life today is impossible. Whenever we get our freedom, science will have a special part to play. Population is growing day by day and its future welfare will depend on science; to give up science and go backwards would be suicide. To close our schools and colleges and open spinning and weaving centres instead would take us straight back into the Dark Ages. But to appeal to students to become revolutionaries is not a bad thing, you must admit that, Shankar.'

'Oh, yes! And what about other kinds of boycott?'

'Boycotting the law-courts is all right; it is a means of showing our foreign rulers our strength and our discontent. And the boycott of British goods is a slap in the face to British capitalists, and helps native enterprise.'

'Safdar, I see you have moved pretty far already!'

'Not yet, but I want to.'

'You want to?'

'Tell me first: are we passing through a revolutionary epoch, or are we not?'

'Brother Saffu, I have been asking you a lot of questions, just to draw you out. But the moment I heard of the Russian Revolution, I began to hunt high and low for communist literature and study it, and still more to think about my own problems from the communist point of view. I believe that this is the way to happiness for India and for the world. I have only been held back by uncertainty as to whether Gandhi's non-cooperation could fulfil its grand object or not; but when you made me think of the people just now as the backbone of revolution, my uncertainty vanished. I don't believe that Gandhi is capable of organizing a revolution, Safdar, to speak frankly, but I do believe the people can do it. In 1857 the fallen feudalists got a lot of our people behind them with their nonsense of greased cartridges and "religion in danger", but today the people are more interested in questions of bread and butter. I think this agitation is right; the revolutionary slogan is right, and even if later on Gandhi shows his real face, he will not be able to turn the current of revolution.'

'That is why I have decided to join in the struggle, and become a non-cooperator.'[15]

'You are in such a hurry?'

'If I had been in a hurry I should have plunged in long ago. I have only come to a decision after thinking it over for a long time, and now after learning your opinion.'

While Safdar, gravely and thoughtfully, was saying this, Shankar's glance wandered away.

'My friend,' Safdar went on, finding him silent, 'you must be thinking about your sister-in-law and the lipstick and silk dress and velvet slippers, or about this house and the servants. I shan't put any pressure on Sakina; she must choose what sort of life she likes. She has her own property and this house, and lands and money. These things have no charm for me. Let her follow her own inclinations.'

'I wasn't thinking about her or you, I was thinking about myself. The stumbling block in my own mind has disappeared. Come! We shall tread the path of revolution together, like two brothers!'

'Shankar,' returned his friend, with glistening eyes, 'I used to long for you at Oxford; now I shall be quite happy even if I have to go to the gallows.'

Sakina came to call them to dinner, and their conference ended.

—2—

From this evening Sakina found her husband much more cheerful; she thought it was just the pleasure of a chat with Shankar that had done it. For Safdar, the hardest task was to inform Sakina of his decision. He himself had been brought up in a sheltered home, but he had lived in the countryside and been touched by the sight of naked misery; he was confident that he would come through the ordeal he was throwing himself into. Her case was different. She had grown up in a wealthy home in the city, and one could say of her as the poet says of Sita – 'She did not touch the hard earth even with her foot'. On Sunday too, he could not summon up courage. Next day, at the High Court he told a few close friends of his intention, and then he had to face the necessity of an explanation to Sakina.

In the evening he sent out for the best champagne to be had in Lucknow. Sakina supposed that some other friends must be coming, but when dinner was over and he told the servant to open the champagne, she was somewhat puzzled.

Safdar put a glass of wine to her lips and said –

'Sakina, my dear, this is the last favour you will ever do me.'

'You mean – you are giving up wine, dearest?'

'Yes, wine and many other things, but not you. From now on you will be my wine; thinking of your beautiful face will be my only intoxication.' He saw distress in her face, and went on – 'Let us drink this champagne together, dear; there is something else we must talk about.'

Sakina could not enjoy wine, though Safdar had recited many a quatrain of Omar Khayyam[16] over her glass.

The servants withdrew, and she came and sat on the floor near Safdar, nervous as if feeling a premonition of ill luck. Safdar put his cards on the table –

'Dear Sakina,' he began, 'I have taken a serious decision, though I admit I was wrong in not asking your opinion beforehand. You will understand why I did it from what I am going to tell you. To put it in a nutshell – I am going to join in the national struggle.'

The words fell on her ears like a thunderbolt; it was easy to see; she could not open her mouth to answer.

'But dear,' he added, as she remained silent, 'you have had a sheltered life from your cradle; I don't want to drag you, into hardship.'

She felt as if a fresh dagger had pierced her heart, and made her forget the first shock. Her self-respect awoke suddenly and made her exclaim –

'Dear! Did you really think me so fond of ease and comfort as to want to sit on a sofa and watch you going into hardship? If I have really loved you, Safdar, my love will give me strength to go with you anywhere. I have used a lot of lipstick, and wasted a lot of my time in dressing and powdering, and never tried to gain knowledge of the hard side of life, but Safdar, you are everything to me. I don't want to be a burden to you. I mean that I want to stay with you. You must be my guide in our new life just as you have been in our old one.'

Safdar had not expected this, though he knew that Sakina was quite strong-willed.

'Well,' he resumed, 'I am not accepting any new briefs, and I am handing over some of the cases I have to other lawyers. I hope to get myself free from the courts during this week. There is something else I must tell you; Shankar is taking the plunge along with me.'

'Shankar!' she repeated in surprise.

'He is a jewel, Sakina! He would go to the end of the world with me. I was always thinking of him at Oxford.'

'But he is making a bigger sacrifice, Safdar!'

'He has chosen a life of self-sacrifice for himself, and on principle he has never budged from it. Otherwise he could have been a good lawyer; or he could have got a better job in his own department.'

'I was very sorry when his two children died, but now I suppose it is good that he is burdened with only the two others, instead of four.'

'How is Champa likely to take the news, Sakina?'

'She will agree blindly; it was she who taught me how to love!'

'We must make some arrangements for our new life.'

'I have had no time to think about it, as you said yourself. You tell me what we should do.'

'We had better give all our servants two months' wages as a present and get rid of them, except for Mangar and our nurse Sharifan, as she is from our own village.'

'Yes, good.'

'We shall have to sell both the cars.'

'Very well.'

'And give away or auction all our furniture except a couple of beds and a few chairs.'

'Yes.'

'We'll go and live in our aunt's house on Latouche Road, and rent this bungalow.'

'All right.'

'There's nothing else I can think of.'

'My clothes and your English suits?'

'I am going in for Gandhi's non-cooperation – is that what you are thinking of? I'm not in favour of burning them, especially when so many bonfires of English clothes have been made already. But I'm having handmade cotton *kurta-pyjama*[17] got ready; I shall have them by the day after tomorrow.'

'What about me? You've grown very selfish!'

'Will you be able to wear a clumsy dress of handwoven cotton cloth?'

'I will come with you to the end of the world.'

'What will you do with these clothes?'

'That's what I can't figure out. If they were auctioned, I could use the money to buy clothes for the poor. Anyway, I'll try to give them away somehow!'

—3—

People were soon chattering about Safdar, the rising barrister, and the great sacrifice he had made, though he himself felt that Shankar was the one who deserved credit. All through October and November Safdar was able to go about appealing to the public, often accompanied by Sakina or Shankar. His interest lay chiefly in the countryside, for he had more confidence in the peasants and village workers than in the educated town folk. But within a week he realized that the rustic could understand barely a quarter of his high-flown Urdu speeches. Shankar from the beginning had addressed them in their own dialect, and when Safdar saw the effect he made he set himself to master the Awadh dialect. At first too many literary words crept into his vocabulary, but by hard effort and with Shankar's help he made himself at home in the idiom before two months were over, recalling many words he had forgotten, and learning new ones. Then the villagers thronged to listen, in thrall to everything he said.

In the first week of December 1920, Safdar and Shankar, with many other political workers, were sentenced to a year's imprisonment, and found themselves in Faizabad jail. Their wives, who were not arrested, continued the work.

In jail Safdar followed the Congress rule of spinning for an hour each day. Those who knew how critical he was of Gandhi in his political views laughed at him and his spinning-wheel. 'I know,' he would answer, 'that the boycott of British cloth is a political weapon, and also that at present our country cannot produce enough cloth for itself, so we must help to produce more, but as soon as our mills begin to manufacture sufficient cloth, I shan't be in favour of going on with the spinning-wheel.'

Too many of the prisoners were sitting idle. They believed in Gandhi's promise of Home Rule within a year, and thought that by going to jail they had done their duty in full. So far 'Gandhism' had not fallen prey to pretence, dishonesty and posturing; so it could be said that among the Non-Cooperation prisoners the majority were honest patriots. Still, the two friends were astonished to find that scarcely any of them were at pains to increase their political knowledge. Many spent their time reciting the *Ramayan*, the Gita[18] or the Quran; some kept on praying with rosary in their hands. Others wasted all their time at cards or chess.

One day Safdar met the learned Vinayak Prasad, an influential Gandhi-ite. Shankar was with them. Vinayak declared that Gandhi's use of the doctrine of non-violence was a great discovery, and that it was a most useful weapon.

'It may be useful in the present circumstances,' Safdar answered. 'But non-violence is not the road to success by itself. In this world animals which can't fight usually fall prey to others.'

'Yes, animals, but in human beings non-violence creates a miraculous power.'

'I see no evidence of that in political history.'

'How can there be evidence, when the discovery is something so new?'

'Not so new either,' remarked Shankar. 'It was preached by Buddh and Mahavir and several other religious leaders.'

'Not as a political theory.'

'If its political utility has increased, it is only because today civilization has spread somewhat and people think it shocking when they read in their newspapers of unarmed crowds being fired on. You see what the firing by the British at Jallianwala Bagh[19] has led to.'

'You think that our non-violent non-cooperation is not enough to bring us freedom?'

'First you tell me what you mean by freedom.'

'You have joined the struggle for freedom yourself, what do you understand by it?'

'The rule of the workers, and no one else.'

'So in your freedom there are to be no rights for students, merchants or landlords who have given body and soul and wealth to the cause, who have borne hardships and gone to jail?'

'In the first place, you see that our merchants and landlords have no time to spare from forming conciliation committees; how could the poor creatures begin coming to jail? And if any of them have come, they ought not to think of their own interests as something apart from those of the workers.'

Shankar and Safdar used to study from books together, and discuss the economic and social problems of the country. Few of the others wanted to listen to them at first. But when the midnight of 31 December 1921 came and went and the prison gates remained shut, many despaired. And when Gandhi learned of the burning of some policemen at Chauri Chaura[20] by a resentful, excited mob, and called off the movement, many were forced to think seriously. Some of them later on came to accept the view of Safdar and Shankar, that the true revolutionary force lay in the people, not in Gandhi's brain; and that Gandhi, by showing lack of confidence in the people's strength, had proved himself an obstacle to the revolution.

20

Sumer

TIME : 1942 CE

—1—

It was August 1941. The monsoon rains this year were particularly heavy. At times you could hardly see the sun for many days. The Ganga had risen too high near the city of Patna and the fear of the river bursting its banks was constant. Staying alert is always required at such times and so the young people of Patna city, most of whom were students, had taken the responsibility of watching the river dam. Sumer was a first-year master's student at Patna College. His duty was near the bank. It was midnight when the sudden rise in the water level was noticed. It kept rising, even the next morning, when its surface remained barely a foot from the upper edge of the dam. There was fear among people and thousands of men were standing ready with their spades and baskets, although it was doubtful they could make the dam higher by even an inch. Worried, Sumer was also on guard at the dam since morning. By midday the water slowly started receding. Sumer, who was very concerned, felt a sigh of relief. Sumer had noticed a gentleman nearby guarding the same area. He did feel like talking to him at times but was so upset due to the risk of the flood that he never wanted to initiate the conversation. Today, when the water level started to go down, and the clouds in the sky also started thinning away, seeing his neighbouring sentinel standing close by, he felt like talking to him.

The complexion of one of them was wheatish and the other's was dark, but they were both of average height, equally tall as each other. Whereas Sumer was a young man of twenty-one, the other appeared to be forty years old, fat and lazy looking. Sumer had on *khaki* shorts and *khaki* T-shirt with inverted collars. He had a raincoat on his shoulders and was wearing black rubber boots. His companion was wearing white *dhoti-kurta*[1] and a Gandhi cap all made of cotton. He also had a blanket on him and was barefoot. Sumer moved forward, expressing joy on his face, and said –

'We are relieved, the flood is going down!'

'And the clouds are also thinning away.'

'Oh yes, how worried were we. I had once read, when this city of Patliputr was being built two and half thousand years ago, Gautam the Buddh, while declaring it well endowed in all respects, had also predicted its three enemies: the fire, the water and the internal feud.'

'So you are a student of history?'

'No, I am a student of politics but I also am fond of history; especially reading translations of ancient documents.'

'Yes, one of the enemies, the water, we are witnessing for a number of days.'

'And the risk of fire must have been great those days when a majority of houses in Patliputr were probably made of wood. That was natural when the city was surrounded by *sal* forests.'

'And the internal feud has defamed the whole of India. Well, may I know your name?'

'My name is Sumer; I am a fifth-year student at Patna College.'

'And I am Rambalak Ojha. I had also been a student at the Patna College sometime in the past but already more than twenty years have passed since then. A friend of mine insisted, otherwise I would have entered the non-cooperation movement without completing my master's degree. Anyway, even if that were the case, I would have no regrets. For some years I have started realizing that the education in these schools and colleges is useless.'

'Then you must have forgotten all that education?'

'I wish I would have, I would have turned into a blank page again. In that case I would have known the truth better.'

'You mean you would have followed a blind belief instead of following your intellect.'

'Do you consider following belief bad, Sumer Babu?'[2]

'I am not any *Babu*, Ojhaji. I am the son of a poor Chamar.[3] I do not own an inch of land. I did have some, but the feudal lord forcibly converted it into his orchard. My mother somehow earns her living by working as a maid. It was only a noble man's kindness and then the receipt of a scholarship for studies that made me come this far. Now you can understand I do not deserve to be addressed as Babu.'

'You can take it as my habit Sumerji but I am so pleased with our acquaintance with each other today. You can understand how great this follower of Gandhiji would have felt seeing a Harijan[4] youth working so hard!'

'Ojhaji, I would like to prolong our conversation cordially but would prefer you to know my differences beforehand. I strongly abhor the word "Harijan". I consider this a dogmatic title that pulls India back into the darkness of her ancient past and Gandhiji – the worst enemy of my community.'

'Don't you recognize Gandhiji's favours to your community?'

'I recognize his favours only as much as a worker should recognize the favours of his factory owner.'

'Gandhiji does not favour the factory owners.'

'What else could it mean when he calls the landlords, the capitalists and the kings as great protectors – "guardians"? Gandhiji showers his love on us fearing that we may renounce Hinduism. His "fast unto death" at Pune was aimed at the same: that we may not create our own state, independent of the Hindus. The Hindus needed cheap slaves and for thousands of years our community has been fulfilling that need. Back then we were called *das*, and now by naming us Harijan, Gandhiji wants to do us a favour. Perhaps this Hari has been our biggest enemy after the Hindus. You can understand why we would not like to be the children of such a god?'

'So you don't believe in God either?'

'In response to what favour? For thousands of years we have been treated worse than animals and considered honourless untouchables in the name of the same God of the Hindus which kept on incarnating himself for minor reasons, riding on mythical chariots; but our women kept on getting molested for hundreds of generations. We kept on getting sold like cattle in the markets and in the funfairs of Sonepur;[5] even today getting abused, beaten and starved is considered God's favour to us. To hell with such a god who did not bother to move even after seeing all this.'

'Then perhaps you like the path of Doctor Ambedkar?'

'Not really. Dr. Ambedkar himself is a victim. I too had faced Hindu boys, bullies, who did not let me stay in the hostel for the first two years, but I don't see any difference between the approach of Ambedkar or the Congress leaders of the untouchable community. In my eyes their path ultimately joins the path of Birla and Bajaj.[6] What this means is that among the untouchables, too, there might be some who'll manage to start drawing salaries of five or six thousand rupees a month. Amongst the untouchables, too, if they cannot become Birlas and Bajajs, some at least would own thousands. The untouchables may manage to own a few landownerships if not the estates. But by doing so the pitiable condition of a hundred million untouchables cannot be improved.'

'Then you mean the exploitation should stop.'

'Yes. Our problems can only be solved when the fat cats getting richer on our labour are eradicated from the face of the earth.'

'That is precisely why Gandhiji is speaking in favour of clothes made by hand, rice and sugar grown by hand and all other goods that are made by the human hand.'

'Yes. He is speaking on behalf of the wealth of Birla-Bajaj. Whenever the Khadisangh[7] goes in deficit, one or the other capitalist offers them a cheque. If they really believed that Gandhiji's handloom could shut their mills, and their wealth such as precious necklaces and silk *sarees* would become things of the past, then, remember Ojhaji, none of these rich men and women would have worshipped Gandhiji.'

'So you consider Gandhians touts?'

'I have no doubt, and if there was any that too is now gone, when they have joined in the howling of the capitalists in their protest against the "house-burning" policy.'

'So you want that all the factories be destroyed in places where the Japanese may enter? How hard it was for the Indians to build these factories, you should take that into account Sumerji.'

'I did take into account all the labour and troubles of Indians and also what the Gandhians are talking about – "not tolerating the existence of machines for a moment". Besides, I also know that the rich creed wants that their factories be captured by the Japanese, unharmed.

The Japanese are staunch supporters of capitalism. After listening to Japanese radio, they are satisfied that they would stay the owners of these factories during the Japanese takeover. Apart from this, you tell me, which other great ideology has inspired them for the sacrifice?'

'They wish to save the wealth of the country.'

'Oh please don't scratch our wounds, Ojhaji. These businessmen are not worried about the country's wealth but of their own. For them the country may go to hell! You better not talk about expecting the "country's wealth" to be saved by such people who get poor strikers run over by cars rather than increase the salary of the worker by a few pennies!'

'Okay, even if we agree about their character, you should not have doubt about Gandhiji's honesty.'

'I judge a man's honesty by his words and actions. I don't think Gandhiji is a child. He was in need of five lakh[8] rupees for the Indus fund. Within five days the businessmen of Bombay offered seven lakh to him. For the amount of work that he is doing for the rich, the millionaires of UK and USA could have offered seventy million. The deal would have been pretty profitable.'

'But this would be deemed a bribe.'

'Yes, but the Indian businessmen have the same thoughts in their mind even when making an offering to God. You would find "*shubh-labh*"[9] written on their doors.'

'So, you don't consider the handlooms to be enemies of exploitation?'

'On the contrary, I consider them the most effective supporters of exploitation.'

'In that case, you may also consider the mills as the enemies of exploitation?'

'Hear me out as to why I consider them exploiters. Just as the world has moved forward leaving stone weapons behind, similarly, the time of handlooms has also gone. I have seen the manuscripts written on palm leaves thousands of years ago displayed in the Patna museum. During those days, the ledgers of the traders, books and notebooks of the students of Nalanda used to be these very palm leaves. Gandhiji may supplicate all his life for a return to the days of the palm leaf, but people would never prefer to go back to the time of the palm leaf, leaving the paper of Titagarh,[10] the monotype and rotary press behind. And it is in their benefit not to return anyway, since these palm leaves may not create hurdles in reciting devotional songs at Sevagram,[11] but education for all – especially modern education – would be made impossible. If Gandhiji insists on combating the tanks, aeroplanes and submarines of fascist bandits with Stone Age weapons, even a nation with minimal brainpower won't accept it, since it would be suicide.'

'So you don't agree with the great principle of non-violence?'

'Gandhiji's "principle of non-violence" ... God save us from it! The principle that supports bullets fired on farmers and workers by the government of the Congress, but advises being unarmed before fascist bandits, is impossible to understand for us. Let me answer your first question. The businessmen know that the handlooms cannot harm them at all. So long as these handlooms do not bring finer and cheaper cloth into the market, their existence is dependent on the charity of these very merchants. This "handloomism" is a major hurdle in the path of communism – the real cure for human exploitation. Idiotically, so many people think that in order to stop human exploitation, handloomism is better than communism which is the "people's ownership of the factories". Following the same principle, the merchants, who provide cloth made in their mills to people, are handloom worshippers themselves and Gandhiji, too, understands this fact very well.'

'But this is an attack on his integrity.'

'His every action is dangerous for an exploited person like me – and for the most exploited group in India, our caste. We should have locked up these temples which are the source of such mental slavery and are a business of the priests who are the nurturers of exploitation. But, on the contrary, in order to entrap us, Gandhiji wants to get them opened for us. If we can't burn away these old books and scriptures written by the so-called saints, fostered by the rich, we can at least lock them away forever; but supplicating for the same books, Gandhiji wants us to go astray. This deadly system called the "*varn vyavastha*"[12] should have been completely uprooted from Indian soil, but Gandhiji, illogically gives his colourful explanation of the same system. In spite of all this, if the "welfare of the untouchables" is not mere posturing, then what is it? A handful of untouchables may get employment but only the blind can hope for salvation through such welfare.'

'So you don't want the untouchables and upper castes to mix?'

'Time has already mixed us up, but Gandhiji's beloved religion, god and dogma are not letting us understand this truth. Just have a look at me Ojhaji: my skin complexion is wheatish and nose is sharp whereas your complexion is dark and the nose quite flat. What does it mean? There is more Aryan blood in my veins. You have more blood of my forefathers. By creating the iron wall of the caste system, your forefathers wished to not let the blood mix, but their desires were not fulfilled and you and me are present as perfect evidence of such admixture. The blood of the banks of the Volga and the Ganga has finally got mixed. Today there is no conflict with respect to skin colour; nobody would excommunicate you from the caste of Brahmins. Everything would be all right if only this religion, god and dogma leave us alone. And this is not possible as long as our exploiters and their protectors like Gandhiji are present.'

'Even your pinching words won't make me angry.'

'Behind this pinch is my defeated heart and youth, Ojhaji. If my words have caused you pain, I am sorry.'

'No, I don't mind. But if you don't consider it possible to re-establish the indigenous system of handlooms then do you think that the Indian soil is fertile for a system like communism imported from abroad?'

'Everything that is disapproved by the exploiters is "imported and impossible". The sugar mills, the aeroplanes, the cars, the glass works, the fountain pens, the footwear, the factories run by electricity or steam worth millions of rupees are no more "imported" for rich traders because thanks to this stuff they became millionaires. As soon as products like the radio, television, films, tanks, etc. start stuffing the pockets of these capitalists with millions of rupees earned by the blood and sweat of the poor workers, they no longer stay "foreign". Everything that helps promote the exploitation is homemade for them but communism, which is the only way to eradicate exploitation, would always be foreign for them. Is that honesty, Ojhaji?'

'But Sumerji, please pay attention to the fact that communism is against religion whereas India has always been a religious country.'

'You talk about dropping all the education you received at college, so what can I say now? Whenever you name religion, you only consider it to be Hinduism. Gandhiji has pledged his support to the cow-welfare organizations of Bajaj where the participants are made to vow to use everything except the meat that comes from cows including the urine and the dung. If we compare the numbers of beef eaters with those who don't, in India, beef eaters would be greater. My community is also beef-eating. Even otherwise, about one fourth of Indians are Muslims, nearly ten million are Christians and a few hundred thousand are Buddhists. If you count these faiths among "religions", where in the world are there no believers? Gandhiji's friends – people like Lord Irwin, the previous Viceroy, and currently, Lord Halifax – are great Christian patrons. Crying foul in the name of religion, these "saints" have always tried to convince people to stay away from communism. The Muslims of Arabia, Turkey, Iran and Afghanistan are no less religious than the Muslims of India. You can't call Japan less religious either where, in order to construct a temple, the wood was collected with ropes made of the hair donated by hundreds of thousands of girls of their own free will. All the muggers are always staunchly religious, Ojhaji, and all the enemies of exploitation are often declared enemies of religion! Even if we consider communism to be foreign, foreign religions like Christianity, Islam and imported things like trains, telegrams, aeroplanes, and factories have become indigenous right before our eyes. Similarly, communism would also turn indigenous. Moreover, it has already become so.'

—2—

There are only two venues in Patna where one can go for an evening stroll, The Patna Lawns and the Hardinge Park; both have been so poorly maintained that no one finds them attractive. However, the ones who wish to come out for leisure, stroll or meet friends, do come to these places. It was getting dark; still, the discussion between the three young men was not coming to an end. They wouldn't budge from the lawns of Bankipur (Patna). One of them was saying –

'Comrade Sumer! I would implore you to think once again, you are going to take a huge step.'

'No step can be bigger than challenging death, and surely I have not rushed. Such a decision could not have been taken in haste anyway.'

'Flying in the air, brother! I get scared even by standing on the roof of the pub.'

'So many people are scared of riding a bicycle, while you race on it with your hands up in the air!'

'Anyway, I don't understand why the son of a maid would sacrifice his life in the war of empires.'

'It is because the future of the maid's son and their entire community is connected with this war. It is because this war would not only decide the fate of the empires but also of the exploiters.'

'So you don't believe that the biggest criminals in this war are the British capitalists?'

'Whose interests were represented by Baldwin and Chamberlain? I admit, these very people are the ones who fostered and nurtured Mussolini, Hitler, so they could rescue the exploiters from communist forces. But the Bhasmasur[13] wished to gulp the Baijnath[14] to start with! And till this drama went on, I did not decide to take this big step. But today, Bhasmasur not only wants to eat up the Baijnath, but intends to attack us too.'

'Attack us? But I don't see any difference in circumstances between now and before.'

'You don't see the difference because your community, the community of the businessmen, expects to enjoy the sunshine even under fascist rule. Krupp and Mitsui[15] are having the best of both worlds thanks to the war; but if the Soviets lose, the workers and farmers exploited at the hands of the rich would have no hope left. Farmers can't dare to fight for their rights under the rule of the murderers Hitler and Tojo, dear Kishor. Neither are the workers allowed to strike against any atrocity! Fascism wishes to enslave the workers in the true sense. For us the Soviet Union is not one of many but just one such country which the workers and farmers can call their own land, their hope. After millions of sacrifices for over one and a half century, this light of communism for humanity, for the sections of society exploited for centuries, finally shone on the world.

You let this light die once, and you'll find out how long the darkness prevails on earth. We cannot allow this ultimate disaster happening before our eyes.'

'But, brother Sumer! There are other socialists too in the country who wish exploitation by the rich to be eradicated from the world.'

'God save us from such socialists, who see light in the darkness emerging from the Sevagram. Even Hitler calls himself a socialist. Gandhiji's followers, too, call him a socialist. One doesn't become a socialist by just naming himself so. Do you know that with the victory of Hitler and Tojo the capitalism and the capitalists of India won't get destroyed but would flourish instead? The fascist goons will not even let the workers and farmers breathe, and to know what will happen to the communists you can see what is happening in Germany and Italy. Not only that, see how the communists are being shot every day in France. All those who wish to stay aloof from this war by calling themselves Marxists, are either cheating others or themselves. We know very well that the price of a Marxist socialist's life is just a bullet under the rule of Hitler and Tojo. If some socialist still calls himself impartial it can only be considered meanness. The ones who are talking about raising the flag of socialism after the defeat of the Soviets, can either be counted insane or cheats!'

'You think that no one can stay non-aligned in this war?'

'Yes, I firmly believe that anybody who is sane has allied himself with one or the other side, because this war would result either in the total destruction of anti-exploitation forces or in increasing their power to such an extent that there would be no place left for Mussolini, Tojo, or their forefathers – Baldwin, Chamberlain or Halifax – in this world. Subhas Chandra Bose[16] and his followers have made up their mind and so have the ones whom you call impartial. They are only pretending to be non-aligned, because they are not ignorant of the attitude of the fascists.'

'But are you watching the attitude of the British in India?'

'These people are blind! They are trying to live in the times of thirty years ago. But what do you think; are we dreaming of a new world after the war for these old fossils? We know they will erect obstacles in our path of preparation for war, because they see everything through the eyes of the past era.

'Yes. Don't you see the people, whose faces were seen only in the peace committees, now roaring before the public posing as some kind of war heroes? Our Governor-General is preaching to people to sacrifice their lives whereas if you see their expenditure you would go mad. For us a day's minimum wage is one *anna*, according to which our yearly income is twenty-five rupees. And their salary:

Designation	*Wages*	*Times the wage of a manual labourer*
Viceroy	Rs. 2,50,800	i.e. 10,000 times
Governor of Bengal	Rs. 1,20,000	i.e. 4,800 times
Governor of the United Provinces	Rs. 1,20,000	i.e. 4,800 times
Governor of Bihar	Rs. 1,00,000	i.e. 4,000 times

'And all this is excluding other expenditures. If you include other expenditures, even excluding the holiday salary and travel expenses for going to and coming (from England), the annual expenditure of the Governor of Bengal is Rs. 6,07,200, i.e. 42,292 times the salary of a manual labourer! Now compare it with the wages of a labourer in England, whose minimum income per week for working in the coal mines has been fixed at 75 to 85 shillings, i.e. more than our 52 to 56 rupees. The farm labourers also take more than 45 rupees per week, which is equal to £200–221 yearly. Considering these figures, their prime minister receives a salary that is thirty-six times the salary of a manual labourer. The Premier of the Soviet Union gets 12,000 roubles and a big number of workers receive a roughly similar amount in salary; even the minimum earners do not get less than one sixth of this amount. Now compare this:

The Governor of Bengal in India	42,292 times the salary of a manual labourer
The Prime Minister of England	36 times the salary of a manual labourer
The Premier of Russia	6 times the salary of a manual labourer

'And if you compare the income of these capitalists with the manual labourer, you would faint.'

'This is sheer loot, brother Sumer.'

'That's why I say that we cannot pin our hopes on these salaried Englishmen in India, who are selfish, coward and unable to foresee the future. We are not going to win this war for them. We are going to sacrifice our lives for that world which has spread over one sixth of the planet and is going to be destroyed by the fascists. We are going to die for that new world where humanity would be free and rich.'

Samad was quiet so far. With a desire to ask a question, he said –

'Comrade Sumer! I agree with you on a lot of issues and disagree on some. However, it's not a secret how I value your opinion. I also think that in this worldwide conflict, we cannot stay non-aligned. But, O' friend! You informed us only when you got selected and admitted in the defence forces; shouldn't you have told us before?'

'I could have told you earlier, but what if I didn't get selected? That's why I disclosed it to friends only after getting inducted and receiving flight training of twenty-four hours. Now there is no harm in disclosing it. I am going to the flight training school at Ambala just the day after tomorrow!'

'Have you informed your mother?'

'Whether Patna or Ambala, both are the same for my mother. Until I tell her frankly that I am going to my death, it would make no difference to her. But writing to her in detail would mean making her life miserable for ever. I have decided, as long as I am alive, I would keep on writing to her, and this would keep her mind at rest.'

'I can't stop thinking about your bravery.'

'Samad! We should always keep on paying back for being born as human beings; however, being visionary idealists, we carry even greater responsibilities on our shoulders.'

'So you think this war would bring a big change in the world order?'

'The change brought by the previous war was not small either. The rule of equality on one sixth of the world – the Soviet Union – came into existence. It was not a small event. But the change that this war would bring would renew the whole world. I have no doubt in the victory of the side which has the support of the Soviet Union and the Red Army, for the victory of which the people of China, England, America are determined to sacrifice their lives today.'

Samad and Roopkishor had an ongoing debate on the topic of Pakistan. Roopkishor brought it up once again –

'Whether it's Gandhian *swarajya* or a Communist one, we can have our difference of opinion on that matter, dear friend Sumer! However, should there be any doubt that self-rule would be for Bharat (India)?'

'"Bharat" is also an abstract term Roop Babu! This word could create many misunderstandings. Self-rule is needed for all Indians, where the citizens can decide their fate themselves. Self-rule acquired in haste should not stay limited to the upper classes only.'

Roop – 'Okay, you may say that, but a united country should not be allowed to be divided into pieces under self-rule.'

'You are using a confusing term once again. Whether India is one or many also depends on her citizens. During the Mauryan period India's western borders went as far as Amu Darya, on the other side of the Hindu Kush mountains, and from the point of view of language, traditions, history the Afghan people are also included in that India. Up until the 10th century CE, Kabul was a Hindu kingdom. Considering this fact, the Hindu Kush is the real border of India. Are the supporters of United India ready to claim land right up to the Hindu Kush? Not just Afghanistan, even the frontier Pathans who live on the west of the Sindh cannot be forced to live in United India against their will. Then why can the same not be said about the provinces of Sindh, Panjab, Kashmir and East Bengal?'

Roop – 'You mean they should be excluded from India?'

Sumer – 'Yes, if they are bent upon it. We are fighting for the people, which means the people of no country can be enslaved against their will. The issue of Pakistan is not to be resolved by the Hindus. The decision is in the hands of the people of those provinces where Muslims are in a majority. If we wish to instal a government of bandits instead of the people, then Pakistan will certainly come into existence. If we wish to establish the rule of working-class people who do mental as well as physical labour, then India would be a united country made up of many independent republics. For having "one nation-one country", a common language, common food, and removal of untouchability to allow inter-caste marriages are required, which only communism can achieve. Even then, based on the languages, we'll have to consider more than eighty nations in independent India.'

'More than eighty! You have gone much further than the idea of creating a Pakistan.'

'Well, I have not made the languages. Under people's rule the mother tongues would be the medium of instruction in education, and the mother tongue is that language in which even a child does not make a grammatical mistake. The Soviet Union is a multicultural country of seventy nationalities. Why is it a surprise for India to be a country of eighty types of people when her population is double that of the USSR?'

'So you are in favour of Pakistan?'

'As long as it is a demand of the Muslim public. Today, all leaders of Islamic organizations of different ideologies are united on the issue. I think that the non-Muslims have no right to reject this genuine demand. If the population of those provinces where the Muslims are in a majority wishes to part ways with the Indian union, they should have that right to do so.'

—3—

There is no sign of life on the quiet waters of the dark ocean underneath and only the endless clouds are in view at the front. Here in the sky there is no way to check your speed except the speedometer which is situated right in front of Sumer. Flying an aeroplane at the speed of three hundred miles an hour, Sumer's thoughts for a moment turned to the era when man considered the roughly-shaped stone weapons his mightiest power. But today he is the king of the skies. How far humanity has progressed! But, at the same time, he thought of the enemies of humanity, the fascists, who are using this wonderful invention of the human brain for enslaving humanity. The thought that the fascist Japanese have already entered Burma, in the neighbourhood of India, made him shudder. Then the houses of Kadamkuan (Patna) and the women that live in those houses, including his beloved, came into his visions. Women who had accepted this brave man of an untouchable mother as their son and brother. His blood boiled with hatred for the fascists. Just then, he saw three aeroplanes with the three red suns marked on them flying ahead of him. Sumer informed his gunner on the phone and within two minutes he positioned himself between the fascists' aeroplanes. It takes time to say it, even longer to write, but one could barely perceive how swiftly Sumer correctly positioned his aeroplane, how his gunner Sharif's machine gun sounded *tr... tr... tr...*, and how, within the next ten minutes, all three enemy planes fell into the sea like dead birds.

It was the first opportunity for Sumer to show his skills, but he felt very satisfied with his success. While walking away from his aeroplane, he said to the gunner Sharif –

'Brother Shuru, we have paid back our debt. How great it would be if each of us kills at least three fascists!'

'I also feel light now. Our death won't be worthless any more.'

'Well, now as long as we live, we'll keep turning profits by killing fascists!'

Sumer lived for two hundred more days. He destroyed a hundred Japanese planes. On his last day, he was on duty over the Bay of Bengal. A Japanese war fleet was passing near the west of the Andaman Islands when Sumer saw that forty-thousand-ton warship. There were security planes flying above the warship, but they could not notice Sumer's eyes that were peeping through the clouds.

Sumer ordered his gunner to prepare the torpedoes. The cloud was spread out above the fleet. Sumer flew his plane at full speed. The enemy's planes never knew when a plane appeared above the warship, and when its pilot crashed his plane into it! The bodies of Sumer and his gunner were never found, but they sunk the warship along with themselves.

Notes

Volga se Ganga: Text and Context

1 Rahul Sankrityayan, *Meri Jeevan-Yatra*, Vol. II, Allahabad: Kitab Mahal, 1950, p. 350.

2 Sankrityayan, 'Buddhist Dialectics', in *Buddhism: The Marxist Approach*, New Delhi: People's Publishing House, 1970.

1. Nisha

1 A typical shape of the Indian plough, which is often used as a simile to compare with beautiful curves.

2 Vrik: Sanskrit word for wolf.

3 'Med' (honey) is an Indo-European word: *madhu* (Skt.), *myod* (Russ.). Medved: the honey-eater (Russ.).

4 An Indian unit of weight. One *ser* is roughly equal to 2 pounds or 900 grams.

2. Diva

1 Diva: day/day-light (lit.).

2 Sur: sun (lit.).

3 Sister (Skt.).

4 Jan: A multiple-meaning word in Sanskrit used here as 'clan'. *Jan* had many applications throughout India's cultural history.

5 Diva-Sunu: son of Diva.

6 Duhita: daughter of Diva.

7 'O... o... o... g... n... a ... A... y... a... a ...': the Fire-god has come. From *agon* (Russ.) or *agni* (Skt.) for fire.

8 *Chashak* (Skt.), *chashka* (Russ.): cup.

9 Devadaru (Skt.): woods of the gods.

10 Bhaga: God, as in 'Bhagvan'; also means vagina.

11 Kuru is one of the most mentioned Vedic tribes, the name of which travelled in Vedic literature and Hindu epics all the way to India.

12 Shambhu is also one of the names for the god Shiv in modern Hindu terminology.

3. Amritashv

1 Farghana valley in today's Uzbekistan, the same place from where the Mughal emperor Babur had come to India in the 15th century CE.

2 Ashv: horse (Skt.): a suffix in all the names that appear in this story. The author has tried to convey how important the horse was in the lives of the Indo-Iranians.

3 Som: a famous alcoholic beverage of the Aryan people.

4 Krichhashv: poor/lazy horse.

5 Riddhashv: 'rich in horses'.

6 Mama: mother's brother.

7 The author wrote 'Maha-pitar' which would literally translate as 'great-father', although the phrase is used here for 'tribal-chief'.

8 Vahlik, Paktha: two of the Vedic tribes.

9 Tat (Skt.): father.

4. Puruhut

1 Danda: The translator did not find a parallel for this word in English. I can't say what the reasons could have been, the most likely of which is the possibility of not having such a thing in Bronze Age England. The author, however, uses this word for a ridge at the mountain top, a herding place/encampment of the Bronze Age Aryan tribes, during the summer months.

2 Puru: one of the Vedic tribes.

3 Madr, or Medes: one of the Indo-Iranian tribes.

4 Parshu/Parsu: a Vedic tribe that has been linked to later Persians.

5 Shvak (Skt.): dog. The same as *sobaka* (Russ.).

6 Karonda: Bengal currant/*Carissa carandas*.

7 'Gur' is jaggery or raw-sugar, but the author may have used it for honey.

8 Pururava: leading character of an ancient myth, a love-tale.

9 Urvashi: the heroine nymph from the same myth as mentioned in the previous note.

10 Mitr, Nasatya, Agni: Aryan gods as mentioned in Vedic literature.

11 Hiranya (Skt.): gold.

12 Rajat (Skt.): silver.

13 Das (Skt.): slave. A word that has taken such deep root in Indian culture, it has become a synonym for 'humble', and even a surname.

14 Indr: considered as one of the Hindu gods today, but the word has many meanings including commander, prince, etc.

5. Purudhan

1 Asur: a controversial term used as a derogatory word for the indigenous people of the Indian subcontinent.

2 Suvastu (Skt.): beautiful architecture (lit.). The area in the north-west of

today's Pakistan is still called Swat.

3 Kos: an Indian unit for distance used since Vedic times. One *kos* is roughly 2.25 miles.

4 Janpati (Skt.): clan-leader. From *jan* (people) + *pati* (owner).

5 Pushkalavati (Skt.): lotus city (lit.). Still exists under the name of Charsadda in the north-west of today's Pakistan.

6 Sindhu (Skt.): river. A word that has not only given a name to the mighty river Indus but to the Hindu belief system as a whole and, consequently, to India as a country too.

7 'Devs' being gods and 'Asurs' being demons, the struggle between Aryans and indigenous Indians gave rise to the myth of Devasur-Sangram.

6. Angira

1 Yojan: an ancient Indian unit of distance, equivalent to about 8 miles.

2 Present day Taxila; originally 'Takshshila' from Sanskrit – Taksh + *shila*. Taksh was the son of Bharat, in the epic *Mahabharat*, who was the king of this area. Shila: stone (lit.). Hence, Takshshila: 'Capital of Taksh'.

3 Indr Maghva: reference to a war leader from the Vedic texts.

4 Shambar: reference to an indigenous Indian ruler mentioned in the Vedic texts.

5 Pur (Skt.): walled city, stronghold, fortress, etc.

6 Jan-parishad (Skt.): popular assembly or council of people.

7 Modern Sialkot (Panjab), now in Pakistan.—*Au.*

8 Rishi: a Sanskrit word for teacher/sage/seer/elder etc.

9 Mangur: a type of fish of dark brown colour that is native to India.

10 Jehlam: wrongly spelled by the British as Jhelum.

11 Takshshila as an academy came to be known as one of the first centres of learning in ancient India.

12 Sauvir: modern Rori near Karachi.

13 Moolsthan (Skt.): from *mool* (native/original) + *sthan* (place) – the 'native place'. Modern-day city of Multan.—*Au.*

7. Sudas

1 State of Uttar Pradesh in modern India.

2 Chandrbhaga: one of the five rivers of Panjab, also known as Chenab, Jhana.

3 Shami: a kind of tree (*Prosopis cineraria*), typical in South Asia.

4 Pitar: a Proto-Indo-European word for 'father'.

5 Duhitar/duhita: Proto-Indo-European words for 'daughter'.

6 Arya: one of the most controversial but common words among Indo-

Aryan cultures, used here as an address of respect or as 'noble'.

7 The author indicates a swap of the sound 's' with 'h', which is very common in most Indic languages.

8 Ahichchhatr or Ahi-kshetr: ancient capital of northern Panchal.

9 Rohilkhand: a region in the north-west of Uttar Pradesh state that later on came to be known as such, which takes its name from an Afghan tribe 'Rohil'. Khanda is Sanskrit for 'part'.

10 Janpad (Skt.): a word used for kingdom or republic during the Vedic period or the late-Bronze Age in India. It could literally mean 'people's place'.

11 Shatadru: ancient name of Satluj, one of the five rivers of Panjab, misspelled by the British as 'Sutlej'.

12 The major rivers of northern India: Ganga is often misspelled as 'Ganges' and Yamuna is sometimes written as Jamuna.

13 *Rig Ved* 6.23.2.—*Au.*

14 Vadhyashv, Divodas and Sudas all are characters from Vedic literature.

15 Palas: a kind of tree (*Butea monosperma*) native to South Asia. *Palas* is associated with many Indian myths.

16 Brahmin: a priest. It is also the caste that later rose to the highest position in the hierarchy of the caste-system.

17 Kshatriya: the ruling/warrior class (caste).

18 Sruva: a wooden service-spoon used during *yajna* – a ritual of offering oblations and libations into sacred fire.

19 Indrani: the wife of the deity Indr.

8. Pravahan

1 Upnishads: the Hindu scriptures that contain central ideas of Vedic philosophy.

2 As per Indian custom a cousin is called a brother/sister.

3 A traditional residential school for learning religious texts.

4 Brahma: the Hindu god of creation.

5 Gargya: one of the clan-names of the Brahmin caste.

6 A reference to the ritual of keeping a *palas* tree branch as a symbol of studentship of the religious schools.

7 Shivi: a democratic republic of ancient India.

8 Kashi: Vedic name for present-day Varanasi.

9 Shabar: a forest-dwelling native tribe of South India.

10 Samidha: ritual firewood.

11 *Rig Ved* 6.26.25.

12 Sadanira: an ancient name of the river Gandak, which flows from Nepal to India and merges into Ganga near Patna.

13 Yajnavalkya or Yagyavalkya: a Vedic-era sage who is believed to have lived near Videh in the 7th century BCE.

14 Janak: a king of the Videh kingdom who is mentioned in later Vedic literature and is also considered to be a foster father of Sita, central female character of the Hindu epic *Ramayan*.

15 Jambu: a fruit tree native to India only. It is believed that the ancient name of India – Jambudvip ('island of *jambu* trees') – was derived from this word.

16 Mallyayuddh: traditional Indian wrestling.

9. Bandhul the Malla

1 Sal: a kind of tree (*Shorea robusta*).

2 Gan (Skt.): a word for 'democratic republic' but had multiple applications throughout Indian history.

3 Nilgai: blue cow (lit.), a kind of deer. Being native to India only, has no parallel word in English, although sometimes called the Indian/Asian antelope.

4 Jambudvip: an ancient name of India.

5 Ganpati (Skt.): republican chief. From *gan* (republic) + *pati* (owner/master).

6 Ayushman: a popular title or form of address that literally meant 'one who is blessed with a long life'.

7 Mallagram: present-day Gorakhpur in the state of Uttar Pradesh.

8 Two of the sixteen republics of ancient India that made a confederation called 'Mahajanpad'.

9 Sahet-Mahet: presently a Buddhist archaeological site in Shravasti district of Uttar Pradesh.

10 Jamun: a fruit tree exclusively native to India; the same as *jambu* explained earlier (see note 15 of chapter 8 above).

11 Ajit Keskambal from *ajit* (unwinnable) + *kes* (hair) + *kambal* (blanket). As the story goes, Ajit always wore a blanket made of hair, hence came to be called Ajit Keskambal.

12 Chakrvarti: paramount ruler. From *chakr* (wheel) + *varti* (suppository): a king whose chariot can roam anywhere unchallenged.

13 Kapilvastu: the capital city of Buddh's father, who was a king.

14 Jain: follower of a faith system known for its extreme measure of non-violence that was contemporary to Buddhism.

15 Niganth: the name of Mahavir, the last spiritual teacher of the Jain faith.

16 Shakya: a clan name of the Kshatriya caste, to which Buddh belonged.

17 As per available information Ajatshatru was the nephew of Prasenjit as well as his son-in-law.

10. Naagdatt

1 The author has used this word for 'Panjab', as he had given the same in brackets. It literally means 'the Northern-Highway'.

2 Yavan, from the word 'Ionian', was used in India for 'Greek' like Yunaan (Per.) was for Greece.

3 Satrap, or Kshatrap: a provincial governor in the ancient Persian empire.

4 During the Sassanid Empire, it was often called Sogdiana, a provincial name taken from the Achaemenid Empire.

5 'King of Kings' for the Persian 'Shahanshah'; it can also be understood as 'Emperor'.

6 Ratti: an Indian unit of weight, equivalent to 8 grams.

7 Ahura-Mazda: the Avestan name for the creator and sole God of Zoroastrianism – Iran's pre-Islamic faith system.

8 Attic: Athens's Greek dialect.

11. Prabha

1 *Ramayan*: an ancient Hindu epic poem.

2 Varanasi: a city in the state of Uttar Pradesh, also called Banaras.

3 *Raghuvamsh*: 'Dynasty of Raghu'.

4 *Kumarsambhav*: 'The Birth of Kumar (the War-god)'.

5 Suvarnakshi (Skt.): the golden eyed. From *suvarn* (gold) + *aksh* (eyes).

6 Chaitr: the first month of the Hindu lunar calendar that falls in March/April.

7 Vaishya: the commercial caste. Tier 3 in the order of the caste hierarchy. See illustration on p. 144.

8 Svayambar/svayamvar (Skt.): from *svayam* (self) + *var* (groom); an ancient tradition where the bride would choose her husband, as a winner of some kind of competition set for prospective grooms to compete in.

9 Saumya: a Sanskrit word for friendly/polite address.

10 Mukhar Veena: Indian stringed instrument similar to *sitar*.

11 Prabhalok (Skt.): from the words *prabha* (light) + *lok* (world).

12 Ur-basi: one who lives in the heart.—*Au.*

13 Ap: in the water of river Saryu; sar: swimmer.—*Au.*

14 Used in the sense of 'Indians' here.

15 Rajput: the princely or ruling caste. From *raj* (king) + *put* (son). See illustration on p. 144.

16 Throwing or putting one's turban at somebody's feet is considered extreme pleading by the turban wearer, since a turban, being a head-cloth, is a symbol in India of great pride.

17 Mlechh: a derogatory word with many meanings – barbarian, untouchable, foreigner, non-Aryan, uncivilized, one who does not know Sanskrit, etc.

18 Dharmrakshit (Pali): protected by Dharm (lit.). A title in Buddhism for a Greek Buddhist missionary.

19 Chandal: another word for the 'untouchables', the lowest of the lowest in a caste-Hindu society.

20 Mahasthavir: a title for the head of the Buddhist monks of the reformist order.

21 Sangh: a Pali word for association, assembly, company, communion, family, etc. The word is also used for Buddhist monasteries.

22 Shruti is Sanskrit for 'that which is heard' and refers to the body of the most authoritative, ancient religious texts comprising the central canon of Hinduism, such as the four Veds.

23 Birch bark manuscripts of Brahminical theology.

24 Peepal: *Ficus religiosa* or sacred fig, a species of fig native to the Indian subcontinent. It is also known as the Bodhi tree.

25 Bhadant: a term of respect applied to a Buddhist scholar.

26 Bakul: *Mimusops elengi*, a medium-sized evergreen tree found in tropical forests in South Asia.

27 Bhikshu-Sangh: the community of mendicant monks.

28 Sarvastivad: an early school of Buddhism that held to the existence of Dharms (Skt.), i.e. the law or doctrine of all three times – present, past and future.

29 Purushpur: present-day city of Peshawar.

30 Turushk: Turkish.

31 The Nyaya and the Vaisheshik: two orthodox systems of Indian philosophy. Both systems are 'committed to common-sense realism and pluralism in their ontology; believe in the creation of the world from material atoms that conjoin to generate this world by the will of God' (*The Oxford Handbook of World Philosophy*, 2011).

32 Fragments of this nine-act play 'Sariputr-prakaran' were discovered in 1911.

12. Suparn the Yaudheya

1 Madhupark: a worshipping practice of the Hindus in which different foods mixed in honey were presented to the deities.

2 Avanti (Malwa): a region in west-central India.

3 Jujhva: a word that literally means 'warrior', but used here as 'quarrelsome', in a derogatory sense. The words *jujhar*, *jujharu* still exist

in contemporary Panjabi and mean 'great fighter'. The translator had put it as 'fighting cock' instead.

4 As per Hindu and Buddhist mythology there exist three worlds – Kamlok (the desire realm), Rooplok (material world) and Arooplok (formless realm).

5 Nirukt (Skt.): explained/interpreted (lit.). A study of interpretation of the etymology of Vedic literature.

6 Yaudheya (Skt.): warrior/soldier (lit.).

7 Vikramaditya: brave as the Sun (lit.). An honorary title.

8 Charm (Skt.): hide.

9 Sanskrit quote:
राज्ञो महान्से पूर्व रन्तिदेवस्य वै द्विज। अहन्यहनि वाध्येते द्वे साहस्त्रे गवां तथा॥
समासं ददतो ह्यन्न रन्तिदेवस्य नित्यशः। अतुला कीर्तिरभवन्नृपस्य द्विजसत्तम॥ – वनपर्व, 208. 8–10
महानदी चर्मराशेरुक्लेदात् संसृजेयतः। ततश्चर्मण्वती त्येवं विख्याता सा महानदी॥ – शान्तिपर्व, 29, 123

10 Sanskrit quote:
सांकृति रन्तिदेवं च मृतं संजय शुश्रुम। द्विशता साहस्त्रा आसन् तस्य सूदा महात्मनः॥
गृहानभ्यागतान् विप्रान् अतिधीन् परिवेषकाः। – द्रोणपर्व, 67. 1–2
तत्र स्म सूदाः क्रोशान्ति सुमृष्ट मणिकुण्डलाः। सुपं भूयिष्टम श्रीघ्व नाद्य मांसं यथा पुरा॥ – द्रोणपर्व, 67. 17–18

11 Nagar (Skt.): town; Naagar (Skt.): town-bred.

12 Shankar: another name of Shiv, the Hindu god.

13 Master as 'teacher', not the 'master' of a slave.

14 Vishnu forms a Hindu trinity along with Shiv and Brahma.

15 Kumar: a reference to Kartikeya (the Hindu god of war).

16 Parambhattarak: paramount sovereign, an ancient honorific title.

17 Achintya: present-day Ajanta.

18 East Asians.

13. **Durmukh**

1 Prayag: present-day city of Allahabad, renamed Prayagraj in October 2018.

2 'Mahavihar' or Buddhist monastery, famous for being an important centre of teaching and learning.

3 As per available information this is a reference to the Chinese monk Hiuen Tsang (Xuanzang) who visited India in the 7th century CE.

4 Baanbhatt: 7th century (CE) Sanskrit poet and prose writer of India.

5 Varn (Skt.): colour (lit.), or caste-group.

6 Ashram (Skt.): hermitage (lit.), or (here) age-based life stages in Hinduism, where life is divided into four *ashrams*.

7 Bania: a derogatory reference to the trader class, Tier 3 in the hierarchy of caste-groups.

8 Asavarn (Skt.): 'not fine coloured', antonym of *savarn*, the fine-coloured

(lit.). *Savarn* refers to the upper-caste groups; hence *asavarn* are the 'lower' castes.

9 Devar: From the combination of *do* (two) + *var* (bridegroom).—*Au.*

10 Akshayavat: 'the indestructible banyan tree'. A sacred fig tree for the Hindus with various myths attached.

11 Lakhchumbi: 'the one who kisses a hundred thousand' (lit.), i.e. the possessor of a hundred thousand women.

12 Durmukh: from *dur* (bad) + *mukh* (mouth).

13 Pandit: used here as 'scholar' although it also is a synonym to Brahmin, the priestly caste.

14 Sanskrit reference from *Pramanvarttik*:
वेदप्रामाण्यं कस्यचित्कर्तृवादः स्नाने धर्मेच्छा जातिवादावलेपः।
सन्तापारम्भः पापहानाय चेति ध्वस्तप्रज्ञानां पंचलिगानि जाड्ये॥

15 Vaitarni: a mythological river in hell.

16 Sinhal: Sri Lanka; Suvarndvip: 'Island of Gold' (in South-East Asia); Kambojdvip: Cambodia; Champadvip: Eastern Indo-China; Cheen: China; Tushar: Himalaya; Parasya: Persia.

17 Sanskrit quote: दिग् व्यपकं तमः.

18 Nirvan (Skt.): liberation from the cycle of rebirths.

19 Bhairvichakr: a tantric mode of goddess worship.

20 Mahayan: greater ship (lit.). The newer version of Buddhism, liberalized from rigid conservatism.

21 Bodhisattv: the one who gets enlightened, but waits for Nirvan for the sake of others.

22 Tri-Ratn: the three jewels (lit.) – Buddh, Dharm and Sangh.

23 Tathagat: an honorific title of Buddh.

24 Rahu-Ketu: two heavenly characters of Hindu mythology that cause solar eclipses.

25 Vinay Pitak: basket of rules (lit.). One of the three parts of the Buddhist holy scriptures.

14. Chakrpani

1 Pamir: a mountain range in Central Asia.

2 Somnath: a Shiv temple on the coast of Gujrat that was destroyed by the Muslim invaders many times.

3 Jagnimitranand.

4 Bhot: Bhutan.

5 Tarini (Taradevi): The Mother Goddess.

6 Rudraksh: dried seeds of a tree (*Elaeocarpus ganitrus*), sacred for the Hindus.

7 A kind of grass (*Eragrostis cynosuroides*) which was offered/accepted as

alms according to Hindu mythology.

8 Sanskrit quote: सर्वेषामाव दानानां भार्यादानं विशिष्यते।

9 Vaishnav (Skt.): worshipper of Vishnu.

10 Sanskrit quote: अन्तः शाक्ता बहिश्शैवाः सभामध्ये च वैष्णवाः।

11 Panchmakar: the five 'M's – *madya* (alcohol), *maans* (meat), *matsya* (fish), *mudra* (gesture), *maithun* (sex).

12 Madhyamik: the philosophy of the Mahayan school of Buddhism, founded by Naagarjun (150–250 CE).

13 Vedantist: an expert in the study of the Veds.

14 A Hindu system of philosophy based on the Upnishads.

15 Pithaura: a Rajput kingdom of Prithviraj Chauhan, who was ruling Delhi.

16 Baba: old man (lit.). But the word is often used in the sense of grandfather, elderly man, father, sage, teacher, etc.

17 Dron: a reference to the royal preceptor Dronacharya in the epic *Mahabharat*.

18 Chandr: moon (lit.). The word is often used as a metaphor to express compassion, to say 'as handsome as the Moon'.

19 In Hindu and Buddhist mythological astrology, Rahu is a planet that attacks the Sun-deity and the Moon-deity.

20 Hindustan: Hindu + *stana* (place); abode of the Hindus (Indians). Name of India given by the Persians.

15. Baba Noordin

1 Ghor province in central Afghanistan.

2 The Mamluk dynasty or the so-called Slave dynasty that ruled northern India after they were left there by Turkish invaders as their slaves to rule from Delhi.

3 Khilji was a Turkic tribe, settled in Afghanistan.

4 Jahanpanah: a Persian phrase to address a person in a position of great authority, such as a king.

5 A province of Afghanistan known for her ruler Mahmud of Ghazni and his raids and plunder of India and Iran.

6 Sultan-e-Zamana; same as note 4 of this chapter.

7 Vazir-ul-mulk: a term equivalent to Prime Minister.

8 Panchayat: from the word *panch* (Skt.), meaning five; a traditional council/managing committee of five representatives of a village.

9 Amir-ul-mominin (Ar.): leader or commander of the faithful.

10 Sufis are the practitioners of Sufism, a mystical dimension of Islam.

11 Raja: king.

12 Hilsa: in the state of Bihar, a place known for being an important Buddhist centre of learning.

13 Kashaya: a red-brown robe typical among Buddhists.

14 Khanqah: a Sufi shrine or a building specifically designed for the gathering of a Sufi brotherhood.

15 Pravaran: a Buddhist holy day celebrated on the full moon at the end of the Monsoon season.

16 Pirs: Muslim saints or holy-men.

17 Baba: used here for Sufi monk.

18 Maulvi: a priest in a mosque.

19 Salaam-Aleikum: Arab greeting.

20 Tasavvuf: mysticism. The origin of this word is disputed but considered as Arabic by most.

21 An-ul-haq (Ar.): related to a Sufi – Mansur Al-Hallaj – who was killed for 'heresy', for uttering these words.

22 Persian.

23 Kufr (Ar.): denial of God.

24 Shams Tabrizi, spiritual instructor of Rumi, a great Persian Sufi poet, and Mansur Al-Hallaj (see note 21 of this chapter).

25 Traditionally, the red spot on a married Hindu woman's forehead is vermilion powder.

26 Amir: prince; a word of Semitic origin that literally means 'to give orders'.

27 Chaudhari: a surname as well as a title for a man of position.

28 Ram-Ram: a Hindu way to greet; from the name of the god Ram.

29 The tradition of addressing a stranger with a word that indicates familial relationship is considered civilized in India. Often a person of the same age is addressed as brother/sister, an elder as uncle/aunty, and so on.

30 'Ji' (please) is a suffix which is added to a name or title as a form of address to show respect.

31 From *labh* (profit) + *din* (faith): blessed religion (lit.). But when the prefix 'a' is inserted in any word of an Indic language, it turns the word into an antonym of the same word. Therefore, Alabhdin is 'unblessed', although the author has used it to indicate an illiterate pronunciation for Ala-ud-Din (Khilji).

32 Begum: an aristocratic title for married Muslim women.

33 Dassehra: a major Hindu festival that falls ten days before Diwali.

34 Neem: a tree native to India.

35 Fakir: mendicant (lit.); but used here in the sense of monk or friar.

36 Haryana: a region north-west of Delhi, far-east of Panjab.

16. Suraiya

1 Chhonkra/shami (*Prosopis cineraria*): a flowering tree, native to western Asia and the Indian subcontinent.

2 Jalal-ud-din Muhammad Akbar, the Mughal emperor Akbar's full name.
3 Bira: a nickname for Birbal.
4 A reference to one of the anecdotes which were popular about Emperor Akbar and his minister Birbal. King Todar Mall, who was one of the nobles of Emperor Akbar, is known for supervising matters of land and revenue during Akbar's reign and also for surveying the farming lands in the country.
5 *Ain-i-Akbari*: biography of Emperor Akbar.
6 Traditional washing was done by beating the wet clothes on a stone.
7 Bairam Khan, father of Abdul Rahim Khan-i-Khana, a Hindi poet in Akbar's court.
8 Ashok: sorrow-less (lit.); a tree (*Saraca asoca*) considered sacred throughout the Indian subcontinent.
9 Kamal: lotus flower (lit.).
10 Sadhuni: female monk.
11 In 1715 CE, the Mughal emperor had conferred the title of 'Jagat Seth' ('Merchant of the World') on a rich trader.
12 A reference to a tradition of putting pennants in the ground to show off one's wealth.
13 Firangi: initially used for the French crusaders in the Arab world, the word came to be used as a synonym for white/European colonialists in South Asia.

17. Rekha Bhagat

1 Gandak/Narayani: one of the major rivers of Nepal and tributary of the Ganga.
2 Hariharnath: a temple of a Hindu deity.
3 Hariharkshetr: an old name of Sonepur, a town in the state of Bihar on the confluence of the rivers Gandak and Ganga.
4 The (British) East India Company.
5 Mooris Ghinavan: only an ordinary name but literally may mean dirty fellow.
6 Satyug: truthful era (lit.), or Golden Age; one of the four mythological eras (*yugs*) of Hinduism, when the world was ruled by the gods.
7 Munshi: a Persian word for 'master of languages', but used here for secretary or teacher in British India.
8 Ravan and Kans: two villains from the two major Hindu epics.
9 Patwari: a village accountant/revenue clerk.
10 Kabir: a revered mystic poet of the 15th century CE.
11 Nazim: a provincial governor during Mughal rule.
12 Sahib: a word of Arabic origin used for showing respect to aristocracy

and to someone in a position of power.

13 Company Bahadur was a popular title for East India Company officials. The word *bahadur* literally means 'brave'.

14 Nawab: an honorific title bestowed by the Mughal rulers on their provincial representatives.

15 Used in the sense of 'his manhood is not worth much now'. But the literal translation was needed to show the manner of speech of the men-folk.

16 Khvas: a barber or a kind of servant in the service of Rajput kings who also acted as a bodyguard.

17 Anna: an Indian monetary denomination; sixteen *annas* made one rupee.

18 'Sahib' is used here for colonialist Englishmen.

19 Bilayat/Vilayat: Hindustani name for England or a general term for 'foreign country'.

20 Satyug, Tretyug, Dvapar Yug, Kalyug: the four *yugs* (eras) in Hindu mythology; *Kalyug* being the last.

21 Teenkaudi: a name that literally means 'three shells', in the sense of 'three pennies' or very little value.

22 De: a Bengali surname.

23 Awadh: the name of a region mispronounced and written as 'Oudh' in British records.

24 Sipahi: solider; mispronounced and popularized by the British as 'Sepoy'.

25 Mandua/ragi: finger millet.

26 Agahan: ninth month of the Hindu calendar, corresponding to November.

27 Sukhari: from the word *sukha*, i.e. dry/drought.

28 Magh: a month of the Hindu calendar that falls in January.

18. Mangal Singh

1 Sati: a Hindu ritual of burning a widow alive!

2 Thaan: an Indian unit for a particular length of a piece of cloth.

3 Purdah (Per.): curtain. The word is also used for 'veil' in the Indian subcontinent.

4 Peshwa: a title equivalent to Prime Minister in the Maratha Empire (west-central India).

5 'Adulterated' could be the nearest possible equivalent for 'jootha' [m.s.adj.], a word used to mean 'already tasted', mostly used for food, but used for 'kissed' here. The translator had opted for the word 'false'.

6 A reference to the prince of Panjab, the last heir to the Sikh Kingdom (Khalsa Raj), who was kidnapped by the colonial British authorities, brought to England and raised as a Christian aristocrat.

7 'States': the kingdoms which ruled independently but swore allegiance to the British throne.
8 Bahadur Shah: the last Mughal emperor, deposed and exiled by the British.
9 A simile from Greek mythology chosen by the translator but not originally mentioned by the author.

19. Safdar

1 Verandah: a kind of awning built as an extension to the main building.
2 Mem-Sahib: a phrase that initially came to be used for the female version of 'Sahib', for the colonial English women, but later for all aristocratic women in India.
3 Saree: a typical Indian dress for women.
4 'Master' is used here to mean teacher.
5 Affectionate address, but not real brother. See note 29 of chapter 15 above.
6 Indian National Congress, later a major political party in pre- and post-Independence India.
7 Swarajya: self-rule (lit.); a slogan popular during the Independence movement.
8 Durbar: Imperial court.
9 Kaiser-i-Hind: German imperial title (Kaiser) used to denote 'Empress of India'.
10 Same as Kaiser.
11 Victor Alexander Bruce, 9th Earl of Elgin.
12 Lala Lajpat Rai, Bal Gangadhar Tilak, Bipin Chandra Pal: three activists of the Indian freedom struggle.
13 Naram Dal: soft group (lit.); from *naram* (soft) + *dal* (group), i.e. a group of moderates or believers in non-violence.
14 Khilafat (Ar.): succession (lit.). The movement (1914–18) was an agitation by the Indian Muslims, allied with Indian nationalists to pressure the British government to preserve the authority of the Ottoman Sultan as Caliph of Islam after the First World War.
15 A reference to the 'Non-Cooperation' movement initiated by M.K. Gandhi against British rule.
16 Omar Khayyam: a revered Persian poet famous for his poetry about the worldly pleasures of life.
17 Kurta-pyjama: an Indian shirt and trouser set, mostly of cotton.
18 Gita: a holy text of the Hindus from the epic of *Mahabharat*.
19 Jallianwala Bagh: a venue in the Indian city of Amritsar known for the infamous massacre of unarmed protesters by the British-Indian military.
20 Chauri Chaura: a town near Gorakhpur in the state of Uttar Pradesh.

The incident took place on 4 February 1922.

20. Sumer

1 Dhoti: a piece of cloth that is wrapped around the lower part of the body; kurta: the Indian long shirt.

2 Babu: a word used to address the rich landowners/aristocrats.

3 Chamar: tanner. One of the prominent untouchable castes of India.

4 Harijan: God's children (lit.); from Hari (god) + *jan* (people).

5 Sonepur: a township in the state of Bihar famous for its funfair.

6 Birla and Bajaj: two major Indian capitalist houses.

7 Khadisangh: a cottage industry of cotton products.

8 Lakh: Indian word for one hundred thousand.

9 Shubh-Labh (Skt.): auspicious profit (lit.).

10 The city of Titagarh was famous for its paper industry.

11 Sevagram: a village in the Vardha district of Maharashtra state where Gandhi had established a place of worship.

12 From *varn* (colour) + *vyavastha* (arrangement): the caste system. This clearly indicates caste initially being based on the colour of the skin.

13 Bhasmasur: this refers to an ancient Indian myth of a demon called Bhasmasur who enjoyed a blessing bestowed upon him that whoever he touches would turn into ash (*bhasm*).

14 Baijnath was an ancient city that Bhasmasur wanted to destroy.

15 Krupp: a prominent German company, an industrialist dynasty which made weapons; Mitsui: one of the largest corporate houses in Japan.

16 An Indian nationalist freedom fighter who allied with the Nazi leadership against British rule.

Appendices

Appendix 1

'A book without compare in any Indian Language'

BY BHADANT ANAND KAUSALYAYAN

(TRANSLATED BY MAYA JOSHI)

'Addendum' to Volga se Ganga
(1942; Allahabad: Kitab Mahal, 2007), pp. 343–6

I had read some of the stories of *Volga se Ganga* in Hindi magazines, and when the book got published, I think it was I who got the first copy. I have read the entire book once and several stories more than once, and read them out to others, to people of all kinds and in all stations of life. My critique was that many of the stories are more history than story. I truly found some of them somewhat crushed under the weight of knowledge – a story should be light and easy. I once wrote this to Rahulji. He answered – were these stories to be taken merely as history engagingly written, I would be satisfied.

I have heard *Volga se Ganga* praised, and done so myself. But the other day when I got to read the opinion of a Maharashtrian scholar, one familiar with world literature, that 'no other Indian language has anything to equal this Hindi book', my Hindi-worshipping heart truly danced.

But, alas! Yesterday, a gentleman sent me a clipping of *Vishwabandhu* in which I got to read '*Nagnvadi Ved-nindak Rahul*' [Rahul, the Nudity-promoting Denouncer of the Veds] – by 'Shri Swamiji'. But why keep his identity secret? It's another matter that one might choose to adopt 'Swamiji' as a proper name.

Liking or not liking a book is as much a matter of personal capacity as of personal interest. Everybody does not take to a book in the same way. Why should *Volga se Ganga* alone be an exception to this?

But I want to know just this regarding Swamiji's desire that the public try their best 'to get this detested book banned' – does bringing this desire to fruition honour us or bring us dishonour? The Arya *jati* specializes, one has heard all along, in overpowering false conceptions solely by force of intellect. '*Vade vade jaayate tattvabodhah* [debate and counter-debate alone bring forth true knowledge]' – is this not the declaration of the Arya ancestors?

I am deeply familiar with this epoch-making creation of Rahulji's and I know that it incorporates the results of an extraordinary thinker's lifetime of study. If we find his conclusions wrong, let us prove them to be so. Independent thinkers – if they are honest and wish to nurture the sapling of honesty – have no other alternative. The first four stories of Rahulji's *Volga se Ganga* are called 'Nisha', 'Diva', 'Amritashv', 'Puruhut'. These four depict society between 6000 BCE and 2500 BCE. It is the prehistoric period; and these are stories. Therefore, it is understood that imagination plays a special role in these stories, but they are not merely works of the imagination. Whatever is original and significant in these stories is a result of Rahulji's studies in Indo-European and Indo-Persian philology. *The Origin of the Family, Private Property and the State* by Engels is a well-known tome. Before we ban these stories, we will have to have to ban that book.

The next four stories are – 'Purudhan', 'Angira', 'Sudas', and 'Pravahan'. All these are also backed up by literary sources – Veds, Brahmans, the *Mahabharat*, Purans, and Buddhist commentarial works known as Atthakatha. The story called 'Sudas' is based on the *Rig Ved* and 'Pravahan Jaivali' [*sic*], the story that provokes everyone – Buddhist and non-Buddhist – is based on *Chhandogya* and *Brihadaranyak Upnishads* and the aforementioned Atthakathas of the Buddhists. These four stories attempt to present the development of society from 2000 BCE to 700 BCE. Readers should notice that we haven't yet reached the Buddh's time.

The next story is 'Bandhul Malla' (460 BCE). All materials for this story have been taken from Buddhist texts. They contain so much material that Rahulji had to write a separate novel called *Singh Senapati* in order to represent that period.

The tenth story is 'Naagdatt'. If you read Kautilya's *Arthshastr*, narratives by Greek travellers, *Hindu Polity* by Jayaswalji [K.P. Jayaswal], or Vincent Smith's history taught in all your schools and colleges, it should come as no surprise that you too would encounter some historical facts presented by Rahulji in 'Naagdatt'.

The eleventh story, 'Prabha', has gained popularity as an independent story as well. Backing it up are two of Ashvghosh's *kavyas* – *Buddhcharit* and *Saundaranand*, all of Sanskrit drama, Winternitz's *A History of Indian Literature* and Rhys Davids's *Buddhist India*. That story is set in 50 BCE.

The twelfth tale is 'Suparn Yaudheya' from the Gupt period. Some of the material for it has been taken from inscriptions dating to the Gupt period, which are indelible, and the perennially read *Raghuvamsh*, *Kumarsambhav*, *Abhijnanshakuntalam*. Panini has contributed to it, as has the Chinese traveller Fa-Hien.

The thirteenth story is 'Durmukh' – one that pierces like an arrow. What can one do? It is backed by *Harshcharit*, *Kadambari*, and the travel-narratives of Hiuen Tsang and I-tsing.

The fourteenth story is set in 1200 CE and is called 'Chakrpani'. The source for that story will have to be found in *Naishadh* [a *mahakavya*, *Naishadhcharit*, by Shriharsh], *Khandan-Khand-Khadya* [a Sanskrit treatise by Shriharsh], and in several records and inscriptions.

'Baba Noordin' to 'Sumer' are six other stories whose period is the 10th century to the 20th century CE. All those stories are also supported by historical evidence, much like the others. But I notice that nobody has any special objection to them. Perhaps because they are all concerned with relatively recent times, and we are worshippers of the past.

The writer of these lines does not have the wherewithal to agree or disagree with all the conclusions drawn in the book and its stories, because to do that requires research that is at least approximate to, if not equal to, that of Rahulji's. These lines have been written merely to request the likes of 'Swamiji' to recognize that these stories contain years of study, and are not just 'random nonsense'.

Just a few days back, some illiterate Jains had made some noises against views expressed by Acharya Dhammanandoji Kosambi. A Jain *panditji* said – 'We will give testimony in favour of Kosambiji.' That turned out to be unnecessary.

I am afraid that our ancient books and their creator *rishi*-

maharishis [sages and seers] are giving testimony in favour of Rahulji – 'Why, he is right! There is no *dharm* greater than the truth.'

Appendix 2

'What Does *Volga se Ganga* Teach Us?'

SHRIPAD AMRIT DANGE

(TRANSLATED BY SHEELA JAYWANT)

Introduction to Volga te Ganga

(Mumbai: Lok Sahitya, 1944), pp. 15–23

In his anthology, *Volga se Ganga*, a book significant in Hindi literature, essayist and traveller Rahul Sankrityayan has traced Mankind's progression over eight thousand years. Sankrityayan describes how primitive man lived, what hurdles he overcame, what struggles he went through and how he evolved through the millennia. He points out how far Man has come and wonders how far he is likely to go. What makes this book different from the others in its category is that Sankrityayan's accounts have been presented through short stories.

It stands apart from other history-based fiction published in Hindi because the stories themselves are unique.

All fiction written about the pre-British era mentions kings and queens, forts and swords, people dressed in short-shirts worn over *dhotis* or *pyjamas* and loincloths, as if by including them in the descriptions, the work can be labelled 'historical'. Actually, many books even today have such misleading details. Sankrityayan's work stands apart because he has represented those times realistically.

One has to take note of more than just the names of places listed in the book. It has historical value because of the way the stories lay bare the basics of how Man lived – really lived – and how he changed his ways through the centuries. They deal with fundamental elements. They are stories, true, but they are authentic – and excellent – depictions of the way Mankind lived through the ages.

This book is not a narration of history; it divulges much more. It brings alive, era by era, Man's passions, thoughts, feelings and behaviour.

Sankrityayan has clarified, in the introduction of the book, that he has put forth his technical (historical) theories in his book *Manav Samaj* (literally, 'The Society of Humans'). In it he has incorporated Marx's well-known treatises on materialism and used them to illustrate the development of the Hindi '*manav samaj*'. The reason behind his writing these stories, he declares, was so that people, informed and aware, know where they stand and how they can and must move ahead.

What does the communist way of thinking have to say about such kind of 'progress'?

Communism believes in five eras:

1. the primal society which had simple groups of people living together,
2. when slavery was the norm,
3. the technological age,
4. when free trade and capitalism came into being, and
5. after the birth of communism.

How are these eras recognized? Does the arrival and decline of each take Mankind towards 'progress' at all? Who or what is responsible for the commencing and culmination of the eras? Are they man-made or otherwise destined? These questions could give rise to many others.

No one can deny the fact that the aim of production of equipment/vessels/implements and clever use of the intellect to make profit was to make Man happy. That is considered progress. If a simple man-on-the-street sees how far Man has come from the time he lived in the dark ages, before history was recorded, till the year 1942, he will quite easily agree that there has been a lot of progress. Who wouldn't say that Man has come a long way since he ate raw meat, chewed on bones, wore no clothes and lived in primitive conditions? Only the very ignorant.

Progress attained and measured over a period of time is called an 'era'. The indicators of eras are the food grown and consumed during those years and the way people enjoy themselves. An era is labelled or known by the techniques used for all of these. Those same means are used to form relationships between people; those, too, are considered indicators of an era. Mankind invents things; inventions and discoveries change Mankind. From the interactions between the two flow the modifications that create history and the advancement of Mankind.

Nature does not automatically provide. The cow and grass are both created by nature, true, but to satisfy hunger, a cow must make the effort to go to where the grass is. Similarly, the cow and Man are both offspring of Nature, but to get milk, it is not sufficient for the latter to turn to the cow for milk or meat. He must domesticate the original, wild form of the bovine and for that he must master the technique of lassoing, tying and taming her. Next he must know how to extract milk from her udders and devise and fabricate a utensil to contain that milk. If a meadow has been overgrazed and there is hardly any grass to eat, there is no way a cow can produce or obtain grass for herself. She doesn't have the intellect for it. Man, however, can grow grass to replace the fodder that has been consumed, and make provisions for the future too. He has the brains and the skill to make the tools required for the job. Both the cow and Man work at obtaining grass. But there is a difference. One follows instinct and lives off whatever nature gives it; there is no intent in its 'work'. There is no cow-society that grows crops, develops methods to harvest it, owns ploughs or fields or forges relationships based on them. Cows form herds, not societies.

Man, on the other hand, is bound by various things: tending to the pasture he owns, protecting its ownership, harvesting the crop, storing it with care, and making optimal use of it all. He slogs, and he enjoys the outcome. Man doesn't form herds; he works with deliberation towards forming a society.

Everybody has to work in combination to combat natural elements, to grow food. Afterwards, everyone enjoys the fruit of that labour. When the tools are rudimentary and non-durable, it isn't possible to use them for more than a day. It's only when Man works collectively, with his kind, in a team, that some kind of benefit is possible. In such a situation, can the sense of 'I, me, myself' be possible? When production falls way below the level of need, how can the thought arise that a man can live off the productive ability of another? There is so little known about how nature works, that one doesn't know the when and how of life and death. To grow things together and eat them together, that is all aboriginal man's life is about. There is no private-personal ownership, no rulers, no families or clans or tribes. Pre-historic people don't have the concept of 'blood'-relatives, class, caste and no sense of strife. There is no need for decisions or judgments to be made. They have poverty of possessions, poverty of thought and ideas. But everyone participates in all activities; they are small of stature, but sturdy and focused. They have to constantly struggle to survive, but are free from discord. That is the very basic society of the Caveman.

Once the population within such a fundamental society grows, people wander away and various branches and clans are formed. Opportunistic sexual relations become less common and humans get bound to each other. Parents, siblings, couples, and other relationships are formed and, besides other associations, the 'family' gets instituted. The foundation of such a family is based not on economic or physical considerations nor on wealth and ownership, but for procreation. To propagate and conserve healthy progeny is the only objective.

This ever-famished community keeps increasing its skill at producing more and better food for itself. It is not possible to stop the evolution of discoveries and developments. Someone finds that fire can be used, that it can be started; someone begins to design and manufacture vessels; others learn how to tame animals. Hides are treated and converted into wraps, bones are chiselled into weapons and tools, fur is woven into fabric and the use of various raw materials increases as does the level of comforts and pleasures. Mankind's ability, whose output was always less than the need, escalates such that, with a little extra effort and the help of technology, at the end of a task's completion, there is some energy left to spare. That gives rise to a breed that has excess energy to spare and another that makes use of the first kind. That is when the era of slavery starts.

Before a particular class or caste can assert its superiority over another and make the latter, lesser class or caste, work and decide under what circumstances the latter will live, the common efforts to own, produce, share and enjoy the gains has to be destroyed.

When a primal tribe (or group or clan) nurtures its ability to produce and slowly, collectively, makes various products in more than sufficient quantities, it feels the need to barter those goods with things other tribes have made or possess. Owners of herds of cows, buffaloes and horses become wealthier than the others, their capacity to work is greater, they are able to have, or do actually have, more manpower. They are able to make additional and better things. These tribes or groups thus develop the ability to exchange what they have in excess for items that they don't have but need or want. In the beginning, such barter is of goods made by the group and collectively owned by all. The headman makes the deals on behalf of the group after taking the opinion and approval of its members.

However, it is difficult for the barterer to weigh and calculate the use of an item needed. Also, how does one put a value to labour, to 'man-hours'? By pointing out the time-and-energy required to make or grow a particular product. It is therefore impossible to estimate the cost of a single animal of a herd jointly owned and tended to by all members of a group. It is not that difficult to put a price to an iron bar made in a furnace. Through the barter system, individual effort and input gets sifted from the work put in through teamwork.

That is not all. As the barter system evolves, things which are needed by common consensus and used by everyone also get drawn into the barter system and have a 'price' put on them; they become a medium of exchange. Over time, those items no longer remain a part of common use or ownership, they take the form of money. Bartering becomes a profession, and barterers from within what was once a conjointly functional group come to be the ones that handle money as a form of wealth. The commonality of contribution of labour and use of the produce lags behind; private-personal efforts and enterprise get more importance. The time comes when the unity of the entity, i.e. the clan or tribe, develops cracks, enough to make it disintegrate. The dawn of private ownership sees two sets form: one has a lot of wealth, i.e. the rich, the other has very little of it, the poor. The friction between the slogging deprived and the privileged moneyed classes begins.

Within primary groups in which people work collectively through teamwork, the various jobs slowly get divided or shared to achieve excellence. Tribes have to constantly battle with other groups; for that they need to nominate leaders and soldiers. For daily guidance, the people need to have frontrunners. The division of labour over generations develops into traditional occupations.

That is not the only reason why classes or disputes between classes take place. The seed of friction between classes or communities is not sowed in the distinctions between occupations; it sprouts when the fruits of labour are unfairly distributed. In a shared-responsibility society, the produce is also commonly shared, so the germ of dissent doesn't grow. Once production increases and bartering sets in, once private wealth and uneven dissemination of that wealth happens, that's when discord starts. A classless society thus gets corrupted by class-consciousness.

In the very elementary societies, there is scope only for inter-group fights. Now arise opportunities for intra-clan quarrels. On the one side are the many who are poor, and on the other the few who have the wealth and so the power. The battles become furious. In the beginning, members of a clan are related by blood. As wealth and its consumption increases, people begin to migrate and reside in the lands of the rich. And they get drawn into the battle. It is not possible to bind them by the rules of those related by blood. Their thoughts, beliefs, behaviour, habits, everything is alien. Their bond to their adopted land is restricted, mercenary. Whereas the community in that land is connected each to the other by blood. How do these divergent peoples find a way through their differences? Only through war.

But at the end of that confrontation, the winning side is likely to be the one with the economic power. That is just what happens. The slogging majority is made slave to the few who are dependent on that slogging. A new system is formed, of master and slave. Kingdoms are formed where hitherto no land was formally owned. It belongs, naturally, to the wealthy class. Put the labourers to work and keep the economy rolling, destroy all signs of communal living and harmony, promote a society that is based on class alone; anyone who disagrees with this philosophy is crushed. That's the new viewpoint.

Why does any society where there is no slavery, no wringing of rights, no coercion, no crime, no punishment, get upturned, and dominance get established and retained by a few who wield the power? Why does the majority accept that? The power of the wealthy doesn't last by using only politics as a weapon. When, in a primary, simple society the produce is divided fairly, the wealth, the strength of all the members and of the entire clan, increases progressively. After violent conflict, in spite of squeezing the downtrodden cruelly, there is still progress, still some benefit for everyone, which is why the class divide can live on. It is possible to keep alive and in good shape even the post-war vanquished (who in bygone days would be left, dying or dead, at war-site graves) to be used as labour, as slaves. The latter, though oppressed, feel indebted to the victors to be alive. Clearly demarcated classes and monarchies survive because, despite the exploitation and living by the unfair rules of money-power, everybody gets some benefit from it.

The older, classless, primary society and the master-slave, king-subject, inequitable society, both, depending on economic events controlled by (powerful) people, give rise to newer institutions. All the members or regulators of such institutions are of the same clan(s) or related by blood; in other words, they 'belong' to each other in some way. Connections by wealth prove stronger than linkages by genes. At one time, everything was decided by arms; for in-house regulations, there was no need for a ruler or king. In the absence of internal strife, greed, self-indulgence or want, such a need was not felt. The group was complete, self-inspired and looking after its own. Now, the wealthy class gets the power of the ruler and of weaponry. Next, a need arises to create a leader who is distinctly apart from the rest, to make rules for maintaining internal order within a group. In the past, common produce and its enjoyment did not have a tax to be kept aside for a monarch or leader; now that became a prerequisite. Then, a criminal was thrown out of the group or, if he was a soldier, sent to be killed in battle; now, jails or workhouses have to be created to fill with dread those who create friction within a group. A society that rectified itself without penalties, now becomes one that antagonizes people of the same kith, becomes punishment-driven.

Just as a primary, simple society cannot survive for long, so also, the master-slave system also perishes with time.

The systems of a society that is dependent on slave-labour fail once it crosses a certain threshold. Internal dissensions come to a boil. Explosions take place. The framework of those systems begins to crumble. And the feudal era is born. It is in the same way that the capitalist era evolves. And, thence, the age of communism. This is the ultimate era of man-to-man economic relationships. Once more, the rule of absolute authority (for example, monarchy) perishes. The concept of 'class' gets erased. Production is high, there is common-public-manufacturing, prosperity is shared. However, the speciality of this era is that the division of the yield is dependent on level of skill; society becomes self-regulatory again.

Between both ends of the spectrum, i.e. the primary and the communist systems, are the three others in which the wealthy ones rest on and enjoy the fruits of the hard labour of the 'lower-in-rank' workers. In these systems, the powerful classes own the methods and tools of production. Both the primary and communist systems are classless. However, the primary society has poverty of technology. In it, there is no opportunity to recognize or appreciate pleasures, culture, glories of the intellect or individual talent. The last era, of communism, rises on the foundations of tremendous use of modern technology and expertise. There is no question of poverty of any sort in it. That is why it has no distinction by class. Which is why a new kind of Man gets churned up in it, who is fully aware of various pleasures, culture, the development of mental abilities and personal aptitudes.

There is another thing the primary and communist systems have in common: the rights and participation of women in all productive activities. That is how women in these systems have complete self-independence. In the three other interim eras the womenfolk don't enjoy such freedom.

Each of these five periods in the history of Mankind has different cultures, laws, arts and ways of thinking. These are created based on economic boundaries and the relations between the classes. As Mankind changes, each age succumbs to progress and gets pushed to a level higher. Rahulji has tried to present these levels in totality, for a combined view, through his stories in this anthology. Objections could be raised regarding some of the inclusions, that they have more than a touch of the logical or philosophical, and lack literary merit. But one finds impressive prose in most of the stories. The description of the very ancient epochs is excellent.

In fact, some of the portrayals of the prehistoric living conditions are so engaging, that complaints have come from some quarters that they are quite unbelievable, difficult to comprehend and that they don't fit into the social documentation of 'Hindi culture'. Those objections are baseless.

Every society of Mankind has gone through primary communism or has been through a phase that comprised small, functional groups or tribes. Ancient 'Hindi' people were no exception to this rule. Joint production, joint sharing of resulting profit, absence of a ruling class, no form of stark authority, no internal strife or discontent, no opposition between teams, connections by blood, a community-family, this is what 'Hindi' society once had. Vedic scholars will easily be able to point out that in Vedic literature the death rites of those eras point to such a society. It has been explained that the Veds – or the meaning of the word 'Ved' – are documentations of the knowledge, including of economics, of that period. '*Ved-Vedsa*' [*sic*] means riches; and the way to acquire the knowledge to get them, of getting what one desires, with faith and integrity. What other information do they give us? What else do they describe? How to do a *yajna*. The term '*yajna*' is not the alm-collecting ritual conducted by the priests of today. What was the real, the ancient *yajna*? How was it conducted? Who participated in it? Who reaped its benefits? When such questions come to mind and their answers are sought, one finds that it means communal labour and joint enjoyment of what is reaped. That's where the Aryan populace came from and that's how it prospered. Their method of making things was the *yajna* method or *yajna-karm*. A civilization like that considers it a part of the larger world of inanimate things and living creatures, and it considered the universe to be '*brahman*'. One can confidently state that '*brahman*' means the way the ancients lived, or commune-living.

There is no need to deliberate on this subject here. One needs to dwell on how authentic the picture is, which Rahulji has projected about the Indo-European civilization, and whether it is based on the truth. It is not difficult to find evidence of how primary man lived in small, independent, class-less, leaderless groups that had cooperative ownership of wealth and impartial distribution of it. It is not difficult to get proof of how he lived and migrated, the quarrels that arose amongst those who lived in those times, their elementary inter-clan fights which grew into more complicated, inter-class ones.

Fire was discovered and tamed, a community-based living labelled *yajna* was created, and ways of producing and sharing yield amongst other things evolved. There was an increase in making prolonged sacrifices and in creating legends of three-night long *yajna* rituals. There were narrations of the doings of gods who were personifications of natural phenomena: the eight '*vasus*' whose chiefs during various periods were Indr or Agni or Vishnu. Stories were woven around Aditya, the sun god who signified the twelve months and Rudr, who represented the dreadful natural forces or storms. The rites around the sacred fire were developed and the precepts of Vedic ceremonies laid down as were the beginnings of the various forms of the Ganpati and the roles of one who led a group. The methods of distributing and enjoying whatever is sacrificed at the raised altar were listed. The allocation of the spoils of victory in war, including prisoners, was done according to the *daansukts* or hymns that praised the act of giving, as also for *yajnas* in which humans were sacrificed (the '*purushmedh*'). The clashes between two classes was portrayed as a battle between the gods. Finally, there was a breakdown of the relationships by blood and the dawn of an authority that drew its power from the slaves it ruled over – examples of these are given in the hymns of the '*Purushsukt*' and the *Mahabharat*. If one applies the principles of Marxism whilst reading these, it is quite easy to get a clear perspective of what life was like in the Indo-European societies of yore.

That's when questions arise in a reader's mind and the answers to those questions are also revealed.

For self-protection, the peripatetic primary tribes had to fight battles; subsequently, they had the burden of in-fighting amongst the classes and some revolutionary movements. The masters of the upper classes got insolent and began to aggressively acquire for their personal benefit slaves, land, businesses, houses and other forms of wealth, which, in the years gone by, were quite unknown. Each class in each era fights its battles with the technology of the times, for contemporary reasons, based on the produce and the methods used for manufacturing it. Will this turmoil end at all? If so, how? Or is it a never-ending cycle?

If one makes a synopsis of the treaties made by the ancients till recent times (which has been touched upon in this anthology) it is observed that Mankind need not be dejected. Presently, one powerful country, Russia, has taken communism to its ultimate level. As a matter of principle, it has pledged to reach out to states in other parts of the world to stop wars, violence, disparity between the classes and promote internal peace amongst people which will lead to a happier world. Russia will keep its promise. The common people of the world, having learnt the lessons and the experiences of long centuries of history, exploitation, bondage, suppression, slavery, will wish for freedom from them. They are clamouring towards a more refined culture and for happiness and they will be successful in their endeavours.

RAHUL SANKRITYAYAN (1893–1963) was an Indian polymath who is often remembered as the father of Hindi travel writing. He was also known for his role in the revival of Buddhism in India, as co-founder of the Bihar unit of the Communist Party, and a pioneering explorer-traveller. His choice of Hindi for the bulk of his writing marks him as a contributor to a popular progressive intellectual discourse in that language. Apart from his iconic travelogues that record journeys into remote Himalayan regions and across Asia and Europe, he wrote on travel (*Ghumakkar Shastr*), made significant contributions to history (including the Sahitya Akademi Award winning *Madhya Asia ka Itihas*), philosophy (*Darshan Digdarshan*), memoir-writing (*Meri Jeevan-Yatra, Mere Asahyog ke Saathi*), polemics (*Bhago Nahin Duniya ko Badlo, Tumhari Kshaya*), biography (of travellers, thinkers, social reformers, political leaders), drama (Bhojpuri), translation (of Tajik novels, as well as *The Communist Manifesto*), lexicography, critical commentary on and emendation of rare Buddhist philosophical texts recovered from Tibet, and diverse fiction, mostly historical. He was imprisoned for his anti-colonial activism for about three years by the British. In 1963, he was conferred the Padma Bhushan.

VICTOR GORDON KIERNAN (1913–2009) was a British Marxist historian. He was part of the famous Communist Party Historians' Group of the 1940s that included E.P. Thompson, Christopher Hill, Rodney Hilton and others. He was described by Hill as 'one of the most versatile of British historians'.

KANWAL DHALIWAL is a painter, sculptor, author, and translator. He did his B.F.A. in Painting (1984) from Government College of Arts, Chandigarh, and an M.A. in Art in Architecture (2002) from the University of East London. He also has a Master's degree in Russian (1991) from the Institute of English and Foreign Languages, Hyderabad. He has previously translated *Volga se Ganga* to Panjabi.

MAYA JOSHI is Associate Professor of English Literature at Lady Shri Ram College, but considers it her good fortune to have been exposed from childhood to literatures other than English and subjects other than Literature. Her publications include a critical edition of Mary Shelley's *Frankenstein*; a co-edited volume on Buddhist philosophy, *Pramana: Dharmakirti and the Indian Philosophical Debate* (Manohar, 2010); a translation with critical introduction of selections from Rahul Sankrityayan's *Baisvin Sadi* for *The Gollancz Book of South Asian Science Fiction*, ed. Tarun Saint (2019); and a chapter on Sankrityayan and Ambedkar's engagements with Buddha and Marx in *India and Civilizational Futures: Papers from The Backwaters Collective on Metaphysics and Politics*, ed. Vinay Lal (2019). In 2017–18, she was Fulbright-Nehru Visiting Scholar at the University of Pennsylvania, working on an intellectual biography of Rahul Sankrityayan, whom she has enjoyed reading, speaking and writing on for over a decade.

ANAND KAUSALYAYAN was a Buddhist monk, scholar, traveller and a prolific writer. He is considered as one of the great activists of Buddhism of the 20th century. He was mentored by Rahul Sankrityayan and continued to work closely with him throughout his life.

S.A. DANGE (1899–1991) was a founding member of the Communist Party of India. He wrote one of the first studies of Lenin in India (*Gandhi v. Lenin*, 1921) and edited one of the first Marxist journals (*Socialist*). Dange and Sankrityayan were interned together while Sankrityayan wrote *Volga se Ganga*.

SHEELA JAYAWANT is a Goa-based humour columnist and writer of short fiction. She also translates from Marathi to English.